MW01014924

Thrift

Thrift
A Cyclopedia

BEING AN EARLY ATTEMPT TO ASSEMBLE THE
BEST OF WHAT IS KNOWN FROM HISTORY AND
LITERATURE ABOUT ONE OF OUR MOST PRO-
VOCATIVE WORDS ∼ FOR THOSE WHO ARE NOT
ASHAMED TO THINK ANEW ABOUT HAPPINESS,
• EXTRAVAGANCE, AND THRIVING •

David Blankenhorn

TEMPLETON FOUNDATION PRESS
WEST CONSHOHOCKEN, PENNSYLVANIA

A COMPANION TO THE TRAVELING EXHIBITION, *THRIFT: IN SEARCH OF THE ART OF LIVING WELL*, AND THE REPORT
TO THE NATION, *FOR A NEW THRIFT: CONFRONTING THE DEBT CULTURE*. VISIT THE WEBSITE: WWW.NEWTHRIFT.ORG

Templeton Foundation Press
300 Conshohocken State Road, Suite 670
West Conshohocken, PA 19428
www.templetonpress.org

© 2008 by the Institute for American Values

All rights reserved. No part of this book may be used or reproduced, stored in a retrieval system, or transmitted in any form or by any means, electronic, mechanical, photocopying, recording, or otherwise, without the written permission of Templeton Foundation Press.

Templeton Foundation Press helps intellectual leaders and others learn about science research on aspects of realities, invisible and intangible. Spiritual realities include unlimited love, accelerating creativity, worship, and the benefits of purpose in persons and in the cosmos.

Designed and typeset by Gopa & Ted2, Inc.
Printed in the United States of America

08 09 10 11 12 13   10 9 8 7 6 5 4 3 2 1

Library of Congress Cataloging-in-Publication Data

Blankenhorn, David.
  Thrift : a cyclopedia : being an early attempt to assemble the best of what is known from history and literature about one of our most provocative words for those who are not ashamed to think anew about happiness, extravagance, and thriving / David Blankenhorn.
      p. cm.
  "A Companion to the traveling exhibition, Thrift: In Search of the Art of Living Well and the Report to the Nation, For a New Thrift: Confronting the Debt Culture."
  Developed after a conference of scholars the author convened in October of 2005, at the request of the John Templeton Foundation, to discuss the history of thrift as an American value and practice.
  Includes bibliographical references and index.
  ISBN-13: 978-1-59947-142-6 (pbk. : alk. paper)
  ISBN-10: 1-59947-142-6 (pbk. : alk. paper) 1. Consumption (Economics)—Social aspects—United States. 2. Saving and investment—United States—United States. 3. Social values—United States—History. 4. Conduct of life—United States—History. 5. Social values—United States—Quotations, maxims, etc. I. Title.
  HC110.C6B57 2008
  332.0240097303—dc22

                                    2008006962

For Arthur and Joann Rasmussen—thrivers who help others to thrive

. . . .

"If a good man thrive, all thrive with him."
—George Herbert

Contents

Thrift

Introduction

THIS BOOK is an extended reflection, and a preliminary bringing together of knowledge, on the English word "thrift." In October of 2005, at the request of the John Templeton Foundation, I helped to convene a conference of nearly forty leading scholars to discuss the history of thrift as an American value and practice. The main thing I learned at the conference is that most leading scholars are not very interested in thrift. Moreover, among those who are interested, thrift is usually viewed as either mildly amusing, worrisomely retrograde, or both.

The very word "thrift" tells its own tale, being derived from the word "to thrive."
JOHN LUBBOCK, *THE USE OF LIFE*, 1894

A prominent professor of political philosophy from Harvard, who adamantly insisted that thrift is not a virtue, and whose commissioned paper did not contain even one mention of the word "thrift," asked me pointedly: "Are you saying that the word 'thrift' has to be on every page?" I told him I'd think about that.

So I went home and thought about it. I eventually decided that the answer to his question is "Yes." A serious paper on the topic of thrift ought to contain the word "thrift" on every page. Or nearly every page. Or at least on one or two pages! This book contains the word "thrift" on nearly every page.

I'm grateful to that Harvard professor, because that conference, and in particular his question, greatly deepened my interest in the subject. What was this odd idea that they could barely be bothered to study and so clearly did not believe in? Moreover, the whole experience of that conference made me realize that leading scholars are not the only ones today who are actively disinterested in thrift. The word "thrift" has largely fallen out of our public conversation. As a result, the whole concept sounds quaintly old-fashioned, like something your great-grandparents might have talked about—but not you, and certainly not your children. I began to wonder, why is this the case? What's the real story behind this funny little word that so many people can't or don't want to say?

a genuine thrift nut. I believe in it passionately. I'm a starry-eyed advocate. For so many of the problems now ailing us—from shameful wasteful-

1. *a. The fact or condition of thriving or prospering; (obsolete)*
   b. Means of thriving;
   c. Prosperous growth, physical thriving;
   d. Growing-pains.
2. *a. Savings, earnings, gains, profit;*
   b. That which is saved (of something); (obsolete)
3. *a. Economical management, economy;*
   b. A U.S. savings and loan association.

"THRIFT," OXFORD ENGLISH DICTIONARY

To pursue the answer to this question, I needed a research methodology. I decided, for lack of a better idea, to keep it simple. Following the implicit guideline contained in the question posed by my irritated Harvard mentor, I began to search everywhere for phrases, sentences, and pages that contained the word "thrift." I confess that I began with *Bartlett's Familiar Quotations*—I knew I could find a few there! It also turns out that, unlike today's leading scholars, Shakespeare liked the word quite a bit. So did Chaucer before him. In fact, amazingly enough, so have many of the English-speaking world's most prominent writers and leaders! Over the centuries, thrift has been repeatedly, passionately, and articulately advocated. It has also been repeatedly, passionately, and articulately denounced. Both proponents and advocates typically agree that thrift is a big idea, with high stakes for individuals and society.

Somewhere in all of my note taking, I became

ness, to growing economic inequality, to independence-killing indebtedness, to runaway mindless consumerism—I believe that the philosophy of thrift is the closest thing we have to a miracle cure. As a result, I want to testify about it. I want to shout it from the rooftops. I want to convert people. And I hope that after you read this book, you will want to do the same.

However, except for an occasional editorial or attempt to clarify the narrative, I myself don't have much to say in this book. The reason is not laziness. It's thrift! First, the way to understand thrift is to get as close to it as possible. As a result, reading what I say about Benjamin Franklin's view of thrift is not nearly as instructive—or as fun!—as reading what Franklin himself says about thrift. No view of mine about the U.S. Savings and Loan League circa 1965 could ever be as revealing, or as interestingly expressed, as the view of the guy who served as president of the League in 1965 and therefore gave the keynote address at the League's 1965 annual convention. Learning what I conclude about thrift-boxes is not as good as actually seeing a thrift-box. (That's why this book has lots of visual images.)

There are several species of plants, such as the sea-pink, Armeria maritima, or March rosemary (Statice) which from their vigorous growth are often termed "thrift."

"THRIFT," *ENCYCLOPAEDIA BRITANNICA*, 1911

Relatedly, there is the question of economy, or what might be called editorial thrift. With this topic, there is a lot of ground to cover. Concision is essential. So in this book I am giving you a box of chocolates, rather than a windy treatise on the history of chocolate. I think you'll like it more.

Moreover, this topic, probably more than any other I've encountered, requires us to attend very carefully to the exact words of people who are (mostly) now dead. Trust me. There is nothing bad that I could possibly say about thrift that has not already been said, far more vividly and powerfully, by people smarter (or at least more famous) than I am. Even more importantly for my more partisan purposes, the finest words in praise of thrift, as well as the words that most precisely convey what thrift is and why it matters, have already been uttered. I can hardly improve on them, so I don't try to. Instead I let the historical actors themselves, using their own best words, duke it out over this contentious issue, and, apart from playing the role of editorial emcee, and occasion-

Do you believe in THRIFT?

Western Electric

A UNIT OF THE BELL SYSTEM SINCE 1882

MANUFACTURER ... PURCHASER ... DISTRIBUTOR ... INSTALLER ...

ally putting in my own good word for thrift, I mostly stay out of the way.

The word has no exact synonym.

"THRIFT," *THE WORLD BOOK*, 1918

I call this book a cyclopedia for several reasons. For starters, the very idea of a cyclopedia—an economical bringing together of the available knowledge on a subject—both embodies and contributes to the thrift ideal. Second, the word "cyclopedia" is an odd, old-style word, and this book, with its eccentric mixing of (mostly) quotes from literature and history with (some) personal commentary, is an odd, old-style book. Third, a number of

Thrift Champions, Pearce School, Washington, DC, 1925

early and what we would now view as primitive encyclopedias, dating back to the seventeenth century, were called "cyclopedias"; this current collection of knowledge is also probably primitive, in the sense of being an early and therefore inevitably partial attempt to bring together, from a modern vantage-point, what is known and relevant regarding the English word "thrift." And finally, "cyclopedia" for me evokes and pays respectful homage to one of the great, practical thrift books of the

twentieth century, *Cyclopedia of Building, Loan and Savings Associations*, first published in 1923.

The book's structure is simple. We begin philologically, with the word itself—its origins, history, and meanings. Next, we hear from some of history's most eloquent opponents of thrift. Then we hear from some thrift visionaries—leaders who like thrift, have thought about it seriously, and have done their best to champion it. Since leaders often build institutions and lead social movements, we next focus on the main thrift institutions in English-speaking societies, followed by a look at some of the main social movements that have been animated by the thrift deal. Then, toward the end, for fun and instruction, we survey history's proverbs and maxims of thrift. Finally, I propose that we briefly think about the question, "What kind of country do we want to be?"

. . . there are few words in the English language that have a more interesting history, or convey a deeper moral than the word "Thrift."

RICHARDSON CAMPBELL, *PROVIDENT AND INDUSTRIAL INSTITUTIONS*, ABOUT 1926

Here is the basic conclusion, the moral, that I draw from this book's analysis. Thrift is a big, important word. We largely ignore it today, to our great loss. Some of the most intelligent people ever to use our language have thought and said a great deal about this word, and for good reasons. The word has helped to create some of our most vital social institutions and fuel some of our most inspiring social movements. Possibly as much as we need any idea today, we need this one. That's the basic conclusion that, in my view, emerges from this little cyclopedia on thrift.

A word about spelling and punctuation: In most (though not all) cases, when the sources readily available to me permitted a choice between the author's original spelling and punctuation, and one or more modernized versions, I chose the original. That will make it harder at times for you as a reader—but also better. It's like watching an old black-and-white movie. Yes, you could probably find a "colorized" version somewhere, but the original is truer.

Thrift, that sovereign bourgeois virtue, is often misunderstood, simply because the word can mean so many different things.

MARIA OSSOWSKA, *BOURGEOIS MORALITY*, 1956

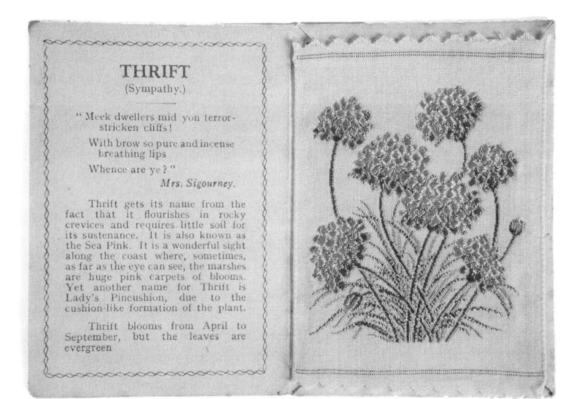

THRIFT
(Sympathy.)

" Meek dwellers mid yon terror-
stricken cliffs !

With brow so pure and incense
breathing lips

Whence are ye ? "

Mrs. Sigourney.

Thrift gets its name from the fact that it flourishes in rocky crevices and requires little soil for its sustenance. It is also known as the Sea Pink. It is a wonderful sight along the coast where, sometimes, as far as the eye can see, the marshes are huge pink carpets of blooms. Yet another name for Thrift is Lady's Pincushion, due to the cushion-like formation of the plant.

Thrift blooms from April to September, but the leaves are evergreen

Thrift, Kensitas Flowers

PART ONE

What Is Thrift?

I N 1910, the U.S. National Bankers Association, at its annual meeting in Los Angeles, invited as a guest lecturer the noted humorist, journalist, and minister Robert J. Burdette. Burdette's lecture to the bankers was entitled "Thrift." His opening query, and the core question that Burdette sought to answer that evening, was "What is thrift?" He confessed that his task was not an easy one.

He began the lecture by reporting, by way of the dictionary, that thrift is "the condition of one who thrives," but admitted with a smile that such a definition was "not quite good enough." Then he offered another: "Luck, fortune, success." Still not quite right. And then another: "Frugality, economical management." Yes, maybe, but not really. And then one more try: "Good husbandry." Finally, Burdette simply gave up. He confessed to the bankers: "Now, after all, what is thrift? Just thrift." The bankers laughed, and Burdette went on his merry way, delivering charming descriptions and anecdotes of thrift, and ending up by suggesting that the highest form of thrift is generosity, since in heaven, according to Burdette at least, they measure a man's thriftiness by "what he gave away."[1]

What (if anything!) can we learn today from these long-forgotten quips delivered to long-deceased bankers after a dinner in Los Angeles nearly a century ago? Well, for starters, let's realize that, in 1910, it was not at all surprising for a well-known person to deliver a public lecture on "Thrift." Quite the contrary. I am focusing here on one such talk by Robert Burdette, but there are many others from this era that I could just as easily have chosen. That fact alone should tell us something. People in the United States used to spend quite a bit of time asking themselves, "What is thrift?" Today, we don't.

Second, earlier generations assumed that the answer to the question, while important, was not easy or straightforward. The topic was complex, not simple. They assumed, therefore, that the question called for some study and reflection,

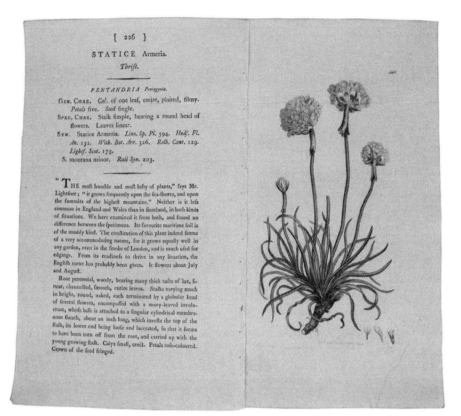

James Edward Smith,
English Botany, vol. 4, 1795

or at least some genuine mental effort. Today, we don't. Quite the contrary. To the degree that people speak of thrift today, they are probably quite certain that thrift means scrimping and saving, usually up to and including being unpleasantly cheap and stingy. So, after all, what is thrift? What to earlier generations of Americans had seemed a difficult, important question has largely become for our generation an easy, unimportant question. That's quite a shift! Burdette, for example, concludes that thrift can mean generosity. So have many other thoughtful people, from Lao Tzu writing in China in about 600 BCE, to the great British statesman William Gladstone in the 1890s, to Dr. John M. Templeton Jr., one of today's very few pro-thrift voices, in his 2004 book, *Thrift and*

Generosity. But is this proposition well known in the United States today? Are very many of us even thinking about it?

So just for the fun of it, and for any thrift (that is, good fortune) that it might provide us, let's try to look with fresh eyes, with innocence even, and ask our ourselves anew, "What is thrift?" When all is properly considered, we will end up with a definition of thrift that is fairly coherent and thrifty (that is, economical), but to get there honestly, we must first work through some complexity. The complexity is necessary for four reasons.

First, thrift is inherently a complex idea. It is a multifaceted philosophical concept for which there is no single precise synonym in the English language. Second, because of this multidimen-

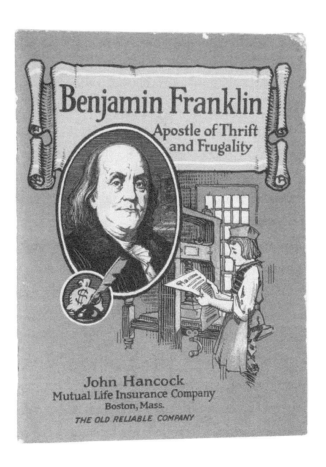

Published 1921

sionality, thrift can mean, and virtually from the beginning has meant, different things to different people. Some tend to emphasize one dimension of the idea, and some another, with still others trying to synthesize. Third, the dominant meaning of the word has steadily evolved over time. "Thrift" in the fourteenth century typically meant something quite different from "thrift" in 1800, which in turn is quite different from the most common meanings of "thrift" in 1950, not to mention the dominant meaning of "thrift" today. To all of these turns and evolutions, due attention must be paid. And finally, unfortunately "thrift" is a word that, especially today, is often defined publicly by peo-

ple who don't like it. (I learned this fact the hard way when I helped to convene that group of prominent scholars to opine on thrift.) The result is like asking a gun-control advocate to define "firearm," or a die-hard Republican to tell you what Democrats truly believe—you are likely to get some nuggets of valid information, but you are unlikely to get the whole story, and often enough you will see streaks of bias infiltrating both the working definitions and the underlying assumptions.

So, to tell our tale thriftily—that is, well, properly, suitably—let's begin by considering four fairly distinct ways of understanding what thrift is.

1. Thrift as Growing

Planting of trees is England's old thrift.
ENGLISH PROVERB

. . . .

On sandy wastes, ere yet the frugal root
Of tender grass can feed the springing shoot
Fringing each sterile bank and rocky rift
Green grows the tufted cushions of the Thrift . . .

THE TIME TO LEARN

Rollin Kirby, 1920

Ah! well named flower, for of a thrift we sing,
Skilled like thyself, a fertile growth to bring
In barren wastes with Hope's sweet verdure rife
The pledge and potency of statelier life.
WALSHAM HOWE, THE FIRST BISHOP OF
WAKEFIELD, "THRIFT—THE PLANT"

. . . .

As we can see, one primary meaning of thrift is growing, blooming, or spreading with vigor, health, and efficiency, either as a part of nature, or as a metaphor stemming from the idea of natural, effective growth.

And if it be asshe, elme, or oke, cut of all
the bowes cleane, and save the toppe hole.
For if thou make hym ryche of bowes,
thou makest hyme poore of thryfe . . .
"HOW TO REMOVE TREES," FITZHERBERT'S *THE BOOK*
OF HUSBANDRY, 1534

. . . .

An Olde Thrift Newly Revived. Wherein is
declared the manner of Planting, Preserving, and
Husbanding Young Trees.
TITLE OF A BOOK BY RICHARD MOORE, ABOUT 1612

No grace has more abundant promises made unto it than this of of mercy, a sowing, a reaping, a thrifty grace.

REV. EDWARD REYNOLDS, A SERMON, MID-SEVENTEENTH CENTURY

. . . .

. . . I would select a wood of young and thrifty trees.

JAMES FENIMORE COOPER, *THE PIONEERS*, 1823

. . . .

This cow had a cough and looked unthrifty all last winter and spring.

REPORT FROM DR. E. E. SALMON, U.S. BUREAU OF ANIMAL INDUSTRY, NOVEMBER 16, 1885

. . . a thrifty growth of the sugar-cane . . .

HERMAN MELVILLE, *OMOO*, 1847

. . . .

. . . in the rear of the row of buildings, the track of many languid years is seen in a border of unthrifty grass . . .

NATHANIEL HAWTHORNE, *THE SCARLET LETTER*, 1850

. . . .

. . . whose old roots furnish still the wild stocks of many a thrifty village tree.

HENRY DAVID THOREAU, *WALDEN*, 1854

O love and summer, you are in the dreams and in me,
Autumn and winter are in the dreams,
*   the farmer goes with his thrift,*
The droves and crops increase, the barns
*   are well-fill'd.*

WALT WHITMAN, "THE SLEEPERS," 1855

. . . .

Farmington seems to us to be suitably named, being a vast conglomeration of farms and farm houses. We could not but notice the thrifty look which bespoke the careful husbandman.

IRVING TODD, DISCUSSING FARMINGTON, MINNESOTA, 1863

Frequently the thrift ideal is compared to cultivation of the soil and to natural growth.

There is a use of the word "thrift" that may help us to realize its best meaning. Gardeners call a plant of vigorous growth a "thrifty" plant. Let us bear this in mind in our charitable work, and remember that anything that hinders vigorous growth is essentially unthrifty. Thrift means something more than the hoarding of small savings. In fact, saving at the expense of health, or training, or some other necessary preparation for successful living, is always unthrifty.

MARY E. RICHMOND, *FRIENDLY VISITING AMONG THE POOR: A HANDBOOK FOR CHARITY WORKERS*, 1903

Poster, 1929

Though neither concerns nature directly, both of the sayings below—one from the late sixteenth century on thrift of revenge, and one from the early twentieth century on thrift of thought—seem to use the word "thrift" primarily in the sense of vigorous and efficient growth.

Phi. What I pray you? and how manie are the names, whereby the Devill allures persones in anie of these snares?
Epi. Even by these three passiones that are within our selves: Curiousitie in great imagines: thrift of revenge, for some tortes deeply apprehended; or greedie appetitie of geare, caused through great poverty.

KING JAMES VI OF SCOTLAND, *DAEMONOLOGIE*, 1597

. . . .

. . . the rules of thought are essentially the rules of thrift. I mean that the best way of taking stock of one's philosophic and artistic estate is analogous to the best way of so dealing with a real estate, especially a small one; it permits of the same terminology and is troubled with the same errors. When we expect a peasant to make the best use of a field, we do not mean he should put up with it, like a prison. That is not making the best use of it, but only accepting the worst. We mean that his thrift thrives; that his land, so to speak, enlarges inward; that, like a cup in a fairy tale, it holds more and more without overflowing. And the same intensive cultivation can be in the thought, and even in the fancy.

G. K. CHESTERTON, "THE THRIFT OF THOUGHT," 1916

Shall we apologize for making two blades of grass grow where one grew before? Shall we look askance at the man who is diligent in business, and whose thrift and energy give him control of productive capital, the use of which ameliorates the condition of an entire neighborhood?

. . . We live in an economic age, and we must not be afraid of it. The business career nowadays is the dominating one.

ALBERT SHAW, *THE OUTLOOK FOR THE AVERAGE MAN*, 1907

2. Thrift as Good Fortune

PROBABLY the oldest meanings of "thrift" in the English language are good fortune, thriving, wealth, being blessed with luck and good favor, and being the best, the most proper, or the most suitable.

For he does men evere schame: sorewe him
  must bifalle
And lesser thrift [bad fortune] upon his heued . . .
"A MIRACLE OF ST. JAMES," ABOUT 1305

. . . .

I kan right now no thrifty [suitable, fitting]
tale seyn . . .
GEOFFREY CHAUCER, CANTERBURY TALES, "THE MAN OF LAW'S TALE," (INTRODUCTION, 46), 1380s

. . . .

Now good thrift [good luck, good fortune] have he,
wherso that he be!
CHAUCER, TROILUS AND CRISEYDE (II, 847), 1380s

. . . .

Of al this noble town the thriftieste [best, finest,
most atttractive].
CHAUCER, TROILUS AND CRISEYDE (II, 737)

She took hire leve at hem ful thriftily [properly, in
the best way].
CHAUCER, TROILUS AND CRISEYDE (III, 211)

. . . .

In his generally excellent biography of Benjamin Franklin, Carl Van Doren suggests that thrift is a "prim, dry" idea, from which Franklin needs to be "rescued."[1] Well, slog your way through the following bit of old English—"Her arms small, her hair straight and soft; her sides long, fleshy, smooth, and white; he began to stroke her, and good thrift came to him, from her snow-white throat and her round, light breasts"—and you'll see that Chaucer's view of thrift is almost anything but "prim and dry."

Hire armes smale, hire streghte bak and
  softe,
Hire sydes longe, flesshly, smothe, and white
He gan to stroke, and good thrift [good luck,
  good fortune] bad ful ofte
Hire snowissh throte, hire brestes round
  and lite.
CHAUCER, TROILUS AND CRISEYDE (III, 1247–50)

Hir chaffare [merchandise] was so thrifty [fine, suitable, serviceable] and so newe.

CHAUCER, *CANTERBURY TALES*, "THE MAN OF LAW'S TALE" (138)

. . . .

I sitte at hoom; I have no thrifty [excellent, suitable] clooth.

CHAUCER, *CANTERBURY TALES*, "THE WIFE OF BATH'S TALE" (238)

. . . .

But by my thrift [an oath: By my fortune!], yet shal I blere hir ye, For al the sleighte in hir philosophye.

CHAUCER, *CANTERBURY TALES*, "THE REEVE'S TALE" (4049–50)

. . . .

The Way to Thrift

THE TITLE OF A POEM, IN WHICH A MOTHER ADVISES HER DAUGHTER ON THE WAYS OF WISE LIVING, LATE FOURTEENTH CENTURY

. . . .

Now good thrifte [luck, fortune] come unto thee, sone deere!

THOMAS HOCCLEVE, *THE REGIMENT OF PRINCES*, 1411

Ye prowd galantts hertless, With your hygh cappis witlesse, And your schort gownys thrifless [without worth], . . . Therfor your thrifte [good fortune] is almost don, And with youre long here into your eyen Have brought this londe to gret pyne.

SONGS AND CAROLS, ABOUT 1470

. . . .

Slip-thrift

A GAME INVENTED IN ENGLAND DURING THE REIGN OF KING HENRY VIII

. . . .

In "Slip-thrift"—apparently also called "slide-thrift"—players in the game pushed groats and, later, shillings across a designated area to reach a desired destination. The game may have involved gambling or betting. Versions of this game eventually became known as "shovel-board" and, still later, "shuffle-board." So these game-players in the mid-sixteenth century were "sliding" and "slipping" (and possibly risking) their "thrift"—that is, their wealth—across the game area.[2]

There are such dicing-houses, also . . . where young gentlemen dice away their thrift; and where dicing is, there are other follies also.

HUGH LATIMER, SERMON PREACHED BEFORE KING EDWARD VI, APRIL 12, 1549

THE TORCH-BEARER

Rollin Kirby, 1920

THE PARTING OF THE WAYS

Rollin Kirby, 1920

But of course thrift can also mean something quite different from material treasure. In this wonderful saying, also from 1549, we see that thrift, in the sense of ultimate blessing or favor, can also be invoked to call into question the value of material things:

The entrie unto immortal thrifte is throughe losse of transitorie thynges.

MILES COVERDALE, *ERASMUS' PARAPHRASES*, 1549

. . . .

Shakespeare, our greatest writer in English, used the word "thrift" in nearly every sense in which

the word can be used, both to praise and to damn. Here he uses "thrift" to mean good fortune:

I have a mind presages me such thrift,
That I should questionless be fortunate!

WILLIAM SHAKESPEARE, *THE MERCHANT OF VENICE* (I, I), ABOUT 1596

. . . .

Fellow, learn to new-live: the way to thrift
For thee in grace is a repentant shrift.

JOHN FORD, *LOVE'S SACRIFICE* (IV, 3), 1633

3. Thrift as Prospering

Here is one of my very favorite thrift sayings:

His thrift waxes thin, that spends before he wins.
"HOW THE GOOD WIFE TAUGHT HER
DAUGHTER," ABOUT 1430

. . . .

I love this saying because, on the one hand, it uses "thrift" in its classical sense of thriving, or being blessed with good fortune, while on the other, it concretely links the condition of thriving to a habit that one should cultivate within the economic sphere of life—that is, the discipline of living within one's means. Which is not just any old habit! Indeed, of all the commonsense guidelines for thrift since the word first emerged in English, this one is certainly one of the most commonly repeated and urgently advised. For example, Robert Louis Stevenson's "Christmas Sermon" from 1888, in which he beautifully adumbrates the "task" in life that requires "fortitude and delicacy," sincerely hopes that each of us are able "to earn a little and to spend a little less."[1]

The idea is an old one. Here is another of my all-time favorite thrift sayings:

Cut my coat after my cloth.
GODLY QUEEN HESTER, ABOUT 1529

. . . .

And here is another wonderful one, spelling out the guideline a bit more fully:

Be thriftie, but not covetous . . .
Never exceed thy income . . .
By no means runne in debt: take thine own
    measure.
Who cannot live on twentie pound a yeare,
Cannot on fortie: he's a man of pleasure,

. . . .

A kinde of thing that's for it self too deere.
    The curious unthrift makes his cloth too wide,
    And spares himself, but would his taylor chide.
GEORGE HERBERT, "THE CHURCH-PORCH," 1633

. . . .

When the "good wife" teaches her daughter in fifteenth-century England that "His thrift waxes thin, that spends before he wins," and when George Herbert sits on "the Church-porch" in the 1630s to advise young people in the ways of thrift and right living, the former is prefiguring by many generations, and the latter is making quite explicit, a broad evolution in the meaning and dominant usages of the word "thrift." This new emphasis begins, roughly speaking, in the seventeenth century, concurrent with the rise in Britain of a more market-based economy and, beginning in the latter decades of the seventeenth century, the Industrial Revolution. The pastor and prominent nineteenth-century British thrift advocate William L. Blackley describes the change:

But to thrive *and be* provided *are, after all, not quite the same thing as to be* thrifty *and* provident. *The former terms refer to a man's condition, the latter to his character. The one pair describe a state, the other imply a habit.*

REV. WILLIAM L. BLACKLEY, *THRIFT AND INDEPENDENCE*, 1885

. . . .

Well put! Blackley is here confirming the gradual but steady evolution, largely completed by the mid-nineteenth century, in how writers commonly use the word "thrift." Using the word in its classical senses of growing and thriving—that is, a status or condition—increasingly gives way to thrift as referring to a set of habits and values, or character traits. This shift is quite significant. The older usages refer to a result; the newer usages refer to ways of getting the result. The older ones are largely descriptive; the newer ones are largely nor-

mative. Instead of wealth and good fortune, thrift now increasingly comes to mean certain pathways to wealth and good fortune.

In brief, the word "thrift" is being gradually moralized. It now overtly implies an "ought"—with the "ought" dimension of the word increasingly taking precedence over the "is" dimension. The novelist W. Somerset Maugham, in 1915, nicely captures this by-now well-established sense of the word when he describes a character, a poor parson, as "thrifty by inclination and economical by necessity."[2] The concept of thrift has also, to use an ugly word, been at least partly economized. Instead of essentially referring to life as a whole, life in all of its flourishing—"Now thrift and speed be thine, my dear child!"[3]—thrift in this new emphasis increasingly comes to mean first and foremost economic prosperity, or prosperity primarily in the material sense.

. . . .

Thrift is the fuel of magnificence.

SIR PHILIP SIDNEY, *COUNTESS OF PEMBROKE'S ARCADIA*, ABOUT 1580

. . . .

For husbandrie weepeth,
where housewifery sleepeth,
And hardly he creepeth,
*   up ladder to thrift.*

THOMAS TUSSER, *FIVE HUNDRED POINTES OF GOOD HUSBANDRIE*, 1580

THE MODERN ST. GEORGE

Rollin Kirby, 1920

UNCONQUERABLE

Rollin Kirby, 1920

Behold th' ensamples in our sightes,
Of lustfull luxurie and thriftlesse wast!

EDMUND SPENCER, *THE FAERIE QUEENE*, 1596

. . . .

I am a man that from my first have been
*   inclined to thrift,*
And my estate deserves an heir more rais'd than
*   one which holds a trencher.*

WILLIAM SHAKESPEARE, *TIMON OF*
ATHENS (I, I), ABOUT 1607

Shakespeare rarely fails to delight. Here he uses what most modern thrift visionaries have concluded is the best antonym of thrift—waste—to make a play on words:

Indeed, I am in the waist two yards about; but I
am now about no waste; I am about thrift.

SHAKESPEARE, *THE MERRY WIVES OF*
WINDSOR (I, 3), ABOUT 1600

It is required that this care [in working diligently] does not proceed from the love of riches, but out of conscience towards God, whose benefits we ought not to abuse, and out of a foresight of providing for our necessities, and doing good for others. For honest thrift does not hinder, but rather promotes liberality and other virtues.

THE PURITAN DIVINE WILLIAM AMES
(1576–1633), ABOUT 1632

. . . .

*Let wealth come in by comely thrift
And not by any sordid shift . . .*

ROBERT HERRICK (1591–1674), "THE
WELL-WISHES AT WEDDINGS"

. . . .

The Earl had a reputation for financial shrewdness, and if he noted down the maxim "in sume cases the best thrift is to be prodigall" it was only in order to make the immediate comment, "a rull often false alwayse unsertayn."

VIEWS OF THE FOURTH EARL OF BEDFORD
(1593–1641), IN *SURVEY OF LONDON*

. . . .

She was so thrifty and good, that her name passed into a proverb.

HENRY WADSWORTH LONGFELLOW, "THE
COURTSHIP OF MILES STANDISH," 1858

Industry is the parent of thrift . . . I never knew an early-rising, hard-working, prudent man, careful of his earnings, and strictly honest who complained of bad luck.

HENRY WARD BEECHER, *LECTURES TO YOUNG
MEN ON VARIOUS IMPORTANT SUBJECTS*, 1844

. . . .

. . . those principles which teach a man to look beyond this world for his highest happiness do really offer the best security for his present enjoyment. The sobriety and reflection which religion enjoins are favourable to the development and improvement of all our mental powers, while the temperance, economy and industry which the precepts of the gospel inculcate are most conducive to our outward prosperity. These results, though not urged as considerations for embracing the offers of the gospel, are still not to be overlooked by those who would rightly estimate their value . . . as a general thing, industry leads to prosperity and happiness, and indolence is the parent of suffering crime.

THE TWO CARPENTERS; *FRUITS OF SLOTH
AND THRIFT ILLUSTRATED*, 1847

. . . .

The scope of thrift is limitless.

THOMAS A. EDISON, 1847

Thrift is the best means of thriving.

ELIZA COOK, DESCRIBING "DIAMOND
DUST" (SHORT WISE SAYINGS), 1849

. . . .

In this respect to what is our poverty ascribable?
To the same cause that has impoverished and
dishonored us in all other respects—the thriftless
and degrading system of human slavery.

HINTON ROWAN HELPER, *IMPENDING*
CRISIS OF THE SOUTH, 1860

. . . .

By all the world contributed—freedom's and law's
    and thrift's society,
The crown and teeming paradise, so far, of time's
    accumulations,
To justify the past.

WALT WHITMAN, "THE PRAIRIE STATES," 1880

. . . .

God pays debts seven for one: who squanders on
Him shows thrift.

ROBERT BROWNING, "DRAMATIC IDYLS," 1880

If much were mine, then manifold
Should be the offering of my thrift.

CHRISTINA ROSSETTI, *POEMS*, 1896

. . . .

the new America of starved children and hollow
    bellies and cracked shoes stamping on souplines,
that has swallowed up the old thrifty farmlands
of Wayne County, Michigan,
as if they had never been.

JOHN DOS PASSOS, WRITING ABOUT
HENRY FORD, *THE BIG MONEY*, 1933

. . . .

To lose sensibility, to see what one sees,
As if sight had not its own miraculous thrift,
To hear only what one hears, one meaning alone,
As if the paradise of meaning ceased
To be paradise, it is this to be destitute.

WALLACE STEVENS, "ESTHETIQUE DU MAL," 1945

4. Thrift as Saving

John Maynard Keynes was one of the greatest public intellectuals of his generation and arguably the most influential economist of the twentieth century. Probably his most respected book is *A Treatise on Money*, published in two volumes in December of 1930. Here is a famous portion of that book:

It has been usual to think of the accumulated wealth of the world as having been painfully built up out of that voluntary abstinence of individuals from the immediate enjoyment of consumption, which we call Thrift. But it should be obvious that mere abstinence is not enough by itself to build cities or drain fens . . .

If Enterprise is afoot, wealth accumulates whatever may be happening to Thrift; and if Enterprise is asleep, wealth decays whatever Thrift may be doing.

Thus, Thrift may be the handmaiden of Enterprise. But equally she may not. And, perhaps, even usually she is not.

JOHN MAYNARD KEYNES, *A TREATISE ON MONEY*, 1930

A few weeks after the book was published, struggling valiantly for ways to overcome the Great Depression that was casting such a blight on the British economy (as well as on the U.S. and other economies), Keynes went on the radio to address the British people directly on this same subject:

There are today many well-wishers of their country who believe that the most useful thing which they and their neighbours can do to mend the situation is to save more than usual . . . Now, in certain circumstances, all this would be quite right, but in present circumstances, unluckily, it is quite wrong. It is utterly harmful and misguided—the very opposite of the truth . . .

The best guess I can make is that whenever you save five shillings, you put a man out of work for a day. Your saving that five shillings adds to unemployment to the extent of one man for one day—and so on in proportion. On the other hand, whenever you buy goods you increase employment— though they must be British, home-produced goods if you are to increase employment in this country. After all, this is only the plainest common sense. For if you buy goods, someone will have to make them. And if you do not buy goods, the shops will not clear their stocks, they will not give repeat orders, and someone will be thrown out of work.

Therefore, O patriotic housewives, sally out tomorrow early into the streets and go to the wonderful sales which are everywhere advertised.

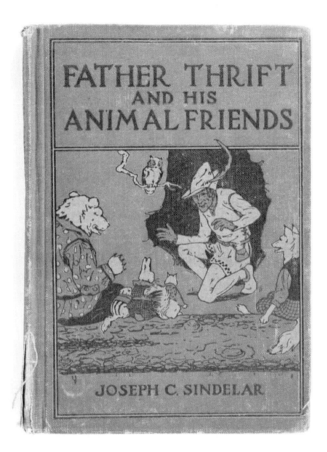

Published 1918

You will do yourselves good—for never were things so cheap, cheap beyond your dreams. Lay in a stock of household linen, of sheets and blankets to satisfy all your needs. And have the added joy that you are increasing employment, adding to the wealth of the country because you are setting on foot useful activities, bringing a chance and a hope to Lancashire, Yorkshire, and Belfast.

JOHN MAYNARD KEYNES, "SAVING AND SPENDING," RADIO ADDRESS, JANUARY 14, 1931

Something remarkable had happened. Leave aside for a moment whether Keynes was right or wrong in his belief that more consumer spending in 1931 would be good for the British economy. (I'm no expert, but I think he was right.) But here we see, quite dramatically, a case in which a distinguished thinker and writer helps in a decisive way to transmogrify, or at least greatly alter, the public meaning of a key word.

In most earlier generations, the thrift ethic most definitely included (though it was not limited to) the principles of hard work, gain-seeking, initiative, and industry, or what Keynes here called "Enterprise." But amazingly, Keynes now treats the two concepts, Thrift and Enterprise, as conceptually separate from one another! Further, he also views them in part as actual opposites, or as concepts that can be in tension with one another and can at times work against each other. He clearly argues, for example, that what finally determines economic outcomes is Enterprise, not Thrift.

For Keynes, "thrift" has thus acquired a much narrower and more restricted meaning. "Thrift" for him now only connotes what most earlier writers would have called "frugality"—saving, self-denial, perhaps even parsimony. In the passage from *A Treatise on Money*, Keynes makes this point with unmistakable clarity when he describes "that voluntary abstinence of individuals from the immediate enjoyment of consumption, which we call Thrift." He even defines thrift as "mere abstinence." Wow! Thrift now only means abstaining, whereas those admirably proactive forces, enterprise and industry, which can be opposed to thrift, mean that we are doing something productive! As we'll see in part three and elsewhere in this book, the majority of thrift advocates prior to this time who had ever written or spoken about the subject, from Daniel Defoe and his "Essay on Projects" to Booker T. Washington and his Tuskegee Institute, would be absolutely bewildered to hear the concept that meant so much to them defined in this curiously limited way. What are we seeing here? It's not just Keynes, of course. Starting, roughly speaking, in the middle decades of the nineteenth century, and gaining much momentum in Keynes's generation, yet another broad, tectonic shift begins in how many English-speaking people understand and use the word "thrift." In brief, the word gets narrower. It shrinks. Instead of typically meaning pathways to material prosperity—or even more classically, growth or good fortune—thrift during these years increasingly comes to mean saving money, economizing, conserving, being careful and sparing, reusing, and avoiding financial and material waste. Most of all, and for many people all that the word ultimately comes to mean, is what the word meant to Keynes: SAVE YOUR MONEY.

And I must needs further say, that considering you live rent free, and I hope free from any future charge from my Brother John or any of your Children but Pall, that 50 pounds a yeare will bee thought a good competence. Especially if all ways of thrift bee studied, as I hope you will all thinke it necessary from hence forward to doe. And by

the way lett mee tell you, that if I understand any thing of thrift, it cannot be any good husbandry to such a family as yours to keepe either hoggs, poultry, sheepe, cowes (or horses more than one) there being meate of all sorts, milke, butter, cheese eggs fowle and every thing elce to bee had cheaper and I am sure with more quiet at the market . . .

SAMUEL PEPYS, LETTER TO HIS FATHER, MAY 16, 1663

· · · ·

We must save the King Money wherever we can, for I am afraid the War is too great for our Purses, if things be not managed with all imaginable Thrift. When the People of England see all things are saved, that can be saved; that there are no exorbitant Pensions, nor unnecessary Salaries, and all this applied to the Use to which they are given; we shall give, and they shall pay whatever his Majesty can want, to secure the Protestant Religion . . .

SIR CHARLES SEDLEY, SPEECH TO PARLIAMENT, MARCH 1690

· · · ·

They who are Sparing in their younger Days seldom fail to be much more thrifty in their Decline.

REV. THOMAS SECKER, SERMON, ABOUT 1768

· · · ·

Whatever might be our points of difference, we all of us seemed to have come to Blithedale with the

one thrifty and laudable idea of wearing out our
old clothes.

NATHANIEL HAWTHORNE, *THE
BLITHEDALE ROMANCE*, 1852

. . . .

Decent burial was what Lisbeth had been thinking
of for herself through years of thrift . . .

GEORGE ELIOT, *ADAM BEDE*, 1859

. . . .

Mrs. Ward mended the torn coat with motherly
zeal, and gave it many of those timely stitches which
thrifty women love to sew.

LOUISA MAY ALCOTT, "THE KING OF CLUBS
AND THE QUEEN OF HEARTS," 1876

. . . .

Paradise is that old mansion
Many owned before—
Occupied by each an instant
Then reversed the Door—
Bliss is frugal of her Leases
Adam taught her Thrift
Bankrupt once through his excesses—

EMILY DICKINSON, ABOUT 1868

Lesson 23: THRIFT

*1. You remember how careful and thrifty Robinson
Crusoe had to be at first on his desert island.
Supposing ten of you were shipwrecked on an
island, and that you only rescued a few sacks of corn
from the wreck. What would you do? . . .*

*17. Yes. If we eat up this year all we produce, we
run a risk of starving next year. How is it that
people do not starve in England, even if they do not
put by in bad or even in good years?*

*18. Because other persons have to keep them out of
what they put by. Must these other persons put by
more or less in consequence?*

19. Is this fair?

*20. Is is right of us to depend if we can help it on
others' savings or thrift?*

*21. Should we not always in plentiful years put by
for less plentiful ones?*

22. What do we call this?

23. Thrift, yes. Is thrift a duty?

GEORGE C. T. BARTLEY, *DOMESTIC ECONOMY: THRIFT
IN EVERY-DAY LIFE* (A BOOK FOR TEACHERS), 1878

. . . .

The whole secret of right thrift lies in the formula:
Save wisely, so as to be able to spend judiciously in
a time of need which will probably be greater than
that of the present.

MARY WILLCOX BROWN, *THE
DEVELOPMENT OF THRIFT*, 1899

Children Should Save

Teach your children early in life the value of thrift. This habit, if formed early, will never be outgrown. Parents should give them a start.

Open an account with us in the youngster's name, give him the bank book and tell him what it is and what it means. Then encourage him to save his pennies. The results will surprise you. One dollar opens an account.

DO IT NOW.

AD, PENNSYLVANIA TRUST COMPANY, EARLY 1900S

. . . .

Thrift is the art of saving a portion of every dollar earned.

J. S. KIRTLEY, "THRIFT," HALF-HOUR TALKS ON CHARACTER BUILDING, 1910

. . . .

My fair, no beauty of thine will last
Save in my love's eternity.
Thy smiles, that light thee fitfully,
Are lost forever—their moment past—
Except the few thou givest to me.
Thy sweet words vanish day by day,
As all breath of mortality;
Thy laughter, done, must cease to be,
And all thy dear tones pass away,
Except the few that sing to me.
Hide then within my heart, O hide
All thou art loth should go from thee.
Be kinder to thyself and me.

My cupful from this river's tide
Shall never reach the long sad sea.

ALICE MEYNELL, "THE LOVER URGES THE BETTER THRIFT," 1913

. . . .

Money saved and put away safely in the bank is a worry-killer and a gloom-dispeller, while common-sense thrift, in the long run, brings greater happiness than extravagance ever can.

T. D. MACGREGOR, THE BOOK OF THRIFT: WHY AND HOW TO SAVE AND WHAT TO DO WITH YOUR SAVINGS, 1915

. . . .

The book will be of great service in schools that are introducing thrift lessons and school savings as a permanent feature of school procedure, in accordance with the program of the National Savings Movement of the United States Treasury Department and the recommendation of the National Education Association.

REVIEW OF PENNIES AND PLANS, IN THE ELEMENTARY SCHOOL JOURNAL, 1920

. . . .

Notice below that the state of Kentucky, in mandating this form of education in the public schools, keeps saying "thrift and industry"—never just "thrift"—as if they have concluded, as Keynes was soon publicly to conclude, that "thrift" and "industry" have become two separate things.

That there shall be taught in the public and high schools of the State a course of lessons to inculcate the habits of thrift and industry.

. . . It shall be the duty of every teacher in the State, paid entirely or in part by the State, to observe at least one fifteen-minute period each week to the teaching of thrift and industry and to keep placards on thrift and industry posted in the school room.

CHAPTER 21, *LAWS OF KENTUCKY*, 1920

. . . .

Little Bo-Peep has lost her sheep,
And doesn't know where to find them.
That's always the way with careless girls,
Who think of only frippery, ribbons and curls.
On a wave of thoughtlessness they drift,
And know not the meaning of "save" or "thrift."

THRIFT—AFTER MOTHER GOOSE, 1920

. . . .

The buyer must cling to thrift ideals, and not buy if there is not specific necessity . . .

MARY SCHENK WOOLMAN, *CLOTHING*, 1920

Thrift means the state of thriving—that is, of prosperity, increase of wealth, and happiness. It has come to be applied particularly to saving money, because everyone has seen that this is one way to prosperity.

THREE BRITISH THRIFT LEADERS, LETTER TO *THE TIMES*, OCTOBER 31, 1933

. . . .

Of course, it is rather difficult to preach thrift to some people in these days. They say, "What's the use? I have too many friends who scrimped and saved, denied themselves all pleasures so that they might have protection in their old age. And now their savings have been wiped out. They put something by for a rainy day, but when the rain came they found themselves as wet as those who had saved nothing."

Now these people who lost their savings through no fault of their own are justified in complaining. They may have invested in insecure securities, because they had no positive way of knowing that the securities would become worthless. They may have been swindled. Or they may have been victims of an economic system that in some respects was none too sound.

But, even in their misfortune, they must not forget that it was not saving which was at fault. The thing to do is not to say that saving is wrong, but to help work out a sounder and fairer business and economic system.

If a man's house burns down, he does not say, "It's foolish to build a house." He says, "We must build better houses, and we must find better ways of preventing and fighting fires."

And it would be wrong to suppose that all our people have lost their savings. On the contrary, it has been savings which have carried thousands of people along until they could begin earning again. It has been savings which have enabled us to help others.

JAMES M. SPINNING, SUPERINTENDENT OF SCHOOLS OF ROCHESTER, NEW YORK, WRITING IN *THE THRIFT ADVOCATE*, JUNE 1934

. . . .

Among the recollections of my childhood are those worthy old men and women, friends and neighbours of my parents, who, after perhaps fifty or sixty years of labour, had been compelled to take the dreaded journey "over the hill to the poorhouse." No human institution was ever more hated and feared by free men than the English workhouse of sixty years ago was hated and feared by those proud peasants, and no one without personal knowledge of them, and without experience of the conditions under which they lived, can appreciate the stern thrift, born of fear and the pride of independence, with which a few coppers were preserved from each week's scanty income for payments to the Friendly Society, the pig-club, or the savings bank. The aged and sick would forgo every comfort, cling despairingly to their damp and often derelict cottage, and pray that death would save them from the crowning indignity of the workhouse.

HENRY SNELL, *MEN, MOVEMENTS AND MYSELF*, 1936

. . . .

Lee, who's also been known to wash and reuse dental floss, hoped to make the point that, as the son of immigrants for whom "thrift was a way of life," he wasn't afraid of potential embarrassment over pinching pennies. "Cutting back on luxuries helps me focus on things that are important to me, enabling me to give more," Lee says.

"ANDREW LEE '07 NAMED TRUMAN SCHOLAR," NEWS RELEASE, CLAREMONT MCKENNA COLLEGE, APRIL 10, 2006

5. Thrift as Hoarding

E. BELFORT BAX was a well-known socialist leader in Victorian Britain. A committed Marxist, he detested capitalism and also, and as a result, detested thrift, even thrift in the form of producer and consumer cooperatives.

As I have said, co-operative experiments reflect what are, from a Socialistic point of view, the worst aspects of the current order. The trade co-operator canonises the bourgeois *virtues, but Socialist vices, "over-work," and "thrift." To the Socialist, labour is an evil to be minimised to the utmost. The man who works at his trade or avocation more than necessity compels him, or who accumulates more than he can enjoy, is not a hero but a fool from the Socialist's standpoint. It is this necessary work which it is the aim of Socialism to reduce to the minimum. Again, "thrift," the hoarding up of the products of labour, it is obvious must be without rhyme or reason, except on a capitalist basis. For the only two purposes which commodities serve are consumption and exchange. Now except under peculiar circumstances (arctic expeditions and the like), it is certain they would not be "saved" to any considerable extent merely for the sake of future consumption. Hence the object of "thrift," or hoarding, must lie in exchange. And, in short, it is the increment obtainable by commodities or realised labour-power when represented by exchange-value or money, that furnishes the only* raison d'etre *of "thrift." The aim of the Socialist, therefore, which is the enjoyment of the products of labour as opposed to that of the* bourgeois *which is their mere accumulation with a view to "surplus-value" is radically at variance with "thrift."*

E. BELFORT BAX, "UNSCIENTIFIC SOCIALISM," 1884

. . . .

Leave aside for now whether Bax was right or wrong in taking such a dim view of cooperatives. (Personally I'm a fan of these thrift institutions.) Let's simply focus for a moment on the fact that, for Bax, "thrift" means "hoarding." Period. To him, that's entirely what the word means.

Despite the best efforts of thrift advocates everywhere to make clear that thrift and hoarding, far from being same thing, and far from being even remotely related, are in fact very close to being opposites, many people over the centuries have insisted otherwise. Especially in the case of people who dislike and distrust thrift anyway, it is common enough, and it has gotten increasingly common since the late nineteenth and early twentieth centuries, to hear that thrift basically means hoarding—being a miser, accumulating money for its own sake, being stingy and cheap, or scrimping and saving in ways that are unpleasant and ultimately futile (since we can't take it with us when we die).

By this reckoning, old Scrooge, before the visits from Marley and the three ghosts, was presumably demonstrating "thrift" by virtue of his penurious self-denial, his harsh treatment of his clerk and nephew, Bob Cratchit, and his adamant refusal to help anyone in the town, for any reason, lest he part with one of his (many! hoarded!) coins. Thrifty old Mr. Scrooge!

It reminds me of a story a minister once told me. People would sometimes tell him with great conviction, "I don't believe in God!" He would always reply: "Tell me more about this God you don't believe in. I probably don't believe in him, either!" Now, I'm a wide-eyed, self-confessed thrift enthusiast—but I intensely dislike, and certainly don't believe in, the idea of hoarding.

I also dislike avarice. But in the following quotation, please note than none other than Max Weber, whose book on *The Protestant Ethic and the Spirit of Capitalism* stands as one of the most important and influential books of the twentieth century, explicitly defines Benjamin Franklin's philosophy of thrift, which Weber also terms "the Protestant ethic," as a "philosophy of avarice" in which the accumulation of wealth is understood as "an end in itself." It is this precise quality, Weber says—this conception of thrift as avarice—which "interests us"—that is, which forms the core subject of his famous book.

The peculiarity of this philosophy of avarice [as exemplified by Franklin's writings on thrift] appears to be the ideal of the honest man of recognized credit, and above all the idea of a duty of the individual toward the increase of his capital, which is assumed as an end in itself. Truly what is here preached is not simply a means of making one's way in the world, but a peculiar ethic. The infraction of its rules is treated not as foolishness but as forgetfulness of duty. That is the essence of the matter. It is not mere business astuteness, that sort of thing is common enough, it is an ethos. This is the quality which interests us.

MAX WEBER, *THE PROTESTANT ETHIC AND THE SPIRIT OF CAPITALISM*, 1905

. . . .

Today in the United States, if you were to convene a reasonable cross-section of prominent academics, and ask them what thrift is, many would reply "Who cares?" and more than a few would reply "Being cheap and stingy." (Trust me—I tried this exercise!) So, the accusations of avarice, hoarding, and selfishness carry real weight. To a significant degree, they have stuck. They have effectively become some of the accepted meanings of the word. Part of the reason for taking this cluster of accusations seriously is to see if there is any truth in them. Are thrift advocates who so loudly deny them protesting too much?

Thrift, thrift, Horatio! the funeral baked meats Did coldly furnish forth the marriage tables.

WILLIAM SHAKESPEARE, *HAMLET* (I, 2), ABOUT 1600

For as a thrifty wench scrapes kitching-stuffe,
And barrelling the droppings, and the snuffe,
Of wasting candles, which in thirty yeare
(Relique-like kept) perchance buyes wedding geare;
Peecemeale he gets lands, and spends as much time
Wringing each Acre, as men pulling prime.

JOHN DONNE, "SATYRE 2," 1590S

. . . .

THRIFTY, an old miser.

A CHARACTER IN THOMAS OTWAY'S
THE CHEATS OF SCAPIN, 1677

. . . .

Two passions, both degenerate, for they both
Began in honour, gradually obtained
Rule over her, and vexed her daily life;
An urelenting, avaricious thrift;
And a strange thraldom of maternal love;
. . . she placed her trust
In ceaseless pains—and strictest parsimony
Which sternly hoarded all that could be spared,
From each day's need, out of each day's least gain.

WILLIAM WORDSWORTH, "THE EXCURSION," 1814

. . . .

It may be said that the soil was originally purchased
by the settlers; but who does not know the nature
of Indian purchases, in the early periods of
colonization? The Europeans always made thrifty
bargains through their superior adroitness in traffic;

and they gained vast accessions of territory by easily-
provoked hostilities.

WASHINGTON IRVING, *THE SKETCH BOOK,* 1820

. . . .

Why should money be hoarded when so many
pockets were empty? . . . Thrift, if it meant
the pushing against and elbowing of men, was
a word not to be found in his vocabulary.

BEN BRIERLY, *TALES AND SKETCHES*
OF LANCASHIRE LIFE, 1884

. . . .

He [Sir William Temple] loved fame, but not with
the love of an exalted and generous mind. He loved
it as an end, not at all as a means; as a personal
luxury, not at all as an instrument of advantage
to others. He scraped it together and treasured it
up with a timid and niggardly thrift; and never
employed the hoard in any enterprise, however
virtuous and useful, in which there was hazard of
losing one particle.

THOMAS B. MACAULEY, ON SIR WILLIAM TEMPLE, 1838

. . . .

[bitterly]
Ay! I have come to my inheritance.
O bloody legacy! and O murderous dole!
Which, like a thrifty miser, must I hoard

OSCAR WILDE, *THE DUCHESS OF PADUA,* 1883

Thrift is the watchword of Jewtown, as of its people the world over. It is at once its strength and its fatal weakness, its cardinal virtue and its foul disgrace. Become an over-mastering passion with these people who come here in droves from Eastern Europe to escape persecution, from which freedom could be bought only with gold, it has enslaved them in bondage worse than that from which they fled. Money is their God. Life itself is of little value compared with even the leanest bank account.

JACOB RIIS, *HOW THE OTHER HALF LIVES*, 1890

· · · ·

Long enough has selfish and greedy thrift dominated the councils of the Republic.

WILLIAM JENNINGS BRYAN, *THE FIRST BATTLE: A STORY OF THE CAMPAIGN OF 1896*, 1896

· · · ·

But the theatre did not often do so well; the people of the town were still too thrifty.

They were thrifty because they were the sons or grandsons of the "early settlers," who had opened the wilderness and had reached it from the East and the South with wagons and axes and guns, but with no money at all. The pioneers were thrifty or they would have perished: they had to store away food for the winter, or goods to trade for food, and they often feared they had not stored enough—they left traces of that fear in their sons and grandsons. In the minds of most of these, indeed, their thrift

was next to their religion: to save, even for the sake of saving, was their earliest lesson and discipline. No matter how prosperous they were, they could not spend money either upon "art," or upon mere luxury and entertainment, without a sense of sin.

BOOTH TARKINGTON, *THE MAGNIFICENT AMBERSONS*, 1918

· · · ·

Mrs. Manson Mingott had long since succeeded in untying her husband's fortune, and had lived in affluence for half a century; but memories of her early straits had made her excessively thrifty, and though, when she bought a dress or a piece of furniture, she took care that it should be of the best, she could not bring herself to spend much on the transient pleasures of the table. Therefore, for totally different reasons, her food was as poor as Mrs. Archer's, and her wines did nothing to redeem it. Her relatives considered that the penury of her table discredited the Mingott name, which had always been associated with good living; but people continued to come to her in spite of the "made dishes" and flat champagne, and in reply to the remonstrances of her son Lovell (who tried to retrieve the family credit by having the best chef in New York) she used to say laughingly: "What's the use of two good cooks in one family, now that I've married the girls and can't eat sauces?"

EDITH WHARTON, *THE AGE OF INNOCENCE*, 1920

Box Top, Crystal Clear Coin Bank

No man of elder years than fifty
Should be empowered with lands and gold,
It turns them shrewd and over-thrifty,
It makes them cruel and blind and cold.

ARTHUR D. FICKE, "YOUTH AND AGE," 1929

. . . .

"So you came to the war to make money?" he said.
"Aweel," MacWyrglinchbeath said, "A wou'na be
wastin' ma time."

WILLIAM FAULKNER, "THRIFT," *SATURDAY*
EVENING POST, SEPTEMBER 6, 1930

For instance, it appears that the 58 thriftiest people
in the United States (laughter)—the 58 thriftiest
people in the United States—and of course we are
all in favor of thrift, the thriftier you are the nearer
you will come to being included among the 58—in
1932 they were all so thrifty that although they had
a million dollars income a year or more, they paid
no tax whatever to the Federal Government on 37
percent of their net incomes.

. . . Furthermore, it turned up in the figures
that one family in this country had 197 family
trusts. They are a very thrifty family. Of course it
is very easy to demonstrate that one of the primary
purposes of these 197 family trusts in this one family
was to reduce their taxes through the reduction
and splitting up of income into a great many parts,
thereby avoiding or greatly reducing the surtaxes.

That family trust method, in the case of that one family, cost the Government of the United States a very large sum of money.

PRESIDENT FRANKLIN D. ROOSEVELT, EXCERPTS
FROM A PRESS CONFERENCE, JULY 31, 1935

. . . .

Let's permit my friends, the thrift enthusiasts, to have the last few words on this point.

So devotion is counterfaited by superstition, good thrift by niggardliness . . .

BISHOP JOSEPH HALL, *MEDITATIONS AND VOWS*, ABOUT 1608

. . . .

I mistook her patience for simplicity, her kindness for wantoness, her thrift for covetousness, her obedience for flattery, her retir'd life for dull stupidity.

MARGARET CAVENDISH, *PLAYES*, 1662

. . . .

Some economists may be selfish, but every spendthrift is.

LORD DERBY, LONDON, MARCH 12, 1880

. . . .

Hoarding millions is avarice, not thrift.

ANDREW CARNEGIE, "THRIFT AS A DUTY," 1900

As for the argument that the inculcation of thrift through school banks is destructive of generosity, experience has shown that it is quite the reverse . . . Generosity, like any other virtue, withers up, perishes from want of exercise. And who can practice it that has nothing to give?

AGNES LAMBERT, "THRIFT AMONG THE CHILDREN," 1886

. . . .

Her thrift was not for hoarding, but for using.

GAIL HAMILTON, IN 1886 DESCRIBING ZILPAH P. GRANT,
AN AMERICAN EDUCATOR WHO IN 1828 FOUNDED
THE IPSWICH FEMALE SEMINARY, ONE OF THE FIRST
MAJOR U.S. EDUCATIONAL INSTITUTIONS FOR WOMEN

. . . .

. . . a wise and elegant thrift—nothing wasted, nothing wanted . . .

A DESCRIPTION IN 1885 OF ZILPAH P.
GRANT, BY HER BIOGRAPHER

. . . .

Whatever thrift is, it is not avarice . . . avarice is not generous; and, after all, it is the thrifty people who are generous.

LORD ROSEBERY, ADDRESS TO THE ANNUAL MEETING OF
THE EDINBURGH SAVINGS BANK, DECEMBER 28, 1908

*Figure out the cost to the average smoker or
the moderate drinker for a period of ten years,
computing interest on the investment at the market
rate. Is saving this expense to be looked upon as
stinginess or as praiseworthy thrift?*

*Does a good living and prosperity come oftener
from high wages or from a habit of saving?
Distinguish carefully between stinginess and thrift.*

*What is the difference between a generous man
and a spendthrift? Which does the most harm to
the community, a stingy man or a spendthrift?*

*Is the conceited or self-centered man more likely
to be stingy or a spendthrift? Is he likely to be a
generous man?*

YMCA, *LIFE QUESTIONS OF SCHOOL BOYS*, 1916

. . . .

*. . . it should be perfectly clear that thrift does not
mean the hoarding of money. To hoard money is
one of the most thriftless things one can do with
it. The miser of romance . . . was, in the strictest
possible sense, a thriftless consumer of wealth . . .*

Thrift, no less than extravagance, consists
*in using money; that is, spending it. The sole
difference is the purpose or purposes for which
it is spent. To spend money for immediate and
temporary gratification is extravagance; to spend
it for things which add to one's power, mental,
physical, moral, or economic, is thrift.*

THE ECONOMIST THOMAS NIXON CARVER,
"THE RELATIONSHIP OF THRIFT TO
NATION BUILDING," 1921

. . . .

*The word thrift has too generally been associated
with stinginess, meanness, parsimony, when its true
significance is the elimination of waste.*

CALIFORNIA BUILDING-LOAN LEAGUE, 1922

. . . .

*Thrift by derivation means thriving; and the miser
is the man who does not thrive. The whole meaning
of thrift is making the most of everything; and the
miser does not make anything of anything.*

G. K. CHESTERTON, *AS I WAS SAYING*, 1936

6. What Thrift Is

CAN THRIFT BE DEFINED? Notwithstanding the various historical shifts and the many and often conflicting usages, does there remain an underlying conceptual core, a set of enduring principles and an ethically coherent way of seeing the world that can legitimately, as if in a dictionary, be called "thrift"? Many learned people will tell you that the answer is no. I disagree. So let me briefly say what I think thrift is, and then to support my definition, let me present to you some formulations from others who (mostly) have thought carefully about thrift, who believe that thrift is a good thing, and who, like me, believe that they know what thrift is.

Thrift is a particular way of seeing the world— a set of principles and ethical guidelines intended to orient us toward certain goals. Thrift concerns not only the material world—the world of material goods and the money to buy them—but also the natural, spiritual, and aesthetic worlds.

Put most simply, thrift is the moral discipline of wisest use. The root of "thrift" is "thrive." Thrift says: Use all that you have in the wisest way, to promote thriving.

To understand thrift's scope, think in terms of "three." Specifically, three groups of three.

Substantively, thrift is made up of three traits or norms: industry, frugality, and trusteeship. These are its pillars, its overarching principles.

INDUSTRY: hard work; the great value and necessity of persistent, diligent, careful, productive labor. (A thrift maxim: the reward for good work is more work.)

FRUGALITY: being sparing as regards using or spending for myself; the worth of conserving and reusing; and the importance of eliminating waste and avoiding extravagance.

TRUSTEESHIP: what is mine, I hold in trust; my wealth (my thrift) is ultimately for the purpose of helping others and contributing to the common good.

Operationally, thrift comes in three main forms, corresponding to three life domains: individual and household, commercial, and public.

INDIVIDUAL AND HOUSEHOLD THRIFT is close to home and largely private; it is reflected mainly in individual character traits and in household norms and practices. Examples of such thrift include mending torn clothing, recycling waste products, and allocating a fixed proportion of personal or household earnings to savings.

COMMERCIAL THRIFT concerns the operation of businesses and the production side of the marketplace. Examples of this form of thrift include changing the workplace to reduce waste or increase quality, forming a food co-op, or making sure that you have a deserved reputation for honest dealing.

PUBLIC THRIFT is, well, public—it involves collective decision-making and social and public institutions aimed at thrift. Examples of this form of thrift include building a public library, mobilizing for sacrifice in times of war or national emergency, or instituting reforms or passing laws to promote conservation.

Finally, thrift contains within it three main beliefs or assumptions about the human person.

The first is that PRODUCTIVE WORK IS GOOD. A thrifty person is anything but passive or idle. (One of the Scandinavian roots of the word means "to seize.") Thrift openly embraces material prosperity, in the sense that thrift strongly values productivity and fruitfulness stemming from steady and good work. Thrift grows things. Where one blade of grass is now growing, thrift works to make two grow. Then three.

The second is that WHAT WE HAVE IS NOT OURS. The Christian doctrine of stewardship teaches us that everything we have, including our own lives, is a gift from God, and must be used for his purposes, not ours alone. Thrift secularizes this power-ful idea, urging us to view ourselves not as owners, but as trustees, who are obliged (entrusted) to use what we have not for ourselves alone, but for the common good and to help those in need.

The third is that GIVING PEOPLE THINGS IS NOT AS GOOD AS HELPING THEM TO HELP THEM-SELVES. Typically, thrift is deeply suspicious of handouts, or acts of charity that require little or nothing from the recipient. From top to bottom, thrift is a virtue tailor-made by, and for, those who want to lift themselves up, and for those who want to help others to do the same.

Thinges thriftie, that teacheth the thriving to thrive.
THOMAS TUSSER, *A HUNDRED POYNTES OF GOOD HUSBANDRY*, 1557

. . . .

This fatherly advise may be my all-time favorite thrift saying:

Wisedome is great wealth. Sparing, is good getting.
Thrift consisteth not in golde, but grace.
. . . those that give themselves to be bookish,
are oftentimes so blockish, that they forget
thrift: Whereby the olde Saw is verified, that
the greatest Clearkes are not the wisest men,
who digge still at the roote, while others gather
the fruite . . .
. . . The stipende that is allowed to maintaine
thee use wisely, be neither prodigall to spende all,
nor covetous to keepe all, cut thy coat according

to thy cloth, and thinke it better to bee accompted thriftie among the wise, then a good companion among the riotous.

. . . Be thriftie and warie in thy expences, for in olde time, they were as soone condemned by law that spent their wives dowry prodigally, as they that divorced them wrongfully.

. . . Now thou art come to that honourable estate, forget all thy former follyes, and debate with thy selfe, that here-to-fore thou diddest but goe about the world, and that nowe, thou art come into it, that Love did once make thee to folow ryot, that it muste now enforce thee to pursue thrifte, that then there was no pleasure to bee compared to the courting of Ladyes, that now there can be no delight greater then to have a wife.

. . . Thus hast thou if thou canst use it, the whole wealth of the world: and he that can not follow good counsel, never can get commoditie. I leave thee more, then thy father left me: For he dying, gave me great wealth, without care how I might keepe it: and I give thee good counsell, with all meanes how to get riches. And no doubt, what so is gotten with witte, will bee kept with warinesse, and encreased with Wisedome.

JOHN LYLY, *EUPHUES AND HIS ENGLAND*, 1580

. . . .

Thy heart's thirst is satisfied with thy hand's thrift.
JOHN LYLY, *SAPHO AND PHAO* (I, I), 1584

Some mouth'd like greedy oystriges; some faste
Like loathly toades; some fashioned in the waste
Like swine: for so deformd is Luxury,
Surfeat, Misdiet, and unthriftie Waste,
Vaine Feastes, and ydle Superfluity:
All those this Sences Fort assayle incessantly.
EDMUND SPENCER, *THE FAERIE QUEENE*, 1596

. . . .

Many men marvell Lynus does not thrive,
That hath more trades than any man alive;
As first a broker, then a petty-fogger,
A traveller, a gamester, and a cogger,[1]
A coyner, a promoter, and a bawd,
A spie, a practiser in every fraud;
And missing thrift by these lewd trades and sinister,
He takes the best, yet proves the worst, a minister.
HARRINGTON'S EPIGRAMS, 1633

. . . .

Why walkes Nick Flimsey like a Male-content?
Is it because his money is all spent?
No, but because the Ding-thrift[2] now is poore,
And knowes not where i'th world to borrow more.
ROBERT HERRICK, "UPON FLIMSEY," 1648

. . . .

Necessary frugality or sparing is an act of fidelity, obedience, and gratitude, by which we use all our estates so faithfully for the chief Owner, so obediently to our chief Ruler, and so gratefully to our chief Benefactor, as that we waste it not any other way.

[Answering the question, How do we know when our expenditure is excessive?] . . . it is excess when any thing is that way expended, which you are called to expend another way.

THE PURITAN DIVINE RICHARD BAXTER (1615–91),
DIRECTIONS ABOUT PRODIGALITY AND SINFUL WASTE

. . . .

. . . carefulness, that handmaiden of generosity . . .

"SIR ROGER DE COVERLEY,"
IN *THE SPECTATOR*, ABOUT 1711

. . . .

. . . the man of thrift shows regularity in every thing.

"HEZEKIAH THRIFT," IN THE
SPECTATOR, OCTOBER 14, 1712

. . . .

But when a man is diligent and frugal, in order to have it in his power to do good; when he is more industrious, or more sparing perhaps than his circumstances necessarily require, that he may have to give to him that needeth; when he labours in order to support the weak; such care of his affairs is itself charity, and the actual beneficence which it enables him to practice is additional charity.

REV. JOSEPH BUTLER, SERMON
DELIVERED MARCH 31, 1748

But in another instance the Roman law goes much beyond the English. For, if a man by notorious prodigality was in danger of wasting his estate, he was looked upon as non compos and committed to the care of curators or tutors by the praetor. But with us, when a man on an inquest of idiocy hath been returned an unthrift and not an idiot, no further proceedings have been had.

WILLIAM BLACKSTONE, *COMMENTARIES
ON THE LAWS*, 1765

. . . .

To catch Dame Fortune's golden smile,
Assiduous wait upon her;
And gather gear by ev'ry wile,
That's justify'd by Honor:
Not for to hide it in a hedge,
Nor for a train-attendant;
But for the glorious privilege
Of being independent.

ROBERT BURNS, "EPISTLE TO A
YOUNG FRIEND," MAY 1786

. . . .

Be assured that it gives much more pain to the mind to be in debt, than to do without any article whatever which we may seem to want.

THOMAS JEFFERSON, LETTER TO HIS
DAUGHTER MARTHA, JUNE 14, 1787

Raw Haste, half-sister to Delay.

ALFRED, LORD TENNYSON, "LOVE THOU THY
LAND, WITH LOVE FAR-BOUGHT," 1833

. . . .

*On the whole, a man must not complain
of his "element," of his "time," or the like;
it is thriftless work doing so.*

THOMAS CARLYLE, "THE HERO AS A MAN
OF LETTERS," 1840

. . . .

*And looks the whole world in the face,
For he owes not any man.*

HENRY WADSWORTH LONGFELLOW, "THE VILLAGE
BLACKSMITH," 1840

*By diligence and self-command, let him put
the bread he eats at his own disposal, that he
may not stand in bitter and false relations to
other men; for the best good of wealth is freedom.
Let him practice the minor virtues.*

RALPH WALDO EMERSON, "PRUDENCE," 1841

. . . .

*Things are in the saddle,
And ride mankind.*

EMERSON, "ODE, INSCRIBED TO
WILLIAM H. CHANNING," 1846

. . . .

*The true thrift is always to spend on the higher
plane; to invest and invest, with keener avarice,
that he may spend in spiritual creation, and not
in augmenting animal existence.*

EMERSON, *THE CONDUCT OF LIFE*, 1860

The virtues are economists.
EMERSON, *THE CONDUCT OF LIFE*

. . . .

Waste is worse than loss.
THOMAS A. EDISON, 1847

. . . .

Your request for eighty dollars, I do not think it best to comply with now. At the various times when I have helped you a little, you have said to me, "We can get along very well now," but in a very short time I find you in the same difficulty again. Now this can only happen by some defect in your conduct. What that defect is, I think I know. You are not lazy, *and still you are an* idler. *I doubt whether since I saw you, you have done a good whole day's work, in any one day. You do not very much dislike to work, and still you do not work much, merely because it does not seem to you that you could get much for it.*

This habit of uselessly wasting time, is the whole difficulty; it is vastly important to you, and still more so to your children, that you should break this habit. It is more important to them, because they have longer to live, and can keep out of an idle habit before they are in it, easier than they can get out after they are in.

You are now in need of some ready money; and what I propose is, that you shall go to work, "tooth and nail," for somebody who will give you money for it.

Let father and your boys take charge of your things at home—prepare for a crop, and make the crop, and you go to work for the best money wages, or in discharge of any debt you owe, that you can get. And to secure you a fair reward for your labor, I now promise you that for every dollar you will, between this and the first of May, get for your own labor either in money or in your indebtedness, I will then give you one other dollar . . .

Now if you will do this, you will soon be out of debt, and what is better, you will have a habit that will keep you from getting in debt again. But if I should now clear you out, next year you will be just as deep in as ever . . . You have always been kind to me, and I do not now mean to be unkind to you. On the contrary, if you will but follow my advice, you will find it worth more than eight times eighty dollars to you.

ABRAHAM LINCOLN, LETTER TO HIS STEPBROTHER JOHN
D. JOHNSTON, DECEMBER 24, 1848

. . . .

To the New England mind, roads, schools, clothes, and a clean face were connected as a part of the law of order or divine system. Bad roads meant bad morals. The moral of this Virginia road was clear, and the boy learned it fully.

HENRY ADAMS, *THE EDUCATION OF HENRY ADAMS*, RECALLING HIS FIRST TRIP TO THE U.S. SOUTH IN 1850

. . . .

He looked like a man who had never cringed and never had had a creditor.

HERMAN MELVILLE, *MOBY-DICK*, 1851

. . . .

A man who saves from principle is likely to be the man who gives from principle.

REV. DR. DAVID KING, AT A MEETING ORGANIZED BY THE GLASGOW SAVINGS BANK, GLASGOW CITY HALL, FEBRUARY 10, 1852

. . . .

Pick up that pin—let that account be correct to a farthing—find out what that ribbon costs before you say "you will take it"—pay that half dime your friend handed you to make change with—in a word, be economical, be accurate, know what you are doing—be honest and then be generous; for all you have or acquire thus belongs to you by every rule of right, and you may put it to any good use if you acquire it justly and honestly, for you have a foundation, a back ground which will always keep you above the waves of evil. It is not parsimonious to be economical. It is not selfish to be correct in

your dealings. It is not small to know the price of articles you are about to purchase, or remember the little debt you owe.

FREEMAN HUNT, *WORTH AND WEALTH*, 1856

. . . .

Now, we have warped the word "economy" in our English language into a meaning which it has no business whatever to bear. In our use of it, it constantly signifies merely sparing or saving; economy of money means saving money—economy of time, sparing time, and so on. But that is a wholly barbarous use of the word . . . Economy no more means saving money than it means spending money. It means, the administration of a house; its stewardship; spending or saving, that is, whether money or time, or anything else, to the best possible advantage.

JOHN RUSKIN, LECTURE ON "THE POLITICAL ECONOMY OF ART," DELIVERED JULY 10, 1857

. . . .

Believe me when I tell you that the thrift of time will pay you in after life with an usury of profit beyond your most sanguine dreams, and that the waste of it will make you dwindle, alike in intellectual and in moral stature, beneath your darkest reckonings.

WILLIAM E. GLADSTONE, RECTORIAL ADDRESS, UNIVERSITY OF EDINBURGH, APRIL 1860

Gladstone's love of order and hatred of waste were most marked in money matters, national and private. His own sons, sent to Eton, had only 10s. each, increased by 1s. every half, but Mrs. Gladstone, who had not the same love of method, saw that they did not run short. Hand in hand with Gladstone's keen thrift went a boundless generosity. Between 1831 and 1898 he gave away 83,000 pounds to charity and religion and set apart 30,000 pounds for the founding of St. Deiniol's Library at Hawarden . . .

"GLADSTONE'S THRIFT AND GENEROSITY," *THE TIMES,*
JUNE 27, 1936

. . . .

There was no man so careful and thrifty in his expenditure, combined with great generosity and liberality. But no man ever saw that great man at work could believe that it was anything but a sin to waste anything, especially time.

LORD ROSEBERY, DESCRIBING WILLIAM GLADSTONE

. . . .

In 1895, when he was eighty-five years old and donating his some 32,000 books to nearby St. Deiniol's Library, which he had founded, Glad-stone, no fan of extravagant spending and unafraid of hard work, reportedly took the books to the new library himself, using his wheelbarrow to transport them. We will hear a bit more from and about this great thrift advocate in part three, when we look at Charles Sikes and the passage of the Post Office Savings Bank Act of 1861.

. . . that thrift, which makes graceful use of common things.

THE GARDENER'S MONTHLY AND
HORTICULTURALIST, MAY 1877

. . . .

Spend upward, that is, for the higher faculties. Spend for the mind rather than the body; for culture rather than amusement. The very secret and essence of thrift consists of getting things into higher values . . . The night supper, the ball, the drink, the billiard table, the minstrels,—enough calls of this sort there are, and in no wise modest in their demands, but they issue from below you. Go buy a book instead, or journey abroad, or bestow a gift. I have not urged thrift upon you for its own sake, nor merely that you may be kept from poverty, nor even for the ease it brings, but because it lies near to all the virtues, and antagonizes all the vices. It is the conserving and protecting virtue. It makes soil and atmosphere for all healthy growths. It favors a full manhood. It works against the very faults it seems to invite, and becomes the reason and inspiration of generosity.

REV. THEODORE T. MUNGER, *ON THE THRESHOLD,* 1881

Upheld by truth and thrift, and gained by pluck
Too shrewd to lean on patronage and luck.
"PLAIN WORDS TO YOUNG MEN," 1883

. . . .

There is a close relationship between generosity
and thrift.
"AN OLD BOY," *NOTES FOR BOYS*, 1885

. . . .

So that the conclusion is this: that thrift is a virtue
and generosity is a virtue, but selfishness may enter
into thrift and generosity and spoil them both.
MISSION SOCIETY, METHODIST EPISCOPAL CHURCH, 1900

. . . .

The penny savings began to be received in 1889.
Two years later the stamp saving system was
introduced. The first "Thrift Society" was the Co-
operative Coal Club founded in 1903 . . . In 1905 a
sick benefit society was started in connection with
the above and has been very successful under the
name of the Rainy Day Society . . . One of our
[supporters] has taken savings in schools under her
wing by paying the Starr Center a sum sufficient
for the salary of a person to collect daily small sums
from the children in the schools of the Seventh
Ward.
ACTIVITIES OF THE STARR CENTER, 725-727-729
LOMBARD STREET, PHILADELPHIA, FOUNDED 1894

To promote right living, thrift, and happiness, by
means of instruction in useful knowledge, industrial
training, wholesome recreation and friendly visits.
MISSION STATEMENT OF THE CHEERFUL HOME
SETTLEMENT, 421 JERSEY STREET, QUINCY,
ILLINOIS, FOUNDED FEBRUARY 1903

. . . .

To inspire higher ideals of manhood and
womanhood, to purify the social condition, and to
encourage thrift and neighborhood pride, and good
citizenship.
MISSION STATEMENT OF THE EMANUEL SETTLEMENT,
2732 ARMOUR AVENUE, CHICAGO, FOUNDED 1908

. . . .

Thrift means making the best of every thing; life,
our faculties, the world in its entirety, made the
most of; and above all other habits, it gives bone
and sinew to the moral character, and enables it to
resist the temptations of life.
JAMES PLATT, "THRIFT," 1889

. . . .

This, then, is held to be the duty of the man of
wealth: To set an example of modest, unostentatious
living, shunning display or extravagance; to
provide moderately for the legitimate wants of
those dependent upon him; and, after doing so,
to consider all surplus revenues which come to
him simply as trust funds, which he is called upon

From a purely economic point of view a saving in the worker's income due to superior housewifery is equivalent to an increase in his earnings; but morally, the superior thrift is, of course, immensely more important.

HORACE PLUNKETT, *IRELAND IN THE NEW CENTURY*, 1904

. . . .

The spirit of thrift is opposed to waste on the one hand and to recklessness on the other. It does not involve stinginess, which is an abuse of thrift, nor does it require that each item of savings should be a financial investment; the money that is spent on the education of one's self or of one's family, in travel, in music, in art, or in helpfulness to others, if it brings real returns in personal development or in a better understanding of the world we live in, is in accordance with the spirit of thrift.

CHANCELLOR DAVID STARR JORDAN OF STANFORD UNIVERSITY, SPEECH AT THE INTERNATIONAL CONGRESS FOR THRIFT, HELD IN CONJUNCTION WITH THE PANAMA-PACIFIC EXPOSITION IN SAN FRANCISCO, AUGUST 1915

to administer, and strictly bound as a matter of duty to administer in the manner which, in his judgement, is best calculated to produce the most beneficial results for the community—the man of wealth thus becoming the mere trustee and agent for his poorer brethren, bringing to their service his superior wisdom, experience, and ability to administer, doing for them better than they would or could do for themselves.

ANDREW CARNEGIE, "THE GOSPEL OF WEALTH," 1889

. . . .

9. A SCOUT IS THRIFTY

He does not wantonly destroy property. He works faithfully, wastes nothing, and makes the best of his opportunities. He saves his money so that he may pay his own way, be generous to those in need, and helpful to worthy objects. He may work for pay, but must not receive tips for courtesies or "Good Turns."

THE NINTH SCOUT LAW, *BOY SCOUT HANDBOOK*, 1916

To earn what you can; spend what you must; give what you should, and save the rest—this is thrift.

J. O. ENGLEMAN, *MORAL EDUCATION IN SCHOOL AND HOME*, 1918

. . . .

Happy Jack shook his head. "Peter," said he, "you haven't yet learned the meaning of the word thrift. Sammy Jay told me all about that pile of clover. He told me how it had spoiled because it wasn't properly taken care of. Doing useless things, no matter how hard you work, is waste of time and not thrift. And allowing a lot of good food to spoil is the very worst kind of thriftlessness. The trouble with you, Peter, is that you didn't begin young enough to learn how to be thrifty. Now you are too old to learn, I guess. It's too bad, Peter; it's too bad. There is nothing like learning thrift when you are young. It will help you all your life.

> *"Oh shiftless, thriftless, heedless Peter,*
> *A pity 'tis you are not neater,*
> *For thrift and neatness go together,*
> *Though bright or stormy be the weather.*

But we love you just the same, Peter, and we're sorry you can't join our club" concluded Happy Jack.

HAPPY JACK'S THRIFT CLUB, PAMPHLET FOR CHILDREN, 1918

What is Thrift? The prudent man looks ahead and gets ready. The frugal man lives carefully and saves persistently. The economical man spends judiciously, buys wisely, and wastes nothing. The industrious man works hard. The miser hoards. But the man of thrift spends wisely, plans carefully, manages economically, and saves consistently. Thrift should be all of prudence, economy, frugality, industry—and more. Thrift is conservation. Thrift is discrimination. Thrift is self-discipline, self-control, self-respect. Thrift is a foundation stone of character—individual and national. Thrift is practical patriotism.

"MATERIAL FOR A THRIFT TALK," U.S. TREASURY DEPARTMENT, 1918

. . . .

Thrift is making the best of what one has in strength, time, or money; getting one hundred percent in one's relations with life. Thrift is an appreciation and application of the accumulative force of little things. Thrift is a constructive force; waste is its destructive opposite. Sometimes thrift is saving, going without; sometimes thrift is spending—"there is a scattering that increaseth"— but always it is something for something. Thrift is the base on which success of every kind is built, for either thrift or waste is used in everything.

DORA MORELL HUGHES, *THRIFT IN THE HOUSEHOLD*, 1918

Summed up: Thrift is a composite virtue. It includes economy, self-denial, and savings; but it is no relative of niggardliness or meanness . . . Any virtue that is carried to extremes becomes undesirable and no longer a virtue. The thrift that does not make a man charitable sours into avarice. Thrift means better homes, better citizens, more comforts, more enjoyments, little waste, little anxiety—peace. Out of it grows energy, steady courage, opportunity, independence, self-respect, aimfulness in life—manhood. It is the one material habit that has no shady side.

M. W. HARRISON, "DO YOU KNOW WHAT
THRIFT IS?" (SCHOOL TEXTBOOK), 1919

. . . .

When I came to the United States as a lad of six, the most needful lesson for me, as a boy, was the necessity for thrift. I had been taught in my home across the sea that thrift was one of the fundamentals in a successful life. My family had come from a land (the Netherlands) noted for its thrift; but we had been in the United States only few days before the realization came home strongly to my father and mother that they had brought their children to a land of waste.

Where the Dutchman saved, the American wasted. There was waste, the most prodigal waste, on every hand. In every street-car and on every ferry-boat the floors and seats were littered with newspapers that had been read and thrown away or left behind . . .

At school I learned quickly that to "save money"

was to be "stingy"; as a young man, I soon found that the American disliked the word "economy," and on every hand as plenty grew spending grew. There was literally nothing in American life to teach me thrift or economy; everything to teach me to spend and waste.

THE AMERICANIZATION OF EDWARD BOK, 1920

. . . .

Old Uncle Thrift said:
"We will be a thrifty nation,
When we all learn conservation."

THE TREASURE TWINS (CHILDREN'S BOOK), 1923

. . . .

We decided that the best definition of thrift for our purposes, indeed a good definition to bear in mind all the while, is that thrift is wise spending. If you spend your time and your strength and your money wisely, you will be thrifty.

HELEN ATWATER, AMERICAN HOME
ECONOMICS ASSOCIATION, 1924

. . . .

We have worked out a thrift chart. This chart is marked and checked each day by the child. She must keep it for three months and then send it to National headquarters, and if it complies with all the requirements she is given an honor card. After having kept the chart for three months it will not be very easy for her to break the habits which she has formed and practiced conscientiously during that period.

MISS E. A. SHELTON, CAMP FIRE GIRLS, 1924

. . . .

They must recognize the obligation of citizenship to see that the public resources of the country, on which depend the possibility of private thrift, of individual thrift, are protected through the practice of public thrift; that is, the conservation of our natural resources.

HERBERT A. SMITH, U.S. FOREST SERVICE, 1924

. . . .

The Persistent Peddler had an argument for the use of everything. Fairy Thrift peeped in the window and called merrily,

> *"Says Fairy Thrift, 'I hope you'll agree*
> *Not to purchase everything you see.'"*

LAURA ROUNDTREE SMITH, *NAN AND ANN IN THRIFT TOWN* (CHILDREN'S BOOK), 1925

. . . .

We believe in the Habit of Thrift because:

1. *It is the foundation of a strong character in that it builds up self-denial, will power, and self-confidence.*
2. *It promotes the growth of individual industry and responsibility.*
3. *It calls for intelligence in spending and results in scientific management of one's personal affairs.*
4. *It develops forethought and removes one of the greatest causes for worry.*
5. *It establishes for the thrifty person a reputation for intelligence, diligence, and dependability.*
6. *It puts one in line for the best positions.*
7. *It enables one to seize business opportunity when it comes.*
8. *It secures great and better planned pleasures.*
9. *It makes one a benefactor to society, not a beneficiary.*
10. *It assures national stability, prosperity, and happiness.*

THRIFT CREED ADOPTED BY ROOSEVELT HIGH SCHOOL IN SEATTLE, 1920S

. . . .

Luxury, Extravagance, Lolly Popp, Candy Barr, Chewing Gumm, and Movie Madd
Villains waylaying a child on his way to the savings bank.

FROM A PLAY PERFORMED IN THE LOS ANGELES PUBLIC SCHOOLS, 1920S

. . . .

Thrift is a word of broader meaning than saving. It denotes a higher and more intelligent use of accumulations, than merely saving them.

HENRY S. ROSENTHAL, *CYCLOPEDIA OF BUILDING, LOAN AND SAVING ASSOCIATIONS*, 1927

Work, earn, make a budget, record expenditures, have a bank account, carry life insurance, own your home, make a will, invest in safe securities, pay bills promptly, and share with others.
"FINANCIAL CREED" RECOMMENDED BY THE NATIONAL THRIFT COMMITTEE OF THE YMCA, 1928

. . . .

. . . wise spending, careful saving, and generous sharing.
THE DEFINITION OF "THRIFT" PROPOSED FOR NATIONAL THRIFT WEEK, 1931

. . . .

Thrift . . . is more than the mere practice of saving money: it implies rather a denunciation of every form of waste, not only of money, but of time, energy, talents, and other assets of mankind.
"WORLD THRIFT DAY," *THE TIMES* (LONDON), OCTOBER 26, 1938

. . . .

How does, or should, the rise in the twentieth century of mass consumer spending—what the economist John Kenneth Galbraith in 1958 called "the affluent society"—affect the ideals of thrift? Many of today's prominent academics will tell you with barely disguised pleasure that mass consumer spending, with its installment-plan and credit-card buying and its nonstop, buy-it-now advertising, means the end of thrift as a persuasive public value. But the great credit union leader Roy F. Bergengren—possibly the most important U.S. thrift organizer of the twentieth century—believed otherwise. Rather than abandon thrift, or smugly write it off, Bergengren worked long and carefully from the 1920s to the 1950s, in both his writing and his organizing, to explore and deepen its meaning.

Bergengren's life goal was to advance economic democracy—his 1952 book about his career is entitled *Crusade: The Fight for Economic Democracy*—by building a vibrant credit union movement in the U.S. that would, in his words, "democratize the control of credit." To him, and to his colleagues in the movement, this goal is intimately linked to thrift.

A credit union cannot become a successful credit agency until it has first attracted the savings of its members. It obviously cannot invest its accumulated saving until it has some accumulated savings. The credit union is, therefore, first a thrift plan which offers to its members machinery which, properly used, makes systematic saving easily possible.

. . . the credit union seeks to promote thrift in the modern and better acceptance of the word . . . Thrift—What Is It?

The word is variously defined as "a thriving condition, prosperity, success, good fortune." It is also defined as "savings, hoarded wealth." With some parts of this definition we can agree, even in a book which has to do with the credit union in the year 1940. Other parts of the definition are obsolete viewed from the 1940 angle.

. . . We can no longer think of thrift in terms of abstinence from buying; that sort of thrift makes for industrial suicide.

Further, when we think in terms of thrift, we must think also in terms of life. In a too earnest effort to provide for the rainy day, we must not drive all the sunshine out of our every day. It is possible to plan so carefully for old age as to take all the joy out of living. Again take a modern device, the electric washing machine. I recall no poet that was ever inspired to write an ode to the scrubbing board . . .

So, when we think of thrift we are thinking also of life; we are thinking of average human happiness, and we are thinking of the work without which we cannot earn our daily bread.

As soon as we give thought to thrift in these terms, we realize that any plan of distributing goods which does not take into account the capacity of individuals to absorb goods, and which sells him the goods on any wasteful plan of installment credit our usurious loans must be eliminated. There must be sanity in purchasing; there must be equal sanity in financing.

ROY F. BERGENGREN, *CREDIT UNION NORTH AMERICA*, 1940

. . . .

One of the most important divergences [between the college-bound boys and the boys who are members of street gangs in a poor Italian neighborhood in Boston] arises in matters involving the expenditure of money. The college boys fit in with an economy of savings and investment. The corner boys fit in with a spending economy. The college boy must save his money in order to finance his education and launch his business or professional career. He therefore cultivates the middle-class virtue of thrift. In order to participate in group activities, the corner boy must share his money with others. If he has money and his friend does not, he is expected to do the spending for both of them. It is possible to be thrifty and still be a corner boy, but it is not possible to be thrifty and yet hold a high position in the corner gang.

WILLLIAM FOOTE WHYTE, *STREET CORNER SOCIETY*, 1943

. . . .

It has been one my deep regrets that Daddy hasn't lived long enough to learn that we wanted to take care of this, or that we couldn't pay it to him when he so badly needed it . . . I know that you and he both wrote it off long ago, but we haven't forgotten and so for his dear sake and yours we want to begin sending you a little check of $5 a month (which is all too small) which would be nice for you to use in any way you choose for your own little personal expenses. We want you to count on this each month unless or until we should find ourselves in financial difficulties again which we don't expect or anticipate, we hope, for many years to come, if ever.

We won't look back with regret & wish we had done differently but we can look forward & do what we can.

EVA CARRIGEN OF CASPER, WYOMING, LETTER TO HER MOTHER, 1944

How would you like to drive an automobile which had only one wheel? You would not get very far with it, would you? Yet there are many people who seem to think that they can drive their "Thrift" automobile on only one wheel—"Saving." You and I know that they will not drive very far nor very happily without the other three wheels— "Spending," "Investing," and "Giving."

HARRY C. MCKOWN, *ADVENTURES IN THRIFT* (A BOOK FOR TEENAGERS), 1946

. . . .

Real thrift is not limited to saving money, which is only the most visible form of this vast concept. To take care of the goods diligently, to save time, to work properly, these are all included in the true concept of thrift, which means the formation of character, habits, and the view of life.

ADVERTISEMENT FROM FINLAND'S CENTRAL ASSOCIATION OF COOPERATIVE BANKS, 1950

. . . .

We are going to put "thrift" back in the dictionary.

PRESIDENT LYNDON JOHNSON, SPEECH, 1964

. . . .

Talk economy and then spend away.

PRESIDENT LYNDON JOHNSON, PRIVATELY INSTRUCTING HIS STAFF ON LEGISLATIVE AND POLITICAL STRATEGY, 1964

The future orientation of the middle-class person presumes, among other things, a surplus of resources to be invested in the future and a belief that the future will be sufficiently stable both to justify his investment (money in a bank, time and effort in a job, investment of himself in marriage and family, etc.) and to permit the consumption of his investment at a time, place and manner of his own choosing and to his greater satisfaction. But the streetcorner man lives in a sea of want. He does not, as a rule, have a surplus of resources, either economic or psychological. Gratification of hunger and the desire for simple creature comforts cannot be long deferred. Neither can support for one's flagging self-esteem. Living on the edge of both economic and psychological subsistence, the streetcorner man is obliged to spend all his resources on maintaining himself from moment to moment.

ELLIOT LIEBOW, *TALLY'S CORNER*, 1967

. . . .

. . . the science of ecology tells us pragmatically that we cannot continue to waste, and the ethics of our Judeo-Christian tradition tell us that we should not.

. . . in its [a less wasteful life-style's] emphasis on simplicity, self-reliance and thrift may well lie the key to our survival.

LAURANCE S. ROCKEFELLER, "THE CASE FOR A SIMPLER LIFE-STYLE," 1976

I've never borrowed a significant amount of money in my life. Never. Never will. I've got no interest in it. The other reason is I never thought I would be way happier when I had 2X instead of X.

WARREN E. BUFFETT, THE CHAIRMAN OF BERKSHIRE HATHAWAY INC. AND ONE OF THE WORLD'S WEALTHIEST MEN, 1991

. . . .

Where did Donald Trump go wrong? The big problem with Donald Trump was he never went right . . . I would suggest that the big successes I've met had a fair amount of Ben Franklin in them. And Donald Trump did not.

WARREN BUFFETT, 1991

. . . .

Warren Buffett's 2001 Lincoln Town Car was sold for $73,200 at a charity auction . . . The deal includes the car's "THRIFTY" license plate . . .

NEW YORK TIMES, SEPTEMBER 23, 2006

. . . .

Whatcha gonna do when the meat gives out, sugar babe?

NORMAN BLAKE, "CHATTANOOGA SUGAR BABE," 1998

Thrift is a universal virtue. Nations must cultivate it. (Only the USA seems to be averse to it.)

THE TRIBUNE, INDIA, MARCH 26, 1999

. . . .

Genuine thrift is rooted in the philosophical understanding that life is a gift to be explored and enjoyed . . . It is hard for me to imagine a greater, nobler purpose than to combine a life of thrift with a commitment to generosity.

DR. JOHN M. TEMPLETON JR., *THRIFT AND GENEROSITY*, 2004

. . . .

Ecology, for example, recognizes the finitude of resources and encourages various forms of rationing—which traditionalists politely term "thrift."

MARK WEGIERSKI, "BEYOND LEFT-RIGHT," 2004

Staying married, not getting divorced, thinking about savings.

ECONOMICS PROFESSOR JAY ZARGORSKY, ON THE MAIN WAYS TO GET RICH, MAY 2007

. . . .

*Stay out of credit card debt.
Save first and spend later.
Have a financial plan.*

GEORGE R. BARNES OF PRUDENTIAL FINANCIAL, THREE FINANCIAL RULES FOR YOUNG FATHERS PRESENTED AT A "MEETING THE FATHERHOOD CHALLENGE" CONFERENCE AT THE APOLLO THEATER, NEW YORK CITY, FEBRUARY 3, 2007

. . . .

Maybe we should start considering our sojourn on earth as a loan. There can be no doubt that for the past hundred years at least, Europe and the United States have been running up a debt, and now other parts of the world are following their example. Nature is issuing warnings [in the form of climate changes] that we must not only stop the debt from growing but start to pay it back.

VACLAV HAVEL, "OUR MORAL FOOTPRINT," *NEW YORK TIMES*, SEPTEMBER 27, 2007

PART TWO

The Cases against Thrift

THRIFT HAS many worthy enemies. For as long as people have been passionately praising thrift, people have been passionately condemning it. Thrift's enemies also tend to be highly articulate and fun to read. Let's find out who they are, and hear them out. Maybe they have a point.

7. The Ascetic's Case

THE GOAL OF MATERIAL PROSPERITY IS ILLUSORY, A DANGER, OR BOTH;
THRIFT EMPHASIZES THINGS THAT SHOULD NOT MATTER.

For we brought nothing into this world, and it is certain we can carry nothing out.

And having food and raiment let us be therewith content.

But they that will be rich fall into a temptation and a snare, and into many foolish and harmful lusts, which drown men in destruction and perdition.

For the love of money is the root of all evil: which while some coveted after, they have erred from the faith, and pierced themselves through with many sorrows.

I TIMOTHY 6:7–10 (KJV)

. . . .

Whoever buys a thing, not that he may sell it whole and unchanged, but that it may be a material for fashioning something, he is no merchant. But the man who buys it in order that he may gain by selling it again unchanged and as he bought it, that man is of the buyers and sellers who are cast forth from God's temple.

CORPUS JURIS CANONICI (CORPUS OF CANON LAW), COMPILED ABOUT 1150

He who has enough to satisfy his wants and nevertheless ceaselessy labors to aquire riches, either in order to obtain a higher social position, or that subsequently he may have enough to live without labor, or that his sons may become men of wealth and importance—all such are incited by a damnable avarice, sensuality, or pride.

A SCHOOLMAN (UNIVERSITY SCHOLAR IN EUROPE), 1300S

. . . .

. . . truth and commerce cannot live together . . . it is impossible for you to serve God, that is, to serve the truth, and be a merchant . . .

STANISLAW ORZECHOWSKI, THE POLITY OF THE KINGDOM OF POLAND, 1564

. . . .

Thrift is care and scruple in the spending of one's means. It is not a virtue, and it requires neither skill nor talent.

IMMANUEL KANT, LECTURE AT KONIGSBERG, 1775

8. The Prophet's Case

THE MOMENT OF ULTIMATE MEANING IS NEARING;
AT SUCH A TIME, THRIFT IS INSIGNIFICANT.

*Consider the ravens: for they neither sow nor reap;
which neither have storehouse nor barn; and God
feedeth them: how much more are ye better than the
fowls? . . .*

*Consider the lilies how they grow: they toil not,
they spin not; and yet I say unto you, that Solomon
in all his glory was not arrayed like one of these.*

*If then God so clothe the grass, which is today in
the field, and tomorrow is cast into the oven, how
much more will he clothe you, O ye of little faith?*

*And seek not ye what ye shall eat, or what ye
shall drink, neither be ye of doubtful mind.*

*For all these things do the nations of the world
seek after; and your Father knowest that ye have
need of these things.*

*But rather seek ye the kingdom of God; and all
of these things shall be added unto you.*

LUKE 12:24, 27–31 (KJV)

*Avaunt, you drudge! Now all may labour'd ends
are at the stake. Is't a time to think of thrift?*

PHILIP MASSINGER, *A NEW WAY TO
PAY OLD DEBTS* (III, 2), 1633

. . . .

*O my friends, there are resources in us on which
we have not yet drawn. There are men who rise
refreshed on hearing a threat; men to whom a crisis
which intimidates and paralyses the majority,—
demanding not the faculties of prudence and thrift,
but comprehension, immoveableness, the readiness
of sacrifice,—comes graceful and beloved as a bride.*

RALPH WALDO EMERSON, DIVINITY SCHOOL ADDRESS,
CAMBRIDGE, MASSACHUSETTS, JULY 15, 1838

9. The Gentleman's Case

A GENTLEMAN OR A GENTLEWOMAN IS DEVOTED TO LEISURE, PLEASURE, AND
THE PURSUIT OF HIGHER THINGS; THRIFT IS VULGAR AND COMMONPLACE.

An unmatched user of the English language, Shakespeare uses the word "thrift" in nearly every sense that it can be used, at times to suggest something good, and at times the opposite. In *Hamlet*, it's mostly the latter.[1]

The instances that second marriage move,
Are base respects of thrift, but none of love.
WILLIAM SHAKESPEARE, *HAMLET* (III, 2), ABOUT 1600

. . . .

Woful profusion! at how dear a rate,
Are we made up! All hope of thrift and state
Lost for a verse.
HENRY VAUGHN, DISCUSSING THE PRICE OF THE POET'S
ART IN "TO HIS FRIEND," 1651

. . . .

I have already computed the Charge of nursing
a Beggar's Child (in which List I reckon all
Cottagers, Labourers, *and Four fifths of the*
Farmers) *to be about two Shilling per Annum,*
Rags included; and I believe no Gentleman would

repine to give Ten Shillings for the Carcase of a
good fat Child, *which, as I have said, will make*
four Dishes of excellent nutritive Meat, when he
hath only some particular Friend or his own Family
to dine with him. Thus the Squire will learn to
be a good Landlord, and grow popular among
his Tenants; the Mother will have Eight Shillings
net Profit, and be fit for Work till she produceth
another Child.

Those who are more thrifty (as I must confess
the Times require) *may flay the Carcase; the Skin*
of which artificially dressed will make admirable
Gloves for Ladies, *and* Summer Boots for fine
Gentlemen.
JONATHAN SWIFT, *A MODEST PROPOSAL*, 1729

. . . .

If the letter below from Oliver Goldsmith in fact endorses thrift, it may be the saddest and most bittersweet endorsement of thrift in the history of the English language.

Above all things, let him never touch a romance or
novel; these paint beauty in colors more charming

than nature, and describe happiness that man never tastes. How delusive, how destructive, are those pictures of consummate bliss! They teach the youthful mind to sigh after beauty and happiness that never existed; to despise the little good which fortune has mixed in our cup, by expecting more than she ever gave; and, in general, take the word of a man who has seen the world, and who has studied human nature more by experience than precept; take my word for it, I say, that books teach us very little of the world. The greatest merit in a state of poverty would only serve to make the possessor ridiculous—may distress, but cannot relieve him. Frugality, and even avarice, in the lower orders of mankind, are true ambition. These afford the only ladder for the poor to rise to preferment. Teach then, my dear sir, to your son, thrift and economy. Let his poor wandering uncle's example be placed before his eyes. I had learned from books to be disinterested and generous before I was taught from experience the necessity of being prudent. I had contracted the habits and notions of a philosopher, while I was exposing myself to the approaches of insidious cunning; and often by being, even with my narrow finances, charitable to excess, I forgot the rules of justice, and placed myself in the very situation of the wretch who thanked me for my bounty.

OLIVER GOLDSMITH, LETTER ADVISING HIS BROTHER, HENRY, REGARDING THE UPBRINGING OF HENRY'S SON (OLIVER'S NEPHEW), JANUARY 1759

But the age of chivalry is gone.—That of sophisters, economists, and calculators, has succeeded and the glory of Europe is extinguished for ever.

EDMUND BURKE, *REFLECTIONS ON THE REVOLUTION IN FRANCE*, 1790

· · · ·

Domestic slavery in the Southern States has produced the same results in elevating the character of the master that it did in Greece and Rome. He is lofty and independent in his sentiments, generous, affectionate, brave and eloquent; he is superior to the Northerner in everything but the arts of thrift.

GEORGE FITZHUGH, *SOCIOLOGY FOR THE SOUTH*, 1854

· · · ·

. . . I was not reading it for its own sake and because I loved it, but for selfish ends of my own, and because I wished to possess myself of it for business purposes, as it were. The reading that does one good, and lasting good, is the reading that one does for pleasure, and simply and unselfishly, as children do. Art will still withhold herself from thrift, and she does well, for nothing but love has any right to her.

WILLIAM DEAN HOWELLS, *MY LITERARY PASSIONS*, 1909

· · · ·

My great-uncle Ben was the meanest of men,
He would never let go of a dollar;
As a grudging resort, he made use of a wart

On his neck, as a stud for his collar.
He would pasture his cows on the grave of his
    spouse,
He would rob a blind babe of its bottle,
And he spoke through his nose, with a voice like a
    crow's,
To avoid wear and tear to his throttle.
But he died worth a million intensely respected
By all who divided the wealth he collected.
My cousin MacNab was as close as a crab,
At the smallest disbursement he grumbled;
He would order cigars at American bars
And allow one to pay, while he fumbled.
But he made a big pile, in this niggardly style,
And at last, when by Fate he was smitten,
He bequeathed (in his will) the contents of his till
To a College of Thrift in North Britain;
And the public of Scotland were loud in their
    praises,
And garnished his tomb with a wreath of cheap
    daisies.

HARRY GRAHAM, "THE SEVEN DEADLY VIRTUES:
NO. I —THRIFT," *THE GRAPHIC MIDSUMMER NUMBER,*
JULY 15, 1911

. . . .

With your neat little safety-vault boxes,
With your faces like geese and foxes,
You,
Short-legged, short-armed, short-minded men,
Your short-sighted days are over,
Your habits of strutting through clover,
Your movie-thugs, killing off souls and dreams,

Your magazines, drying up healing streams,
Your newspapers, blasting truth and splendor,
Your shysters, ruining progress and glory, —
Babbitt, your story is passing away,
The Virginians are coming again.

. . . Babbitt sold Judas. Babbitt sold Christ.
Babbitt sold everything under the sun.
The Moon-Proud consider a trader a hog.
The Moon-Proud are coming again.

VACHEL LINDSAY, "THE VIRGINIANS
ARE COMING AGAIN," 1928

. . . .

This was increased by the intense economy practiced
in our household where to save matches we always
used "spills" from six to ten inches long made
by rolling up the margins of old newspapers . . .
But apart from the use of "spills" thrift was not
only encouraged but enforced by the most rigid
discipline, thus engendering a parsimony akin to
avarice . . .

ARTHUR TRAIN, *PURITAN'S PROGRESS,* 1931

. . . .

"A lost cent is a lost chance" is his favorite
expression, the aphoristic lecture with which he
chastises his children (is that how Marjorie's father
made his million?): a lost cent is a lost chance. And
you might as well substitute "soul" for "chance" so
grave and theological is the cast to his voice.

DAVID BOSWORTH, *FROM MY FATHER, SINGING,* 1986

10. The Sensualist's Case

NOTHING IS GIVEN TO US BUT TODAY, WHICH IS MEANT FOR US TO EXPERIENCE
FULLY; THRIFT IS THE ENEMY OF JOY AND THE KILLER OF SPONTANEITY.

Let the world slide, let the world go;
A fig for care, a fig for woe!
If I can't pay, why, I can owe,
And death makes equal the high and low.

JOHN HEYWOOD, "BE MERRY, FRIENDS,"
PROBABLY 1570S

. . . .

These thriftles birds, which spend the day
in needless notes.

GEORGE GASCOIGNE, *THE COMPLAYNT OF PHILOMENE*,
1576

. . . .

WILL SUMMER: A small matter. I know one
spent, in less than a year, eight and fifty pounds in
mustard, and another that ran in debt in the space
of four or five year above fourteen thousand pound
in lute-strings and gray paper.
SUMMER: O monstrous unthrift, who e're
heard the like?
The sea's vast throat, in so short tract of time,
Devoureth nor consumeth half so much.

How well mightst thou have liv'd within thy bounds!
VER: What talk you to me of living within my
bounds? I tell you, none but asses live within their
bounds: the silly beasts, if they be put in a pasture
that is eaten bare to the very earth and where there
is nothing to be had but thistles, will rather fall
soberly to those thistles and be hunger-starved, than
they will offer to break their bounds; whereas the
lusty courser, if he be in a barren plot and spy better
grass in some pasture near adjoining, breaks over
hedge and ditch, and to go, ere he will be pent in,
and not have his belly full . . .
VER: Tell me, I pray, wherefore was gold laid
under our feet in the veins of the earth, but that
we should contemn it and tread upon it, and so
consequently tread thrift under our feet? . . . I will
prove it, that an unthrift of any comes nearest
a happy man, insomuch as he comes nearest to
beggary. Cicero saith . . . the chiefest felicity that
may be to rest from all labors . . . Who rests so
much? Who hath so little to do as the beggar?
Who can sing so merry a note, As he that cannot
change a groat? Cui nil est, nil deest: "he that hath
nothing, wants nothing." . . . All alchemists and
all philosophers are beggars: Omnia mea mecum

porto, quoth Bias, when he had nothing but bread and cheese in a leathern bag, and two or three books in his bosom. Saint Francis, a holy Saint, and never had any money. It is madness to dote upon muck. That young man of Athens (Aelianus makes mention of) may be an example to us, who doted so extremely on the image of fortune, that, when he might not enjoy it, he died for sorrow. The earth yields all her fruits together, and why should not we spend them together? I thank heavens on my knees, that have made me an unthrift.

THOMAS NASHE, *SUMMERS LAST WILL AND TESTAMENT*, 1600

. . . .

'Tis even a second hell to part from pleasure
When man has got a smack on't: as many holydays
Coming together make your poor heads idle
A great while after, and are said to stick
Fast in their fingers' ends,—even so does game
In a new-married couple; for the time
It spoils all thrift, and indeed lies a'bed
T'invent all the new ways for great expense.

THOMAS MIDDLETON, *WOMEN BEWARE WOMEN* (I, 3), ABOUT 1622

. . . .

Hang consideration!
When this is spent, is not our ship the same,
Our courage too the same, to fetch in more?
The earth, where it is fertilest, returns not
More than three harvests, while the glorious sun
Posts through the zodiac, and makes up the year.

But the sea, which is our mother, (that embraces
Both the rich Indies in her outstretch'd arms,)
Yields every day a crop, if we dare reap it.
No, no, my mates, let tradesmen think of thrift,
And usurers hoard up; let our expenses
Be, as our comings in are, without bounds.

PHILIP MASSINGER, *THE RENEGADO* (I, 3), 1624

. . . .

Now I shall laugh at those that heap up wealth
By lazy methods and slow rules of thrift:
I'm grown the child of wit, and can advance
Myself, by being votary to chance.

SIR WILLIAM D'AVENANT, *THE WITS* (II, 3), 1636

. . . .

. . . he [Mr. Hunt] told me some ridiculous pieces of thrift of Sir G. Downing's, who is his countryman, in inviting some poor people, at Christmas last, to charm the country people's mouths; but did give them nothing but beef, porridge, pudding, and pork, and nothing said all dinner, but only his mother would say, "It's good broth, son." He would answer, "Yes, it is good broth." Then, says his lady, "Confirm all, and say, Yes, very good broth." By and by she would begin and say, "Good pork:" "Yes," says the mother, "good pork." Then he cries, "Yes, very good pork." And so they said of all things; to whch nobody made any answer, they going there not out of love or esteem for them, but to eat his victuals, knowing him to be a niggardly fellow . . .

DIARY OF SAMUEL PEPYS, FEBRUARY 27, 1667

I am a lusty lively lad,
   Now come to one-and-twenty,
My father left me all he had,
   Both gold and silver plenty;
Now he's in grave, I will be brave,
   The ladies shall adore me,
I'le court and kiss, what hurt's in this?
   My dad did so before me.
My father was a thrifty sir,
   Till soul and body sundred,
Some say he was a usurer
   For thirty in the hundred;

He scrapt and scratcht, she pinch'd and patch'd,
   That in her body bore me,
But I'll let flie, good cause why,
   My father was born before me.
My daddy had his duty done
   In getting so much treasure;
I'le be as dutiful a son
   For spending it in pleasure . . .
I'll dice and drab, and drink, and stab,
   No Hector shall out-roar me;
If teachers tell me tales of hell,
   My father is gone before me.

A SONG FROM A LONDON PAGEANT, ABOUT 1672

Let neist day come as it thinks fit,
The present minute's only ours;
On pleasure let's employ our wit
And laugh at fortune's feckless powers.

SCOTTISH POEM FROM THE EIGHTEENTH CENTURY

. . . .

. . . I am writing now in little Ireland. The dialect on the neighbouring shores of Scotland and Ireland is much the same, yet I can perceive a great difference in the nations, from the chambermaid at this nate toone kept by Mr Kelly. She is fair, kind and ready to laugh, because she is out of the horrible dominion of the Scotch Kirk. A Scotch girl stands in terrible awe of the Elders—poor little Susannas, they will scarcely laugh, and their Kirk is greatly to be damn'd. These Kirkmen have done Scotland good. They have made men, women; old men, young men; old women, young women; boys, girls; and all infants careful—so that they are formed into regular Phalanges of savers and gainers. Such a thrifty army cannot fail to enrich their Country, and give it a greater appearance of Comfort than that of their poor rash neighbourhood—these Kirk-men have done Scotland harm; they have banished puns, and laughing, and kissing, etc. (except in cases where the very danger and crime must make it very gustful). I shall make a full stop at kissing, for after that there should be a better parenthesis, and go on to remind you of the fate of Burns—poor unfortunate fellow, his disposition was Southern—how sad it is when a luxurious imagination is obliged, in self defence, to deaden its delicacy in vulgarity, and rot (?) in things attainable, that it may not have leisure to go mad after things which are not. No man, in such matters, will be content with the experience of others—It is true that out of suffering there is no dignity, no greatness, that in the most abstracted pleasure there is no lasting happiness—Yet who would not like to discover over again that Cleopatra was a Gipsey, Helen a Rogue, and Ruth a deep one? I have not sufficient reasoning faculty to settle the doctrine of thrift, as it is consistent with the dignity of human Society—with the happiness of Cottagers. All I can do is by plump contrasts; were the fingers made to squeeze a guinea or a white hand?—were the lips made to hold a pen or a kiss? and yet in Cities man is shut out from his fellows if he is poor—the Cottager must be dirty, and very wretched, if she be not thrifty—the present state of society demands this, and this convinces me that the world is very young, and in a very ignorant state—We live in a barbarous age—I would sooner be a wild deer than a girl under the dominion of the Kirk; and I would sooner be a wild hog, than be the occasion of a poor Creature's pennance before those execrable elders.

THE POET JOHN KEATS, LETTER TO HIS BROTHER, THOMAS, DESCRIBING HIS VISIT TO SCOTLAND, JULY 6, 1818

. . . he laughs at thrift, and counts industry a colder companion than pleasure.

A BOOK REVIEW IN *THE LITERARY GAZETTE*, JANUARY 7, 1826

. . . .

I never was more tired of a house than of Clifton Villa; and for Mrs. Hume's sake, I shall forever retain a detestation of thin slices of bread and butter. She is an awfully thrifty woman, and nobody can sit at her table without feeling that she both numbers and measures every mouthful that you eat; . . .

NATHANIEL HAWTHORNE, *ENGLISH NOTE-BOOKS*, 1853–58

. . . .

The utilitarian habits of New England, originating in necessity, and far outliving the circumstances in which they had their birth, have tended more than any other cause to make New England character unlovable . . . There are those who will not allow their families to cultivate flowers, because flowers are not useful . . . They will not have an instrument of music in their homes, because music is not useful, and it involves an expenditure of money . . . They will not buy pictures . . . They will not attend a lecture . . . They will not attend a concert . . . They will not hire a minister who possesses fine gifts . . . So they take up with ministerial dry nursing, and one another's dry experiences, as spiritual food, in order to save a few more dollars.

There are a few of the severer virtues that will live upon a diet of this kind. Endurance, industry, a negative purity, thrift, integrity—these can live, and do live, after a sort, on a plain and scanty diet, and these, as we know, abound in New England. But generosity, hospitality, charity, liberality—all these qualities that enrich the character, and all those virtues that enlarge it and give it fullness and beauty and attractiveness, are always wanting among the class that sacrifices every thing for use.

JOSIAH GILBERT HOLLAND ("TIMOTHY TITCOMB"), *LESSONS IN LIFE*, 1861

. . . .

(Passionately seen and yearn'd for by one poor little child,
While others remain busy or smartly talking,
forever teaching thrift, thrift . . .)

WALT WHITMAN, "SONG OF THE BANNER AT DAYBREAK," 1865

. . . .

He said, "I will not save!
The liberal sun
Is richer for the light he gave
And gives the world. I choose to hold
The mine, and not to hoard the gold.
Can I be one
To dry my heart to coffered dust,
Or cling to hidden coin, a rust?
"Ask June to stint her bloom
Against the day

Whereof no lingering drop would stay
Shut from the generous flood away."
He said, "If I give all
    Open to sight,
The everything men riches call,
'T is clearing rubbish from my way
Into the avenues of day,
    The door of light.
Thriftless he can afford to be
Who find's the universe's key.

LUCY LARCOM, "THRIFTLESS," 1881

Taught to wanton, taught to play,
    By the young year's wanton flower,
      We will take no heed to-day,
        Have no thought for thrift this hour;
          Thrift, whose uncongenial power
            Laws on youth imposes.

J. A. SYMONDS, "AN EXHORTATION TO LIBERALITY BY
THE EXAMPLE OF THE ROSE," 1884

. . . .

We owe something to extravagance, for thrift and
adventure seldom go hand in hand.

JENNIE JEROME CHURCHILL, ABOUT 1915

. . . .

In his passion for thrift, the pioneer confuses thrift
with life.

ZONA GALE, *YALE REVIEW*, SEPTEMBER 1933

Of sorrowful November gloom!
Free blossom yields abundant seed;
June's thriftlessness is thrift indeed.
    There is no way
To count November's added sighs,
Should lavish June turn pennywise.
"Among the immortal gods
    Unthrift is thrift;
Worst poverty—with them at odds.
No wealth but this: to feel the flow
Of life's deep well to torrents grow,
    A current swift,

I found out some time back that it's idleness breeds all our virtues, our most bearable qualities—contemplation, equableness, laziness, letting other people alone; good digestion mental and physical: the wisdom to concentrate on fleshly pleasures—eating and evacuating and fornication and sitting in the sun—than which there is nothing better, nothing to match, nothing else in all this world but to live for the short time you are loaned breath, to be alive and know it—oh, yes, she taught me that; she has marked me too forever—nothing, nothing. But it was only recently I have clearly seen, followed out the logical conclusion, that it is one of what we call the prime virtues—thrift, industry, independence—that breeds all the vices—fanaticism, smugness, meddling, fear, and worst of all, respectability.

WILLIAM FAULKNER, *THE WILD PALMS*, 1939

. . . .

*The further through life I drift
The more obvious it becomes that I am lacking
   in thrift.*

OGDEN NASH, "A PENNY SAVED IS IMPOSSIBLE," 1942

. . . .

Finally, the very notion of thrift has lost much of its enticement, because the contemporary man discounts the future at an inordinantly high rate. [Today we prefer] what Adam Smith called "the passion for present enjoyment."

"SAVINGS BANKS," *ENCYCLOPEDIA BRITANNICA*, 1954

It is stupid to pile up treasures that we can enjoy only in old age, when we have lost the capacity for enjoyment. Better to seize the moment as it comes, to dwell in it intensely, even at the cost of future suffering. Better to live extravagantly.

MALCOLM COWLEY, *EXILE'S RETURN*, 1961

. . . .

*No, I ain't gonna work for Maggie's brother
   no more.
Well, he hands you a nickel,
He hands you a dime,
He asks you with a grin
If you're havin' a good time.
Then he fines you every time you slam
   the door.
I ain't gonna work for Maggie's brother
   no more . . .*

BOB DYLAN, *MAGGIE'S FARM*, 1965

. . . .

. . . money won is twice as sweet as money earned.

"EDDIE FELSON," IN THE MOVIE *THE COLOR OF MONEY*, 1986

11. The Economist's Case

STEADILY GROWING CONSUMER SPENDING KEEPS THE ECONOMY HEALTHY; PARADOXICALLY, THRIFT RETARDS GROWTH.

Prodigality is a vice that is prejudicial to the Man, but not to trade.

NICHOLAS BARBON, *A DISCOURSE OF TRADE*, 1690

. . . .

. . . prodigality,
That noble sin; whilst luxury
Employ'd a million of the poor . . .
The prodigality I call a noble sin is . . . that
agreeable good-natured vice that makes the chimney
smoke and all the tradesmen smile; I mean the
unmixed prodigality of heedless and voluptuous
men, that being educated in plenty, abhor the vile
thoughts of lucre and lavish away only what others
took pains to scrape together . . .

Frugality is like honesty, a mean starving virtue
. . . It is an idle dreaming virtue that employs
no hands, and therefore very useless in a trading
country, where there are vast numbers that one way
or other must be all set to work. Prodigality has a
thousand inventions to keep people from sitting still
that frugality would never think of . . .

The Dutch may ascribe their present grandeur
to the virtue and frugality of their ancestors as

they please; but what made that contemptible spot
of ground so considerable among the principal
powers of Europe has been their political wisdom
in postponing everything to merchandise and
navigation, the unlimited liberty of conscience
among them, and the unwearied application which
which they have always made use of the most
effectual means to encourage and increase trade in
general.

BERNARD MANDEVILLE, *THE FABLE OF THE BEES*, 1714

. . . .

Excessive Saving a Cause of Commerical Distress
A COLLECTION OF ARTICLES BY THE ECONOMICS
WRITER URIEL H. CROCKER, 1884

. . . .

The identification of depression in trade with
insufficient consumption or excessive thrift is, we
venture to assert, unassailable . . . This conclusion
is of critical importance to the community: it
means neither more nor less than the community
could at once and permanently enjoy a larger

income. It means that the East End problem, with its concomitant of vice and misery, is traced to its economic cause, and that this economic cause is the most respectable and highly extolled virtue of thrift.

A. F. MUMMERY AND J. A. HOBSON, *THE PHYSIOLOGY OF INDUSTRY*, 1889

. . . .

So that the doctrine of universal thrift is once more seen to be a futility . . .

JOHN M. ROBERTSON, *THE FALLACY OF SAVING*, 1892

. . . .

Dr. [Alvan L.] Barach declared that the nation was in the sinister grip of a habit of excessive thrift . . . He said this habit, born of want and fear in the deepest period of the depression, was retarding recovery, and must be broken.

"THRIFT HABIT HELD RETARDING RECOVERY," *NEW YORK TIMES*, JANUARY 29, 1934

. . . .

Remember from an earlier chapter our friend John Maynard Keynes, who famously argued that thrift at times can retard enterprise and thus harm the economy? Due in part to Keynes's great stature, this idea—which was often termed the "paradox of thrift"—deeply influenced several generations of economists, including those who wrote economics textbooks.

By attempting to increase its rate of saving, society may create conditions under which the amount it can actually save is reduced. This phenomenon is called the paradox of thrift . . . [T]hrift, which has always been held in high esteem in our economy, now becomes something of a social vice.

CAMPBELL R. MCCONNELL, *ELEMENTARY ECONOMICS*, A LEADING COLLEGE TEXTBOOK, 1960

. . . .

It is a paradox because in kindergarten we are all taught that thrift is always a good thing. Benjamin Franklin's Poor Richard's Almanac *never tired of preaching the doctrine of saving. And now comes a new generation of alleged financial experts who seem to be telling us that black is white and white is black, and that the old virtues may be modern sins.*

PAUL A. SAMUELSON, *ECONOMICS* (4TH EDITION), THE NATION'S LEADING COLLEGE ECONOMICS TEXTBOOK, 1958

. . . .

Before moving on, let's give a few final words to those pro-thrift economists who dispute "the economist's case against thrift":

But things are changing. The 14th edition of Paul A. Samuelson's Economics *. . . does not even mention the so-called paradox of thrift. Instead of disparaging saving, this edition contains an extensive discussion of the low U.S. saving rate*

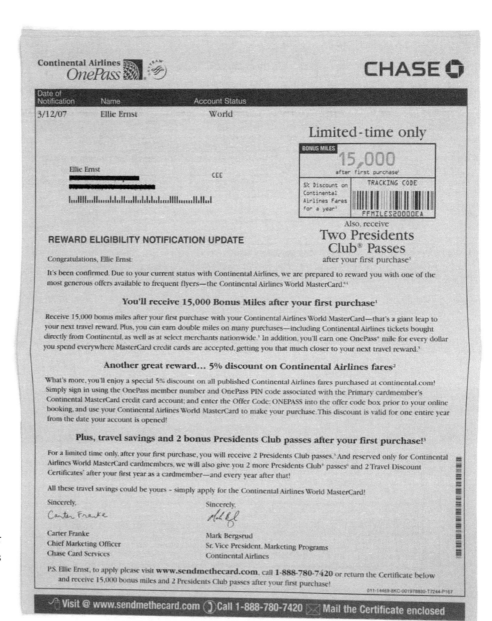

Credit card offer for
Ellie Ernst, age 6 months

and a comparison of that rate to the much higher
savings rates in Germany and Japan.

CLIFFORD F. THIES, "THE PARADOX OF THRIFT:
RIP," 1996

Keynes's successors took delight in teaching their
students about the paradox of thrift—whereby the
effect of an increase in each individual's savings
rate would be a shortfall of aggregate demand,
resulting in lower incomes and savings than before
. . . But given our current willingness to use
monetary and fiscal stabilization tools when

needed, the empirical fact is that the economy has operated at very close to full employment during most of the years since World War II. And with near full employment the norm, the [older] logic . . . reasserts itself. Higher savings leads to higher investment, which in turn stimulates faster economic growth and higher incomes for all. It is thus no surprise that modern economics textbooks have again begun to emphasize the importance of long-run growth and downplay the importance short-run stabilization policy. Given our ability to manage economic downturns, savings is once again a good thing, not a threat to economic stability.

ROBERT H. FRANK, PROFESSOR OF MANAGEMENT AND ECONOMICS, CORNELL UNIVERSITY, 2006

. . . .

. . . the most serious problem we have faced in the last 50 years is that of low national saving, resulting dependence on foreign capital, and fiscal sustainability . . . Private saving has been trending downward for many years, with breaks in the trend associated with periods when the stock market performed poorly. But the clear change in national saving, which has declined precipitously in recent years, comes from the increase in the federal budget deficit, which accounts for the fact that the United States now has the lowest rate of national saving in its history.

LAWRENCE H. SUMMERS, SPEECH AT THE INSTITUTE FOR INTERNATIONAL ECONOMICS, MARCH 23, 2004

There is a widespread fallacy to the effect that extravagance gives employment to labor. This fallacy is probably due to the opinion that thrift consists of hoarding money or hiding it away. This, however, is not thrift at all. To hide money away, and keep it out of use, is a very thriftless thing to do. The thrifty person is not a miser. He is one who spends money just as freely as the extravagant man, but he spends it wisely instead of unwisely . . . When we realize that thrift consists in spending money wisely, instead of unwisely, we shall very easily see that the thrifty man spends exactly as much money as the thriftless man, provided he has as much money to spend. Moreover, in the long run, the thrifty man will spend more, because he will have more to spend than the thriftless man; and the thrifty community will be a community in which more money is spent than in the thriftless community.

T. N. CARVER, "THE RELATION OF THRIFT TO NATION BULDING," 1920

. . . .

The rapid increases in inflation in the U.S. in the 1970s gave rise to another important economic argument against thrift: It doesn't pay, because rapid inflation wipes out the gains accrued from saving.

I was brought up to regard thrift as a virtue . . . [Yet] I now smile benignly as the children spend their allowances on comic books, cheap costume jewelry, model kits, mice, accessories for Barbie and Superman cards. Kids' stuff. They are buying

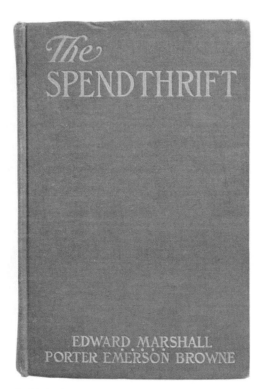

Published 1910

something now and enjoying it now. Instant gratification: not how I was raised.

But if they put the money, instead, into their savings accounts, would it be worth anything, even with interest, in a few years when they might want to take it out? . . . How can I encourage them to save for tomorrow, when tomorrow outruns their savings? . . . Thus inflation makes hedonists of us all . . . Instead of building character, thrift today builds disillusion.

JOAN STRIEFLING, "THOUGHTS ON THRIFT," *NEW YORK TIMES*, MAY 29, 1980

12. The Socialist's Case

THRIFT IS A FALSE PROMISE, MADE IN BAD FAITH, AIMED AT KEEPING THE POOR,
POOR, AND THE RICH, RICH; THRIFT IS AN ENEMY OF RADICAL TRANSFORMATION.

One school [of economic thought] . . . advocates thrift and execrates luxury . . . [but] it advocates thrift in order to produce wealth—i.e., luxury . . . [It] advances earnest and detailed arguments to show that through prodigality I diminish rather than increase my possessions; but its supporters hypocritically refuse to admit that production is regulated by caprice and fancy; they forget the "refined needs" and forget that without consumption there can be no production . . .

And you must not only be parsimonious in gratifying your immediate senses, such as eating, etc. You must also be chary of participating in affairs of general interest, showing sympathy and trust, etc., if you want to be economical . . . You must make everything which is yours venal—i.e., useful. I might ask the political economist: am I obeying economic laws if I make money by prostituting my body to the lust of another (in France, the factory workers call the prostitution of their wives and daughters the nth working hour, which is literally true), or if I sell my friend to the Moroccans (and the direct sale of men in the form of trade in conscripts, etc., occurs in all civilized countries)?

His answer will be: your acts do not contravene my laws . . .

KARL MARX, *ECONOMIC AND PHILOSOPHICAL MANUSCRIPTS*, 1844

. . . .

Political economy, this science of wealth, is therefore at the same time the science of denial, of starvation, of saving, and it actually goes so far as to save man the need for fresh air or physical exercise. This science . . . is at the same time the science of asceticism, and its true ideal is the ascetic but rapacious skinflint and the ascetic but productive slave. Its moral idea is the worker who puts a part of his wages into savings . . . the denial of life and of all human needs, is its principal doctrine. The less you eat, drink, buy books, go to the theatre, go dancing, go drinking, think, love, theorize, sing, paint, fence, etc., the more you save and the greater will become the treasure that neither moths nor maggots can consume—your capital . . . Everything which the political economist takes from you in terms of life and humanity,

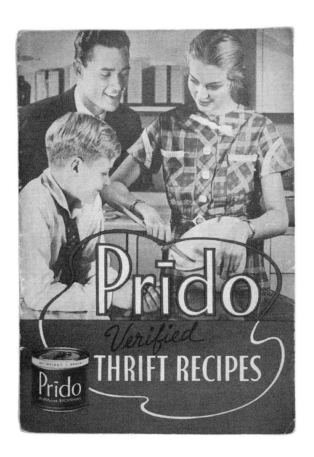

Fun-Full Thrift Game

he restores to you in the form of money and wealth . . .

MARX, *ECONOMIC AND PHILOSOPHICAL MANUSCRIPTS*, 1844

. . . .

The palliatives over which many worthy people are busying themselves now are useless: because they are but unorganized partial revolts against a vast wide-spreading grasping organization which will, with the unconscious instinct of a plant, meet every attempt at bettering the condition of the people with an attack on a fresh side; new machines,

new markets, wholesale emigration, the revival of grovelling superstitions, preachments of thrift to lack-alls, of temperance to the wretched; such things as these will baffle at every turn all partial revolts against the monster we of the middle classes have created for our own undoing.

WILLIAM MORRIS, "ART AND SOCIALISM," LECTURE DELIVERED JANUARY 23, 1884

. . . .

Sometimes the poor are praised for being thrifty. But to recommend thrift to the poor is both grotesque and insulting. It is like advising a man *who is starving to eat less. For a town or country labourer to practice thrift would be absolutely immoral.*

OSCAR WILDE, *THE SOUL OF MAN UNDER SOCIALISM*, 1891

. . . .

Each class would have preached the importance of those virtues, for whose exercise there was no necessity in their own lives. The rich would have spoken on the value of thrift, and the idle grown eloquent over the dignity of labour.

OSCAR WILDE, *THE PICTURE OF DORIAN GRAY*, 1891

. . . .

Intemperance, unthrift, idleness, and inefficiency are indeed common vices of the poor. If therefore we could teach the poor to be temperate, thrifty, industrious, and efficient, would not the problem of poverty be solved? Is not a moral remedy instead of an economic remedy the one to be desired?

. . . This "moral view" has much to recommend it at first sight. In the first place, it is a "moral" view, and as morality is admittedly the truest and most real end of man, it would seem that a moral cure must be more radical and efficient than any merely industrial cure. Again, these "vices" of the poor, drink, dirt, gambling, prostitution, &c., are very definite and concrete maladies attaching to large numbers of individual cases, and visibly responsible for the misery and degradation of the vicious and their families. Last, not least, this aspect of poverty, by representing the condition of the poor to be chiefly "their own fault," lightens the sense of responsibility for the "well to do." It is decidedly the more comfortable view, for it at once flatters the pride of the rich by representing poverty as an evidence of incompetency, salves his conscience when pricked by the contrast of the misery around him, and assists him to secure his material interests by adopting an attitude of stern repression towards large industrial or political agitations in the interests of labour, on the ground that "these are wrong ways of tackling the question."

The question is this, Can the poor be moralized, and will that cure Poverty? . . . In the first place, it is very difficult to ascertain to what extent drink, vice, idleness, and other personal defects are actually responsible for poverty in individual cases. There is, however, reason to believe that the bulk of cases of extreme poverty and destitution cannot be traced to these personal vices, but, on the other hand, that they are attributable to industrial causes for which the sufferer is not responsible . . . The Rev. S. A. Barnett, who knows East London so well, does not find the origin of poverty in the vices of the poor. Terrible as are the results of drunkenness, impurity, unthrift, idleness, disregard of sanitary rules, it is not possible, looking fairly at the facts, to regard these as the main sources of poverty. If we are not carried away by the spirit of some special fanaticism, we shall look upon these evils as the natural and necessary accessories of the struggle for a livelihood, carried on under the industrial conditions of our age and country.

. . . We cannot go to the lowest of our slum population and teach them to be clean, thrifty,

industrious, steady, moral, intellectual, and religious, until we have first taught them how to secure for themselves the industrial conditions of healthy physical life. Our poorest classes have neither the time, the energy, or the desire to be clean, thrifty, intellectual, moral, or religious. In our haste we forget that there is a proper and necessary order in the awakening of desires. At present our "slum" population do not desire to be moral and intellectual, or even to be particularly clean. Therefore these higher goods must wait, so far as they are dependent on the voluntary action of the poor. What these people do want is better food, and more of it; warmer clothes; better and surer shelter; and greater security of permanent employment on decent wages. Until we can assist them to gratify these "lower" desires, we shall try in vain to awaken "higher" ones.

JOHN A. HOBSON, *PROBLEMS OF POVERTY*, 1891

. . . .

Another panacea for social ills is thrift, under which term may be included the virtues of manliness, intelligence, temperance, frgality, efficiency, etc. . . . Of all the remedies proposed to heal the gaping wounds of society the exhortation to manliness and thrift is the most insipid and jejeune.

F. M. SPRAGUE, *SOCIALISM*, 1893

Thrift was invented by capitalist rogues to beguile fools to destruction, and to deprive honest fools of their diet and their proper comfort.

JOHN BURNS, ADDRESS TO THE BRITISH TRADES UNION CONGRESS, 1894

. . . .

But this lady visitor [social worker], who pretends to be good to the poor, and certainly does talk as though she were kind-hearted, what does she come for, if she does not intend to give them things which so plainly are needed? The visitor says, sometimes, that in holding her poor family so hard to a standard of thrift she is really breaking down a rule of higher living which they formerly possessed; that saving, which seemed quite commendable in a comfortable part of the town, appears almost criminal in a poorer quarter, where the next-door neighbor needs food, even if the children of the family do not. She feels the sordidness of constantly being obliged to urge the industrial view of life.

. . . The sense of prudence, the necessity for saving, can never come to a primitive, emotional man with the force of a conviction, but the necessity of providing for his children is a powerful incentive. He naturally regards his children as his saving-bank; he expects them to care for him when he gets old . . . Another tailor whom I know, a Socialist, always speaks of saving as a bourgeois virtue, one quite impossible to the genuine workingman. He supports a family, consisting of himself, a wife and three children, and his parents, on eight dollars a week. He insists that it would be criminal not to expend every penny of this amount upon food and shelter, and he expects his children later to take care of him.

JANE ADDAMS, "THE SUBTLE PROBLEMS
OF CHARITY," 1899

. . . .

. . . thrift is an impossibility, and to preach thrift when there is no chance of saving is pure cant and cruelty.

WILLIAM H. DAWSON, DESCRIBING THE VIEWS OF
KARL JOHANN RODBERTUS, ONE OF THE FOUNDERS OF
MODERN GERMAN SOCIALISM, 1899

. . . .

I know the miners in the north of England, and the workers in the south and the agricultural labourers. I would complain of their miserly thrift—yes, thrift is a mean, starving virtue. The women wear themselves out body and soul by their forsight and prudent care. Up the first thing in the morning, cooking and polishing and scrubbing all day, sitting up half the night mending, patching, and darning. The men just as bad—with their club and sick benefits and the rest of it.

Many a time I have rounded on a Cumberland miner's wife for her thrift—I have urged her to spend all the man's wages—to give the children some extra fun and jollity in the early days—for it's little enough they get of it as they grow older. But the women were always having an eye to the future—to the time when he'd not be able to

work or some equally pleasant prospect. The thrifty middle class . . . are the most extravagant of all our English castes. The cost of human flesh and blood is never counted—they deny themselves everything, they slave and worry all the years of their life— become sour and miserable, ill-tempered before they are thirty. And to what end? That their children may carry on the tradition of grudging care.

The extravagance of the upper classes is disgusting, and the thrift of the working classes is stupid. The Lancaster operatives' midway shows dignity—a good time when the money's there, and a drawing in when it's gone.

Had he drunk no beer all his days, would my old shovel-guard now be any better off?

M. D. EDER, "ON THRIFT," 1909

. . . .

Most esteemed Mr. Filene! are you fully convinced that the workers of the whole world are such fools?

VLADIMIR I. LENIN, THE RUSSIAN REVOLUTIONARY AND
THE FIRST LEADER OF THE SOVIET UNION, CRITICIZING
THE PROGRESSIVE U.S. BUSINESS LEADER AND THRIFT
ADVOCATE EDWARD FILENE OF BOSTON, A FOUNDER OF
THE MODERN U.S. CREDIT UNION MOVEMENT, "THE
IDEAS OF PROGRESSIVE CAPITAL," 1913

. . . .

Thrift is very well when thrift brings greater power; but when that virtue simply means greater exploitation, then thrift is a vice. The Irish tenant lost the habit of thriftiness because every time he *made a saving, that saving was taken away from him by his landlord. When one class is subject to another class, the thrift of the subject class only adds to the wealth of the master class.*

. . . [Therefore] . . . In the morality of the working-class the word thrift will not be found.

<small>ALGERNON SIDNEY CRAPSEY, *THE RISE OF THE WORKING-CLASS*, 1914</small>

. . . .

. . . a poor person cannot become a capitalist. A poor person is one who has less than enough to live on. I can remember a bishop, who ought to have known better, exhorting the poor in the East End of London, at a time when poverty there was even more dreadful that it is at present, to become capitalists by saving. He really should have had his apron publicly and officially torn off him, and his shovel hat publicly and officially jumped on, for such a monstrously wicked precept . . .

Poor people cannot save, and ought not to try. Spending is not only a first necessity but a first duty. Nine people out of ten have not enough money to spend on themselves and their families; and to preach saving to them is not only foolish but wicked. School-mistresses are already complaining that the encouragement held out by Building Societies to poor parents to buy their own houses has led to the underfeeding of their children. Fortunately most of the poor neither save nor try to. All the spare money invested in the Savings Banks and Building Societies and Co-operative Societies and Savings Certificates, though it sounds very

Published 1951

imposing when it is totalled up into hundreds of millions, is such a mere fleabite compared to the total sums invested . . .

<small>GEORGE BERNARD SHAW, DISCUSSING "THRIFT" IN *THE INTELLIGENT WOMAN'S GUIDE TO SOCIALISM AND CAPITALISM*, 1928</small>

. . . .

The doctrine of thrift for the poor is dumb and cruel, like advising them to try and lift themselves by their bootstraps.

<small>THE U.S. SOCIALIST LEADER AND PRESIDENTIAL CANDIDATE NORMAN THOMAS</small>

13. The Spendthrift's Case

WHAT I WANT IS WHAT I DESERVE; THRIFT DENIES ME,
AND PREVENTS ONE FROM HAVING THE BEST.

*Yet above al thinges, new fashions I love well,
And to were them, my thryft I wyl sell.*

THE FYRST BOKE OF THE INTRODUCTION
OF KNOWLEDGE, 1542

. . . .

*I reckon few will have good Malt in Scotland; as
thrift will make them mix heated Barley with good.*

LETTER OF JOHN COCKBURN OF ORMISTOUN, SCOTLAND,
TO HIS GARDENER, OCTOBER 9, 1739

. . . .

*I suppose you design little poor Windows and Doors
that nobody can go in or out without breaking their
head except they remember to duck like a goose. It is
a common wise practice which proceeds from their
wise heads and noble way of thinking in Scotland,
that if any thing is made look ugly, or if neat is
spoiled in dressing, it is thrift. Losing a hog for a
halfpenny worth of Tar is with them a mark of
judgement . . .*

COCKBURN TO HIS GARDENER, 1742

*It was not his idea that he could get rich by saving.
From the first he had the notion that liberal
spending was better, and that somehow he would
get along.*

THEODORE DREISER, *THE FINANCIER*, 1912

. . . .

*In fact, the whole town grew prosperous, extremely
prosperous, by heeding Father Thrift's advice.
You would suppose that the queer little old man
would be well rewarded. Not so! For when these
people became very, very prosperous, they felt that
the queer little old man was only in their way.
What further need had they of his advice? He had
taught them to live simply, to spend wisely, and
to waste nothing. He had taught them to enjoy
simple pleasures and to form simple habits . . .
But the townspeople would not listen to him now.
Young Mr. Spendthrift had come to town and they
followed him. They only laughed at Father Thrift.*

JOSEPH C. SINDELAR, *FATHER THRIFT AND HIS ANIMAL
FRIENDS* (CHILDREN'S BOOK), 1918

Published 1931

How can the organization man be thrifty? Other people are thrifty for him. He still buys most of his own life insurance, but for the bulk of his rainy-day saving, he gives his proxy to the financial and personnel departments of his organization. In his professional capacity also thrift is becoming a little un-American. The same man who will quote from Benjamin Franklin on thrift for the house organ would be horrified if consumers took these maxims to heart and started putting more money into savings and less into installment purchases. No longer can he afford the luxury of damning the profligacy of the public; not in public, at any rate. He not only has to persuade people to buy more but persuade them out of any guilt feelings they might have for following his advice. Few talents are more commercially sought today than the knack of describing departures from the Protestant Ethic as reaffirmations of it.

In an advertisement that should go down in social history, the J. Walter Thompson agency has hit the problem of absolution head-on. It quotes Benjamin Franklin on the benefits of spending. "Is not the hope of being one day able to purchase and enjoy luxuries a great spur to labor and industry? . . . May not luxury therefore produce more than it consumes, if, without such a spur, people would be, as they are naturally enough inclined to be, lazy and indolent?" This thought, the ad says, in a meaningful aside, "appears to be a mature after-thought, qualifying his earlier and more familiar writings on the importance of thrift."

WILLIAM H. WHYTE JR., *THE ORGANIZATION MAN*, 1956

. . . greed, for lack of a better word, is good.
"GORDON GEKKO," IN THE MOVIE *WALL STREET*, 1987

. . . .

In recent weeks, immense riches have been rained upon top bankers and traders. After a year of record profits, investment houses like Goldman Sachs, Lehman Brothers and Morgan Stanley are awarding bonuses as high as $60 million. And a select group of hedge fund managers and private equity executives may be taking home even more.

That is serious money. And the serious luxury goods markets are feeling the impact.

Miller Motorcars, in Greenwich, Conn., is fielding more requests for the $250,000 Ferrari 599 GTB Fiorano than it can possibly fill. One real estate broker laments a dearth of listing for two clients trying to spend $20 million on Manhattan properties. Financiers already comfortably settled in million-dollar apartments and town houses are buying $5 million apartments for their children.
"WALL ST. BONUSES: SO MUCH MONEY, TOO FEW FERRARIS," *NEW YORK TIMES*, DECEMBER 25, 2006

. . . .

. . . Hasbro is about to launch its new, new, new game of human life . . . Money is a big part of the [forthcoming] Game of Life: Twists & Turns. But there's no cash. Instead, each player gets a Life-Visa-brand "credit card" to insert in the game's electronic Life Pod, which keeps track of Life Points—earn more, spend more! "We are not marketing to kids," a Visa spokesman, Michael Rolnick, has said . . . " We are helping to educate kids. It's never too early." Hmm. Let's just say that Twists & Turns has a rather forgiving attitude toward the rather highly leveraged player. "If you're bankrupt in Monopoly, you're watching," a Hasbro Games vice-president, George Burch, says. "In this game, you can be hugely in debt, but you're still playing!" In the Mansion of Happiness [a nineteenth-century children's "game of life"] there's a square for that kind of thing. It's called the "Road to Folly."
JILL LEPORE, "THE MEANING OF LIFE," *THE NEW YORKER*, MAY 21, 2007

. . . .

Dismissed by sophisticates as anachronistic and sharply accused of these various failings, often bloodied, stands thrift: temperamentally middle-class, democratic, egalitarian, reformist, future-minded, cheerfully promising prosperity for all who are willing and able to strive, and guided by an ethical code of conservation and duty to the common good. As we've seen, many clever people have viewed it as either irrelevant or harmful. I disagree.

Some people say that thrift is about saving money. It is. It is also about saving ourselves, and our society.

PART THREE

Visionaries

THRIFT IS MADE prominent in society in three main ways. The first is through **individual leaders**—those gifted people who, through their words and deeds, make a compelling case for why thrift matters. The second is through **institutions**—those relatively stable societal structures conveying behavior-guiding rules that are intended, at least in large part, to advance the ideals and practices of thrift. And the third is through **social movements**—those larger and comparatively fluid groupings of individuals and organizations working together over periods of time to achieve pro-thrift social changes.

All three are important. Together, they embody our society's thrift tradition. Because the foundation on which the others are built is individual leaders, let's start with them. I often think of them, affectionately, as thrift nuts. But maybe in this book we should be more dignified. Let's call them thrift visionaries, and visit with a few.

From a painting by
HERBERT PAUS

© ARCO 1922

THRIFT!

WISE old BENJAMIN FRANKLIN, apostle of thrift, set the heating industry one step forward by the invention of the Franklin stove.

The American Radiator Company has carried on the work he so well began. Out of its Institute of Thermal Research has come a long procession of better boilers, culminating in the IDEAL TYPE A HEAT MACHINE—the most perfect heating equipment ever developed.

It, too, is a contribution to thrift; it pays for itself in the fuel it saves.

Send your name to either address below for a finely illustrated book describing the IDEAL TYPE A HEAT MACHINE.

AMERICAN RADIATOR COMPANY

IDEAL Boilers and AMERICAN Radiators for every heating need

104 West 42d Street, New York   Dept. 55   816 So. Michigan Avenue, Chicago

"Mention The Geographic—It identifies you"

Published 1922

14. By Dint of His Thrift

DANIEL DEFOE

DANIEL FOE was born in London in the late summer of 1660, the son of James and Alice, both of whom, in their religious convictions, were strong Dissenters, or Puritans. James Foe earned his living as a butcher. In midlife, Daniel changed his last name to "Defoe."

Defoe is one of the most influential pamphleteers, journalists, and novelists in British history. His first important work was his *Essay on Projects*, published in 1697. The novel *Robinson Crusoe*, his most famous achievement and the first and greatest thrift novel in the English language, was published in 1719. Throughout his writings, Defoe is a passionate, articulate advocate of thrift. He died on April 21, 1731, and is buried in London.

European thrift really began with Daniel Defoe. His essays marked the first crystalization of public thrift impulses.

S. W. STRAUS, PRESIDENT, AMERICAN SOCIETY FOR THRIFT, 1920

. . . .

. . . Daniel Defoe, the renowned author of Robinson Crusoe, *published a work entitled* Essay on Projects, *in which he advocated a plan for the formation of societies "formed by mutual assistance for the relief of the members in seasons of distress," and there is no doubt that his essay led to the formation of life insurance companies, and also had its influence in regard to Friendly Societies.*

RICHARDSON CAMPBELL, *RECHABITE HISTORY*, 1911

. . . .

It is but a small matter for a man to contribute, if he gave 1s. 3d. out of his wages to relieve five wounded men [seamen] of his own fraternity; but at the same time be assured that if he is hurt or maimed he shall have the same relief, is a thing so rational that hardly anything but a hare-brained fellow, that thinks of nothing, would omit entering himself into such an office.

. . . Suppose [also] an office to be erected, to be called an office of insurance for widows, upon the following conditions . . .

I have named these two cases [seamen and widows] as special experiments of what might be done by assurances in way of friendly society; and I believe I might, without arrogance, affirm that the same thought might be improved into methods that should prevent the general misery and poverty of mankind, and at once secure us against beggars, parish poor, almshouses, and hospitals; and by which not a creature so miserable or so poor but should claim subsistence as their due, and not ask it of charity.

. . . There is a poverty so far from being dispicable that it is honourable, when a man by direct casualty, sudden Providence, and without any procuring of his own, is reduced to want relief from others, as by fire, shipwreck, loss of limbs, and the like.

. . . Want of consideration is the great reason why people do not provide in their youth and strength for old age and sickness; and the ensuing proposal is, in short, only this—that all persons in time of their health and youth, while they are able to work and spare it, should lay up some small inconsiderable part of their gettings as a deposit in safe hands, to lie as a store in bank to relieve them, if by age or accident they come to be disabled . . . If an office in the same nature within this were appointed in every county in England, I doubt not but poverty might easily be prevented, and begging wholly suppressed.

DANIEL DEFOE, *ESSAY ON PROJECTS*, 1697

But I was gotten home to my little tent, where I lay with all my wealth about me very secure. It blew hard all that night, and in the morning, when I looked out, behold, no more ship was to be seen. I was a little surprised, but recovered myself with this satisfactory reflection, viz., that I had lost no time, nor abated no diligence, to get everything out of her that could be useful to me, and that indeed there was little left in her that I was able to bring away if I had had more time . . .

. . . I carefully saved the ears of this corn, you may be sure, in their season, which was about the end of June; and laying up every corn, I resolved to sow them all again, hoping in time to have some quantity sufficient to supply me with bread. But it was not until the fourth year that I could allow myself the least grain of this corn to eat, and even then but sparingly . . .

. . . This will testify for me that I was not idle, and that I spared no pains to bring to pass whatever appeared necessary for my comfortable support; for I considered the keeping up a breed of tame creatures thus at my hand would be a living magazine of flesh, milk, butter, and cheese for me for as long as I lived in the place, if it were to be forty years; and that keeping them in my reach depended entirely upon me perfecting my enclosures to such a degree, that I might be sure of keeping them together; which, by this method, indeed, I so effectually secured, that when these little stakes began to grow, I had planted them so thick, I was forced to pull some of them up again.

In this place I also had my grapes growing,

which I principally depended on for my winter store of raisins, and which I never failed to preserve very carefully, as the best and most agreeable dainty of my whole diet. And indeed they were not agreeable only, but physical, wholesome, nourishing, and refreshing to the last degree.

DANIEL DEFOE, *ROBINSON CRUSOE*, 1719

. . . .

Lesson 22: THRIFT—No. 1

1. Have you ever read Robinson Crusoe? *[Enter into the story, particularly his being left on the desert island with such provisions &c. as he could secure from the wreck.] . . .*

10. Then both the goods which he got out of the wreck and the corn which he grew he preferred using very sparingly at first, so that he might have them the longer. What do we call this?

11. Thrift or foresight, yes. Was it a good thing for Robinson Crusoe that he had thrift and foresight?

12. Is it a good thing for us to have?

GEORGE C. T. BARTLEY, *DOMESTIC ECONOMY: THRIFT IN EVERY-DAY LIFE* (A BOOK FOR TEACHERS), 1878

. . . .

But he saved from aboard an old gun and a sword,
And another odd matter or two, so

That, by dint of his thrift he just managed to shift,
And keep alive Robinson Crusoe.

"ROBINSON CRUSOE," FROM *THE GOLDEN BOOK OF FAVORITE SONGS*, 1915

. . . .

Modern Robinson Crusoes

CHAPTER TITLE, *ADVENTURES IN THRIFT* (A BOOK FOR TEENAGERS), 1946

. . . .

As I have mentioned Sir Robert Clayton, with whom I had the good fortune to become acquainted on account of the mortgage which he helped me to, it is necessary to take notice that I had much advantage in my ordinary affairs by his advice, and therefore I call it my good fortune. For as he paid me so considerable an annual income as £700 a year, so I am to acknowledge myself much a debtor, not only to the justice of his dealings with me, but to the prudence and conduct which he guided me to, by his advice, for the management of my estate; and as he found I was not inclined to marry, he frequently took occasion to hint how soon I might raise my fortune to a prodigious height, if I would but order my family economy so far within my revenue as to lay up every year something to add to the capital.

I was convinced of the truth of what he said, and agreed to the advantages of it. You are to take it as you go that Sir Robert supposed by my own discourse, and especially by my woman Amy, that

I had £2,000 a year income. He judged, as he said, by my way of living, that I could not spend above £1,000; and so, he added, I might prudently lay by £1,000 every year to add to the capital, and by adding every year the additional interest or income of the money to the capital, he proved to me that in ten years I should double the £1,000 per annum that I laid by. And he drew me out a table, as he called it, of the increase, for me to judge by; and by which, he said, if the gentlemen of England would but act so, every family of them would increase their fortunes to a great degree, just as merchants do by trade; whereas now, says Sir Robert, by the humour of living up to the extent of their fortunes, and rather beyond, the gentlemen, says he, ay, and the nobility too, are, almost all of them, borrowers, and all in necessitous circumstances.

. . . I considered his scheme very well, though I said no more to him at that time, and I resolved, though I would make a very good figure—I say, I resolved to abate a little of my expense and draw in, live closer, and save something, if not so much as he proposed to me.

DANIEL DEFOE, *ROXANA*, 1724

· · · ·

Expensive living is a kind of slow fever; it is not so open, so threatening and dangerous, as the ordinary distemper which goes by that name, but it preys upon the spirits, and, when its degrees are increased to a height, is as fatal and as sure to kill

as the other: it is a secret enemy, that feeds upon the vitals; and when it has gone its full length, and the languished tradesman is weakened in his solid part, I mean his stock, then it overwhelms him at once . . .

In short, good husbandry and frugality is quite out of fashion, and he that goes about to set up for the practice of it, must mortify every thing about him that has the least tincture of frugality; it is the mode to live high, to spend more than we get, to neglect trade, contemn care and concern, and go on without forecast, or without consideration; and, in consequence, it is the mode to go on to extremity, to break, become bankrupt and beggars, and so going off the trading stage, leave it open for others to come after us, and do the same.

DANIEL DEFOE, *THE COMPLETE ENGLISH TRADESMAN*, 1726

· · · ·

[Benjamin Franklin's] great English counterpart and fellow spirit, Daniel Defoe, whose Essay on Projects—*a classic document of the rising middle class—might well have been Franklin's first textbook . . .* Robinson Crusoe, *that practically efficient man making himself master of his environment, was the dream of Daniel Defoe; Franklin was the visible, new-world embodiment of that dream.*

VERNON LOUIS PARRINGTON, *MAIN CURRENTS IN AMERICAN THOUGHT*, 1927

One of the narrow lanes running off the Bowery was once called Robinson Crusoe's Alley—perhaps in honor of the first proponent of savings banks!

A HISTORY OF THE BOWERY SAVINGS BANK OF NEW YORK, 1934

Defoe was always short of money.

JAMES SUTHERLAND, *DEFOE* (A BIOGRAPHY), 1937

15. The More Treasure They Will Lay Up in Heaven

JOHN WESLEY

JOHN WESLEY, the famous Anglican preacher (significantly influenced by Puritanism) who became the primary founder of the Methodist Church, was an almost exact contemporary of Benjamin Franklin. Wesley was born in 1703, three years before Franklin was born, and died in 1791, one year after Franlin died.

Wesley's famous formulation—"Gain all you can, Save all you can, then Give all you can"— is one of the most concise, important, and influential thrift sayings in the English language. Wesley's teachings on the uses of money also constitute one of the purest examples of what scholars would later call "the Protestant ethic." Moreover, while Franklin, as we'll see, largely secularized the philosophy of thrift, detaching it from much of its Christian theological context, Wesley most emphatically did not. Finally, Wesley's moving reflections on the core irony of thrift—religiously informed thrift produces affluence, which can produce worldliness and dissipation—are, for my money, much better than Max Weber's, and quite deserving of our consideration today.

1. Be frugal. Save every thing that can honestly be saved.

2. Spend no more than you receive. Contract no debts.

3. Have no long accounts. Pay every thing within the week.

4. Give none that asks for relief either an ill word or an ill look. Do not hurt them if you cannot help them.

JOHN WESLEY, RULES FOR THE "STEWARDS" (OR ADMINSTRATORS) OF THE METHODIST MOVEMENT, 1748

. . . .

Wesley was a gifted organizer. Early in his ministry, he started a school for children and a rest home for "feeble, aged widows." He also organized what he called a "lending stock," which foreshadowed the creation of what thrift advocates more than a century later would call credit unions.

A year or two ago [in 1746] I observed among many a distress . . . They frequently wanted, perhaps in order to carry on their business, a present supply of money. They scrupled to make use of a pawnbroker; but where to borrow it they knew not. I resolved to try if we could not find a remedy . . . Fifty pounds were contributed [to the lending stock]. This was immediately lodged in the hands of two stewards, who attended every Tuesday morning in order to lend to those who wanted any small sum, not exceeding twenty shillings, to be repaid within three months . . . Will not God put it into the heart of some lover of mankind to increase this little stock? If this is not "lending unto the Lord," what is?

WESLEY, 1748

· · · ·

For I look upon all this revenue [of the church], be it what it may, as sacred to God and the poor; out of which, if I want any thing, I am relieved, even as another poor man.

WESLEY, 1748

· · · ·

Gain all you can . . . Save all you can . . . Then give all you can . . . Brethren, can we be either wise or faithful stewards unless we thus manage our Lord's goods? . . . I entreat you, in the name of the Lord Jesus, act up to the dignity of your calling! No more sloth! Whatsoever your hand findeth to do, do it with your might! No more waste! Cut off every expense which fashion, caprice, or flesh and blood demand! No more covetousness! But employ whatever God has entrusted you with, in doing good, all possible good, in every possible kind and degree to the household of faith, to all men! This is no small part of the "wisdom of the just." Give all

ye have, as well as all ye are, a spiritual sacrifice to Him who withheld not from you His Son, His only Son: so "laying up in store for yourselves a good foundation against the time to come, that ye may attain eternal life!"

WESLEY, THE USE OF MONEY, 1760

· · · ·

Never let your expenses exceed your income. To servants I would give full as much as others give for the same service; and not more.

WESLEY, LETTER TO A METHODIST, FEBRUARY 7, 1776

· · · ·

. . . I do not see how it is possible, in the nature of things, for any revival of true religion to continue long. For religion must necessarily produce both industry and frugality, and these cannot but produce riches. But as riches increase, so will pride, anger, and love of the world in all its branches.

How then is it possible that Methodism, that is, a religion of the heart, though it flourishes now as a green bay tree, should continue in this state? For the Methodists in every place grow diligent and frugal; consequently they increase in goods. Hence they proportionately increase in pride, in anger, in the desire of the flesh, the desire of the eyes, and the pride of life. So, although the form of religion remains, the spirit is swiftly vanishing away.

Is there no way to prevent this? this continual decay of pure religion? We ought not to prevent people from being diligent and frugal; we must exhort all Christians to gain all they can, and to save all they can; that is, in effect, to grow rich! What way then (I ask again) can we take, that our money may not sink us to the nethermost hell? There is one way, and there is no other under heaven. If those who "gain all they can," and "save all they can," will likewise "give all they can"; then, the more they gain, the more they will grow in grace, and the more treasure they will lay up in heaven.

WESLEY, AUGUST 4, 1786

. . . .

Wesley was not the only leader to ponder this question. John Adams (1735–1826) was a leader of the American Revolution and served as the second president of the United States. The third president of the U.S. was Thomas Jefferson.

Will you tell me how to prevent riches from becoming the effects of temperence and industry? Will you tell me how to prevent riches from producing luxury? Will you tell me how to prevent luxury from producing effeminacy, intoxication, extravagance, vice and folly?

JOHN ADAMS, LETTER TO THOMAS JEFFERSON, DECEMBER 1819

. . . .

Yet as we see in this excerpt, Wesley, though obviously troubled, gives an answer the question he poses, while Adams, at least in this instance, does not. The issue is quite poignant, for Adams personally was a great proponent of thrift.

I must double and redouble my Diligence. I must be more constant to my office and my Pen. Constancy accomplishes more than Rapidity. Continual Attention will do great Things. Frugality, of Time, is the greatest Art as well as Virtue. This Economy will produce Knowledge as well as Wealth.

JOHN ADAMS, DIARY, MAY 24, 1773

16. The Art of Making Money Plenty

BENJAMIN FRANKLIN

BENJAMIN FRANKLIN may be the most important American. He is almost certainly the most
famous American. He is without doubt America's,
and the world's, most important and famous thrift
nut. Every American who has ever worked in the
field of thrift has worked, at least to some degree,
in Franklin's capacious shadow. He was born in
1706 in Boston. He died in 1790 and is buried in
Philadelphia.

*He was the greatest of all teachers of industry and
thrift.*

WAYNE WHIPPLE, *THE STORY OF YOUNG BENJAMIN
FRANKLIN* (CHILDREN'S BOOK), 1916

. . . .

*Ben Franklin is our greatest example of thrift. He
wrote more on it and wrote better about it than
any man we know.*

ELBERT HUBBARD, *LET THRIFT BE
YOUR RULING HABIT*, 1917

. . . .

Remember that TIME is Money . . .
Remember that CREDIT is Money . . .
*Remember that Money is of a prolific generating
Nature. Money can beget Money, and its Offspring
can beget more, and so on . . .*

Remember this Saying, That the good pay-
master is Lord of another Man's Purse. *He that
is known to pay punctually and exactly to the
Time he promises, may at any time, and on any
Occasion, raise all the Money his friends can spare.
This is sometimes of great Use . . .*

*Beware of thinking all your own that you possess,
and of living accordingly. 'Tis a mistake that many
People who have Credit fall into. To prevent this,
keep an exact Account for some Time of both your
Expences and your Incomes. If you take the Pains at
first to mention Particulars, it will have this good
Effect; you will discover how wonderfully small
trifling Expences mount up to large Sums, and
will discern what might have been, and may for
the future be saved, without occasioning any great
Inconvenience.*

*In short, the Way to Wealth, if you desire it, is as
plain as the Way to Market. It depends chiefly on
two Words, INDUSTRY and FRUGALITY; i.e. Waste*

neither *Time* nor *Money*, but make the best Use of both . . .

BENJAMIN FRANKLIN, *ADVICE TO A YOUNG TRADESMAN*, 1748

. . . .

As the Stamp Act is at length repeal'd, I am willing you should have a new Gown, which you may suppose I did not send sooner, as I knew you would not like to be finer than your Neighbours, unless in a Gown of your own Spinning. Had the Trade between the two Countries totally ceas'd, it was a Comfort to me to recollect that I had once been cloth'd from Head to Foot in Woolen and Linnen of my Wife's Manufacture, that I never was prouder of any Dress in my Life, and that she and her Daughter might do it again if it was necessary.

FRANKLIN, LETTER TO HIS WIFE, APRIL 6, 1766

. . . I live here as frugally as possible not to be destitute of the comforts of life, making no dinners for anybody and contenting myself with a single dish when I dine at home; and yet such is the dearness of living here in every article, that my expenses amaze me . . . In short, with frugality and prudent care we may subsist decently on what we have, and leave it entire to our children; but without such care we shall not be able to keep it together; it will melt away like butter in the sunshine, and we may live long enough to feel the miserable consequences of our indiscretion.

FRANKLIN, LETTER TO HIS WIFE, JUNE 22, 1767

. . . .

Be industrious and frugal, and you will be rich.

FRANKLIN, LETTER TO JOHN ALLEYNE, AUGUST 9, 1768

. . . .

The Parliament remains fix'd in their Resolution not to repeal the Duty Acts this Session, and will rise next Tuesday. I hope my Country folks will remain as fix'd in their Resolutions of Industry and Frugality till these Acts are repeal'd. And, if I could be sure of that, I should almost wish them never to be repealed; being pursuaded, that we shall reap more solid and extensive Advantages from the steady Practice of those two great Virtues, than we can possibly suffer Damage from all the Duties the Parliament of this kingdom can levy on us.

FRANKLIN, LETTER TO SAMUEL COOPER, APRIL 27, 1769

Great frugality and great industry are now become fashionable here: Gentlemen who used to entertain with two or three courses, pride themselves now in treating with simple beef and pudding. By these means, and the stoppage of our consumptive trade with Britain, we shall be better able to pay our voluntary taxes for the support of our troops.

FRANKLIN, LETTER TO JOSEPH PRIESTLY, JULY 7, 1775

. . . .

I was charmed with the account you gave me of your industry, the table-cloths of your own spinning, &c.; but the latter part of the paragraph, that you had sent for linen from France, because weaving and flax were grown dear, alas, that dissolved the charm; and your sending for long black pins, and lace, and feathers! disgusted me as much as if you had put salt in my strawberries . . . The war indeed may in some degree raise the prices of goods, and the high taxes which are necessary to support the war may make our frugality necessary; and, as I am always preaching that doctrine, I cannot in conscience or in decency encourage the contrary, by my example, in furnishing my children with foolish modes and luxuries. I therefore send all the articles you desire, that are useful and necessary, and omit the rest; for as you say you should "have great pride in wearing any thing I send, and showing it as your father's taste," I must avoid giving you an opportunity of doing that with either lace or feathers. If you wear your cambric ruffles as I do, and take care not to mend the holes, they will come in time to be lace; and feathers, my dear girl,

may be had in America from every cock's tail.

FRANKLIN, LETTER TO HIS DAUGHTER, MRS. SARAH BACHE, JUNE 3, 1779

. . . .

. . . we should draw all the Good we can from this World. In my Opinion we might all draw more Good, from it than we do, & suffer less Evil, if we would but take care not to give too much for our Whistles. For to me it seems that most of the unhappy People we meet with, are become so by Neglect of that Caution.

You ask what I mean?—You love Stories, and will excuse my telling you one of my self. When I was a Child of seven Years old, my Friends on a Holiday fill'd my little Pocket with Halfpence. I went directly to a Shop where they sold Toys for Children; and being charm'd with the Sound of a Whistle that I met by the way, in the hands of another Boy, I voluntarily offer'd and gave all my Money for it. When I came home, whistling all over the House, much pleas'd with my Whistle, but disturbing all the Family, my Brothers, Sisters & Cousins, understanding the Bargain I had made, told me I had given four times as much for it as it was worth, put me in mind what good Things I might have bought with the rest of the Money, & laught at me so much for my Folly that I cry'd with Vexation; and the Reflection gave me more Chagrin than the Whistle gave me Pleasure.

This however was afterwards of use to me, the Impression continuing on my Mind; so that often when I was tempted to buy some unnecessary thing,

I said to my self, Do not give too much for the Whistle; and I sav'd my Money.

As I grew up, came into the World, and observed the Actions of Men, I thought I met many who gave too much for the Whistle.—When I saw one ambitious of Court Favour, sacrificing his Time in Attendance at Levees, his Repose, his Liberty, his Virtue and perhaps his Friend, to obtain it; I have said to my self, This Man gives too much for his Whistle.—When I saw another fond of Popularity, constantly employing himself in political Bustles, neglecting his own Affairs, and ruining them by that Neglect, He pays, says I, too much for his Whistle.—If I knew a Miser, who gave up every kind of comfortable Living, all the Pleasure of doing Good to others, all the Esteem of his Fellow Citizens, & the Joys of benevolent Friendship, for the sake of Accumulating Wealth, Poor Man, says I, you pay too much for your Whistle.—When I met with a Man of Pleasure, sacrificing every laudable Improvement of his Mind or of his Fortune, to mere corporeal Satisfactions, & ruining his Health in their Pursuit, Mistaken Man, says I, you are providing Pain for your self instead of Pleasure, you pay too much for your Whistle.—If I see one fond of Appearance, of fine Cloaths, fine Houses, fine Furniture, fine Equipages, all above his Fortune, for which he contracts Debts, and ends his Career in a Prison; Alas, says I, he has paid too much for his Whistle.—When I saw a beautiful sweet-temper'd Girl, marry'd to an ill-natured Brute of a Husband; What a pity, says I, that she should pay so much for a Whistle!—In short, I conceiv'd

that great Part of the Miseries of Mankind, were brought upon them by the false Estimates thay had made of the Value of Things, and by their giving too much for the Whistle.

FRANKLIN, LETTER TO MADAME BRILLON, NOVEMBER 10, 1779

· · · ·

. . . it is prodigious the quantity of Good that may be done by one Man, if he will make a Business of it.

FRANKLIN, LETTER TO THOMAS BRAND HOLLIS, OCTOBER 5, 1783

· · · ·

For my own part, I wish the Bald Eagle had not been chosen as the representative of our Country; he is a Bird of bad moral Character; he does not get his living honestly; you may have seen him perch'd on some dead Tree, near the River where, too lazy to fish for himself, he watches the Labor of the Fishing-Hawk; and, when that diligent Bird has at length taken a Fish, and is bearing it to his Nest for the support of his Mate and young ones, the Bald Eagle pursues him, and takes it from him. With all this Injustice he is never in good Case; but, like those among Men who live by Sharping and Robbing, he is generally poor, and very often lousy.

FRANKLIN, LETTER TO HIS DAUGHTER, MRS. SARAH BACHE, JANUARY 26, 1784

I send you herewith a Bill for Ten Louis d'ors. I do not pretend to give such a Sum; I only lend it to you. When you shall return to your Country with a good Character, you cannot fail of getting into some Business, that will in time enable you to pay all your Debts. In that Case, when you meet another honest Man in similar Distress, you must pay me by lending this Sum to him; enjoining him to discharge the Debt by a like operation, when he shall be able, and shall meet with such another opportunity. I hope it may thus go thro' many hands, before it meets with a Knave that will stop its Progress. This is a trick of mine for doing a deal of good with a little money. I am not rich enough to afford much in good works, and so am obliged to be cunning and make the most of a little.

FRANKLIN, LETTER TO BENJAMIN WEBB,
APRIL 22, 1784

. . . .

So many aspects of Franklin's understanding of thrift, and of his winning character, are present in this short letter to Benjamin Webb—generosity, wit, sympathy for human failings combined with earnest efforts to foster moral perfection, carefulness with money blended with a keen appreciation of its generative power, the willingness to help those who are willing to help themselves and in turn help others, and, to top it all off, a specific scheme to promote thrift by extending credit to those who will use it well and pass it on, the basic insight of which, several generations later, led

thrift advocates working in Franklin's shadow to create institutions such as credit unions and building and loan associations.

I began now gradually to pay off the Debt I was under for the Printing-House.—In order to secure my Credit and Character as a Tradesman, I took care not only to be in Reality Industrious & frugal, but to avoid all Appearance of the Contrary. I drest plainly; I was seen at no Places of idle Diversion; I never went out a-fishing or shooting; a Book, indeed, sometimes debauch'd me from my Work; but that was seldom, snug, & gave no Scandal; and to show that I was not above my Business, I sometimes brought home the Paper I purhas'd at the Stores, thro' the Streets on a Wheelbarrow. Thus being esteem'd an industrious thriving young Man, and paying duly for what I bought, the Merchants who imported Stationery solicited my Custom, others propos'd supplying me with Books, I went on swimmingly . . .

FRANKLIN, *AUTOBIOGRAPHY*, 1784

. . . .

5. FRUGALITY.
Make no Expense but to do good to others or yourself: i.e., Waste nothing.
6. INDUSTRY.
Lose no Time.—Be always employ'd in something useful.—Cut off all unnecessary Actions.

FROM HIS LIST OF THIRTEEN VIRTUES, FRANKLIN,
AUTOBIOGRAPHY, 1784

Who then are the kind of Persons to whom an Emigration to America may be advantageous? . . . hearty young Labouring Men, who understand the Husbandry of Corn and Cattle . . . may easily establish themselves here. A little Money sav'd of the good Wages they receive here, while they work for others, enables them to buy the land and begin . . . in which they are assisted by the Good-Will of their Neighbors, and some Credit. Multitudes of poor People from England, Ireland, Scotland, and Germany, have by this means in a few years become wealthy Farmers . . .

Tolerably good Workmen in any of those mechanical Arts are sure to find Employ, and to be well paid for their Work, there being no Restraints preventing Strangers from exercising any Art they understand, nor any Permission necessary. If they are poor, they begin first as Servants or Journeymen; and if they are sober, industrious, and frugal, they soon become Masters, establish themselves in Business, marry, raise Families, and become respectable Citizens.

. . . The almost general Mediocrity of Fortune that prevails in America obliging its People to follow some Business for subsistence, those Vices, that arise usually from Idleness, are in a great measure prevented. Industry and constant Employment are great preservatives of the Morals and Virtue of a Nation. Hence bad Examples to Youth are more rare in America, which must be a comfortable Consideration to Parents.

FRANKLIN, "INFORMATION TO THOSE WHO WOULD REMOVE TO AMERICA," 1782

At this time when the general complaint is that "money is scarce" it will be an act of kindness to inform the moneyless how they may reinforce their pockets. I will acquaint them with the true secret of money-catching, the certain way to fill empty purses, and how to keep them always full. Two simple rules, well observed, will do the business. First, let honesty and industry be thy constant companions; and Secondly, spend one penny less than thy clear gains. Then shall thy hide-bound pocket soon begin to thrive, and will never again cry with empty belly-ache; neither will creditors insult thee, nor want oppress, nor hunger bite, nor nakedness freeze thee. The whole hemisphere will shine brighter, and pleasure spring up in every corner of thy heart. Now, therefore, embrace these rules and be happy.

FRANKLIN, "THE ART OF MAKING MONEY PLENTY IN EVERY MAN'S POCKET," 1791

. . . .

The diligent Spinner has a large Shift . . .
FRANKLIN, *THE WAY TO WEALTH*, 1758

. . . .

A fat Kitchen makes a lean Will . .
FRANKLIN, *THE WAY TO WEALTH*

. . . .

. . . he that goes a borrowing goes a sorrowing.
FRANKLIN, *THE WAY TO WEALTH*

What maintains one Vice, would bring up two Children.

FRANKLIN, *THE WAY TO WEALTH*

. . . .

Buy what thou hast no Need of, and ere long thou shalt sell thy Necessaries.

FRANKLIN, *THE WAY TO WEALTH*

. . . .

Many have been ruined by buying good Pennyworths.

FRANKLIN, *THE WAY TO WEALTH*

. . . .

. . . always taking out of the Meal-tub, and never putting in, soon comes to the Bottom;

FRANKLIN, *THE WAY TO WEALTH*

. . . .

Women and Wine, Game and Deceit,
Make the Wealth small, and the Wants great.

FRANKLIN, *THE WAY TO WEALTH*

. . . .

Keep thy Shop, and thy Shop will keep thee.

FRANKLIN, *THE WAY TO WEALTH*

Fond pride of Dress, is sure a very Curse;
E'er Fancy you consult, consult your Purse.

FRANKLIN, *THE WAY TO WEALTH*

. . . .

Pride is as loud a Beggar as Want, and a great deal more saucy.

FRANKLIN, *THE WAY TO WEALTH*

. . . .

'Tis easier to suppress the first Desire, than to satisfy all that follow it.

FRANKLIN, *THE WAY TO WEALTH*

. . . .

Remember that Franklin often borrowed and adapted thrift maxims from writers of previous generations. Consider:

Did I gain my wealth by ordinaries? no: by exchanging of gold? no: by keeping of gallant company? no: I hir'd me a little shop, fought low, took small gain, kept no debt-book, garnished my shop, for want of plate, with good, wholesome, thrifty sentences: as, Touchstone, keep thy shop, and thy shop will keep thee. Light gains make heaving purses.

GEORGE CHAPMAN, BEN JOHNSON, AND JOHN MARSTON, *EASTWARD HOE* (I, I), 1605

Franklin maxim plate for children, mid-1800s

Pride breakfasted with Plenty, dined with Poverty, and supped with Infamy.

FRANKLIN, *THE WAY TO WEALTH*

. . . .

*Hope of gain
Lessens pain.*

FRANKLIN, *POOR RICHARD'S ALMANAC*, 1734

. . . .

*The thrifty maxim of the wary Dutch,
Is to save all the Money they can touch.*

FRANKLIN, *POOR RICHARD'S ALMANAC*, 1734

Avarice and happiness never saw each other, how then should they become acquainted.

FRANKLIN, *POOR RICHARD'S ALMANAC*, 1734

. . . .

Early to bed and early to rise, makes a man healthy, wealthy, and wise.

FRANKLIN, *POOR RICHARD'S ALMANAC*, 1735

. . . .

Also who soo woll use the game of anglynge [fishing]: he must ryse erly, whiche thyng is proffytable to man in this way, That is to wit: moost to the heele [profit, healing] of his soule. For it shall cause him to be holy, and to the heele of his body, For it shall cause him to be hole. Also to the encrease of his goodys. For it shall make hym ryche. As the olde englysshe proverbe says in this way.

Who soo woll ryse erly shall be holy, helthy, and zely [fortunate].

THE TREATYSE OF FYSSHINGE WYTH AN ANGLE, MID-FIFTEENTH CENTURY

Deny Self for Self's sake.

FRANKLIN, POOR RICHARD'S ALMANAC, 1735

. . . .

Fly pleasures, and they'll follow you.

FRANKLIN, POOR RICHARD'S ALMANAC, 1738

. . . .

Diligence is the Mother of Good-Luck.

FRANKLIN, POOR RICHARD'S ALMANAC, 1736

. . . .

Wealth is not his that has it, but his that enjoys it.

FRANKLIN, POOR RICHARD'S ALMANAC, 1736

. . . .

Industry need not wish.

FRANKLIN, POOR RICHARD'S ALMANAC, 1739

. . . .

Every little makes a mickle.

FRANKLIN, POOR RICHARD'S ALMANAC, 1737

He that idly loses 5 s. worth of time, loses 5 s., & might as prudently throw 5 s. in the River.

FRANKLIN, POOR RICHARD'S ALMANAC, 1737

. . . .

A penny sav'd is Twopence clear, A Pin a day is a Groat a Year. Save & have.

FRANKLIN, POOR RICHARD'S ALMANAC, 1737

. . . .

The noblest question in the world is What Good may I do in it?

FRANKLIN, POOR RICHARD'S ALMANAC, 1737

. . . .

Now I have a sheep and a cow, every body bids me good morrow.

FRANKLIN, POOR RICHARD'S ALMANAC, 1736

. . . .

Employ thy time well, if thou meanest to gain leisure.

FRANKLIN, POOR RICHARD'S ALMANAC, 1740

. . . .

Be always asham'd to catch thy self idle.

FRANKLIN, POOR RICHARD'S ALMANAC, 1741

Have you somewhat to do to-morrow;
do it to-day.

FRANKLIN, *POOR RICHARD'S ALMANAC*, 1742

. . . .

He that riseth late, must trot all day, and shall
scarce overtake his business at night.

FRANKLIN, *POOR RICHARD'S ALMANAC*, 1742

. . . .

Content and Riches seldom meet together,
Riches take thou, contentment I had rather.

FRANKLIN, *POOR RICHARD'S ALMANAC*, 1743

. . . .

Who is rich? He that rejoices in his Portion.

FRANKLIN, *POOR RICHARD'S ALMANAC*, 1744

. . . .

Beware of little Expences, a small Leak will sink a
great Ship.

FRANKLIN, *POOR RICHARD'S ALMANAC*, 1745

. . . .

Again, Franklin the cheerful borrower from earlier
thrift proponents:

Live with a thrifty, not a needy Fate;
Small shots paid often, waste a vast estate.

ROBERT HERRICK, "EXPENCES EXHAUST," 1648

. . . .

Sloth, like Rust, consumes faster than Labour wears,
while the used Key is always bright . . .

FRANKLIN, *POOR RICHARD'S ALMANAC*, 1745

. . . .

Dost thou love Life? then do not squander Time; for
that's the Stuff Life is made of.

FRANKLIN, *POOR RICHARD'S ALMANAC*, 1746

. . . .

The second Vice is Lying; the first is Running into
Debt.

FRANKLIN, *POOR RICHARD'S ALMANAC*, 1748

. . . .

The Art of getting Riches consists very much in
THRIFT. All Men are not equally qualified for
getting Money, but it is in the Power of every one
alike to practise this Virtue.

FRANKLIN, *POOR RICHARD'S ALMANAC*, 1749

. . . .

Franklin borrowed the above sentences, lock,
stock, and (almost) barrel from the pages of the

famous London publication, *The Spectator*, which Franklin read avidly. Here is Eustace Budgell writing in *The Spectator* in 1712:

. . . the subject of my present paper, which I intend, as an essay on The Ways to raise a Man's Fortune; or The Art of growing Rich . . .

The first and most infallible method toward the attaining of this end is Thrift; all men are not equally qualified for getting money, but it is in the power of every one alike to practice this virtue, and I believe there are very few persons, who, if they please to reflect on their past lives, will not find that had they saved all those little sums, which they have spent unnecessarily, they might at present have been masters of a competent fortune. Diligence justly claims the next place to Thrift. I find both these excellently well represented to common use in the following three Italian proverbs.

Never do that by proxy which you can do yourself.

Never defer that til to morrow which you can do to day.

Never neglect small matters and expenses.

. . . I must not however close this essay, without observing, that what has been said is only intended for persons in the common ways of thriving, and is not designed for those men who from low beginnings push themselves up to the top of states, and the most considerable figures in life. My maxim of saving is not designed for such as these, since nothing is more usual than for thrift to disappoint the ends of ambition, it being almost impossible that the mind should be intent upon trifles, while it is at the same time forming some great design . . . I would however have all my readers take `*`great care how they mistake themselves for uncommon genius's, and men above rule, since it is very easy for them to be deceived in this particular.*

EUSTACE BUDGELL, *THE SPECTATOR*, JANUARY 24, 1712

. . . .

Despite having flattered Budgell by lifting some of his prose, Franklin almost certainly would have disagreed with Budgell's suggestion that thrift "disappoints the ends of ambition," and that men of genius typically do not and need not practice thrift. Indeed, Franklin viewed himself as living proof of the contrary. Nor, as a matter of conceptual clarity, would Franklin be likely to view "diligence" as something separate and distinguishable from "thrift."

For Age and Want save while you may; No Morning Sun lasts a whole Day.

FRANKLIN, *POOR RICHARD'S ALMANAC*, 1755

. . . .

God helps them that help themselves.

FRANKLIN, *POOR RICHARD'S ALMANAC*, 1758

. . . .

Lost Time is never found again.

FRANKLIN, *POOR RICHARD'S ALMANAC*, 1758

And I hope it; for I, too, with your Poet, trust in God. And when I observe, that there is great Frugality, as well as Wisdom, in his Works, since he has been evidently sparing both of Labour and Materials; for by the various wonderful Inventions of Propagation, he has provided for the continual peopling his World with Plants and Animals, without being at the Trouble of repeated new Creations; and by the natural Reduction of compound Substances to their original Elements, capable of being employ'd in new Compositions, he has prevented the Necessity of creating new Matter; so that the Earth, Water, Air, and perhaps Fire, which being compounded form Wood, do, when the Wood is dissolved, return, and again become Air, Earth, Fire, and Water; I say, that, when I see nothing annihilated, and not even a Drop of Water wasted, I cannot suspect the Annihilation of Souls, or believe that he will suffer the daily Waste of Millions of Minds ready made that now exist, and put himself to the continual Trouble of making new ones. Thus finding myself to exist in the World, I believe I shall, in some Shape or other, always exist; and, with all the inconveniences human Life is liable to, I shall not object to a new Edition of mine; hoping, however, that the Errata of the last may be corrected.

FRANKLIN, LETTER TO GEORGE WHATLEY, MAY 23, 1785

. . . .

Franklin hoped and planned that, even after his death, he might be able to influence ideas and create institutions to promote thrift.

The said sum of one thousand pounds sterling, if accepted by the inhabitants of the town of Boston . . . [is to be] let out the same at interest of five per cent. per annum, to such young married artificers, under the age of twenty-five years . . . [with] good moral character . . . these loans are intended to assist young married artificers in setting up their business . . . These aids may therefore be small at first; but as the capital increases by the accumulated interest, they will be more ample. And in order to serve as many as possible in their turn, as well as to make the repayment of the principal borrowed more easy, each borrower shall be obliged to pay with the yearly interest one tenth part of the principal; which sums of principal and interest so paid in, shall be again let out to fresh borrowers . . . it is hoped that no part of the money will at any time be dead, or diverted to other purposes, but be continually augmenting by the interest . . . [therefore] there may in time be more [in the loan fund] than the occasion in Boston shall require, and then some may be spared to the neighboring or other towns . . .

FRANKLIN'S WILL, JUNE 23, 1789

. . . .

Above all, he [Franklin] was the author of that pitiful system of Economics, the adoption of which has degraded our national character.

JOSEPH DENNIE, *THE PORT FOLIO*, 1802

. . . a philosophical Quaker full of mean and thrifty maxims . . .

JOHN KEATS, CRITICIZING FRANKLIN, LETTER TO GEORGE AND GEORGIANA KEATS, OCTOBER 25, 1818

. . . .

The frugality of his manner of life did not lose him the good opinion even of the voluptuaries of the showiest of capitals, whose very iron railings are not free from gilt. Franklin was not less a lady's man, than a man's man, a wise man, and an old man. Not only did he enjoy the homage of the choicest Parisian literati, but at the age of seventy-two he was the caressed favorite of the highest born beauties of the Court; who through blind fashion having been originally attracted to him as a famous savan, were permanently retained as his admirers by his Plato-like graciousness of good humor. Having carefully weighed the world, Franklin could act any part in it. By nature turned to knowledge, his mind was often grave, but never serious. At times he had seriousness—extreme seriousness—for others, but never for himself. Tranquillity was to him instead of it. This philosophical levity of tranquillity, so to speak, is shown in his easy variety of pursuits. Printer, postmaster, almanac maker, essayist, chemist, orator, tinker, statesman, humorist, philosopher, parlor man, political economist, professor of housewifery, ambassador, projector, maxim-monger, herb-doctor, wit:—Jack of all trades, master of each and mastered by none— the type and genius of his land. Franklin was everything but a poet. But since a soul with many

qualities, forming of itself a sort of handy index and pocket congress of all humanity, needs the contact of just as many different men, or subjects, in order to the exhibition of its totality; hence very little indeed of the sage's multifariousness will be portrayed in a simple narrative like the present. This casual private intercourse with Israel, but served to manifest him in his far lesser lights; thrifty, domestic, dietarian, and, it may be, didactically waggish. There was much benevolent irony, innocent mischievousness, in the wise man. Seeking here to depict him in his less exalted habitudes, the narrator feels more as if he were playing with one of the sage's worsted hose, than reverentially handling the honored hat which once oracularly sat upon his brow.

HERMAN MELVILLE, *ISRAEL POTTER*, 1855

. . . .

His maxims were full of animosity towards boys. Nowadays a boy cannot follow out a single natural instinct without tumbling over some of those everlasting aphorisms and hearing from Franklin on the spot. If he buys two cents' worth of peanuts, his father says, "Remember what Franklin has said, my son—'A groat a day's a penny a year'"; and the comfort is all gone out of those peanuts. If he wants to spin his top when he has done work, his father quotes, "Procrastination is the thief of time." If he does a virtuous action, he never gets anything for it, because "Virtue is its own reward." And that boy is hounded to death and robbed of his natural rest, because Franklin once said, in one of his inspired flights of malignity:

Early to bed and early to rise
Makes a man healthy and wealthy and wise.
  As if it were any object to a boy to be healthy
and wealthy and wise on such terms. The sorrow
that that maxim has cost me, through my parents,
experimenting on me with it, tongue cannot
tell . . . When I was a child I had to boil soap,
notwithstanding my father was wealthy, and I had
to get up early and study geometry at breakfast, and
peddle my own poetry, and do everything just as
Franklin did, in the solemn hope that I would be a
Franklin one day. And here I am.

MARK TWAIN, "THE LATE BENJAMIN FRANKLIN," 1870

· · · ·

New England has had two great inspiring
minds,—Jonathan Edwards and Benjamin
Franklin. Far apart in spirit and character, they
formed a grand unity in their influence. One
taught religion, the other thrift; one clarified
theology, the other taught people how to get on.
Edwards tided New England over the infidelity
that prevailed in the last century; Franklin created
the wealth that feeds society today by inspiring a
passion for thrift.

REV. THEODORE T. MUNGER, *ON THE THRESHOLD*, 1881

· · · ·

. . . here was Franklin, poorer than myself, who by
industry, thrift and frugality had become learned
and wise, and elevated to wealth and fame. The
maxims of "poor Richard" exactly suited my

sentiments. I read [Franklin's Autobiography]
again and again . . . After that I was more
industrious when at school, and more constant than
ever in reading and study during leisure hours. I
regard the reading of Franklin's Autobiography *as*
the turning point of my life.

THOMAS MELLON, FOUNDER OF THE MELLON BANK, 1885

· · · ·

One of the fundamental elements of the spirit of
modern capitalism, and not only of that but of
all modern culture: rational conduct on the basis
of the idea of the calling, was born—that is what
this discussion has sought to demonstrate—from
the spirit of Christian asceticism. One has only
to re-read the passage from Franklin, quoted at
the beginning of this essay, in order to see that the
essential elements of the attitude which was there
called the spirit of capitalism are the same as what
we have just shown to be the content of the Puritan
wordly asceticism, only without the religious basis,
which by Franklin's time had died away.

MAX WEBER, *THE PROTESTANT ETHIC AND THE SPIRIT*
OF CAPITALISM, 1905

· · · ·

  To show how Benjamin Franklin through the
practice of thrift was able to rise from poverty
to comfortable financial circumstances.

TEACHING THRIFT IN ELEMENTARY SCHOOLS
(GRADE FIVE), 1919

*The keynote of Frankin's character was thrift—
real thrift that means wise use of one's gifts
and opportunities.*

MARY R. PARKMAN, *CONQUESTS OF INVENTION*, 1923

. . . .

*I can remember, when I was a little boy, my father
used to buy a scrubby yearly almanac with the sun
and moon and stars on the cover. And it used to
prophesy bloodshed and famine. But also crammed in
corners it had little anecdotes and humorisms, with a
moral tag. And I used to have my little priggish laugh
at the women who counted her chickens before they
were hatched and so forth, and I was convinced that
honesty was the best policy, also a little priggishly.
The author of these bits was Poor Richard, and Poor
Richard was Benjamin Franklin, writing in Philadelphia well over a hundred years before.*

*And probably I haven't got over those Poor
Richard tags yet. I rankle still with them. They are
thorns in young flesh.*

*Because, although I still believe honesty is the best
policy, I dislike policy altogether; though it is just as
well not to count your chickens before they are
hatched, it's still more hateful to count them with
gloating when they are hatched. It has taken me
many years and countless smarts to get out of that
barbed wire moral enclosure that Poor Richard
rigged up. Here I am now in tatters and scratched to
ribbons, sitting in the middle of Benjamin's America
looking at the barbed wire, and the fat sheep
crawling under the fence to get fat outside and the
watchdogs yelling at the gate lest by chance anyone*

*should get out by the proper exit. Oh America! Oh
Benjamin! And I just utter a long loud curse against
Benjamin and the American corral.*

D. H. LAWRENCE, "BENJAMIN FRANKLIN," 1923

. . . .

*His mighty answer to the New World's offer
of a great embrace was THRIFT. Work night
and day, build up, penny by penny … our wise
prophet of chicanery, the great buffoon, the face
on the penny stamp.*

WILLLIAM CARLOS WILLIAMS, *IN THE AMERICAN GRAIN*, 1925

. . . .

*Bankers who preach the gospel of savings are
interested in National Thrift Week which each
year begins January 17, the birthday of Benjamin
Franklin, the American apostle of thrift.*

CALIFORNIA BANKERS ASSOCIATION BULLETIN, 1926

. . . .

*The Credit Union League of Massachusetts had
designated Franklin's birthday, January 17, as
Credit Union Day, and it was duly celebrated with
meetings in Boston, Indianapolis, Minneapolis, and
a few other places.*

THE STORIED CREDIT UNION ORGANIZER AND THRIFT
LEADER ROY F. BERGENGREN, RECALLING THE YEAR 1927

Franklin represented the least praiseworthy qualities of the inhabitants of the New World: miserliness, fanatical practicality, and lack of interest in what are usually known as spiritual things. Babbittry was not a new thing in America, but he made a religion of it, and by his tremendous success with it he grafted it upon the American people so securely that the national genius is still suffering from it.

CHARLES ANGOFF, *A LITERARY HISTORY OF THE AMERICAN PEOPLE*, 1935

. . . .

Poor Richard appeals now only to vulgar minds . . . His narrow principles of conduct are as outworn as apprenticeships.

EDITORIAL, *NEW YORK TIMES*, JANUARY 21, 1938

. . . .

Though Franklin was an excellent and successful business man, he retired from active business at forty-two and spent forty-two years more in the service of the public. He might have made a fortune had he patented his stove or his lightening-rod. He refused to patent anything which he thought might be of benefit to mankind. As he did not hungrily gather wealth . . .

CARL VAN DOREN, "MEET DR. FRANKLIN," 1943

By a credible though partial perception of Benjamin Franklin's philosophy, the later nineteenth century made that great American its high priest of the religion of commercial success. But first it stripped him of his urbanity, his humor, his understanding of intellectual values, and his genuine wisdom. An age which was fond of quoting "A Psalm of Life" to prove that "Life is real! Life is earnest!" and we must "Learn to labor and to wait," could easily interpret Franklin through one work alone, "The Way to Wealth." By a curious irony, one of the least ascetic of Americans became the scriptural authority for the least desirable of all types of asceticism, that which ended in mere material acquisition.

LOUIS B. WRIGHT, "FRANKLIN'S LEGACY TO THE GUILDED AGE," 1946

. . . .

Fifteen years ago, savings and loan associations throughout the nation commemorated Benjamin Franklin as their patron saint. More financial institutions bear his name than of any other American.

HOME LIFE, NEWSLETTER OF THE NILES (MICHIGAN) FEDERAL SAVINGS AND LOAN ASSOCIATION, JANUARY 1946

17. Duncan of Ruthwell

HENRY DUNCAN

HENRY DUNCAN, the son and grandson of Presbyterian ministers, was born on October 8, 1774, in Kirkcudbrightshire, Scotland. He attended a grammar school in Dumfries, studied briefly at the University of St. Andrews, and, for a short while, worked as a clerk in a Liverpool bank—an experience that led him to decide to study for the ministry.

At the University of Edinburgh, Duncan imbibed some of the spirit of the Scottish Enlightenment, studying with the famous professor of moral philosophy, Dugald Stewart, and joining the celebrated Speculative Society. In 1799, at age twenty-five, he was ordained minister of Ruthwell, a rural, and very poor, parish in Dumfrieshire, in the Scottish border country.

Duncan was a man of many gifts and protean interests. When the French appeared poised to invade, he organized, captained, and wrote an anthem for the "Ruthwell Volunteers." Using his own money, he imported Indian corn from Liverpool to help feed the poor. He worked to increase employment opportunities for his parishioners. He revived the previously dormant local friendly society. He organized a Bible society. He joined the antislavery movement. He founded, and for seven years edited, a weekly newspaper, the *Dumfries and Galloway Courier*. (The young Thomas Carlyle was a contributor.) He wrote a series of short tracts—the *Scotch Cheap Repository*, in some ways a precursor of penny magazines—as well as short stories and other popular publications intended to convey moral lessons to the young. He wrote an extremely popular devotional book, *The Sacred Philosophy of the Seasons*. He greatly improved the parish manse (the minister's house). He was an avid gardener and an accomplished geologist. He discovered, buried and in fragments in the churchyard, what turned out to be an eighth-century Runic Cross—the cross had been cast down by church authorities in 1642 as being too suggestive of Catholicism—and spent decades, at considerable personal expense, studying and restoring this priceless piece of Christian heritage. (It stands in the Ruthwell parish church today.) Over the course of his ministry, he became steadily more devout, gradually shifting from the "moderate" to the "evangelical" wing of the church. During the "disruption" of 1843, the culmination of years of intrachurch disputes, in large measure precipitated by the state's insistence upon the exercise of patronage in the selection of pastors, Duncan left the established church, becoming one of the founders and main leaders of the Free Church of Scotland. He spent the last part of his life as a parish minister for the Free Church, living in a laborer's cottage.

Oh, and one more thing—he was the main founder of the savings bank movement.

Henry Duncan died on February 12, 1846, and was buried in the Ruthwell churchyard.

. . . the name of the Rev. Dr. Henry Duncan, parish minister of Ruthwell, near Dumfries, will ever be gratefully remembered by all interested in the welfare and progress of the industrial classes of the people, in so far as that progress can be furthered by the agency of Savings Banks. For to Dr. Duncan belongs the great merit of having been the first person to introduce the thrift-plant into Scottish soil, and to demonstrate that it needed only the necessary spade-work and careful tending to make it grow successfully, in England and elsewhere.

MEMORIAL IN 1910 TO THE REV. DR. HENRY DUNCAN, WHO FOUNDED THE WORLD'S FIRST MODERN SAVINGS BANK IN RUTHWELL, SCOTLAND, IN MAY OF 1810

. . . .

Although Dr. Duncan was a man of many talents (he wrote well, was an editor, excelled in sports, was a keen gardener, and something of a scientist) his widest reputation was achieved in connection with his bank and the world today honors him chiefly as the founder of a system of thrift which has proved of incalculable benefit to humanity.

MODERN STORY OF MUTUAL SAVINGS BANKS, 1934

At first sight, it may seem superfluous to speak of thrift and independence to men of your race and in a university that produced Duncan of Ruthwell . . .

RUDYARD KIPLING, ADDRESS AT ST. ANDREWS UNIVERSITY, 1923

. . . .

It was in the beginning of the year 1810 that [Duncan] . . . found an ingenious paper giving an account of a scheme proposed by John Bone, Esq. of London, for gradually abolishing poor rates in England, called by its inventor "Tranquility," of a nature, however, too complicated for general adoption. On perusing this little work, he observed a subordinate provision which struck him as worthy of attention. This was the proposed erection of an economical bank for the savings of the industrious . . . He saw here in prospect a means of improvement and amelioration dependent on no begrudged and degrading poor-law subsidies—not even on the Christian charities of the rich and benevolent— but on the prudent forethought and economy of the people themselves.

MEMOIR OF HENRY DUNCAN, 1848

. . . .

No sooner were these ideas matured in his own mind, that he published a paper . . . in which he proposed to the gentlemen of the county the establishment of Banks for Savings in the different parishes of the district. The paper contained a sketch of rules and regulations which were to form the groundwork of the future institution. But being sensible of the difficulty of inducing any large body of men to engage in an untried scheme, however plausible in theory, he . . . took immediate measures for giving an experimental proof of its practicability and usefulness, by the establishment of a bank, on this plan, in his own parish.

. . . The scheme was drawn up and put into execution in May 1810 . . .

MEMOIR OF HENRY DUNCAN

. . . .

Entering the shop of a bookseller [in Harwick], he found, to his surprise and pleasure, copies, damp from the press, of the Ruthwell Rules, and of a detailed account of this institution, which he himself had published in the Dumfries Courier some months before. On inquiry, he ascertained that these had just been printed by order of the gentlemen of Selkirkshire in their county meeting, with a view to recommend the establishment of similar institutions throughout their district.

MEMOIR OF HENRY DUNCAN

. . . .

Two funds shall be connected with this Institution; the first to be called the Deposit Fund, consisting of the payments of those who are to derive benefit from it; and the second to be called the Auxillary Fund, consisting of the contributions of the benevolent,— together with the surplus interest . . .

The Office-bearers . . . shall be chosen . . . from among the Honorary and Extraordinary Members; but should a sufficient number of such Members not be found willing to accept these offices, the deficiency shall be made up out of those Ordinary Members who make payments, on their own account . . .

The General Meeting shall consist of the Honorary and Extraordinary Members, together with the whole of the Ordinary Members . . . These shall meet once every year . . .

A subscription to the Auxillary Fund of Five Shillings per annum, or a donation of Two Pounds Sterling, shall, ipso facto, constitute an Extraordinary Member . . .

Each Member shall have a right to demand payment of the sum he shall have deposited, together with compound interest, at the rate of 4 per cent. at the General Meeting . . . As soon as the sums deposited amount to Five Pounds, that sum, or any part of it, shall become payable . . . at the rate of 5 per cent. under the following circumstances, provided the depositor shall have been a Member for three years . . . In case a Member die [with the sum going to her or his heir] . . . In case of marriage . . . after the depositor shall have attained the age of fifty-six . . . In case the possession of the money shall appear to the [Bank officers], after due inquiry, to be advantageous to the depositor or his family . . . [Or] When the depositor shall have become incapable of maintaining himself, from sickness or otherwise . . .

After [normal Bank] expenditure, should the Auxillary Fund admit of further application, it shall be employed in giving rewards to regular *depositors, who shall have exhibited proofs of superior industry or virtue . . .*

Should the Auxillary Fund be in a state sufficiently flourishing, occasional loans may be made, to enable deserving Members to repair some causal misfortune (Such as the loss of cow, the wearing of an expensive implement of trade, &c.) or to prosecute their lawful business with advantage . . .

DUNCAN'S "RULES AND REGULATIONS" FOR PARISH BANKS, 1815

. . . .

That every depositor shall be obliged to add to his account a sum, not less than four shillings per annum, under penalty of one shilling, to be forfeited to the auxiliary fund, for each year in which he shall neglect to comply with this regulation.

AMENDMENT TO THE "RULES AND REGULATIONS," ADOPTED BY THE RUTHWELL PARISH BANK ABOUT 1816

. . . .

It may be laid down as a solid practical maxim, that, in all great pecuniary concerns, the jealous and active operation of self-interest is of the utmost consequence.

HENRY DUNCAN, TESTIMONY TO PARLIAMENT, ABOUT 1816

It has been alleged, that, in guarding against the idleness and profligacy of the lower orders, we are attempting to erect a system calculated to excite and to cherish the opposite vice of selfish niggardliness. Were this objection made to an institution, the tendency of which was to increase the parsimony of those already blessed with independent fortunes, or even with a competency, no person could be more ready than myself to admit its force; but it must not be forgotten that the Parish Bank is intended for the benefit of the lower orders, in whom industry and frugality are not only themselves moral virtues of the first class, but also the foundation of many kindred virtues. There is something noble and affecting in the struggle which a poor man makes to preserve his independence, and to rise superior to the difficulties and discouragements incidental to his situation. The end he has in view, and the privations he must undergo before he can attain that end, are such as must attract the applause of every good man. When, from the scanty pittance which he has earned by his honest industry, and which, though it suffices to supply the common wants of nature, is inadequate to procure the conveniences or comforts of life,—when, from that scanty pittance, he is able, by the exercise of a virtuous self-denial, to lay up a provision for the exigencies of his family, he exhibits a pattern of prudence and manly resolution, which would do honour to the highest station.

DUNCAN, A PAMPHLET DEFENDING PARISH BANKS, ABOUT 1815

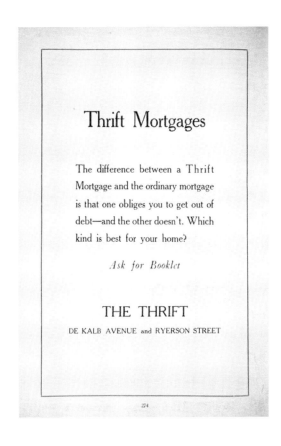

Advertisement from the yearbook
of the Pratt Institute
(founded by Charles Pratt), 1921

*From this time [about 1815] banks for savings
begin to be rapidly established on all sides . . .
Letters of inquiry or information arrived
by every post. Almost every county in Scotland
furnished a few clergymen who sought his
advice in commending the Ruthwell scheme
to their parishioners.*

MEMOIR OF HENRY DUNCAN

. . . .

*Justice leads us to say that we have seldom heard
of a private individual in a retired sphere, with*

*numerous avocations and a narrow income,
who has sacrificed so much ease, expense,
and time, for an object purely disinterested,
as Mr. Duncan has done.*

QUARTERLY REVIEW, OCTOBER 1816

. . . .

*. . . the most ridiculous project that ever
entered into the mind of man.*

WILLIAM COBBETT, ON "THE SAVINGS BANK
SCHEME," JANUARY 4, 1817

And next, a great Hull and Yorkshire man, William Wilberforce, M.P., the Slave Liberator, became the supporter and ally of Dr. Duncan himself in founding Savings Banks, and greatly assisted him in passing through Parliament the first Savings Bank Acts of 1817 and 1819.

MR. J. AVON CLYDE, M.P., SPEAKING TO CONFEREES ASSEMBLED IN THE MUSIC HALL IN EDINBURGH, SCOTLAND, TO COMMEMORATE THE CENTENARY OF SAVINGS BANKS, JUNE 9, 1910

. . . .

Why he [my father] used to tell us what reason we had to be thankfu' that we didna live langsyne, when the lairds could do just what they liket . . . "When," he would say, "was there ever more sic care ta'en o' the education of our bairns, and sae muckle siller spent to suppor the aged and infirm? When was there sae mony institutions for behoof of the poor . . . Surely this is the age of charity; and the only fear is, no that owre little, but that owre muckle may be done for the wants of the poor and needy."

DUNCAN, THE YOUNG SOUTH COUNTRY WEAVER (A NOVEL FOR YOUNG PEOPLE), 1821

. . . .

The proposal to open a bank was made early in 1834, when a committee mostly composed of the leaders of the Temperance Society was formed to prepare a constitution, rules and regulations, and to take the necessary steps for instituting the bank.

The committee in due course completed their task, the constitution and rules being similar to those of savings banks already established on the model of the Rev. Dr. Duncan's scheme.

JAMES KNOX, THE TRIUMPH OF THRIFT, 1927, ON THE FOUNDING OF THE SAVINGS BANK OF AIRDRIE, SCOTLAND, IN 1835

. . . .

That strange and wayward propensity which makes me to neglect my own immediate duties, for objects, good in themselves perhaps, but less within my proper sphere, she [my mother] must have observed, and I feel it is my besetting failing. Yet that conviction does not lead me to amendment. In truth, I have a notion that if I should curb it, my character would rather deteriorate than gain by the restraint.

DUNCAN, LETTER TO MARY LUNDIE, 1833

. . . .

What does your excellent spouse say to all this rout about Savings Banks? I fear she will think we are forgetting the more needful occupation of saving souls.

DUNCAN, LETTER TO HIS FRIEND THE REV. ROBERT LUNDIE, THE PARISH MINISTER IN NEARBY KELSO, MAY 12, 1819—THE "KELSO SAVINGS BANK FRIENDLY SOCIETY" (SCOTLAND'S THIRD SUCH INSTITUTION) HAD OPENED, WITH DUNCAN'S ASSISTANCE, IN NOVEMBER OF 1814; AND SOME YEARS LATER, AFTER BOTH DUNCAN AND MARY LUNDIE HAD BEEN WIDOWED, THE TWO WERE MARRIED.

18. Knox's Bank

JAMES, WALTER, AND JAMES KNOX

THE HAT AND CAP manufacturer James Knox was a founder of the Savings Bank of Airdrie, Scotland, in 1835. He became a bank director in 1838, the bank's president in 1848, and served as the bank's treasurer from 1861 until his death in 1866. His son, Walter—a devoted missionary for the Free Church of Scotland, one of whose founders was Henry Duncan—succeeded him as treasurer. Walter was president of the bank when he died at age forty-five in 1878.

Walter's precocious son, James, was appointed secretary of the bank on January 26, 1876—at the age of fourteen! Twenty years later, in December of 1896, James Knox II was appointed to the position of bank manager, the bank's first-ever salaried position.

James Knox II loved thrift. His 1927 book, *The Triumph of Thrift*, a wonderful homage to thrift and a richly detailed history of the Airdrie Savings Bank and of the three generations of Knox men with which that history is intertwined, is in my view far and away the best book of its kind.

The next name I would mention as prominent amongst the "old brigade" who founded the bank is that of my grandfather, James Knox, hat and cap manufacturer . . . until his death on 10th November, 1866, he was universally regarded as one of the principal mainstays of the institution. No better evidence can be adduced than the fact that, the bank in his day became popularly known as "Knox's Bank"—a term it has never lost.

JAMES KNOX, RECALLING HIS GRANDFATHER

· · · ·

My father succeeded my grandfather in the Treasurership [in 1866] . . .

Another new feature introduced by my father, was the distribution of thrift literature on a more extensive scale. I recall on one occasion when I was yet a boy being requisitioned by him to search through his bookcase for a certain volume which contained a collection of Scottish proverbs. Having found it, I was then told to put a pencil mark opposite the proverbs which I thought had a bearing on the subject of thrift. Afterwards he made his own selection, and though I did not venture to say it, I thought in my young mind that my list had not got full justice. The extracts were utilized in a series of cards setting forth the value of saving habits and the advantages offered by the Bank. A door to door

PLATE 1.

"THRIFT."

BRONZE GROUP ABOVE MAIN DOORWAY OF HEAD OFFICE.

From James Knox, *The Triumph of Thrift*, 1927

distribution was made throughout the town and district.

JAMES KNOX, RECALLING HIS FATHER

. . . .

The next day I conceived the idea of opening a savings bank of my own—a formidable venture for a boy of eleven summers. The Bank was to be named the "Knox Street Savings Bank," and my grannie's cottage was to be its headquarters . . . I

found my first need was for some capital, so I applied to my "bank" which stood on the kitchen mantlepiece and I emptied it. With the contents I bought a cash book and ledger and a supply of small passbooks . . . The minimum deposit was to be one penny . . .

The first two persons to join as depositors were naturally my grannie and myself. If we did not show our confidences in the concern how could I expect the public to have any? . . . I had ten customers the first week and in a short time the number increased to fifty. The funds began to accumulate and, as there was no "strong room" attached to my office, I deemed it prudent to open an account in the name of the "Knox Street Savings Bank" with the Airdrie Savings Bank . . . It was only then that my father learned of the rival bank. He had to know all about it, and while he said little I have no doubt his chief thought was "I'll have to keep my eye on this escapade."

. . . My experience as a bank manager at the age of eleven seems to have commended me to the Directors of the Savings Bank of Airdrie, for at the Annual Meeting on 26th January, 1876, they selected me for the onerous position of Secretary of that institution.

JAMES KNOX, RECALLING THE YEAR 1873, WHEN HE WAS ELEVEN YEARS OLD

. . . .

They imagine that savings banks were established and exist solely as convenient receptacles for the safe custody of money. That is undoubtedly one of their

functions. But, all important as the function is, it is only, after all, a detail of their organization. The Savings Bank Movement and Savings Banks have a much wider scope. Their real end and purpose is to inculcate the spirit of thrift amongst the people. (Applause.)

Thrift is one of the highest of the human virtues. It is something altogether different from the mere piling up and safe keeping of money. On the contrary, thrift is the right usage of all wealth—money included. A fetish devotion to mere money hording kills thrift, and withers the very soul of any individual who is deceived thereby. (Applause.) Thrift is a most potent and moral educator. It fosters and promotes other virtues. It is the great builder up of character. It is the enemy of all selfishness. The Scottish people have been a thrifty race. Hence we find in their character such fine qualities as caution, prudence, foresight, perserverance, self-reliance, and generosity, which are all products of thrift.

JAMES KNOX, SPEECH ON THE OCCASION CELEBRATING HIS FIFTY YEARS OF SERVICE TO THE AIRDRIE SAVINGS BANK, DECEMBER 15, 1926

I appreciate very, very highly the honour the Directors of the Airdrie Savings Bank have conferred upon me in asking me to open their splendid new Palace of Thrift. Who would have thought that pennies and shillings could have done it, and yet it is to the wonderful results of thrift, inspired by the wisdom and foresight of Airdrie folk since 1835, that we owe that splendid building. Men do not realize how great a benefit is thrift.

EMMA, LADY WILSON, OF KIPPEN HOUSE, DUNNING, ON THE OCCASION OF THE OPENING OF THE BANK'S NEW HEADQUARTERS, NOVEMBER 12, 1925

. . . .

. . . one of the most illuminating of our national documents.

GEORGE BLAKE, 1935, DESCRIBING JAMES KNOX'S BOOK, *THE TRIUMPH OF THRIFT*

19. Those Rules of Thrift and Economy

CATHARINE BEECHER

THE EDUCATOR and author Catharine E. Beecher was born on September 6, 1800, in East Hampton, New York, into one of the most impressive American families of the nineteenth century. Her younger sister, Harriet Beecher Stowe, wrote *Uncle Tom's Cabin*. Her father, the Rev. Lyman Beecher, was a prominent writer and religious leader, as were her two brothers, Henry Ward Beecher and Charles Beecher.

In 1823, Catharine Beecher founded the Hartford Female Seminary, where she taught until 1831. She went on to found the American Women's Educational Association in 1852, aimed at creating new educational opportunities for women, and to help found educational institutions for women in Ohio, Iowa, Illinois, and Wisconsin. She wrote many books. Probably her two most important are *A Treatise on Domestic Economy* (1842) and, coauthored with her sister Harriet, *The American Woman's Home* (1869).

Catharine Beecher took thrift very seriously. From its higher purposes—for Beecher, training women to thrive as individuals and to cultivate high morals in the home—to its smallest details, such as eating healthful foods and the proper care of yards and gardens, the topic interested Beecher

greatly and helped to orient her overall work as an educator and as a public intellectual. Catharine Beecher died in Elmira, New York, on May 12, 1878.

. . . young girls, especially in the more wealthy classes, are not trained for their profession. In early life, they go through a course of school training which results in great debility of constitution, while, at the same time, their physical and domestic education is almost wholly neglected.

. . . When young ladies are taught the construction of their own bodies, and all the causes in domestic life which tend to weaken the constitution; when they are taught rightly to appreciate and learn the most convenient and economical modes of performing all family duties, and of employing time and money; and when they perceive the true estimate accorded to these things by teachers and friends, the grand cause of [their suffering] will be removed. Women will be trained to secure, as of first importance, a strong and healthy constitution, and all those rules of thrift and economy that will make domestic duty easy and pleasant.

A TREATISE ON DOMESTIC ECONOMY, 1842

Christianity teaches that, for all the time afforded us, we must give account to God; and that we have no right to waste a single hour.

THE AMERICAN WOMAN'S HOME, 1869

. . . .

Moreover, would not the fine arts, in the end, be better supported by imparting culture and refined taste to the neglected ones [in society]? Teaching industry, thrift, and benevolence is far better than scattering alms, which often does more harm than good; and would not enabling the masses to enjoy the fine arts and purchase in a moderate style serve the interests of civilization as truly as for the rich to accumulate treasures for themselves in the common exclusive style?

THE AMERICAN WOMAN'S HOME

. . . .

Many were opposed to it [slavery] from conscientious principle—many from far-sighted thrift, and from a love of thoroughness . . . People, having once felt the thorough neatness and beauty of execution which comes of free, educated, and thoughtful labor, could not tolerate the clumsiness of slavery.

THE AMERICAN WOMAN'S HOME

. . . .

I have a personal confession to make: I like to sleep late. I've never been an early riser, and I intend

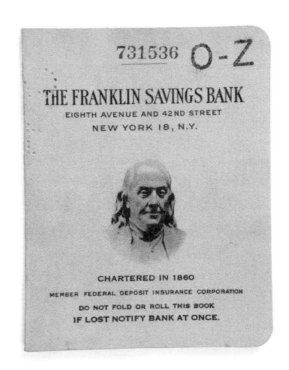

Issued 1947

never to become one. Accordingly, my least favorite thrift maxim is, "Early to bed, early to rise . . ." But Catharine Beecher disagrees. She disagrees quite strongly, and for many well-founded reasons. If anyone could ever reform me on this topic, it would be her. Her arguments on this question, all of which might as well be in the dictionary under "This is Thrift," are quite wonderful.

This practice [of early rising], which may justly be called a domestic virtue, is one which has a peculiar claim to be styled American and democratic . . . in aristocratic countries, especially in England, labor is regarded as the mark of the lower classes, and indolence is considered as one mark of a gentleman . . . From this circumstance, while the lower orders [in aristocracies] labor by day and sleep at night, the rich, the noble, and the honored sleep by day, and follow their pursuits and pleasures by night. It will be found that the aristocracy of London breakfast near midday . . .

Shall we ape the customs of aristocratic lands, in those very practices which result from principles and institutions that we condemn? Shall we not rather take the place to which we are entitled, as the leaders, rather than the followers, in the customs of society, turn back the tide of aristocratic inroads, and carry through the whole, not only of civil and political but of social and domestic life, the true principles of democratic freedom and equality?

. . . [Consider next] the health of a family. It is a universal law of physiology, that all living things flourish best in the light. Vegetables, in a dark cellar, grow pale and spindling . . .

. . . To this we must add the great neglect of economy as well as health in substituting unhealthful gaslight, poisonous, anthracite warmth, for the life-giving light and warmth of the sun. Millions and millions would be saved to this nation in fuel and light, as well as health, by returning to the good old ways . . . to rise with the sun . . .

. . . It thus appears that the laws of our political condition, the laws of the natural world, and the constitution of our bodies, alike demand that we rise with the light of day to prosecute our employments, and that we retire in time for the requisite amount of sleep.

. . . Let any teacher select the unpunctual scholars—a class who most seriously interfere with the interests of the school—and let men of business select those who cause them the most waste of time and vexation, by unpunctuality; and it will be found that they are generally among the late risers . . . Thus, late rising not only injures the person and family which indulge in it, but interferes in the rights and convenience of the community; while early rising imparts corresponding benefits of health, promptitude, vigor of action, economy of time, and general effectiveness both to the individuals who practice it and to the families and communities of which they are a part.

THE AMERICAN WOMAN'S HOME

. . . .

I was pleased to see this general concern for economy, for I love economy exceedingly.

BENJAMIN FRANKLIN, "AN ECONOMICAL PROJECT," A HUMOROUS LETTER TO A PARIS NEWSPAPER IN WHICH HE CALCULATES THE LOSS OF WORK TIME AND WASTE OF CANDLES CONNECTED TO LATE RISING, AND PROPOSES ACCORDINGLY THAT EVERYONE RISE WITH THE SUN, MARCH 20, 1784

20. Those Who Are Not Ashamed of Economy

LYDIA MARIE CHILD

THE POET and novelist, scholar, editor, antislavery leader, champion of women's rights, and popular thrift advocate Lydia Marie Child was born in Medford, Massachusetts, on February 11, 1802. Speaking of Child, the poet John Greenleaf Whittier in 1886 wrote: "It is not too much to say that half a century ago she was the most popular literary woman in the United States."[1] She died in Wayland, Massachusetts, on October 20, 1880.

Child believed deeply in thrift, and throughout her life remained, as she put it, "not ashamed of economy." Yet few of her biographers, it seem, can make the same claim! Quite the contrary. Child's advocacy of thrift, these later admirers regularly imply, was done mainly to get herself published as a young woman, or because writing on such themes was expected of literary women of Child's generation, or in order to pay the debts run up by her loving but hopelessly improvident husband, David Child. But wait a minute. Child herself, as far as I can determine, says exactly the opposite! In the opening pages of her most popular book, *The American Frugal Housewife*, first published as *The Frugal Housewife* in 1829, she writes:

The writer has no apology to offer for this cheap little book of economical hints, except her deep conviction that such a book is needed. In this case, renown is out of the question, and ridicule is a matter of indifference.[2]

Interestingly, Child some years later says exactly the same thing about the antislavery cause that she by then had fervently embraced—that she was writing what she deeply believed, and cared not a fig whether the world criticized her for it—and her biographers seem to take her at her word. Similarly, when she still later says the same thing once again about her study of the world's religions and her plea for religious tolerance and understanding—few are likely to read this book, she (accurately) predicted, but no matter, I write about what I think is important—no one coming after her seems to have doubted that she was telling the truth. But for some reason, Child's advocacy of thrift is treated as an exception: an odd, slightly embarrassing and out-of-place facet of her personality and work that we today should either ignore, or explain away, or try to diminish—perhaps even be ashamed of.

But that's not right. In fact, it's the exact opposite of right. Child's life and work were of one piece. She makes perfectly clear that her thrift fit with, and even made possible, her political commitments, her generosity to others, and yes, even her marriage to the unlucky, debt-producing David. So let us now fully appreciate Lydia Marie Child, an admirable champion of progressive causes and one of the great public intellectuals of her era, who was not ashamed of economy.

Her summary of her thrift philosophy could just as aptly be part of the "What Thrift Is" section of part one of this book:

The true economy of housekeeping is simply the art of gathering up all the fragments, so that nothing be lost. I mean fragments of time, as well as materials. Nothing should be thrown away so long as it is possible to make any use of it, however trifling that use may be; and whatever be the size of a family, every member should be employed either in earning or saving money.

CHILD, *THE AMERICAN FRUGAL HOUSEWIFE: DEDICATED TO THOSE WHO ARE NOT ASHAMED OF ECONOMY*

. . . .

Child strongly stresses cutting your coat after your cloth:

. . . No false pride, or foolish ambition to appear as well as others, should ever induce a person to live one cent beyond the income of which he is certain. If you have two dollars a day, let nothing

but sickness induce you to spend more than nine shillings; if you have a dollar a day, do not spend but seventy-five cents; if you have half a dollar a day, be satisfied to spend forty cents.

. . . The consideration that many purchase by living beyond their income, and of course living upon others, is not worth the trouble it costs. The glare there is about this false and wicked parade is deceptive; it does not in fact procure a man valuable friends, or extensive influence. More than that, it is wrong—morally wrong, so far as the individual is concerned; and injurious beyond calculation to the interests of our country.

CHILD, *THE AMERICAN FRUGAL HOUSEWIFE*

. . . .

What is the ultimate goal of what Child calls true economy?

True economy is a careful treasurer in the service of benevolence.

CHILD, *THE AMERICAN FRUGAL HOUSEWIFE*

. . . .

And yet this princely giver kept til death the cheap, plain fashion of dress which early narrow means had enforced, used an envelope twice, and never wrote on a whole sheet when a half one would suffice. "I do not think, Mrs. Child, you can afford to give away so much now," I said to her once, when in some exigency of the freedman's cause she told me to send them from her a hundred dollars.

"Well," she answered, "I will think it over and send you word to-morrow." To-morrow word came, "Please send them two hundred."

Her means were never large, never so large that a woman of her class would think she had anything to give away. But her spirit was Spartan. When she had nothing for others she worked to get it. She wrote to me once, "I have four hundred dollars to my credit at my publisher's for my book on *Looking Toward Sunset*. Please get it and send it to the freedmen."

WENDELL PHILLIPS, REMARKS AT CHILD'S FUNERAL, OCTOBER 23, 1880

. . . .

Her [Child's] donations for benevolent causes and beneficent reforms were constant and liberal; and only those who knew her intimately could understand the cheerful and unintermitted self-denial which alone enabled her to make them.

JOHN GREENLEAF WHITTIER, 1886

. . . .

Pig's head is a profitable thing to buy. It is despised, because it is cheap; but when well cooked it is delicious. Well cleaned, the tip of the snout cut off, and put in brine a week, it is very good for boiling: the cheeks, in particular, are very sweet; they are better than any other pieces of pork to bake with beans. The head is likewise very good baked about an hour and a half. It tastes like roast pork, and yields abundance of sweet fat, for shortening . . .

. . . Had the young lady been content with Kidderminster carpets, and tasteful vases of her own making, she might have put one thousand dollars at interest; and had she obtained six percent., it would have clothed her as well as the wife of any man, who depends merely upon his own industry, ought to be clothed. This would have saved much domestic disquiet; for, after all, human nature is human nature; and a wife is never better beloved, because she teases for money.

CHILD, *THE AMERICAN FRUGAL HOUSEWIFE*

. . . .

So Mrs. Child published in 1829 her Frugal Housewife, *a book which proved so popular that in 1836 it had reached its 20th edition, and in 1855 its thirty-third.*

THOMAS WENTWORTH HIGGINS, "LYDIA MARIE CHILD," 1900

21. The Prophet of Victorian England

SAMUEL SMILES

THE TITLES of some of Samuel Smiles's most famous books—*Self-Help, Character, Thrift, Duty, Men of Invention and Industry*—convey his message quite well. He was one of the most influential authors and reformers of his generation, both in Britain and around the world. As the poet W. H. Auden put it when describing the death of Sigmund Freud, Smiles's impact on his era was so pervasive that, after he died, he became "no more a person" but "a whole climate of opinion." Samuel Smiles was born on December 23, 1812, in Haddington, Scotland, and died in London on April 16, 1904.

The man who thinks at all of his own future and of social conditions generally, will be found, through his Friendly Society, his Co-operative Store, or his Savings Bank, to be paying some homage to those arts of thriving of which Dr. Smiles will always be regarded as a foremost panegyrist.

THOMAS MACKAY, PREFACE TO *THE AUTOBIOGRAPHY OF SAMUEL SMILES*, 1905

I know that the cost will be objected to. I only speak of the extreme desirableness of our having a Town Hall, with a Public Library, and accommodation for a Public Museum. What was the cost of our jail? What of our pauper training schools? We have built these irrespective of the question of cost . . . Is not the founding of a Public Library as creditable, as necessary, and as beneficial a work as the erection of a jail?

SMILES, LETTER TO THE *LEEDS MERCURY*, NOVEMBER 1850

. . . .

Although Smiles is often described as (and frequently criticized for) exclusively promoting individual or personal thrift, here the young Smiles is advocating a public library based on a vision of public thrift. Championing individual thrift need not, and in this case does not, prevent one from also championing public thrift.

Such progress as was made in thrift propaganda and practice in the last quarter of the 19th century owed not a little to Samuel Smiles.

H. OLIVER HORNE, *A HISTORY OF SAVINGS BANKS*, 1947

My object in writing out Self-Help . . . *was principally to illustrate and enforce the power of George Stephenson's great word—PERSEVERANCE. I had been greatly attracted when a boy by Mr. Craik's* Pursuit of Knowledge Under Difficulties. *I had read it often, and knew its many striking passages almost by heart. It occurred to me, that a similar treatise, dealing not so much with literary achievements and the acquisition of knowledge, as with the ordinary business and pursuits of common life, illustrated by examples of conduct and character drawn from reading, observation, and experience, might be equally usable to the rising generation. It seemed to me that the most important results in daily life are to be obtained, not through the exercise of extraordinary powers, such as genius and intellect, but through the energetic use of simple means and ordinary qualities, with which nearly all human individuals have been more or less endowed.*

THE AUTOBIOGRAPHY OF SAMUEL SMILES

. . . .

There was nothing in the slightest degree new or original in this counsel [in Self-Help*], which was as old as the Proverbs of Solomon, and possibly quite as familiar.*

SMILES, *SELF-HELP*, 1859

. . . .

The power of money is, on the whole, overestimated.

SMILES, *SELF-HELP*

Many popular books have been written for the purpose of communicating to the public the grand secret of making money. But there is no secret whatever about it, as the proverbs of every nation abundantly testify. "Take care of the pennies and the pounds will take care of themselves." "Diligence is the mother of good luck." "No pains no gains." "No sweat no sweet." "Work and thou shalt have." "The world is his who has patience and industry." "Better go to bed supperless than rise in debt." Such are specimens of the proverbial philosophy, embodying the hoarded experience of many generations, as to the best means of thriving in the world. They were current in people's mouths long before books were invented; and like other popular proverbs they were the first codes of popular morals. Moreover, they have stood the test of time, and the experience of every day still bears witness to their accuracy, force and soundness.

SMILES, *SELF-HELP*

. . . .

Economizing for the purpose of being independent is one of the soundest indications of manly character.

SMILES, *SELF-HELP*

. . . .

Simple industry and thrift will go far toward making any person of ordinary working faculty comparatively independent in his means.

SMILES, *SELF-HELP*

To provide for others and for our own comfort and independence in old age, is honorable and greatly to be commended; but to hoard for mere wealth's sake is the characteristic of the narrow-souled and the miserly. It is against the growth of this habit of inordinate saving that the wise man needs most carefully to guard himself: else, what in youth was simple economy, may in old age grow into avarice, and what was a duty in the one case, may become a vice in the other.

. . . He who recognizes no higher logic than that of the shilling may become a very rich man, and yet remain all the while an exceedingly poor creature. For riches are no proof whatever of moral worth; and their glitter often serves only to draw attention to the worthlessness of their possessor, as the light of the glow-worm reveals the grub.

SMILES, *SELF-HELP*

. . . .

The respectable man is one worthy of regard, literally worth turning to look at. But the respectability that consists merely in keeping up appearances is not worth looking at in any sense. Far better and more respectable is the good poor man than the bad rich one—better the humble silent man than the agreeable, well-appointed rogue who keeps his gig.

. . . There are men "in society" now, rich as Croesus, who have no consideration extended toward them, and elicit no respect. For why? They are but as money bags; their only power is in their

till. The men of mark in society—the guides and rulers of opinion—are not necessarily rich men; but men of sterling character, of disciplined experience, and of moral excellence. Even the poor man, like Thomas Wright, though he possesses but little of this world's goods, may, in the enjoyment of a cultivated nature, of opportunities used and not abused, of a life spent to the best of his means and ability, look down, without the slightest feeling of envy, upon the person of mere worldly success, the man of money-bags and acres.

SMILES, *SELF-HELP*

. . . .

National progress is the sum of individual industry, energy, and uprightness, as national decay is of individual idleness, selfishness, and vice. What we are accustomed to decry as great social evils, will for the most part be found to be but the outgrowth of man's own perverted life; and though we may endeavor to cut them down and extirpate them by means of Law, they will only spring up again with fresh luxuriance in some other form, unless the conditions of personal life and character radically improved. If this view be correct, then it follows that the highest patriotism and philanthropy consist, not so much in altering laws and modifying institutions, as in helping and stimulating men to elevate and improve themselves by their own free and independent individual action.

SMILES, *SELF-HELP*

Within a short time [of its publication in 1859] this book, Self-Help, *became of the world's best sellers. Before his death [in 1904] about a quarter of a million copies of the book had been sold in Britain and innumerable foreign editions had been published.*

OLIVER HORNE, *A HISTORY OF SAVINGS BANKS*

. . . .

But a very small portion of the three hundred millions estimated to be annually earned by the working-classes finds its way to the savings-bank, while at least thirty times the amount is spent annually at the beer-shop and the public-house.

. . . In 1859 there were throughout the kingdom 152,222 houses licenced to sell intoxicating drink, and only 606 savings-banks in which to deposit spare money. Thus thriftlessness finds abundant openings for gratification, whilst thrift has perhaps to travel a mile or so to a savings-bank, which opens its door, it may be, for only a few hours once or twice a week.

. . . The extend to which Penny Banks have been used by the very poorest classes, wherever started, affords a further illustration of how much may be done by merely providing increased opportunities for the practice of thrift.

SMILES, "WORKMEN'S EARNINGS AND SAVINGS," *QUARTERLY REVIEW,* 1860

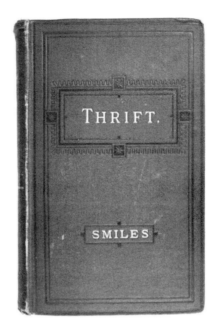

Published 1875

Misery is the result of moral causes. Most commonly it is the offspring of individual vice and improvidence; and it to be cured, not so much by conferring greater rights, as by implanting better habits . . .

SMILES, "WORKMEN'S EARNINGS AND SAVINGS"

. . . .

. . . I bethought me whether I might not enlarge the above article ["Workmen's Earnings and Savings"], and devote a special treatise to the subject of Thrift. I consulted with my friend, Mr. (afterwards Sir) Charles W. Sikes, Banker, Huddersfield, the initiator or inventor of the Post Office Savings Bank system; and he urged me to proceed . . .

THE AUTOBIOGRAPHY OF SAMUEL SMILES

Thrift began with civilization.

SMILES, *THRIFT*, 1875

. . . .

Prodigality is much more natural to man than thrift.

SMILES, *THRIFT*

. . . .

Some of man's best qualities depend upon the right use of money—such as his generosity, benevolence, justice, honesty, and forethought. Many of his worst qualities also originate in the bad use of money—such as greed, miserliness, injustice, extravagance, and improvidence.

SMILES, *THRIFT*

. . . .

Thrift is in no way connected with avarice, usury, greed, or selfishness. It is, in fact, the very reverse of these disgusting dispositions. It means economy for the purpose of securing independence. Thrift requires that money should be used, and not abused.

SMILES, *THRIFT*

. . . .

Thrift does not end with itself, but extends its benefits to others. It founds hospitals, endows charities, establishes colleges, and extends educational influences.

SMILES, *THRIFT*

Idleness consumes more men than rust does iron.

SMILES, *LIFE AND LABOR*, 1889

. . . .

Samuel Smiles was the prophet of Victorian England. There has not yet arisen a prophet who will interpret for us in the same way the new conception of "self-help." The new "self-help" must not be individual but collective; it must result, not in the raising of one man above his fellows by personal "push" or "abstinence," but in the raising of a whole class . . .

G. D. H. COLE, *LABOUR IN THE COMMONWEALTH*, 1919

. . . .

. . . . Smile's Self-Help *was a wonderful stimulus to me, and I believe it has proved the turning point in the careers of tens of thousands of youths.*

ORISON SWETT MARDEN, *PUSHING TO THE FRONT,* 1911

. . . .

He [Orison Swett Marden] wanted to become the Samuel Smiles of America.

MARGARET CONNOLLY, *THE LIFE STORY OF ORISON SWETT MARDEN*, 1925

22. Sikes of Huddersfield

CHARLES SIKES

CHARLES WILLIAM SIKES was born in 1818 in the town of Huddersfield, in Yorkshire, England. In 1833, he began working for the Huddersfield Banking Company, becoming a cashier in 1837, and the company's managing director in 1882.

Charles Sikes loved thrift. He became a tireless advocate of penny savings banks, establishing rules and procedures for these institutions and helping to spread them across Yorkshire. More than any other individual, he originated the idea, and made possible the establishment, of the national system of postal savings banks in Britain—that is, turning every post office in Britain into a place where people can open savings accounts. His work on this issue with the then–chancellor of the exchequer (and later prime minister) William E. Gladstone, culminating in Parliament's passage of the Post Office Savings Bank Act of 1861, ranks as arguably the most fruitful partnership in the history of British thrift movements. For his work in the area of thrift, Charles Sikes was knighted in 1881, upon Gladstone's recommendation. He died in 1889.

Sikes promoted penny banks and helped to create post-office savings banks because philosophically he had embraced two big ideas. The first is self-help. Thrift institutions are not charities that give things away; they can only benefit people who are willing and able to help themselves. The second is localism. For most people, opportunities to save need to be immediate, familiar, and close by—not in another part of town, or in another county, too far away to reach conveniently by walking. For Sikes, then, character matters most, but character can also be shaped by institutions. Both are important.

His first idea [in 1850] was to institute a system of penny banks to act as feeders to the savings banks. To carry out his object he proposed to enlist the help of the Mechanics' Institutes, which by this time were common in most industrial areas . . . If each Institute set up a Savings Bank Committee . . . they could conduct "Preliminary Savings Banks" once a week and help their members accumulate in small sums the pound which could later be deposited in the nearest Trustee Savings Bank.

H. OLIVER HORNE, *A HISTORY OF SAVINGS BANKS*

· · · ·

If a committee at each [Mechanics'] institution were to adopt this course, taking an interest in

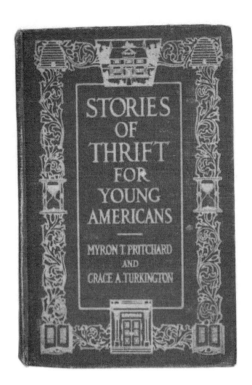

Published 1915

The idea was taken up in a number of places. The Yorkshire Union of Mechanics' Institutes warmly supported it and there was a considerable growth in penny banks and preliminary banks all over the country . . . Sikes went to some trouble in advising a simple and effective system of book-keeping.

HORNE, *A HISTORY OF SAVINGS BANKS*

. . . .

Mr. Sikes' cheap little handbook *[published in 1854] entitled* Good Times, or the Savings Bank and the Fireside, *has already been circulated by thousands, and well deserves the careful perusal of every working man and woman in the kingdom.*

SAMUEL SMILES, *WORKMEN'S EARNINGS, STRIKES, AND SAVINGS*, 1861

. . . .

their humble circumstances, and in a sympathizing and kindly spirit suggest, invite, nay win them over, not only to reading the lesson, but forming the habit of true economy and self-reliance (the most noble lesson for which classes could be formed), how cheering would be the results! Once established in better habits, their feet firmly set in the path of self-reliance, how generally would young men grow up with the practical conviction that to their own advancing intelligence and virtues must they mainly look to work out their own welfare!

CHARLES SIKES, ADVOCATING PENNY BANKS
IN A LETTER PUBLISHED IN THE *LEEDS MERCURY*,
FEBRUARY 23, 1850

. . . he gave his attention very closely to the existing system of savings banks, and in the year 1856 he addressed a very able and exhaustive letter to the then Chancellor of the Exchequer— Sir G. Cornewall Lewis—on Savings Banks Reforms . . . In [1859], Mr. Sikes formulated a plan for a system of savings banks under the control of the Government . . . Mr. Sikes had long cherished the idea of bringing a savings bank "within less than an hour's walk of the fireside of every working man in the Kingdom"; and he tells us the organization of the Post Office suddenly occurred to him as a means to this end.

ARCHIBALD G. BOWIE, *THE ROMANCE OF THE SAVINGS BANKS*, 1898

The summer of 1859 passed and the [postal savings scheme] might even yet have been pigeon-holed. Sikes therefore determined to approach Mr. Gladstone himself. In September he wrote the Chancellor of the Exchequer at great length, expounding his views with force and skill.

. . . The letter made an immediate appeal to Mr. Gladstone . . . Sikes continued his exertions to influence public opinion in favor of his proposals. He gave them wider publicity through the Press and circularized the savings banks, chambers of commerce, and other representative bodies, together with many individuals of standing.

HORNE, *A HISTORY OF SAVINGS BANKS*

. . . .

. . . at the present time there are in the United Kingdom fifteen counties in which there are no Savings Banks, and although difficult to ascertain the exact number of towns, there are probably one hundred with a population varying from 10,000 to 30,000 each, and towards two thousand other towns or places with populations ranging between 1,000 to 10,000, all without Savings Banks! . . . in none of them does there exist a Savings Bank to aid in promoting those habits of forethought and thrift so essential to the progress and prosperity of the people.

SIKES, LETTER TO GLADSTONE ADVOCATING POST-OFFICE SAVINGS BANKS, 1859

The Post Office Savings Bank Act . . . received the Royal Assent on 17 May 1861. Its passing was enthusiastically acclaimed by a large section of the Press, including The Times. *Edwin Chadwick, the Poor Law reformer, applied to it Peel's cynical aphorism that it was "so thoroughly good a measure, he wondered how ever it passed."*

HORNE, *A HISTORY OF SAVINGS BANKS*

. . . .

The post-office savings bank is the most important institution which has been created in the last 50 years for the welfare of the people and the State.

WILLIAM E. GLADSTONE, REMARKS TO THE HOUSE OF COMMONS, 1888

. . . .

Equally with Duncan of Ruthwell, therefore, the name of Sikes of Huddersfield will ever be honorably remembered by all interested in the progress of national thrift.

ALEXANDER CARGILL, "A CENTURY OF NATIONAL THRIFT," *THE TIMES*, MAY 17, 1910

. . . .

Sikes's powerful supporter and colleague in founding the British postal savings system, William E. Gladstone, widely regarded as one of the greatest of all British statesmen, also spoke frequently and with genuine insight on the subject of thrift.

. . . popular thrift is a large part of popular virtue, and is connected with the exercise, and, through the exercise, with the growth of a large portion of those qualities that make a man—whatever his position may be—both good and great.

GLADSTONE, ADDRESS TO THE ANNUAL MEETING OF THE DEPOSITORS IN THE SAVINGS BANKS CONNECTED WITH THE SOUTH-EASTERN AND METROPOLITAN RAILWAY COMPANIES, LONDON, JUNE 18, 1890

It is self-help which make the man; and man-making is the aim which the Almighty has everywhere impressed upon Creation. It is thrift by which self-help for the masses, dependent upon labour, is principally made effective. In them thrift is the symbol and the instrument of independence and liberty—indispensable conditions of all permanent human good.

But thrift is also the mother of wealth, and here comes a danger into view, for wealth is the mother of temptation and leads many of its possessors into a new form of slavery . . .

WILLIAM E. GLADSTONE, REMARKS (VIA PHONOGRAPH) TO A MEETING IN NEW YORK CITY OF THE AMERICAN CO-OPERATIVE BUILDING AND LOAN ASSOCIATIONS, MARCH 31, 1890

23. Who Catches the Vision?

ALONZO, WILMOT, AND WILMOT EVANS

ALONZO H. EVANS was born in Allenstown, New Hampshire, in 1820. He began working for the Boston Five Cents Savings Bank in 1854, the year the bank was founded, serving as its founding treasurer. He was elected president of the bank on April 14, 1874. His son, Irving, who later became a stockbroker, worked at the bank as a teller. Alonzo Evans was also the first mayor of Everett, Massachusetts, represented Everett for a number of years in the Massachusetts legislature, and, in 1892, ran unsuccessfully for the post of Massachusetts state auditor on the Prohibition Party ticket. He died on May 27, 1907.

In the month of November, 1853, the writer . . . with a few other persons, met to consult upon the expediency of establishing an additional savings-bank in the city of Boston, to induce the young and the industrial classes to make a beginning to save by encouraging deposits as small as five cents.

ALONZO H. EVANS, "HISTORICAL ADDRESS," MAY 2, 1904

Whenever any deposits shall be made by any minor, the trustee of said corporation may, at their discretion, pay to such depositor such sum as may be due to him or her, although no guardian shall [be present].

CHARTER, BOSTON FIVE CENTS SAVINGS BANK, 1854

· · · ·

At the annual meeting of the corporation in 1907, Mr. Evans, in his eighty-seventh year, and after fifty-three years of continuous service with the bank, declined election as president. He survived but a short time, his death occurring in May of that year. None who ever saw Mr. Evans will forget his appearance—old-fashioned, we might call it now, but always distinctive: high silk hat, black broadcloth, Prince Albert coat with trousers to match, and boots—yes, boots that were always carefully polished. And none can forget his punctuality . . . nor can they forget his forceful character and competent service.

Alonzo H. Evans was succeeded in the presidency by his son, Wilmot R. Evans.

A HISTORY OF THE BOSTON FIVE CENTS SAVINGS BANK, 1926

Wilmot R. Evans did not seek the light of publicity as many men seek it. Of plain personal habits, he brought to his tasks a keenness which made his own affairs successful and which he generously shared with others. "He had an insight into human nature which made him a leader of men, and his judgement was sought as the final word." Smiling, cordial, democratic in his relations with men of large or small affairs, he was deeply respected by many. His confidence, not easily won, was a splendid thing to have . . .

Mr. Evans [who died on March 24, 1926] was succeeded in the presidency on April 6, 1926, by his son, Wilmot R. Evans Jr.

A HISTORY OF THE BOSTON FIVE CENTS SAVINGS BANK

. . . .

Three or more generations of service to a bank within one family, with leadership passing from father to son to grandson, is more common than one might imagine in the history of mutual savings banks. In Buffalo, New York, for example, Charles Diebolt Jr. served as president from 1924 to 1948. His son, Charles R. Dielbolt, served as president from 1948 to 1967. His grandson, Charles Diebolt III, served as president from 1967 until the bank merged with the Buffalo Savings Bank in 1982. Diebolts were at the helm of this bank for 58 of its 130 years of existence.[1]

Of all financial institutions, mutual savings banks are closest to human beings,—from the boy whose chin barely reaches the counter who wants "to join", or the serious, black-eyed girl who interprets for her grandmother, to those who bring the tales of joy, sickness, death and sin that come daily to the counter to be met and solved as best they may. And to whom do these come, who occupies the first line? To whom comes the thrill that must come to one who opens a savings account for a boy or girl? Who catches the vision of the possibilities of these events? Who are the first to inspire loyalty? The men and women serving at the counter of the bank. Many have come and gone; many are standing at the counters today who by tact, efficiency and example often serve their bank and its depositors and their country better than they will ever know. The dean of these in The Boston Five Cents Savings Bank is Edwin F. Sawyer, with a record of fifty-eight years of service.

A HISTORY OF THE BOSTON FIVE CENTS SAVINGS BANK

24. A Constant Lesson in Thrift

CLARA BARTON

THE EDUCATOR, battlefield nurse, and humanitarian reformer Clara Barton, who in 1881 founded the American Red Cross, was born on Christmas Day, 1821, in Oxford, Massachusetts. She was one of the greatest Americans of her generation. She died in Glen Echo, Maryland, on April 12, 1912.

"Miss Barton, where did you get your money? They are going to ask this, and I had better know. I want no surprises sprung."

"Surely," said Miss Barton, "it is right that they should know. I was brought up in New England, and I have the New England thrift. I began teaching school when I was fourteen and taught for a number of years. I saved my money and invested it successfully. I had a government position in Washington, being the first woman clerk. I saved my earnings and invested them well. I lectured for several years. The people wanted to hear what I had to say, and I received one hundred dollars for every lecture I could give, and this money I saved . . ."

. . . Clara Barton's New England thrift caused her to be able to do consummate work with the money and means that many waste. She has given us a constant lesson in thrift. There was not a woman in that great audience at the Memorial

Service [for Clara Barton, on May 14, 1912, in Philadelphia] who did not feel the crime of waste. We realized the economies which Clara Barton lived and practiced, that she might give life and aid to those who were in dire need. Her herculean work was done with means that most men would scorn as too trivial to begin a work with.

ALICE HUBBARD, TRIBUTE TO CLARA BARTON, JULY 1912

. . . .

At first I used to be shocked over her penuriousness but when I discovered the motive, that it was to save for others in need, no words could describe my conscience-stricken feeling and my admiration of that self-sacrificing woman.

GENERAL W. H. SEARS, A MEMBER OF THE BOARD OF DIRECTORS OF THE AMERICAN RED CROSS

. . . .

The main interest of these reports [of Red Cross activities in 1893 in the wake of a hurricane that devastated much of the Sea Islands, off the coast of South Carolina] will consist in showing the methods of work adopted, not only to preserve so

many people in life with so small means as we had at hand, but to preserve them as well from habits of begging and conditions of pauperism; to teach them independence, economy, and thrift; how to provide for themselves against future want . . .

CLARA BARTON, *THE RED CROSS*

. . . .

We went over shoe-tops in mud to their rude home, to find it one room of logs . . . The Government boats [which came after the flood] had left them rations. There was an air of thrift, even in their desolation, a plank walk was laid about the door, the floor was cleanly swept, and the twenty-five surviving hens, for an equal number was lost in the storm, clucked and craiked comfortably about the door . . . We stood, as we had done so many scores of times during the last few weeks, and looked

this pitiful scene in the face. There was misfortune, poverty, sorrow, want, loneliness, dread of future, but fortitude, courage, integrity, and honest thrift.

CLARA BARTON, DESCRIBING HER VISIT IN THE WAKE OF SEVERE FLOODING TO CAVE-IN-ROCK, ILLINOIS, ON THE OHIO RIVER, IN A LETTER TO THE *ERIE DISPATCH*, MARCH 18, 1884

. . . .

There must be no more big hotel bills; the money must be saved for the sufferers.

CLARA BARTON

. . . .

Economy, prudence, and the simple life are the sure masters of need.

CLARA BARTON

. . . .

. . . she was the acme of New England thrift.

DESCRIPTION IN 1917 OF CLARA BARTON

25. The Greater Thrift

CHARLES PRATT

CHARLES PRATT was born on October 2, 1830, in Watertown, Massachusetts. His father was a cabinetmaker who had come to the United States from Britain. Charles began work at age ten, on a neighbor's farm. He also worked as a grocery store clerk and an apprentice in a machine shop as a young man in Boston. He saved his money from these jobs to pay for several years of education, during which time, he recalled, he lived on a dollar a week.

He developed an innovative method of refining crude oil and organized a refinery business. A major competitor of Pratt's was John D. Rockefeller. In 1872, Charles Pratt & Co. became a part of the Standard "alliance" (formally the Central Association of Refiners), and, ten years later, became one of the founding entities of what would become Standard Oil. Charles Pratt had become a very rich man. He died on May 4, 1891, in New York City.

Pratt Institute was established in 1887 by Mr. Charles Pratt, of Brooklyn. Its object is to promote manual and industrial education, as well as literature, science, and art; to inculcate habits of industry and thrift, and to foster all that makes for right living and good citizenship.
AMERICAN ART ANNUAL, 1898

· · · ·

Mr. Pratt was a firm believer in economy and thrift and was greatly interested in inculcating the habits of thrift in all with whom he came into contact in the Institute, and especially among children. He early formulated a plan for saving by the purchase of stamps. A desk and a small safe, with one person in charge, were located in the General Office. This plan of teaching thrift rapidly developed into a Savings and Loan Association call "The Thrift"...
PRATTONIA, 1921

· · · ·

The Thrift, organized with a membership of 349 had, in 1915, a total of 8,701 members and deposits amounting to $ 4,287,755.52. Today this organization occupies a solid position among the financial institutions of Brooklyn.
CYCLOPEDIA OF AMERICAN BIOGRAPHY, 1918

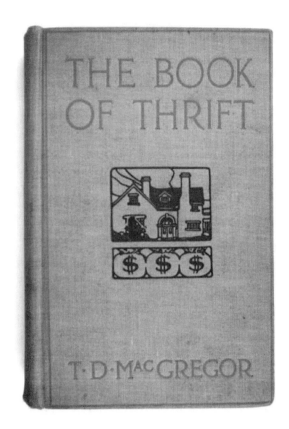

Published 1915

. . . to promote habits of thrift, and encourage people to become prudent and wise in the use of money and time.

STATEMENT OF PURPOSE OF "THE THRIFT"

The difference between a Thrift Mortgage and the ordinary mortgage is that one obliges you to get out of debt—and the other doesn't. Which kind is best for your home?

AD, *THE THRIFT*, 1921

. . . .

Waste Neither Time Nor Money

CHARLES PRATT'S MOTTO, INSCRIBED ABOVE THE FIREPLACE IN THE READING ROOM OF "THE ASTRAL," THE MODEL HOUSING PROJECT FOR WORKING-CLASS RESIDENTS OF BROOKLYN, FINANCED BY PRATT, AND COMPLETED IN 1886

. . . .

Here was a man who knew the value of thrift, not alone the thrift that made it possible for him to rise from surroundings of abject poverty to the heights of wealth and power, but the broader, greater thrift through which he was impelled to turn that wealth and that power for the betterment of mankind, by giving people an opportunity to make the most of themselves.

S. W. STRAUS, DESCRIBING CHARLES PRATT, 1920

. . . .

Thrift Hall

THE LOCATION OF THE OFFICE OF THE REGISTRAR, TODAY, AT THE PRATT INSTITUTE

26. Always Had a Broom in My Hand

JOHN WANAMAKER

JOHN WANAMAKER was born near Philadelphia on July 11, 1838. His parents' financial condition was modest—John's father, Nelson, was a brickmaker and his mother, Elizabeth, was a homemaker. John attended school for only a few years and, at age fourteen, began working full-time as an errand boy in a Philadelphia publishing firm at a salary of $1.25 per week. John's favorite book as a boy was Daniel Defoe's *Robinson Crusoe*. During those years as an errand boy, he began a small magazine, *Everybody's Journal*, full of maxims and practical advice, patterned in part on Franklin's "Poor Richard."

In 1858, he became the first full-time secretary of the Young Men's Christian Association, an organization that Wanamaker supported his whole life. That same year, he founded the Bethany Mission Sunday School, which eventually became the largest Sunday School in the nation. In 1861, when he was not yet twenty-three years old, he and his brother-in-law, Nathan Brown, using only money they had saved from their earnings, opened a clothing store in Philadelphia.

John Wanamaker became one of the most successful merchants of his generation. A number of key merchandizing concepts that are familiar to us today—the everything-under-one-roof "depart-

ment store," the standard of one fixed and easy-to-see price per item (as opposed to individual bargaining with customers), and the money-back guarantee—were originated by John Wanamaker. He also appears to have been a genius at advertising. He worked very hard, and became very rich.

Wanamaker loved thrift. He practiced it his entire life and preached it constantly. He was one of the nation's most committed and creative philanthropists.

For his employees, he created first a benefits association, and then a foundation, to provide health, retirement, and death benefits. He also set up innovative savings programs for employees, including one in which employees' deposits into their savings accounts were matched by contributions from the company.

In 1887, he instituted a profit-sharing plan for employees. In 1891, he created a school for young employees, with courses focusing on thrift and industrial education. In 1896, he opened a free library for employees. In 1888, he founded, and for many years afterward served as president of, the Penny Savings Bank of Philadelphia, intended originally to serve the low-income children attending Bethany Sunday School and their families, but eventually serving many thousands of area depositors.

In 1889, President Benjamin Harrison appointed Wanamaker to the office of postmaster general. In that capacity, Wanamaker urged the creation of a national postal savings system (based on the British model), worked to reduce Sunday operations (he firmly believed in no work on Sunday), expanded rural delivery, and—most of all—led the effort to abolish the use of the mails by lotteries, institutions that Wanamaker detested.

In 1895, he founded the "Men's Friendly Inn" for unemployed, and in particular alcohol-addicted, men seeking work and recovery. He was a lifelong temperance advocate. He founded and supported several large men's ministries, one of which, the Brotherhood of Andrew and Philip, operated its own building and loan association for the benefit of the members. He helped to found the Free Library of Philadelphia, John Wanamaker Branch. He worked diligently for the U.S. Sunday School movement throughout his adult life. John Wanamaker died in Philadelphia on December 12, 1922.

Robinson Crusoe *was the first book I ever read, aside from the Bible.*

JOHN WANAMAKER

. . . .

He was very saving even while a boy, denying himself many a comfort, that he might take as much as possible of his pay to his mother at the end of the week.

HENRY W. RUOFF, DESCRIBING WANAMAKER IN HIS BOOK, *LEADERS OF MEN*, 1903

I regard the Sunday School as the principal educator of my life.

WANAMAKER, WRITING TO THE WORLD'S SUNDAY SCHOOL CONVENTION, 1920

. . . .

While still in his teens John Wanamaker took out his first insurance policy.

JOSEPH H. APPEL, *THE BUSINESS BIOGRAPHY OF JOHN WANAMAKER*, 1930

. . . .

To do a full day's work every day in the year, and to use its product for the uplifting and bettering of my fellow-men.

WANAMAKER'S ANSWER TO THE QUESTION, "WHAT DO YOU CONSIDER TO BE YOUR MISSION IN LIFE?"

. . . .

Many young people believe that a good appearance is more important than anything else, but unless it is supplemented by habits of thrift, it will not get very far.

JOHN WANAMAKER

. . . .

John Wanamaker maintains two savings funds [for his employees], one for men and women, and the other for boys and girls of the establishment. The employees themselves conduct a savings and loan association for the double purpose of encouraging saving and making it unnecessary that any one in temporary difficulties should fall into the hands of money lending sharks.

WILLIAM H. TOLMAN, *SOCIAL ENGINEERING*, 1909

. . . .

Arithmetic problems are largely motivated by store needs. They indirectly call attention also to such matters as waste, carelessness, and extravagance.

A DESCRIPTION OF THE CURRICULUM IN WANAMAKER'S SCHOOL FOR YOUNG EMPLOYEES

. . . .

. . . the [Penny Savings] bank [founded by Wanamaker] has the distinction of doing the largest business in small accounts of any savings bank in the world. It is, in brief, a living monument of thrift.

RUSSELL H. CONWELL, *THE ROMANTIC RISE OF A GREAT AMERICAN*, 1924

. . . .

I am more than ever convinced of the wisdom of allowing to the frugal and thrifty workingman, and especially to working women and youths, the privilege of using the post-offices as places of deposit for small sums.

WANAMAKER, IN HIS CAPACITY AS U.S. POSTMASTER GENERAL, 1891

The habit of thrift taught him as a boy never left him. He had no patience with waste or extravagance. One night shortly after the opening of the Grand Depot he met the bookkeeper as he was leaving. The man had the month's bills in his hand ready to mail. Mr. Wanamaker took the envelopes, examined the addresses, saw that a number of these credit customers lived within walking distance of the store, and sent the man back in the building to remove the stamps from the envelopes and deliver the bills in person.

CONWELL, *THE ROMANTIC RISE OF A GREAT AMERICAN*

. . . .

It is told of him that, in the earlier days of Oak Hall, he used to gather up short pieces of string that came in on parcels, make them into a bunch, and see that they were used when bundles were to be tied. He also had a habit of smoothing out old newspapers, and seeing that they were used as wrappers for such things as did not require a better grade of paper.

ORISON SWETT MARDEN, WRITING ABOUT WANAMAKER, 1905

. . . .

He was always prompt.

MARDEN

. . . .

I have always had a broom in my hand.

JOHN WANAMAKER

27. A Day Labourer So Long

EDWARD BRABROOK

EDWARD BRABROOK was born on April 10, 1839, in Cornhill, England. He began his career working in an insurance company. In 1869, he was appointed assistant registrar of friendly societies, a civil service post. He served as chief registrar of Friendly Societies from 1891 until his retirement in 1904. He was also active in the Society of Antiquaries, the Folk-Lore Society, the Royal Society for Literature (whose history he wrote), the Royal Anthropological Institute, and the Charity Organization Society. In 1904, he served as president of the economic section of the British Association. Late in life, he received the honor of knighthood. Sir Edward Brabrook died in Surrey at the age of ninety-one on March 20, 1930.

His great accomplishment in the area of thrift is detailing the structures and legislative and legal histories of British thrift institutions, particularly friendly societies and building societies. His books include *Institutions for Thrift, Provident Societies and Industrial Welfare* and *The Law of Building Societies*. His knowledge of these institutions was extensive, and he was deeply committed, over many decades, to their purposes. He lectured frequently on the subject of thrift and was a strong advocate of teaching thrift in the schools.

In 1908, when Britain began providing old age pensions to all its older citizens, Brabrook unsuccessfully advocated for a pension scheme that would require financial contributions to the pension fund from all British citizens during their younger, higher-earning years—a requirement that would have made the program more similar in structure to the friendly societies that Brabrook knew and loved so well, and that, as he put it, "would be an assertion and enforcement of the doctrine that the right way to provide for old age is by thrift, self-denial and forethought in youth."[1]

*I must, however, single out one person [to thank],
namely, Mr. E. W. Brabrook, the Chief Registrar
of Friendly Societies, whose ready help in the
preparation of Model Rules, alike for People's
Banks and Village Banks, has proved invaluable.*

HENRY W. WOLFF, IN THE PREFACE OF THE 1896
EDITION OF *PEOPLE'S BANKS*, HIS BOOK ON THE
METHODS AND VIRTUES OF COOPERATIVE BANKING

. . . .

*Thrift: . . . that small corner of the great
field of economics in which I have been
a day labourer so long.*

EDWARD BRABROOK, "THRIFT," PRESIDENTIAL
ADDRESS TO THE ECONOMIC ASSOCIATION
OF THE BRITISH ASSOCIATION, 1904

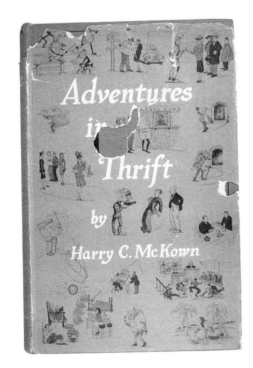

Published 1946

28. The Idea of Thrift

ORISON SWETT MARDEN

ORISON SWETT MARDEN was born on a farm in Thornton Grove, New Hampshire, in 1850. Both of his parents died before he was eight years old; he began working to support himself at about that time. As a young person, he was greatly inspired by the book *Self-Help* by Samuel Smiles.

His first book, *Pushing to the Front*, published in 1894, was a phenomenal success. Many more books followed, including *Thrift, Economy*, and *Cheerfulness as a Life Power*. In 1897, he founded *Success* magazine, which had a large circulation. Marden died at age seventy-four in 1924.

In his writings, Marden strongly emphasized what Norman Vincent Peale would later call "the power of positive thinking"—the idea that, as Marden put it, "he can who thinks he can." In my view, his assertions in this area go too far. But Marden wrote carefully, sensitively, and often about thrift. He clearly cared deeply about the topic, appreciated more than most its complexity as an idea and its serious moral anchoring, and wanted others to benefit from it, as he had done in his own life.

The term thrift is not only properly applied to money matters, but to everything in life—the wise use of one's time, the wise use of one's ability, one's energy, and this means prudent giving, careful habits of life. Thrift is scientific management of one's self, one's time, one's money, the wisest possible expenditure of what we have of all of life's resources.
ORISON SWETT MARDEN, *THRIFT*, 1918

. . . .

The art of saving is essentially the art of wise spending.
MARDEN, *THRIFT*

. . . .

The great thing in making expenditures is to spend upward, to invest in oneself . . . If one is after the largest, completest possible manhood, well-rounded, full-orbed, broad, then he will regard any expenditure to this end as the best kind of paying investment, and he will not be held back by a false sense of economy or deceptive notions of extravagance . . . Stuffing

the pocketbook and starving the mind is
a pretty poor business . . .

MARDEN, *THRIFT*

. . . .

*Thrift is neither extravagance nor meanness.
It is being good to ourselves in as large and
scientific way as possible. Whatever cuts down
power, whatever depletes our vitality, whatever
cuts down our energy, is a niggardly, vicious
economy or a wicked dissipation. Thrift means
that you should always have the best you can
possibly afford, when the thing has any reference
to your physical and mental health, to your
growth in efficiency and power. When these are
concerned you cannot afford the second best.*

ORISON SWETT MARDEN, "BE GOOD TO YOURSELF"

. . . .

*The habit of economy is one that ought
to be cultivated, for careful saving makes
lavish giving possible.*

MARDEN, *ECONOMY: THE SELF DENYING
DEPOSITOR AND PRUDENT PAYMASTER
AT THE BANK OF THRIFT,* 1901

. . . .

*Ignorance is the mortal enemy of thrift. A
thoroughly educated mind is usually a creator of
values, material, mental, and spiritual.*

MARDEN, *ECONOMY*

Published 1918

*Cheerfulness and hopefulness are true
economists; their opposites are among
the greatest of spendthrifts.*

MARDEN, *ECONOMY*

. . . .

Liberality often pays good returns.

MARDEN, *ECONOMY*

The word thrift in its origin means the grasping or holding fast the things that we have. It implies economy, carefulness, as opposed to waste and extravagance. It involves self-denial and frugal living for the time being, until the prosperity which grows out of thrift permits the more liberal indulgence of natural desires.

ORISON SWETT MARDEN, *PUSHING TO THE FRONT*, 1911

. . . .

Among the sworn enemies of thrift may be named going into debt, borrowing money, keeping no itemized account of daily expenditures, and buying on the installment plan.

. . . It is not so much for the money, as for what it means to have earned and saved money; it is the idea of thrift. If we have not been thrifty, if we have not saved anything, the world will look upon us as good for nothing, as partial failures, as either lazy, slipshod, or extravagant.

. . . But let us remember that thrift is not parsimony nor miserliness. It often means very liberal spending. It is a perpetual protest against putting emphasis on the wrong thing.

MARDEN, *PUSHING TO THE FRONT*

29. That We May Save the Greatest

BOLTON HALL

BOLTON HALL was born in Armagh, Ireland, on August 5, 1854. He and his parents, John and Mary, moved to the United States in 1867, when his father was called to become pastor of the Fifth Avenue Presbyterian Church in New York City. Bolton Hall died in Georgia in 1938.

Bolton Hall was a complex, multifaceted man. He spent a few years in business. He became a lawyer who specialized in defending unpopular causes. He wrote many books, both fiction and nonfiction. He was a founder of the American Longshoreman's Union. He was a major-league agitator. He was a long-time follower of Henry George, the single-tax reformer. He got arrested for handing out literature supporting Margaret Sanger, the birth control advocate. He befriended and assisted various anarchists as well as the prominent socialist leaders Eugene V. Debs and Emma Goldman—in 1905 he provided Goldman with a farmhouse retreat in Ossining, New York. He strongly disapproved of traditional charities.

Hall believed fervently in subsistence farming, gardening, and simple and rural living. He used his resources and connections to help organize the "Little Land League"—a philanthropy that purchased farmland near cities and then resold the land to the working poor at reduced prices. He championed school gardens, urban playgrounds, and camping programs for city children, and "was one of the promoters of the movement to utilize the vacant lots in and about cities for the benefit of the industrious poor."[1]

In 1910, he donated about seventy-five acres of land to, and helped to found, a community called Free Acres, a rural commune located near Watchung Hills, New Jersey, about thirty-five miles from New York. Based on philosophical principles including Henry George single-taxism, racial and sexual equality, participatory democracy, environmental conservation, and getting back to the land, Free Acres attracted a steady stream of reformers and political radicals and artists such as Paul Robeson, James Cagney, Michael Gold, and Alexander Calder. The place still exists.

Bolton Hall loved thrift. He wrote about it insightfully and at length, and thrift is a theme running through almost all of his otherwise quite disparate vocations and enthusiasms.

If you have a back yard, you can do your part and help the world and yourself by raising some of the food you eat. The more you raise the less you will

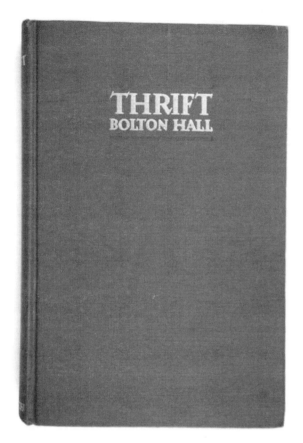

Published 1916

. . . most of us find glass jars the more satisfactory and economical containers for canned vegetables and fruit . . . For use in the storing of products which are already sterilized, such as jellies, jams, and preserves, and the bottling of fruit juices, housewives may practice effective thrift by saving all jars in which they received dried beef, bacon, peanut butter, and other products and bottles that have contained olives, catsup, and kindred goods.
HALL, *THREE ACRES AND LIBERTY*

. . . .

When it comes to combining concision with accuracy and respect for complexity, here is the single best definition of *thrift* that I know of:

The prudent man looks ahead and gets ready. The frugal man lives carefully and saves persistently. The economical man spends judiciously and uses wisely. The careful man buys only what he needs, and wastes nothing. The industrious man works hard and saves hard; the miser hoards; but the man of thrift earns largely, plans carefully, manages economically, spends wisely and saves consistently. Thrift is all frugality, prudence, economy, and industry—and "then some."

We don't speak accurately, perhaps because we don't think accurately. We use "frugality," "carefulness," "prudence," "economy," "industry," as though they all meant the same thing—they don't.

I wanted to extract the meaning of thrift, so I rigged up a derrick and hoisted Noah Webster's Unabridged Dictionary *on to my table, and it*

have to buy, and the more there will be left for some of your fellow countrymen who have not an inch of ground on which to raise anything.

If there is a vacant lot in your neighborhood, see if you cannot get the use of it for yourself and your neighbors, and raise your own vegetables. An hour a day spent in this way will not only increase wealth and help your family, but will help you personally by adding to your strength and well-being and making you appreciate the Eden joy of gardening. An hour in the open air is worth more than a dozen expensive prescriptions by an expensive doctor.
BOLTON HALL, *THREE ACRES AND LIBERTY*, 1907

said that "Thrift is a thriving state." Well, that sounded so strange that I read on further: it said, "Good husbandry," and then it paused, for I did not look satisfied, and it went on, "Economical management, frugality." "Try again, Dick," I said, and the Dictionary hit it at last, "Prosperity."

BOLTON HALL, *THRIFT*, 1916

. . . .

Thrift, economy, saving! unless it is done at the expense of our nobler things or of our fellow men, it is never mean, never contemptible: but we can make it great by making its object grand.

HALL, *THRIFT*

. . . .

Pleasure is expensive, happiness costs nothing. The real thrift consists of giving and thereby getting as much happiness as possible.

HALL, *THRIFT*

Thrift, the power to save, which means self-restraint, is mainly important, not because it means wealth in the end, not because it enables you to make others work while you watch or play, but because it gives you peace of mind. Without peace of mind no one can do his best work or lead a life really worth while.

HALL, *THRIFT*

. . . .

Let us save; save each little thing if we will, but only that we may save the greatest. The greatest to each is not even his own life. Like Him who saved others, but himself he would not save, let our saving be the salvation of the world.

HALL, *THRIFT*

30. A Person Who Makes Beautiful Things

ELBERT HUBBARD

ELBERT HUBBARD was born in Bloomington, Illinois, on June 19, 1856. As a young man he worked on a farm, in a printing office, in the West as a cowboy, and in a soap factory, of which he later became manager, and, several years later, partner. He sold his interest in the soap factory in order to attend Harvard College. On a trip to Europe in 1892, he met the artist, writer, printer, and socialist leader William Morris, whose ideas deeply influenced Hubbard.

In 1895, seeking to emulate Morris and inspired by the larger arts and crafts movement of the period, Hubbard founded the Roycrofters in East Aurora, New York—a residential community built around a cluster of cooperative businesses, including a printing press, a publishing house, a bookbinding business, a lecture program, blacksmithing, carpentry, and basket weaving. From this base in East Aurora, Hubbard wrote many books, pamphlets, articles, and "preachments" and in the early years of the twentieth century became one of the most popular lecturers in the United States.

He did not drink or smoke. He told everyone who would listen that at Roycrofters, "fresh air is free, and outdoor exercise is not discour-

aged." Most of the money he made as a lecturer and author, he gave to Roycrofters, which operated financially on share-and-share-alike, cooperative principles. Hubbard and his wife Alice died on May 7, 1915, in the Irish Sea when the ship on which they were passengers, the *Lusitania*, was sunk by German torpedoes.

Hubbard understood thrift and wrote about it eloquently. He also practiced thrift in multiple and interesting ways, both personally and in his conception and leadership of the Roycrofters.

He valued every cent of every dollar for what it would do, for the good it could be made to accomplish. He was thrifty, and that he had once endured poverty his abstemious habits clearly betrayed. He wasted nothing, and wanted nothing wasted.

FELIX SHAY, *ELBERT HUBBARD OF EAST AURORA*

· · · ·

An employee may subscribe for as many shares [of the Roycroft Press] as he desires, but if he leaves the service of the company he must sell the shares to Mr. Hubbard at the price paid. This is a

Published 1916

somewhat indirect method of profit sharing, and the experiment might be more accurately defined as a case of producers' cooperation . . .

A TEXTBOOK ON U.S. LABOR ISSUES, 1905

. . . .

So a Roycrofter is a person who makes beautiful things, and makes them as well as he can.

ELBERT HUBBARD

. . . .

The habit of thrift is simply the habit which dictates that you shall earn more than you spend

. . . The thrift habit is a sister to a good many other beautiful habits. Thrift implies industry, and of course thrift is economy, and economy means the care of things and their proper use. You do not waste anything that can be used. You save it, care for it, reserve it.

. . . Children should early be taught the savings-bank habit. Such children will grow up—at least, most of them will—able, courageous, helpful, willing, and a few of them will evolve into strong and able people, leaders . . . Thrifty people, other things considered, have good health. Thrift implies that you do not overeat, that you sleep at least eight hours, that you go to bed early and get up early . . . The habit of thrift tends to give clear eyes, good

digestion, efficient muscles. People on moderate
salaries have no business to patronize taxicabs.
Leave that to elderly people who can not easily
board the street-car; also leave it to the people
who have pride plus and who wear clothes
they are afraid will get soiled.

ELBERT HUBBARD, *THRIFT*, 1916

. . . .

In point of all-round development, Franklin
must stand as the foremost American.

ELBERT HUBBARD

. . . .

The Reward for Good Work is More Work

FELIX SHAY, *ELBERT HUBBARD OF EAST AURORA*

The Joy of Originating
The Value of Time
The Success of Perseverance
The Pleasure of Working
The Dignity of Simplicity
The Worth of Character
The Power of Kindness
The Influence of Example
The Obligation of Duty
The Wisdom of Economy
The Virtue of Patience
The Improvement of Talent

HUBBARD, "TWELVE THINGS FOR ROYCOFTERS
TO REMEMBER"

. . . .

A man who gives his money away is not
necessarily more foolish than he who saves it.

HUBBARD, *THE PHILOSOPHY OF ELBERT HUBBARD*

. . . .

The cheap article, I will admit, ministers to a
certain grade of intellect; but if the man grows,
there will come a time when, instead of a great
many cheap and shoddy things, he will want
a few good things.

HUBBARD, *THE LITTLE JOURNEYS*

31. Character in the Highest and Best Sense

BOOKER T. WASHINGTON

As the United States entered the twentieth century, two charismatic men, advocating sometimes overlapping and sometimes clashing strategies for social change, had emerged as key leaders of African Americans. One was W. E. B. DuBois. The other was Booker T. Washington. Historians in recent decades have been kinder to DuBois than to Washington, in part because most recent historians have been either indifferent or hostile to thrift, which was near the very center of Washington's personality and mission. If Benjamin Franklin was the first truly great American champion of thrift, Booker T. Washington was the second.

Booker T. Washington was born a slave in Hale's Ford, Virginia, in about 1856. In 1881, he became the leader of the newly formed Tuskegee Institute, where he served for the rest of his life, and 1900 he wrote *Up from Slavery*, one of the most important books in U.S. history. He died in Tuskegee, Alabama, on November 14, 1915.

The slave system on our place, in large measure, took the spirit of self-reliance and self-help out of the white people. My old master had many boys and girls, but no one, so far as I know, ever mastered a single trade or special line of productive industry.

The girls were not taught to cook, sew, or to take care of the house. All of this was left to the slaves. The slaves, of course, had little personal interest in the life of the plantation, and their ignorance prevented them from learning how to do things in the most improved and thorough manner. As a result of the system, fences were out of repair, gates were hanging half off the hinges, door creaked, window-panes were out, plastering had fallen but was not replaced, weeds grew in the yard. As a rule there was food for whites and blacks, but inside the house, and on the dining-room table, there was wanting that delicacy and refinement of touch and finish which can make a home the most convenient, comfortable, and attractive place in the world. Withal there was a waste of food and other materials which was sad.

BOOKER T. WASHINGTON, *UP FROM SLAVERY*, 1900

. . . .

But, of course, when I saw how all the other boys were dressed, I began to feel quite uncomfortable. As usual, I put the case before my mother, and she explained to me that she had no money with which to buy a "store hat," which was a rather new institution at that time among the members of my race and was considered quite the thing for young and old to own, but that she would find a way to help me out of the difficulty. She accordingly got two pieces of "homespun" (jeans) and sewed them together, and I was soon the proud owner of my first cap.

The lesson that my mother taught me in this has always remained with me, and I have tried as best I could to teach it to others. I have always felt proud, whenever I think of the incident, that my mother had strength of character enough not to be led into the temptation of seeming to be that which she was not—of trying to impress my schoolmates and others with the fact that she was able to buy me a "store hat" when she was not. I have always felt proud that she refused to go into debt for that which she did not have the money to pay for. Since that time I have owned many kinds of caps and hats, but never one of which I have felt so proud as of the cap made of two pieces of cloth sewed together by my mother.

WASHINGTON, *UP FROM SLAVERY*

. . . .

On this same topic, see above, Benjamin Franklin's letter to his wife of April 6, 1766, and his letter to his daughter-in-law of June 3, 1779.

As soon as possible after reaching the grounds of the Hampton Institute, I presented myself before the head teacher for assignment to a class. Having been so long without proper food, a bath and change of clothing, I did not, of course, make a very favorable

impression upon her, and I could see at once that there were doubts in her mind about the wisdom of admitting me . . . In the meantime I saw her admitting other students, and that added greatly to my discomfort, for I felt, deep down in my heart, that I could do as well as they, if I could only get a chance to show what was in me.

After some hours had passed, the head teacher said to me: "The adjoining recitation-room needs sweeping. Take the broom and sweep it."

. . . I swept the recitation room three times. Then I got a dusting-cloth and dusted it four times. All the woodwork around the walls, every bench, table, and desk, I went over four times with my dusting-cloth. Besides, every piece of furniture had been moved and every closet and corner in the room had been thoroughly cleaned . . . When I was through I reported to the head teacher. She was a "Yankee" woman who knew just where to look for dirt. She went into the room and inspected the floors and closets; then she took her handkerchief and rubbed it on the woodwork about the walls, and over the table and benches. When she was unable to find one bit of dirt on the floor, or one particle of dust on any of the furniture, she quietly remarked, "I guess you will do to enter the institution."

WASHINGTON, *UP FROM SLAVERY*

. . . .

In 1878, a book for schoolteachers published in Britain, *Domestic Economy: Thrift in Every-Day Life*, contains a lesson on "How To Set About Cleaning":

1. *When you scrub a floor, what do you want?—*
   A pail of hot water, some hard soap, soda,
   and a good stiff scrubbing brush, a flannel
   and cloth.
2. *How do you set to work?—This should be*
   an experimental lesson; and the children should
   be shown how to work, how to change the water
   when dirty, and how to scrub quickly and
   efficiently . . .
3. *Can we be too particular as regards pure air*
   and health, to say nothing of appearance and
   comfort in keeping everything inside our houses
   clean?[1]

. . . .

The students [at Tuskegee] were making progress
in learning books and in developing their minds;
but it became apparent at once that, if we were
to make any permanent impression upon those
who had come to us for training, we must do
something besides teach them mere books . . . Aside
from this, we wanted to give them such a practical
knowledge of some industry, together with the spirit
of industry, thrift, and economy, that they would
be sure of knowing how to make a living after they
had left us.

WASHINGTON, *UP FROM SLAVERY*

. . . .

For a long time one of the most difficult tasks was
to teach the students that all buttons were to be kept
on their clothes, and that there must be no torn

places and no greasy-spots. This lesson, I am pleased
to be able to say, has been so thoroughly learned and
so faithfully handed down from year to year by one
set of students to another that often at the present
time, when the students march out of chapel in the
evening and their dress is inspected, as it is every
night, not one button is found to be missing.

WASHINGTON, *UP FROM SLAVERY*

. . . .

The night-school [at Tuskegee] was organized on
a plan similar to the one I had helped to establish
at Hampton. At first it was composed of about a
dozen students. They were admitted to night-school
only when they had no money with which to pay
any part of their board in the regular day-school.
It was further required that they must work for ten
hours during the day at some trade or industry, and
study academic branches for two hours during the
evening . . . They were to be paid something above
the cost of their board, with the understanding that
all of their earnings, except a very small part, were
to be reserved in the school's treasury, to be used for
paying their board in the regular day-school after
they had entered the department.

WASHINGTON, *UP FROM SLAVERY*

. . . .

The thing that impressed itself most on me in
Holland was the thoroughness of the agriculture
and the excellence of the Holstein cattle. I never
knew, before visiting Holland, how much it was

possible for people to get out of a small plot of ground.

WASHINGTON, *UP FROM SLAVERY*

. . . .

Mr. Washington called upon me a few days after my gift of six hundred thousand dollars was made to Tuskegee and asked if he might be allowed to make one suggestion. I said: "Certainly."

"You have kindly specified that a sum from that fund be set aside for the future support of myself and my wife during our lives, and we are very grateful, but, Mr. Carnegie, the sum is far beyond our needs . . . Would you have any objection to changing that clause, striking out the sum, and substituting 'only suitable provision'? I'll trust the trustees. Mrs. Washington and myself need very little."

ANDREW CARNEGIE, *AUTOBIOGRAPHY*

. . . .

. . . the most remarkable man living today . . .

ANDREW CARNEGIE, DESCRIBING BOOKER T. WASHINGTON, 1910

. . . .

In meeting men, in many places, I have found that the happiest people are those who do the most for others; the most miserable are those who do the least . . . I often say to our students, in the course of my talks to them on Sunday evenings in the chapel, that the longer I live and the more experience I have of the world, the more I am convinced that, after all, the one thing that is most worth living for—and dying for, if need be—is the opportunity of making someone else more happy and more useful.

WASHINGTON, *UP FROM SLAVERY*

. . . .

My friends, do any of you [teachers] feel discouraged, disheartened—do any of you feel that your work is a drudgery—that your school work this past year has been a failure, have any of you had such miserable surroundings that your heart sinks whenever you enter your school house or boarding place? If these things have been true of any of you, let me suggest that you cannot imagine what a change, yes, what a revolution it will make in your feelings and influence, if, instead of going about your task merely to have so much geography or history, or arithmetic, mastered or memorized, you teach with the idea uppermost of training a human soul—of forming character in the highest and best sense of changing habits of falsifying into habits of truth, of changing dishonesty into honesty, of changing laziness into thrift, of changing sin into righteousness, of teaching pupils to "LOOK UP and not DOWN, To look out and not in, To look forward and not back." My friends, let me urge you as teachers to get near as many human souls as possible.

WASHINGTON, ADDRESS TO THE ALABAMA STATE TEACHERS' ASSOCIATION, JUNE 8, 1892

On New Year's day they had their first Emancipation Celebration in this region and about 3000 it seems to me marched through the town and came to the school where I spoke to them and I tried to press the importance of thrift, economy, and the value of a home upon them.

WASHINGTON, LETTER TO EMILY HOWARD OF TUSKEGEE, ALABAMA, THANKING HER FOR HER GIFT TO THE SCHOOL, JANUARY 12, 1894

. . . .

But what are the actual needs of the people in the black belt of the South? I refer to those who are on these large cotton, rice, and sugar plantations, rather than those in the cities and larger towns. A large majority of the people on these plantations are ignorant, without habits of thrift. They are industrious but they are in debt; they have mortgaged their crops to keep them alive and they are attempting to pay a rate of interest that often ranges from 15 to 40 per cent., and, of course, they come out at the end of the year in debt. The schools in the plantation districts are rarely in session more than three months.

WASHINGTON, ADDRESS TO THE NATIONAL EDUCATIONAL ASSOCIATION, JULY 10, 1896

. . . .

The young women teachers [at Tuskegee] occupy themselves much with a propaganda for cleanliness and good housekeeping among the mothers of families, and argue powerfully for the two-room house as against the one-room shanty. Mr. Booker T. Washington, out of the depth of much experience and knowledge of his race, would probably assent to the proposition that the adoption of two-room houses in place of one-room cabins by the plantation negroes of the South would mean in the present generation ten times more for the real progress of the race in all that belongs to a true civilization, than the possession of the elective franchise. I confess that there is nothing in all the work done by Tuskegee that appeals more strongly to my sympathy or to my imagination as a friend of social reform, than this earnest propoganda for the two-room houses . . .

THE JOURNALIST ALBERT W. SHAW, DESCRIBING HIS VISIT TO TUSKEGEE TO ATTEND THE THIRD TUSKEGEE NEGRO CONFERENCE, HELD ON FEBRUARY 21, 1894

. . . .

If through me . . . seven millions of my people in the South might be permitted to send a message to Harvard—Harvard that offered upon death's altar, young Shaw, and Russell, and Lowell and scores of others, that we might have a free and united country, that message would be, "Tell them that the sacrifice was not in vain. Tell them that by way of the shop, the field, the skilled hand, habits of thrift and economy, by way of industrial school and college, we are coming. We are crawling up, working up, yea, bursting up.

Often through oppression, unjust discrimination and prejudice, but through them all we are coming up, and with proper habits, intelligence and property, there is no power on earth that can permanently stay our progress."

WASHINGTON, ADDRESS TO HARVARD UNIVERSITY
ALUMNI, JUNE 24, 1896

. . . .

. . . we are learning that standing ground for the race, as for the individual, must be laid in intelligence, industry, thrift and property, not as an end, but as a means to the highest privileges . . .

WASHINGTON, SPEECH AT THE UNVEILING OF THE
ROBERT GOULD SHAW MONUMENT, MAY 31, 1897

. . . .

We must make up our minds that in order to be respected we must cultivate habits of economy, thrift, and industry. No people who spend all that they make, can ever attain to any high degree of success. No matter how much education they may receive, they will not be respected so long as they are without bank accounts and without homes. There is no question but that one of the weak points of the race is that we lack in too large a degree the saving habit. We are too much inclined to spend all that we earn at the end of the week or yield too often to the temptation when we get a few dollars ahead to cease work until all of that is spent. I must earnestly advise you to save money, not so much for money's sake, but because a bank account represents foresight, self-denial, thrift, and economy.

The people who save money, who make themselves intelligent, and live moral lives, are the ones who are going to control the destinies of the country.

WASHINGTON, ADDRESS IN BIRMINGHAM,
JANUARY 1, 1900

. . . .

We should not overlook the gospel of thrift. As a race we are not, I fear, willing enough to sacrifice today for tomorrow, and to do without this year, in order that we may possess in years to come . . . It is in the savings bank, as well as in the school and the church; in the home and the farm, that New England today finds her greatness and power. If the colored people of Boston owned as many shoe factories as they own churches, I suspect that the race in this city would be immensely advanced. We do not need fewer churches, but more farms and factories.

WASHINGTON, ADDRESS IN BOSTON, JULY 30, 1903

. . . .

So far as Mr. Washington preaches Thrift, Patience, and Industrial Training for the masses, we must hold up his hands and strive with him, rejoicing in his honors and glorying in the strength of this Joshua called of God and of man to lead the heedless host. But as far as Mr. Washington apologizes for injustice, North or South, does not rightly value the privilege and duty of voting, belittles the emasculating effects of caste distinctions, and opposes the higher training and ambition of our brighter minds—so far as he, the South, or the Nation, does this—we must unceasingly and firmly oppose him.

W. E. B. DUBOIS, ABOUT 1903

. . . .

No man ever performed more notably to bring to pass a practical manifestation of Christian ethics as applied to the uplift of the Negro than did Booker T. Washington, the great Negro educator.

THE CREDIT UNION ORGANIZER AND THRIFT LEADER ROY F. BERGENGREN, 1945

In short, Washington believed that material advancement, achieved through thrift, hard work, Christian character, and economic chauvinism would bring recognition of the Negro's constitutional rights, and break down oppression and segregation.

AUGUST MEIER, *THE JOURNAL OF NEGRO HISTORY*, 1953

32. Beauty in Homespun

MARTHA BERRY

WHAT BOOKER T. WASHINGTON did for rural poor black children in Alabama, Martha Berry decided to do for rural poor white children in Georgia. Martha Berry was born on October 7, 1866, and grew up in relative privilege near Rome, Georgia, at Oak Hill, her parents' plantation. Her father, Thomas, fought for the Confederacy in the Civil War. In about 1900, in her mid-thirties, Martha Berry began teaching Bible stories on Sundays to illiterate mountain children from the region. The woman whom these children called "the Sunday Lady" had found her life's mission. In 1902, she founded the first of what later became the Berry Schools. In 1926, she founded Berry Junior College, and in 1930, she founded Berry College, which today is still going strong. Martha Berry died on February 27, 1942. Her understanding of thrift, and in particular its role in educating children who lack privilege and wealth, reminds me strongly of Booker T. Washington and (see below) Laurence C. Jones.

He [my father] never allowed me to waste even an apple peeling, and I had to save the bread crumbs for the birds. He made me feel that if I wasted anything that a living creature could use it was sinful.

MARTHA BERRY, REMEMBERING HER FATHER, THOMAS BERRY

MISS MARTHA BERRY
FOUNDER

BIRTHPLACE OF BERRY SCHOOLS
MOUNT BERRY, GA.

The aim of my institution is . . . to meet the educational and industrial needs of the poor white country-boys of Georgia; to . . . teach them useful and remunerative trades and ways of making a living, to make them independent, thrifty, and self-respecting.

MARTHA BERRY, 1904

. . . .

They need to know how to scrub, to cook, to care for their rooms, to dress neatly, to farm, to build houses, to save money—in short to do the practical things of life in the best possible way.

MARTHA BERRY

. . . .

. . . it is of the utmost importance to work with economy, frugality, neatness, promptness, and thoroughness. As an example of how such discipline is heeded and carried out, we had a boy who complained of his assistant in the kitchen as being wasteful. He declared that he would "peel his potatoes too thick"— a thing which to his mind and teaching means a loss to him personally and to every boy in the school.

MARTHA BERRY

. . . .

Be a lifter and not a leaner.

MOTTO OF THE BERRY SCHOOLS, ADOPTED BY THE STUDENTS AFTER FORMER PRESIDENT THEODORE ROOSEVELT VISITED THE SCHOOLS ON OCTOBER 8, 1910, AND URGED EACH STUDENT TO BECOME "A LIFTER AND NOT A LEANER."

The Bible for prayer
The Lamp for learning
The Plow for labor
The Cabin for simplicity

MOTTOS ON THE SHIELD
OF THE BERRY SCHOOLS

. . . .

. . teaching the dignity of labor, so that in later years the students will have a sympathetic understanding with all who have to work . . . My life work has been to help poor boys and girls who are willing to help themselves.

MARTHA BERRY, 1925

. . . .

Everything that has been done under Miss Martha Berry's direction has the touch of beauty and fitness.

ALBERT SHAW, "MARTHA BERRY AND HER PATRIOTIC WORK," 1925

. . . .

Culture may rest in the seeing and seeking of beauty in homespun.

MARTHA BERRY, 1935

33. Creative Economy

S. W. STRAUS

THE BANKER and realty financier Simon William Straus was born in Ligonier, Indiana, on December 23, 1866. He attended public schools in Chicago and later attended the Hughes High School in Cincinnati. He entered his father's Chicago-based business (F. W. Straus and Co.) in 1884, and two years later, when his father retired, took over the management of the firm and changed its name to S. W. Straus and Company. The company for many years exerted a strong influence on the U.S. building industry. By 1922, in Chicago alone, Straus had financed more than four thousand buildings. In New York, Straus and Company financed the Chrysler Building, at the time the tallest building in the world.

Straus was a major thrift leader and visionary—and one who generously put his money and time at the service of his convictions. To encourage thrift among his employees, he added bonuses to their savings accounts. In 1913, he founded the American Society for Thrift, and for years wrote, spoke, and organized tirelessly on behalf of thrift. His book, *History of the Thrift Movement in America*, was published in 1920. S. W. Straus died at age sixty-four in New York City on September 7, 1930.

My first thrift efforts arose in my own business experience . . . nearly all of our employees became members of [our company's] Profit-Sharing and Thrift Society.

S. W. STRAUS

. . . .

The American people as a nation dislike to be told that they are unthrifty, and yet it is true that they are unthrifty in the extreme. They boast of their money-making powers, and the facts justify them. American know how to make money, no doubt about it, but they don't know how to spend it— and that is equivalent to saying they don't know how to save it—for money gets its chief value from its use.

. . . Thrift is not a mere forced rule: it is a virtue; it is a principle. Thrift is not an affair of the pocket, but an affair of character. Thrift is not niggardliness, but wisdom. Thrift is not so much a matter of money as an attitude of mind . . . My friends, thrift is creative economy.

STRAUS, ANNOUNCING THE FORMATION OF THE AMERICAN SOCIETY FOR THRIFT, NOVEMBER 1913

. . . the American Society for Thrift has inaugurated a propaganda looking to the encouragement of genuine conservation . . . [The Society's] officers and organization committees include many of the most prominent college presidents and social workers in America. The first bulletin of the society is based, very logically, upon a resolution in the National Association of Retail Grocers, deploring the prodigal tendencies of the times . . .

ATLANTA CONSTITUTION, JANUARY 25, 1914

. . . .

We are going to hold a National Thrift Congress at the Panama Exposition in 1915, and since I came here [to Europe] to study the thrift movements on this side of the water we have determined to make the congress international . . . The most notable example of thrift is Great Britain's splendid system of co-operative associations. They have 2,500,000 members, and the amount of annual business done is just a little less than the business of the United States Steel Corporation. This gives some indication of the scope of this great thrift method.

STRAUS, JUNE 1914

. . . .

Straus and the American Society for Thrift did in fact organize an International Thrift Congress as a part of the Panama-Pacific International Exposition. The Thrift Congress was held on August 11–13, 1915, in Festival Hall on the Exhibition Grounds in San Francisco.

Laying aside a few dollars each week does not necessarily make one a thrifty person. Thrift means so much more than merely saving money—it means personal efficiency—it means plans—it means self-control—it means foresight—it means prudence—it means sane and legitimate self-confidence—it means all that makes for character. It is much removed from miserliness on the one hand as it is from extravagance on the other. As we build the ideals of thrift we build character.

STRAUS, ADDRESS TO THE INTERNATIONAL THRIFT CONGRESS, SAN FRANCISCO, AUGUST 1915

. . . .

At one meeting [held during the International Exposition] S. W. Straus of Chicago, President of the American Society for Thrift, offered to pay the expenses of a committee to study the methods by which instruction in thrift might best be introduced into the public schools, and to furnish cash prizes of $750, $250, and $100 for essays on the subject.

FRANK MORTON TODD, *THE STORY OF THE EXPOSITION*

. . . .

As a result of these deliberations [at the International Thrift Congress] it was decided . . . that overtures should be made to the National Education Association . . . with the request that this body, which represented the great pedagogical

profession in the United States, take such steps
as might be necessary to give thrift a place in the
curricula of the public schools of the nation.

STRAUS, *HISTORY OF THE THRIFT MOVEMENT IN AMERICA*

. . . .

As a result of these "overtures," in late 1915 the National Education Association, partnering with the National Council of Education and the American Society for Thrift, formed a Committee on Thrift Education, chaired by Dr. Arthur H. Chamberlain, which began producing pro-thrift material for school curricula and holding annual meetings to discuss and advocate for thrift education in the schools.

The thrift essay contest, funded by Straus and administered by the National Education Association, did take place. The essays were submitted by March 1, 1916. The entries were judged by a nine-member "Thrift Board" established by the NEA. By 1917, more than 150,000 U.S. school children had participated in this contest.[1]

Saving money is one of the foundation stones in the building of a thrifty character—but it is no more the sum total of thrift than one stone is the sum total in the foundation of a great house. A man may be a money saver, and yet if he dissipates, or is immoral, he is not thrifty. A man may save money, yet if he works 18 hours a day, to the detriment of his health, he is not thrifty. True thrift consists in the judicious use of all our mental, material, and physical resources, and when we merely save money

we have gone only part of the way. A miser is an undesirable citizen. What, pray, would be the fate of a nation of misers? The wheels of industry are turned by those men and women who spend time and employ their money wisely and live sanely.

. . . In Chicago a man died recently and left $700,000 to the Orchestra Association of that city . . . That man has given impetus to artistic development, he has exemplified the greater thrift. The man who is penurious and tight-fisted is a dead weight to civilization. We who have the interests of the great thrift movement in America at heart must realize that one of our chief problems is to teach our fellow men that merely putting money in a savings bank is not the sum total of thrift.

STRAUS, "THE GREATER THRIFT," AN ADDRESS DELIVERED TO THE ANNUAL CONVENTION OF THE NATIONAL EDUCATION ASSOCIATION, JULY 1, 1916

. . . .

No human virtue, no economic force, no patriotic impulse had more to do with the successful outcome of the war than thrift.

STRAUS, JUNE 30, 1918

. . . .

If we are to develop thrift in America along lasting lines, we must begin at the foundation. We must make use of that most important laboratory, the schoolroom. We must learn to teach thrift in the classroom, not as a separate subject, but in its relationship to such branches as arithmetic, history, chemistry, biology, geography, grammar, household economics and business practice.

STRAUS, 1920

. . . .

To this end [gaining public support for thrift education in the schools] there had for many months been planned a National Conference on Thrift and Conservation. This is perhaps the first time in history where there have assembled under auspices of a great National Educational Association, representative of numerous national organizations to consider the problems relating to the school. Some 150 of these national organizations interested themselves in the Conference.

REPORT OF THE NATIONAL CONFERENCE ON THRIFT EDUCATION, SEPTEMBER 1924

. . . .

The National Conference on Thrift and Conservation—under the leadership of Straus's American Society for Thrift and leaders from the National Education Association, the American Bankers Association, the General Federation of Women's Clubs, the American Federation of Labor, the American Library Association, the U.S. Chamber of Commerce, the YMCA, the National Catholic Welfare Council, the Jewish Welfare Board, the U.S. National Parks Service, and many other national organizations—met in Washington, DC, on June 27–28, 1924.

. . . .

More than 4,000,000 children were depositors in school savings banks in 10,000 cities of the country during the last year, Arthur H. Chamberlain, Education Director for the American Society for Thrift, said today. He spoke to an assemblage of bankers and educators attending the National Thrift Conference in connection with the convention of the National Education Association. More than 8,000,000 pupils are now studying thrift in some form, Mr. Chamberlain estimated.

NEW YORK TIMES, JUNE 30, 1926

. . . .

Individual thrift is his hobby.

PROFILE OF S. W. STRAUS, NEW YORK TIMES, NOVEMBER 2, 1913

34. Take the Nickels and Turn Them into Dollars

MAGGIE L. WALKER

MAGGIE L. DRAPER was born in Richmond, Virginia, on July 15, 1867. At age fourteen, she joined the Independent Order of Saint Luke, an African American fraternal society that had been formed in Baltimore after the Civil War. She was a devoted (and lifelong) member of the Baptist Church. She graduated from high school in 1883, and became a teacher. In 1886, she married Armstrong Walker, a brick contractor. She resigned from teaching, had the first of their three children in 1890, and began to devote more time to the Order of Saint Luke. In 1899, Maggie L. Walker became grand secretary, the Order's highest leader.

Under her leadership, the Order grew rapidly and undertook a wide range of initiatives centering on thrift and economic cooperation and empowerment. Walker's vision for the Order in part reflected the influence and legacy of William Washington Browne, some eighteen years older than Walker, and, until he died in 1897, the leader of another Richmond-based African American fraternal society, the United Order of True Reformers. (Browne is discussed further in the next part of this book, under "Friendly and Fraternal Societies.")

In 1903, the Order of Saint Luke under Walk-er's leadership founded the St. Luke Penny Savings Bank, making Walker the first African American woman in U.S. history to serve as the president of a bank. By 1920, the bank had financed 645 black-owned homes, and its assets by 1924 had reached $3.5 million. The Order during Walker's tenure as grand secretary also founded a newspaper, the *St. Luke Herald*, a printing press, and a department store, the St. Luke's Emporium. The Order's juvenile auxiliary, which had been founded in 1895, had enrolled up to 20,000 children by the 1920s. As early as 1909, children constituted about one-third of the approximately 300,000 depositors of the St. Luke Penny Savings Bank.

Maggie L. Walker died at the age of sixty-seven on December 15, 1934.

In my view, few if any calls to cooperative thrift are more compelling than this one from 1901 from Maggie Walker:

Let us have a bank that will take the nickels and turn them into dollars. Then, as our patron saint went about doing good, how easily can this great organization now start and do good in our ranks. Who is so helpless as the Negro woman? Who is so circumscribed and hemmed in, in the race of life, in the struggle for bread, meat and clothing as the Negro woman? They are even being denied the work of teaching Negro children. Can't this great Order, in which there are so many good women, willing women, hard-working women, noble women, whose money is here, whose interests are here, whose hearts and souls are here, do something toward giving employment to those who have made it what it is?

WALKER, CALLING FOR THE ESTABLISHMENT OF THE ST. LUKE'S PENNY SAVINGS BANK, 1901

. . . .

Succor and Employment for the Negro Women

MOTTO OF THE INDEPENDENT ORDER OF SAINT LUKE

. . . .

I felt like a spendthrift. I knew I had the energy to do a lot of things for my people that needed doing, and I felt I ought to be about it in some way. Yet I didn't know what I could do or where to begin. I was restless and wanted work that was of some account.

WALKER, LOOKING BACK ON HER DECISION IN THE MID-1880S TO DEVOTE MORE OF HER TIME AND ENERGY TO THE ORDER OF SAINT LUKE

Over fifteen thousand children who are members, scattered through many states, meet weekly with a regular program which includes Bible instruction and lessons in thrift and hygiene. Each child is given a card-board "rainy-day bank"; as soon as he has a dollar, the leader encourages him to put it in a regular savings bank just as is done with adult members.

L. H. HAMOND, DESCRIBING THE "THRIFT WORK" CARRIED OUT THROUGH THE ORDER OF ST. LUKE'S JUVENILE AUXILIARY, 1922

. . . .

We teach them to save with the definite purpose of wise use of the money. We try to give them a sense of moral responsibility for its wise use. Of course we can't do that without religious teaching.

WALKER, EXPLAINING THE PURPOSES OF THE JUVENILE AUXILIARY

. . . .

. . . save some part of every dollar you have and the practice will become a habit—a habit which you will never regret, and of which you will never grow shame.

WALKER, 1909

35. Some Reflection of the Simple Virtues

LAURENCE C. JONES

LAURENCE C. JONES was born on November 21, 1882, in St. Joseph, Missouri. His mother, Mary, was a seamstress, and his father, John, worked as a porter in a local hotel. As a child, Laurence shined shoes and sold rabbits and pigeons until he had saved enough money to buy a paper route from an older boy. He attended public schools in St. Joseph and later (while living with relatives) in Marshalltown, Iowa. In 1907, he graduated from the University of Iowa, where he had become deeply interested in industrial arts education and was particularly inspired by the mission and success of the Hampton Institute (founded in Virginia in 1868 by Samuel C. Armstrong) and the Tuskegee Institute (founded in Alabama in 1881 and led by Armstrong's student, Booker T. Washington). In the spring of 1909, at the age of twenty-four and with $1.65 in his pocket, Jones moved to the Piney Woods region of Mississippi to become an organizer and educator. He taught the first class of what would become the Piney Woods School outdoors, sitting on a log beneath a cedar tree, with three pupils. The school's first building was completed in 1910.

As an African American starting a school for the children of rural black Mississippians, Jones faced numerous and formidable obstacles, not least of which was the fervent racism of white Mississippi political leaders of that era such as James K. Vardaman and Theodore Bilbo. But he overcame, and succeeded. Dr. Jones died in 1975. Today the Piney Woods School is the largest, as well as the longest continually operating, African American boarding school in the United States. As it was for Booker T. Washington, the concept of thrift is central to Jones's thinking and mission.

[My father gave] me a penny and a nickel—the penny, according to established custom, to be spent for candy or chewing gum, while the nickel was to go into the iron pig on the shelf at home to be used at some distant day when I might be starting out for college, or when I might want to be an expressman and buy a big span of Missouri mules.
LAURENCE C. JONES, PINEY WOODS AND ITS STORY, 1922

. . . .

His childhood hero, Robinson Crusoe, had made a deep impression because he had "made things to suite his needs" and in imitation of him the boy had built many back-yard coops and shelters, raised

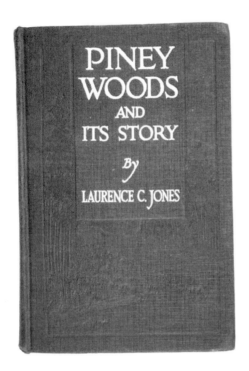

Published 1922

chickens and pigeons, and made a garden. In Iowa he had been fascinated by the accent on thrifty farming and the many agricultural developments.

THE LITTLE PROFESSOR OF PINEY WOODS

. . . .

It was clear that the basis of operation [for my work as an educator] must be in the kitchen, the household, the garden, and the farm. So I talked diversified farming and around the fireside at night we figured out the cost of raising ten-cent cotton and buying fifteen-cent bacon, and ninety-cent corn from the meat-houses and corn-cribs of the North. I showed the folly of saving the worst land for the corn crop, from which they must derive their living, and of going to the crib in the spring and picking up anything left for seed

corn, instead of selecting their seed in the field . . . Meanwhile in the homes I told the women about sanitary cooking and whitewash, and sometimes I applied the whitewash myself.

JONES, PINEY WOODS AND ITS STORY

. . . .

It appears that seed corn interests people who are interested in thrift. For example, see (above) the excerpt from Daniel Defoe's *Robinson Crusoe* regarding the issue of seed corn.

. . . he started out over the back-country trails, going from cabin to cabin, country church to services held under groves—sometimes on muleback, sometimes by oxcart, more often afoot, walking eighteen and twenty miles a day, carrying

his message of better living, better corn, better stock, better poultry, and the need for a school that would teach these things.

THE LITTLE PROFESSOR OF PINEY WOODS

. . . .

We closed the [first] year free of debt and had an average of eighty-five students. We taught common English branches and sewing, basketry, broom-making, and woodwork. There was also a beginning in flower gardening. Our closing exercises consisted of essays on housekeeping, cooking, sewing, gardening, and manual training.

. . . Not any of us had drawn salaries, but we received a living and had the satisfaction of knowing that we had tried to do a little good.

JONES, PINEY WOODS AND ITS STORY

. . . .

The things that impressed me most while there were:
1. *His [Jones'] speeches on honesty, high morals, dependability, initiative and industry.*
2. *The zest and industrial effort put into the building of the school by him and Mrs. Jones.*
3. *A speech made by him at a business club meeting in Jackson, and quoted by the* Daily News: *"Not only is he idle who does nothing, but he is also idle who could be better employed."*

DR. J. R. OTIS, PRESIDENT OF ALCORN A & M COLLEGE IN ALCORN, MISSISSIPPI, RECALLING THE NINE MONTHS HE SPENT AT PINEY WOODS DURING THE SCHOOL YEAR 1915–16

So many times since my visit I have thought of how Christ took those "five loaves and two fishes" and fed the hungry, tired multitude, for beginning as you did out there under that famous little cedar tree with no money and only a few pupils, you are now bringing the knowledge of truth which sets men free and feeding the "bread of life" to hundreds . . .

CHARLES E. BARKER, LETTER TO LAURENCE JONES, MAY 10, 1916

. . . .

It is hoped that in all [Piney Woods students] there may be found some reflection of the simple virtues, thrift, honesty, and diligence . . .

JONES, THE SPIRIT OF PINEY WOODS, 1931

. . . .

When we speak of successful men let us not forget a little colored man, who the members of his race term as "Fesser," counselor, and guide. To have brought thrift and purpose into a hidden corner of the Black Belt, to have set Negroes raising their own corn, raising their own pigs, putting windows and floors into their cabins and sacrificing to send their children to learn books and farms and trades . . . is no mean accomplishment for any man.

THE TIMES REPUBLICAN, MARSHALLTOWN, IOWA, 1930S

To be good, to do good, and to make some money.

MOTTO OF THE ASA TURNER SOCIETY, A STUDENT CLUB
AT THE PINEY WOODS SCHOOL

. . . .

Taking what you have and making what you need.

THEME OF THE 1954 GRADUATION EXERCISES AT PINEY
WOODS

. . . .

*. . . to make two blades of grass grow where only
one grew before . . .*

JONES, REFLECTING ON "THE DESIRE OF HIS HEART"

. . . .

*. . . they [my parents] had always indoctrinated in
us that "we want you to grow up and be somebody."
We had a Thrift Club at school where we were
encouraged to save. Each of us had banks and we*
would take them to the bank to open them to put
money in our savings account. This encouraged
us to save throughout the elementary grades. Our
parents signed for us to participate. We met once a
week after having saved up our pennies throughout
the week. Records were kept of all deposits.

*. . . if you work hard, know how to be punctual,
how to make time, you will make it particularly
with the three B's—behave, be there, and be clean.
Sayings such as this by our parents and community
people were pounded into us.*

JAMES S. WADE, BORN ABOUT 1918 IN RURAL WEST
VIRGINIA, WHO IN 1974 SUCCEEDED DR. LAURENCE C.
JONES AS PRESIDENT OF THE PINEY WOODS SCHOOL

. . . .

Piney Woods School, $85
Martha Berry Schools, $152

CHARITABLE GIFTS FROM IOWA CHAPTERS OF THE
DAUGHTERS OF THE AMERICAN REVOLUTION, 1918

36. George Never Leaves Bedford Falls

FRANK CAPRA

Through the grammar school years I sold papers—mornings, evenings, and Sundays. I gave every penny to Mama . . . At college, I still managed to pay my own way and contribute several hundred dollars a year to my family.

FRANK CAPRA'S MEMOIRS

. . . .

FRANK CAPRA is my favorite film director. And Capra's 1946 movie, *It's a Wonderful Life*, is by far the best movie that anyone has ever made about thrift. Not only the best, but also the most nuanced, appreciative, and well-rounded. It contains tragedy and inner conflict as well as hope and resolution. Nearly every aspect and every scene of the film—the Building and Loan helping ordinary people in Bedford Falls gain financial independence and own their own homes; George's unsought-after fate of giving up his dream of world travel and expansive living, along with Mary's spur-of-the-moment decision to give away their honeymoon money ("How much do you need?") in order to save the Building and Loan during the Great Depression; George's and (mostly) Mary's decision to move into and conserve and restore the decaying old Granville home; the eerie dystopia of Pottersville, in which libraries and other thrift organizations such as the Building and Loan have been supplanted by pawn shops, saloons, and gambling establishments (Does any of that sound familiar?); and many others besides—are deeply connected to the theme of thrift. It's almost as if Capra told himself, "I'm going to make an entire movie about, and in favor of, thrift." And to top it all off—for Capra clearly understood that the word "thrift" in the 1940s was often abused and misunderstood—it's only the movie's villain, Mr. Potter, who actually utters the word "thrift!" Perfect.

Capra confected *It's a Wonderful Life* from a slender short story—really not much more than an extended Christmas card greeting—written by Philip Van Doren Stern called "The Greatest Gift." In Stern's version, by the way, George works at a commercial bank, not a building and loan, and Mary is a spendthrift. It's clear that Capra did not inherit what is arguably the movie's core theme, the theme of thrift, from the writer. Capra put in that part himself.

Frank Capra was born in Sicily, Italy, on May 18, 1897. He died in California on September 3, 1991.

POTTER
Have you put any real pressure on those people of yours to pay those mortgages?

PETER BAILEY
Times are bad, Mr. Potter. A lot of these people are out of work.

POTTER
Then foreclose!

PETER BAILEY
I can't do that. These families have children.

MEDIUM CLOSE SHOT—Potter and Peter Bailey.

GEORGE
Pop!

POTTER
They're not my children.

PETER BAILEY
But they're somebody's children.

POTTER
Are you running a business or a charity ward?

PETER BAILEY
Well, all right . . .

POTTER (interrupting)
Not with my money!

CLOSE SHOT—Potter and Peter Bailey.

PETER BAILEY
Mr. Potter, what makes you such a hard-skulled character? You have no family, no children. You can't begin to spend all the money you've got.

POTTER
So I suppose I should give it to miserable failures like you and that idiot brother of yours to spend for me.

George cannot listen any longer to such libel about his father. He comes around in front of the desk.

GEORGE
He's not a failure! You can't say that about my father!

* * * * *

PETER BAILEY
Of course, it's just a hope, but you wouldn't consider coming back to the Building and Loan, would you? . . .

GEORGE
Oh, now, Pop, I couldn't. I couldn't face being cooped up for the rest of my life in a shabby little office.

He stops, realizing that he has hurt his father.

Oh, I'm sorry, Pop. I didn't mean that remark, but this business of nickels and dimes and spending all your life trying to figure out how to save three cents on a length of pipe . . . I'd go crazy. I want to do something big and something important.

PETER BAILEY *(quietly)*
You know, George, I feel that in a small way we are doing something important. Satisfying a fundamental urge. It's deep in the race for a man to want his own roof and walls and fireplace, and we're helping him get those things in our shabby little office.

GEORGE *(unhappily)*
I know, Dad. I wish I felt . . . But I've been hoarding pennies like a miser in order to . . . Most of my friends have already finished college. I just feel like if I don't get away, I'd bust.

* * * * *

POTTER
You see, if you shoot pool with some employee here, you can come and borrow money. What does that get us? A discontented, lazy rabble instead of a thrifty working class. And all because a few starry-eyed dreamers like Peter Bailey stir them up and fill their heads with a lot of impossible ideas. Now, I say . . .

George puts down his coat and comes around to the table, incensed by what Potter is saying about his father.

GEORGE
Just a minute, just a minute. Now, hold on, Mr. Potter. You're right when you say my father was no

business man. I know that. Why he ever started this cheap, penny-ante Building and Loan, I'll never know. But neither you nor anybody else can say anything against his character, because his whole life was . . . Why, in the twenty-five years since he and Uncle Billy started this thing, he never once thought of himself. Isn't that right, Uncle Billy? He didn't save enough money to send Harry to school, let alone me. But he did help a few people get out of your slums, Mr. Potter. And what's wrong with that? Why . . . Here, you're all businessmen here. Doesn't it make them better citizens? Doesn't it make them better customers? You . . . you said . . . What'd you say just a minute ago? . . . They had to wait and save their money before they even ought to think of a decent home. Wait! Wait for what? Until their children grow up and leave them? Until they're so old and broken-down that they . . . Do you know how long it takes a working man to save five thousand dollars? Just remember this, Mr. Potter, that this rabble you're talking about . . . they do most of the working and paying and living and dying in this community. Well, is it too much to have them work and pay and live and die in a couple of decent rooms and a bath? Anyway, my father didn't think so. People were human beings to him, but to you, a warped, frustrated old man, they're cattle. Well, in my book he died a much richer man than you'll ever be!

* * * * *

ERNIE *[the cab driver]*
By the way, where are you two going on this here honeymoon?

GEORGE

*Where are we going? (takes out a fat roll of bills)
Look at this. There's the kitty, Ernie. Here, come
on, count it, Mary. [It's $2,000 dollars.]*

MARY

*I feel like a bootlegger's wife. (holding up the
money) Look!*

GEORGE

*You know what we're going to do? We're going to
shoot the works. A whole week in New York. A
whole week in Bermuda. The highest hotels—the
oldest champagne—the richest caviar—the hottest
music, and the prettiest wife! . . .*

The cab passes the bank, and Ernie sees a crowd
of people around the door. He stops the cab.

LONG SHOT—scurrying people under
umbrellas, swarming around the bank doors.
Panic is in the air. Attendants are trying to close
down. Several people come running past the cab.

INTERIOR CAB

CLOSE SHOT—George, Mary, and Ernie.

ERNIE

*Don't look now, but there's something funny going
on over there at the bank, George, I've never really
seen one, but that's got all the earmarks of a run.*

* * * * *

GEORGE

*. . . Can't you understand what's happening here?
Don't you see what's happening? Potter isn't selling.
Potter's buying! And why? Because we're panicky
and he's not. That's why. He's picking up some
bargains. Now, we can get through this thing all
right. We've got to stick together, though. We've got
to have faith in each other.*

MRS. THOMPSON

*But my husband hasn't worked in over a year, and
I need money.*

WOMAN

How am I going to live until the bank opens?

MAN

I got doctor bills to pay.

MAN

I need cash.

MAN

Can't feed my kids on faith.

During this scene Mary has come up behind
the counter. Suddenly, as the people once more
start moving toward the door, she holds up a
roll of bills [the $2,000 they had saved for their
honeymoon] and calls out:

MARY

How much do you need?

George jumps over the counter and takes the money from Mary.

GEORGE
Hey! I got two thousand dollars! Here's two thousand dollars. This'll tide us over until the bank reopen. (to Tom) All right, Tom, how much do you need?

* * * * *

CLOSE SHOTS—Mary is busy hanging wallpaper and painting the old place.

JOSEPH'S VOICE
Day after day she worked away remaking the old Granville house into a home.

MONTAGE SEQUENCE
Over the following SERIES OF SHOTS we hear the voices of Joseph and Clarence in Heaven.

JOSEPH'S VOICE
Now, you've probably already guessed that George never leaves Bedford Falls.

CLARENCE'S VOICE
No! . . .

* * * * *

HARRY (cont'd) Good idea, Ernie. A toast . . . to my big brother, George. The richest man in town!
THE MOVIE *IT'S A WONDERFUL LIFE*, 1946

. . . .

. . . a figment of simple Pollyanna platitudes . . . NEW YORK TIMES

. . . convince movie audiences that American life is exactly like the Saturday Evening Post covers of Norman Rockwell . . . THE NEW REPUBLIC

. . . so mincing as to border on baby talk . . . THE NEW YORKER
REVIEWS OF *IT'S A WONDERFUL LIFE*

. . . .

But I didn't give a film-clip whether critics hailed or booted Wonderful Life. *I thought it was the greatest film I ever made . . . It wasn't made for the oh-so-bored critics, or the oh-so-jaded literati. It was my kind of film for my kind of people . . .*
FRANK CAPRA, *THE NAME ABOVE THE TITLE*

PART FOUR

Institutions

For better or worse, individuals really do share their thoughts and they do to some extent harmonize their preferences, and they have no other way to make the big decisions except within the scope of institutions they build.

THE ANTHROPOLOGIST MARY DOUGLAS,
HOW INSTITUTIONS THINK

37. Thrift Boxes

SOME THRIFT INSTITUTIONS are quite complex. But let's start with a simple idea: take some thrift, put it in a box, and call it a thrift box. Thrift boxes may be the oldest and simplest institutional expression of the thrift idea in English-speaking societies.

. . . the thrift-box of St. Cuthbert.

A SMALL, LOCKED BOX WITH A NARROW SLIT IN THE LID, CONTAINING THE INSCRIPTION "PRAY REMEMBER THE POOR," LOCATED IN THE FERETORY OF THE SHRINE OF ST. CUTHBERT, IN DURHAM, ENGLAND, FROM AT LEAST AS EARLY AS 1378 TO ABOUT 1514

· · · ·

In the British Museum are specimens of "Thrift Boxes," small and wide bottles with imitation stoppers, from three to four inches in height, made of thin clay, the upper part covered with green glaze. On one side is a slit for the introduction of money . . .
ALL THE YEAR ROUND, 1887

· · · ·

Thrif or Thrift-box: an earthen pot or box in which money is kept by young persons.
A GLOSSARY OF NORTH COUNTRY WORDS, 1825

[In] the Barber Shops . . . a thrift-box, as it is called, is put by the Apprentice boys against the wall, and every customer according to his inclinations puts in something . . .
THE HISTORY OF RICHMOND IN THE COUNTY OF YORK, 1814

· · · ·

The Thrift Box

TITLE OF A PAMPHLET ON THE BEST WAYS TO ACHIEVE "HEALTH, WEALTH, AND COMFORT" FOR TEXTILE WORKERS AND OWNERS, ON THE ADVANTAGES OF "INSTITUTION [FRIENDLY] SOCIETIES," AND ON MORAL ADVICE FOR THE YOUNG AND FOR PARISHIONERS, ABOUT 1804

· · · ·

They that know how to mend, and are not too proud to wear old clothing at work, nor too slothful to keep them well washed, shall the longer deny misorder to their habiliments, and likewise have shillings a plenty for the greengrocer, as the saying goes, with pennies to spare for the thrift-box.
WHEN MAYFLOWERS BLOSSOM, A 1914 HISTORICAL NOVEL OF EARLY AMERICA

When you were a girl, had you a thrift-box? . . . Some thrift-boxes are made of pot, and must be broken in order to reach the treasure. Some thrift-boxes are so incorrectly constructed that pence will slip out almost as easily as slip in. The best thrift-boxes are those which contain the treasure under lock and key, especially if the key be held by one who is loving and wise.

A BOOK OF MORAL ADVICE FOR MAIDSERVANTS, 1872

· · · ·

Thrift-boxes of various shapes, sizes, and materials, are employed by children, taught by their elders to save their little spare money . . . It is not, however, of that sort of thrift-box that we would now think. The thrift-boxes of which we now chiefly write are alive!

As people grow older, if of a saving disposition, the thrift-box assumes a somewhat different form. A working man takes a share in a Building Society. Henceforth that is to be his thrift-box . . .

Many persons . . . treat their children as their thrift-boxes. All that they can acquire is employed for the benefit of these children. Money is not all that they lavish on their children, but that, so far as they can obtain it, is freely used for their benefit . . . the children form the thrift-box into which mother and father place, from day to day, all the good things they can secure . . . Very lamentable is it when such a thrift-box is missing when most needed.

"THE MISSING THRIFT-BOX (KINDNESS TO PARENTS)," *THE WESLEYAN SUNDAY-SCHOOL MAGAZINE*, 1872

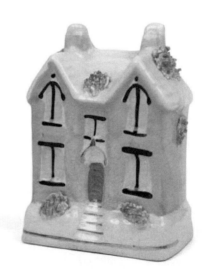

There was at that time an excellent system of teaching young folks the value of thrift. This consisted in saving for some purpose or another the Saturday's penny—one penny being our weekly allowance of pocket-money. The feats we could perform in the way of procuring toys, picture-books, or the materials for constructing flying kites, would amaze the youngsters of the present day, who are generally spoiled by extravagance. And yet we obtained far more pleasure from our purchases. We had in my time "penny pigs," or thrift boxes. They were made in a vase form, of brown glazed earthenware, the only entrance to which was a slit—enough to give entrance to a penny. When the Saturday's penny was not required for any immediate purposes, it was dropped through the slit, and remained there until the box was full. The maximum of pennies it could contain was

about forty-eight. When that was accomplished, the penny pig was broken with a hammer, and its rich contents flowed forth. The breaking of the pig was quite an event. The fine fat old George the Third penny pieces looked thoroughly substantial in our eyes. And then there was the spending of the money—for some long-looked-for toy, or pencils, or book, or painting materials.

JAMES NASMYTH, "MY SCHOOL-DAYS," 1883

. . . .

. . . he and his twin brother became joint owners of a "pinner pig," into which were consigned their pennies. The "pig" on being first opened produced as much money as bought a "pinch back" watch, which he and his brother wore alternately—a week each time. They then discovered that putting

their savings into the Paisley Savings Bank was a more profitable investment that the "pinner pig," for when they were both ready to go to school at Edinburgh they found that each had 10 pounds saved to help the expenses of their education.

SHERIFF LUDOVIC MAIR OF AIRDRIE, SCOTLAND— DESCRIBED BY A NEIGHBOR AS "WELL KNOWN AS A MAN OF THRIFT; AT ANY RATE, HE KNEW HOW TO SAVE A PENNY"—RECALLING HIS AND HIS TWIN BROTHER'S BOYHOODS IN COMMENTS DELIVERED AT THE JUBILEE CELEBRATION OF THE SAVINGS BANK OF AIRDRIE, JANUARY 7, 1886

. . . .

Although I have written a book about "Thrift" when a man, I was not at all thrifty when a boy. We children all had penny-pigs, or thrift boxes, to implant the idea of saving spare money. I thought the principal use of money was to be spent. I occasionally put a few pennies into the slit, but I soon worked them out again by means of a table knife. My brother Jack filled his to the top, and when it was quite filled the pig had to be broken to get out the contents. Mine was usually empty. I suppose years and discretion brought the idea of "Thrift," but I continued to spend money pretty freely.

THE AUTOBIOGRAPHY OF SAMUEL SMILES, 1905

. . . .

Has no child ever saved money in a money-box? . . . Never, after the first few days of saving, did I look on a money-box as anything but an enemy to

be out-witted and, if necessary, to be destroyed . . . It would have seemed to me a kind of meanness to deny my stomach a bar of chocolate or a box of sherbert merely in order that at some future date I might be prosperous . . . The stomach is human, sensitive, and warm. The pocket is inhuman, unfeeling, and cold. It is better that the pocket should serve the stomach than the stomach should serve the pocket. Every child who has ever broken into its own money-box knows this . . . The only money-box consonant with virtue is a box out of which one can get money when one wants it.

ROBERT LYND, *THE MONEY-BOX*, 1925

. . . .

The American [savings] banks first thought of the idea of issuing bank money-boxes of a solid metal type of which the keys would be kept at the bank. The innovation caught on and news of this development was passed on in 1905 to Mr. John Sinclair, Chairman of the Belfast Savings Bank . . . Mr. Sinclair took up the idea with enthusiasm . . . The first of these [in Britain] were issued to depositors on 1 January 1906, and the whole issue was exhausted in about six months . . . By 1909 twenty-one Trustee Savings Banks were issuing home safes. In 1911 the Post Office Savings Bank followed suit . . . The more attractive-looking home safes of the "book" and "recording" type issued within more recent years have helped to increase the popularity of these adjuncts to thrift.

H. OLIVER HORNE, *A HISTORY OF SAVINGS BANKS*, 1947

I send you my money-box. It will be safer for you and better for me, for father is always trying to open it with a sardine-tin knife.

LETTER FROM A BOY TO THE MANAGER OF A SAVINGS BANK, EARLY 1900S

. . . .

The money-box now works for the Saving Bank because it collects small coins with the intention of dropping, sooner or later, at the Savings Bank window the small treasure collected in order to place it in safety and give it a chance to increase there. In this way through this novel function and under the modern form of a metallic box, the key of which remains in the hands of the Savings Bank, the money box has in recent years enjoyed a new life and an even greater diffusion. Thousands of money-boxes are distributed by the Savings Banks themselves and they reign in the families as a symbol of thrift, instrument of education and a harbinger of fortunes.

"THE MONEY-BOX IN HISTORY AND IN ETHNOGRAPHY," *WORLD THRIFT*, THE JOURNAL OF THE INTERNATIONAL THRIFT INSTITUTE, 1928

. . . .

. . . the introduction of the Home Safe has completed a marvelously efficient system of thrift. There are of these useful and modest articles 10,632 in circulation in connection with the Airdrie Savings Bank alone, and the numbers increase continually.

A CENTURY OF THRIFT, REPORTING ON THE AIRDRIE SAVINGS BANK OF SCOTLAND, 1935

1. That thrift is essential to prosperity, perpetuity, and power. That this vigorous growth, as of a plant, we may attain as an association, if we will, and this should be our aim.

2. That, therefore, our aim should be to establish the association on a firm and flourishing financial basis. "Thrift is the best means of thriving," is a significant saying; and the surest sign of an association's permanency and progressiveness is a thrift-box.

KENDRICK C. HILL, SECRETARY-TREASURER OF THE NEW YORK STATE STENOGRAPHERS' ASSOCIATION, PRESENTING THE FIRST TWO OF "A SCORE OF SUGGESTIONS" TO THE ASSOCIATION'S TWENTIETH ANNUAL MEETING, AUGUST 22–23, 1895

38. Gardens

THERE'S SOMETHING about the thrift ethic that likes a garden. If a core metaphor for thrift is making two blades of grass grow where only one had grown before, then planting and growing your flowers, or raising your vegetables, either on your own or cooperatively, takes us to the very heart of the thrift ideal. Find a thrift person and, more likely than not, you are also looking at a garden person. Beautiful gardens are institutions of thrift.

Robinson Crusoe "by the dint of his thrift" famously cultivated a garden on his island.

Two centuries later in the United Sates, the thrift ethic was helping to inform and inspire organizations such as the School Garden Association of America and the Women's National Farm and Garden Association. So, by all means put your spare coins in a thrift box. But also, go outdoors and grow something!

There is nothing better fitted [than gardening] for the healthy development of children. It affords opportunity for spontaneous activity in the open air, and possibilities for acquiring a fund of interesting and related information; it engenders habits of thrift and economy; develops individual responsibility, and respect for the rights of others;
requires regularity, punctuality, and constancy of purpose.
LOUISE KLEIN MILLER, *CHILDREN'S GARDENS FOR SCHOOL AND HOME*, 1904

. . . .

The first school garden was established, in 1891, at the George Putnam School, Roxbury Massachusetts . . . Probably some fifty of the larger cities [today] are equipped with school gardens . . .
HAROLD WALDSTEIN FOGHT, *THE AMERICAN RURAL SCHOOL*, 1910

. . . .

The school garden should be a sort of outdoor laboratory, a place for the outdoor study of growing plants, soil, insects, weeds, etc., and for the application of the facts learned in in-door nature study . . . It can be made one of the best means to develop in the pupils thrift and responsibility, gentleness, and a love for the beautiful and for growing things.
FREDERICK L. HOLTZ, *NATURE-STUDY*, 1908

The first activities of the [American Society for Thrift] were the encouragement of school gardening, a movement which later became one of the great factors of our war-time thrift.

S. W. STRAUS, RECALLING THE FORMATION IN 1913 OF THE AMERICAN SOCIETY FOR THRIFT, *HISTORY OF THE THRIFT MOVEMENT IN AMERICA*

. . . .

Your food bill can be decreased appreciably, the vegetables you grow will be richer in food values and will taste better, much grocery shopping time can be saved, and you will have the assurance of luscious home-canned foods during the winter when you may not be able to buy as many vegetables as you want and need. The exercise will be good for you, and you will really be helping solve our national food problem.

"VICTORY GARDENING PAYS BIG DIVIDENDS," *HOME LIFE*, A MONTHLY PUBLICATION OF THE NILES (MICHIGAN) FEDERAL SAVINGS AND LOAN ASSOCIATION, APRIL 1945

. . . .

Thrift is not only a matter of saving and of properly using the various products, but it is a matter of production as well . . . It is estimated the average village, town, and city family spends $138 per year

for vegetables. If one-fourth of the 12,000,000 such families could produce half of what they use by having a home garden, find the total amount thus produced.

"PROBLEMS OF THRIFT AND ECONOMY," *JUNIOR HIGH SCHOOL MATHEMATICS* (A SCHOOL TEXTBOOK), 1922

. . . .

When one wanders through English gardens and feels all their delight, one cannot but be convinced that common-sense and thrift are the roots on which the beauty has grown and thrived.

R. CLIPSTON STURGIS, "ENGLISH GARDENS," 1902

. . . .

. . . she always meant to have thrift, honesty and abundance in her garden.

ALICE M. RATHBONE, "OUR HARDY FLOWERS," 1903

. . . .

Our motto was, and is, "Thrift and Beauty."

MRS. FRANCIS KING, *PAGES FROM A GARDEN NOTE-BOOK*, DESCRIBING THE PHILADELPHIA BRANCH OF THE WOMEN'S NATIONAL FARM AND GARDEN ASSOCIATION, 1921

39. Friendly and Fraternal Societies

AMONG WAGE EARNERS and their families in the English-speaking world, the first popular economic institution explicitly devoted to thrift was the friendly society. In these organizations, for the first time, the philosophy of thrift became embodied in a complex social institution, created by and for people of modest means.

When I was a graduate student in England studying history in the late 1970s, I wrote my thesis on the Friendly Society of Operative Cabinet Makers, which was founded in Liverpool in 1833. This organization combined the activities of a trade union—such as bargaining with employers for fairer wages and supporting members who went out on strike—with a wide range of cooperative thrift schemes, including sickness, burial, and retirement ("supperannuation") benefits, insurance for tools, and what the men called "tramping" benefits, which was money for unemployed members who had to travel to other places in search of work.

These organizations were democratic, run by the men themselves and paid for by money from their (meager) wages. They combined commonsense thrift with high idealism, even a sense of brotherhood. These men would have had no trouble understanding that the root of thrift is "thrive." I spent many hours in a dusty basement full of trade union records stored in cardboard boxes, reading their annual reports and other copious records, and I came to respect them enormously.

We have mostly forgotten the names of these men, but let us now praise friendly societies.

Friendly Societies are associations formed for promoting the mutual advantage of their members and are based upon the principle that the contributions of the members paid into one common fund is the most effective method of guaranteeing such benefits as these societies insure to their members in times of sickness or distress or at the period of death when such benefits are required.

The good the Friendly Societies are doing and have done in the country are simply incalculable. They teach Thrift. They assist to provide for the proverbial Rainy Day . . . They do more, they cultivate a friendly feeling among the members and become means of interchange of millions of kindly acts.

They do still more. They teach Self Help and Self Government. They were and are instituted by workmen who know the requirements and wants of workmen.

RICHARDSON CAMPBELL OF THE INDEPENDENT ORDER
OF RECHABITES (A FRIENDLY SOCIETY), DISCUSSING
FRIENDLY SOCIETIES IN BRITAIN

The Archbishop of York preaching at Sheffield yesterday, before members of the Friendly Societies of the town, said that thrift had something more in it than just this world's business. Thrift was a branch of justice, and justice was a part of Christian love. It was not a question of a mere worldly nature. They were trying to alter the looser and less careful customs of the world by introducing providence and care for the future. So far from this being alien to religion, it was a fair first step to a well-ordered life according to the law of God.

"THE ARCHBISHOP OF YORK ON THRIFT," *THE TIMES,* LONDON, JANUARY 29, 1883

. . . .

Among various forms of public or social service to which many West Ham residents devoted their leisure, especially before the First World War, was the promotion of temperance, thrift, or mutual aid among a population living in conditions which made it difficult to cultivate such habits. Before the First World War there were some 75 temperance societies and 100 friendly societies in the borough.

A HISTORY OF THE COUNTY OF ESSEX

. . . .

The parish was well supplied with provident societies from about 1850: a coal club, and later a provident fund and a clothing club. As a result the vicar was able to claim in 1893 that his parishioners were relatively well off: there was overtime work

throughout the summer, most of the old people had savings, thrift was generally practised, and there was no begging.

A HISTORY OF THE COUNTY OF SUSSEX

. . . .

In 1890, there were approximately 26,000 registered friendly societies in Great Britain.

Friendly societies, or organizations closely resembling them, also emerged as robust institutions in other places besides Great Britain, especially Belgium, France, Holland, Germany, and Spain, as well, of course, as in many of Britain's colonial possessions. In the United States, these types of institutions, emerging mostly in the latter decades of the nineteenth century, tended to be called fraternal associations, carrying names such as the Oddfellows, the Maccabees, and the Masons.

The fraternal beneficial societies are in truth the societies of the people. They are born of economy, thrift, and fraternal love.

GEORGE W. WALTS, COMMISSIONER OF THE CALIFORNIA BUREAU OF LABOR STATISTICS, 1890

. . . .

There is, however, more notably in the United States than elsewhere, a highly successful form of cooperative insurance, more particularly that conducted by the so-called mutual beneficiary secret fraternities. This form of protection of the families

PROVIDENT AND INDUSTRIAL INSTITUTIONS

BEING RECORDS AND HISTORICAL SKETCHES OF VARIOUS THRIFT
ASSOCIATIONS, INCLUDING THE SOCIAL, RELIGIOUS, MERCHANT
AND CRAFT GUILDS OF THE PAST, THE INCORPORATED
TRADES NOW EXISTING, AND ALSO MARINE, FIRE AND
LIFE INSURANCE COMPANIES, TRADE UNIONS,
BANKS, BUILDING, CO-OPERATIVE, AND
FRIENDLY SOCIETIES, WITH NOTES ON
THEIR SPECIAL IDEALS AND
METHODS OF OPERATION

BY
RICHARDSON CAMPBELL
(Past High Secretary of the Independent Order of Rechabites)

PUBLISHED BY THE BOARD OF DIRECTORS,
RECHABITE BUILDINGS, MANCHESTER

RICHARDSON CAMPBELL

Published about 1926

of members of these organizations constitutes
cooperation in the broadest sense of the word . . .
ALBERT C. STEVENS, "FRATERNAL INSURANCE," 1900

. . . .

The reach of these societies by the early years of the twentieth century was astonishingly broad. An estimated one-third of the adult males in the United States were members of fraternal societies in 1910.[1] A survey of Chicago wage earners in 1919 found that about 40 percent carried insurance through their fraternal societies.[2]

Ancient Order of Hiberians
Ancient Order of United Workmen
Fraternal Order of Eagles
Grand United Order of Galilean Fisherman
Independent Order of Rechabites
International Order of Twelve Knights and
  Daughters of Tabor
Knights and Ladies of Security
Knights of Sobriety, Fidelity and Integrity
Ladies Catholic Benevolent Association
Loyal Order of the Moose
Modern Woodmen of America
Mosaic Templars

Mystic Workers of the World

Nobles of the Mystic Shrine

Order of the Eastern Star

Order of Knights of Pythias

Patriotic and Protective Order of Stags

Order of the Patrons of Husbandry

Order Sons of Italy in America

Thrivent Financial for Lutherans

Tribe of Ben Hur

SOME OF THE APPROXIMATELY SIX HUNDRED U.S.
FRATERNAL SOCIETIES, EARLY TWENTIETH CENTURY

. . . .

*One by one, the household articles found their way
to the pawnbroker or the second hand man. What
of the future now?*

FROM A SLIDE SHOW THAT WAS PART OF THE INITIATION
CEREMONY FOR THE LADIES OF THE MACCABEES,
WARNING MEMBERS OF WHAT CAN HAPPEN IF THEY DO
NOT JOIN TOGETHER FOR MUTUAL PROTECTION, 1910

. . . .

*Our Order is proud to feel that its members
have exercised thrift in the securing of protection
[insurance] for their homes in the best Order on
earth.*

LADIES REVIEW, THE JOURNAL OF THE LADIES OF THE
MACCABEES, JANUARY 1916

In 1916, the Ladies of the Maccabees also endorsed the "noble" efforts of the American Society for Thrift, led by S. W. Straus.

To discipline the young, to train them to practice of thrift and economy, and to give lessons early in the business methods of life . . .

THE PURPOSE OF THE "ROSEBUD DEPARTMENT," THE
CHILDREN'S DIVISION OF THE UNITED ORDER OF TRUE
REFORMERS, AN AFRICAN AMERICAN FRATERNAL SOCIETY
LED BY THE REV. WILLIAM WASHINGTON BROWNE, 1885

. . . .

William Washington Browne was born a slave on a plantation in Habersham County, Georgia, in 1849. He escaped from slavery and served in the Union Army during the Civil War. He taught after the war in a freedman's school in Georgia. He became a Methodist pastor in 1876, and was active in the temperance movement. In 1881, he became the leader of the United Order of True Reformers, an African American temperance society based in Richmond, Virginia. Under his leadership, and focusing on issues of economic cooperation and thrift, the True Reformers grew rapidly across the Upper South and in northern cities. Cooperative insurance was an important part of the True Reformers' program—the group became the nation's first African American society to provide broad life insurance (that is, more than burial insurance) to its members. William Washington Browne died of cancer at the age of forty-eight on December 21, 1897.

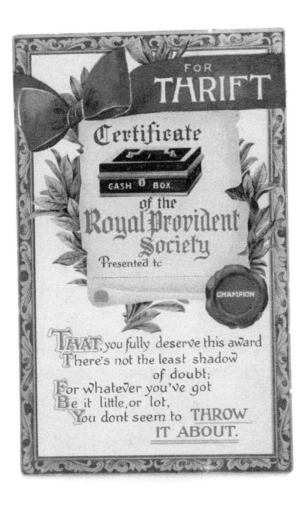

The True Reformers' overall aim was to pool members' resources and then work together cooperatively to buy land and build economic assets. In 1889, the society under Browne's leadership founded the True Reformers Savings Bank, located in Richmond—in part in order to avoid entrusting the Order's funds to white-run financial institutions that did not, to speak with moderation, wish the African American community well. Between the early 1880s and 1910, the True Reformers also founded and operated a building and loan association, a hotel (the Reformer Hotel, located at 900 North Sixth Street in Rich-

mond), a four-story office building, a real-estate department, a subscriber-based newspaper (*The Reformer*), a printing office, several wholesale and retail stores (the Mercantile and Industrial Association), a retirement home (the Old Folks Home), a juvenile department enrolling as of 1900 children from ages three to fourteen (the Rosebud Department), and a cooperative residential community (Browneville). In 1907, W. E. B. DuBois reportedly called the True Reformers "probably the most remarkable Negro organization in the country."[3]

40. Mutual Savings Banks

To UNDERSTAND the role of savings banks as a driver of social change and both a shaper and reflection of key cultural values, particularly during the nineteenth century, let's begin with three powerful statements—the first, from a local savings bank leader, noting the intellectual origins of the savings bank movement; the second, from a scholar, describing that movement's remarkable success over the course of the nineteenth century in promoting its core idea; and the third, from a famous writer, vigorously denouncing that same idea.

. . . the idea of making the advantages of saving and investment available to all people, as well as the dream of making the ownership of homes open to all, sprang from the intellectual revolution achieved by the great liberal philosophers and writers of the 18th century . . . the whole force and significance of our thrift movement derives from this revolution in thought . . .

LEVI P. SMITH, BURLINGTON SAVINGS BANK, 1952

· · · ·

The promotion of thrift, at the end of the 18th century an experiment by a few far-seeking individuals, was by the 20th century almost

universally adopted, and was regarded practically as an adjunct to the institutions of every civilized community.

ENCYCLOPAEDIA BRITANNICA, 11TH EDITION, 1911

· · · ·

He was a mere sign, a portent. There was nothing in him. Just about that time the word Thrift was to the fore. You know the power of words. We pass through periods dominated by this or that word—it may be development, or it may be competition, or education, or purity or efficiency or even sanctity. It is the word of the time. Well just then it was the word Thrift which was out in the streets walking arm in arm with righteousness, the inseparable companion and backer up of all such national catch-words, looking everybody in the eye as it were. The very drabs of the pavement, poor things, didn't escape the fascination . . . However! . . . Well the greatest portion of the press were screeching in all possible tones, like a confounded company of parrots instructed by some devil with a taste for practical jokes, that the financier de Barral was helping the great moral evolution of our character towards the newly-discovered virtue of Thrift. He was helping it by all these great establishments of his, which made the moral merits of Thrift manifest to the most

A TYPICAL SAVINGS-BANK—A GREAT PROMOTER OF THRIFT

From *Stories of Thrift for Young Americans*, 1915

callous hearts, simply by promising to pay ten per cent interest on all deposits. And you didn't want necessarily to belong to the well-to-do classes in order to participate in the advantages of virtue. If you had but a spare sixpence in the world and went and gave it to de Barral it was Thrift! It's quite likely that he himself believed it. He must have. It's inconceivable that he alone should stand out against the infatuation of the whole world.

JOSEPH CONRAD, *CHANCE*, 1913

What was the main nineteenth-century institutional result of that eighteenth-century revolution in thought? What single type of organization, more than any other, transformed the promotion of thrift from "an experiment by a few far-seeking individuals" in 1800 to an idea "almost universally adopted" by 1900? What, concretely, was inspiring such ire and ridicule from Joseph Conrad? The answer in all three cases is: the rise of the savings bank and of the savings bank idea.

Start a Home Fund

By purchasing shares in the Roger Conant Co-operative Bank.
Any number of shares from one to 'twenty-five, at $1 per share a month.

NEW SHARES ON SALE MAY 9TH, OR MAY BE RESERVED ON APPLICATION BY MAIL OR AT THE BANK.

Roger Conant Co-operative Bank

39 CHURCH STREET, SALEM.
Open every Tuesday afternoon and evening.

The Workingmen's Friend Is the Savings Bank

365-¼ days each year this Bank is working for you.

Enroll as a Depositor Now

Salem Savings Bank

125 Washington Street, Salem.
Hours: Daily, 8.45 A. M. to 1.15 P. M.
Saturday Evenings from 7 to 9.

Advertisements, about 1911

By the end of the eighteenth century the notion that the savings banks could significantly benefit the lower classes and play a leading role in society's crusade against pauperism gained popularity among leading British social thinkers, including Jeremy Bentham, David Hume, Robert Torrens, Thomas Malthus, and David Ricardo.

. . . the Reverend Henry Duncan is generally credited with founding the first modern, self-supporting savings bank at Ruthell, Scotland, in 1810. From there the idea began to spread . . . [into] one of the most rapid spontaneous social movements in British history, as savings bank enthusiasts spread their gospel with an almost missionary-like zeal. By the end of 1818 there were 465 savings banks in the British Isles. It was on the crest of this expansionary wave that the savings bank movement came to the United States.

ALAN L. OLMSTEAD, *NEW YORK CITY MUTUAL SAVINGS BANKS,* 1819–1861

Salem Co-Operative Bank

New Series of Shares for Sale

FRIDAY, APRIL 14, 1911.

ASSETS $786,593.45   2210 SHAREHOLDERS

The forty-seventh series now on sale. A safe investment paying never less than five per cent. Home seekers encouraged and advised. The co-operative plan of loans at our office. Buy your new shares today.
GEORGE W. PICKERING, Pres.   ALBERT C. MACKINTIRE, Sec.

A Young Man making application for a position was asked for his references. He produced his Savings Bank Book, which proved him to be a systematic money saver.
He got the position.
The best prizes in the business world are for those with stability of character. The self restraint practiced in money saving is a strong factor in character building.
This bank offers excellent opportunities to money savers.

Salem Five Cents Savings Bank
210 ESSEX STREET

. . . to induce habits of economy by receiving the savings of labourers & domestics & putting them out to interest . . .

JOHN PINTARD, LETTER OF APRIL 3, 1816, PROPOSING THE CREATION OF THE FIRST SAVINGS BANK IN NEW YORK CITY

. . . .

Savings Banks: Under this novel title, it is proposed to form an institution in Boston, for the security and improvement of the savings of persons in humble life, until required by their wants and desires. A meeting of gentlemen has been called, and a large and respectable committee appointed to apply to the Legislature (now in session) for an act of incorporation . . . Similar institutions exist in England and Scotland; in the former place under the appellation of "Provident Institutions for Savings," and in the latter "Savings Banks." In Philadelphia it is proposed to establish one of these societies. We agree in the following sentiment, and wish every success to the laudable schemes contemplated: "It is not by the alms of the wealthy that the good of the lower classes can be generally promoted. By such donations, encouragement is far *oftener given to idleness and hypocrisy than aid to suffering worth. He is the most effective benefactor to the poor, who encourages in them habits of industry, sobriety, and frugality."*

ANNOUNCEMENT IN THE BOSTON *CHRISTIAN DISCIPLE*, DECEMBER 1816

. . . .

A pamphlet, laced with homilies from Franklin, publicized the bank's founding and trumpeted the virtues of "gradual accumulation and ultimate provision for the casualties of life and the wants of age." In a series of examples of accumulation based on regular deposits, the pamphlet shows how an apprentice could save enough to set up his own business and a family could provide dowries for children.

AN ACCOUNT OF THE FOUNDING, IN DECEMBER OF 1816, OF THE PHILADELPHIA SAVING FUND SOCIETY

. . . .

It [the savings bank] will help none but those who are willing to help themselves.

AN "ADDRESS TO THE PUBLIC" BY THE BANK FOR SAVINGS IN THE CITY OF NEW YORK, JUNE 1819

. . . .

"The hand of the dililgent maketh rich" (Prov. 10:4) was adopted as the motto of the Bank for Savings of the City of New York in 1819.

Total Number of Depositors in 1819:   *1,572*

Largest groups of depositors, by occupation:

Clerks	*65*
Cooks	*354*
Domestics	*143*
Labourers	*27*
Seamen	*20*
Seamstresses	*34*
Shoemakers	*21*
Taylors	*21*

By other statuses:

Minors, male	*287*
Minors, female	*276*
Widows	*98*
Orphans	*20*
"Coloured"	*184*

FIRST REPORT OF THE BANK FOR SAVINGS IN THE CITY OF NEW YORK, 1820

. . . .

In four years the new house was built, new furniture bought and paid for, and Charles is considered one of the most thrifty young men in the town—all of which propitious events, we honestly believe, had their origin in the beneficent influence of the Saving's Bank, whose circular had opened his eyes, and stimulated him to carry out his resolution.

OLIVER OPTIC, *THE SAVINGS BANK; OR HOW TO BUY A HOUSE*, EARLY NINETEENTH CENTURY

This is the picture of thrift suggested by depositors of the Boston Five. It shows three generations of a typical American family, planning for the future and enjoying more and more of the things that thrift can build.

THE
BOSTON FIVE
CENTS SAVINGS BANK

Thrift Writes the American Story   Painted by Dwight C. Shepler

Lessons of Thrift, by a member of the
Save-All Club.

A BOOK PUBLISHED IN 1820

. . . .

The Portsmouth [New Hampshire] Savings
Bank was incorporated in June, 1823. It was
the first Savings Bank incorporated or organized
in this State . . . The bank organized here soon
after the Sunday School was established, and for
the same purposes, and, to a considerable extent,
by the same persons.

W. H. Y. HACKETT, IN 1869 RECALLING THE FORMATION
OF THE PORTSMOUTH SAVING BANK IN JUNE OF 1823

This is the Poor Man's Bank . . . to enable him
to save the earnings of his honest industry, to
promote economy, temperance, and enterprise, to
raise him in the world, to provide for his old age.
Let the friends of the poor, who cry out against
the monopolies of the rich, give the poor their iron
chest, where they too might get interest on their
money no matter how small the sum may be.

EDITORIAL, NEW YORK TIMES, ON THE FOUNDING
OF THE BOWERY SAVINGS BANK, 1834

. . . .

We see that all these plans [for opening savings
banks in the early nineteenth century] were meant

for the encouragement of thrift, and were calculated to help the poor help themselves. In every case the need was recognized of a secure depository for the savings of those who were willing to save. The way to encourage thrift was to hold out the certainty that the results of thrift and self-denial would be safely held against the time of need. And this security was to be offered to those least able to take care of their own savings . . . [The founding of the banks] opened up an opportunity for service of a new kind.

WILLIAM E. COX, "THE ETHICS OF THE SAVINGS BANK," SPEECH TO AMERICAN BANKERS ASSOCIATION, NOVEMBER 23, 1911

. . . .

The great English novelist Charles Dickens had a few things to say, some flattering and some not, about thrift in general and savings banks in particular.

At some distance from the factories, and on the highest and pleasantest ground in the neighbourhood, stands their hospital . . . The weekly charge in this establishment for each female patient is three dollars, or twelve shillings English; but no girl employed by any of the corporations is ever excluded for want of the means of payment. That they do not very often want the means, may be gathered from the fact, that in July, 1841, no fewer than nine hundred and seventy-eight of these girls were depositors in the Lowell Savings Bank: the amount of whose joint savings was estimated at

one hundred thousand dollars, or twenty thousand English pounds.

CHARLES DICKENS, *AMERICAN NOTES*, 1842

. . . .

Annual income, twenty pounds; annual expenditure, nineteen-six; result—happiness. Annual income, twenty pounds; annual expenditure, twenty pounds ought and six; result—misery.

CHARLES DICKENS, *DAVID COPPERFIELD*, 1850

. . . .

. . . wrote leaden little books for them, showing how the good grown-up baby invariably got to the savings-bank, and the bad grown-up baby invariably got transported.

CHARLES DICKENS, *HARD TIMES*, 1854

. . . .

In business Richard Mott was thrifty and prosperous. Though through sweeping reverses, at the age of fifty, he gave up his entire property to his creditors, he speedily rallied and died possessed of a handsome competence. For twenty years ending with his death [in January of 1888] he was the president of the Toledo Savings Bank, which he organized May 1868, and devoted eight hours a day, gratuitously, to its service.

KATE BROWNLEE SHERWOOD, "CHARACTER-ISTICS OF RICHARD MOTT," MAY 1889

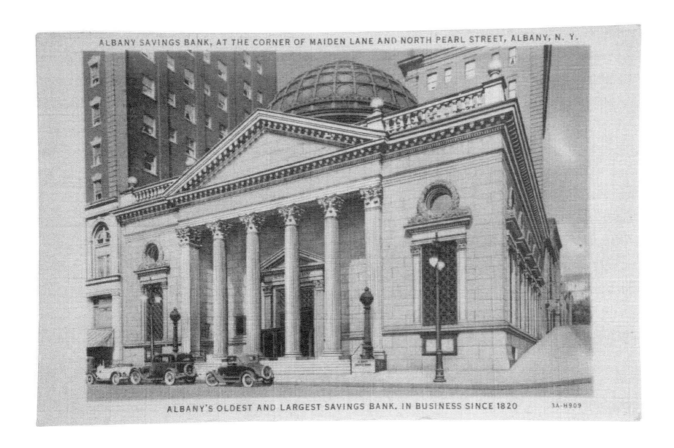

ALBANY SAVINGS BANK, AT THE CORNER OF MAIDEN LANE AND NORTH PEARL STREET, ALBANY, N. Y.

ALBANY'S OLDEST AND LARGEST SAVINGS BANK. IN BUSINESS SINCE 1820   3A-H909

Richard Mott was born in Mamaroneck, New York, on July 21, 1804. He moved to the pioneer town of Toledo, Ohio, in 1836. He was a Quaker. He served two terms as the mayor of Toledo during the 1840s. Lucretia Coffin Mott, the famous abolitionist and early feminist leader, was his sister-in-law, married to his eldest brother James. Richard Mott broke with the Democratic Party in the 1850s over the slavery issue, and the first meeting of the Ohio State Republican Party took place in his home.

Some of the other organizations to which Richard Mott gave his time and money—we are told that he "did not believe in encouraging the idle and vicious by prodigal almsgiving and blind benefactions"—include the Toledo Woman Suffrage Association, the New Century Club (a literary discussion group), the Protestant Orphan's Home, the Home for Friendless Women, the Industrial School, the Humane Society, and the Protestant Hospital and Temperance Association.[1]

The primary law for everyone to achieve business success is to live within his income. When outgo exceeds income, the game is desperate, the fate inevitable. The two per cents crush all in the end.

No person can be idle and unemployed without danger . . . Better be overtasked than undertasked.

*There is more danger from the millionaire
than from the impecunious classes; from gigantic,
entrenched monopolies than imported ignorance
and superstition.*

MAXIMS OF RICHARD MOTT

. . . .

*It is strictly a Society for Savings—a [in the words
of the bank's charter] "benevolent institution . . .
managed by trustees without salary in the interest
of depositors only . . ."*

SAMUEL H. MATHER, WHO FOUNDED THE SOCIETY FOR
SAVINGS IN THE CITY OF CLEVELAND IN MARCH OF 1849
AND WAS PRESIDENT OF THE SOCIETY WHEN HE DIED IN
JANUARY OF 1894

. . . .

Samuel Holmes Mather was born on March 20, 1813, in New Hampshire. He graduated from Dartmouth College in 1834. As early as 1841, he served as member of the school board in Cleveland, and as late as 1891, as treasurer of the Episcopal Diocese of Ohio. He founded the Society for Savings in the city of Cleveland on March 1849. At some point early in the Society's years, as a result of the demand of that institution, he significantly reduced his for-profit business interests and activities.

Leading a savings bank typically seems to go hand in hand with other forms of service to the community. Mather's son (or perhaps other relation), also named Samuel, later himself became a prominent Cleveland businessman, as well as an important philanthropic and civic leader. The younger Mather served as the president of the Citizens Committee of Cleveland, a leader of the Cleveland Chamber of Commerce, and the chairman of the board of Cleveland's Lakeside Hospital. On the national stage, at the request of Andrew Carnegie, he also served as a founding trustee of the Carnegie Endowment for International Peace. In May of 1897, his wife founded the Goodrich Social Settlement, a settlement house serving the poor of Cleveland.

Finally, it appears that these two Samuel Mathers are also direct descendants of the famous Puritan divine Cotton Mather, the author of *Essays to Do Good*, a 1711 tract that deeply influenced Benjamin Franklin. We can therefore detect a straight line from Cotton Mather's teaching on stewardship and doing good in the early eighteenth century, to Benjamin Franklin's thrift maxims in the next generation, to Samuel Mather's Society for Savings in the nineteenth-century Western Reserve.[2]

*My life work is now practically finished . . .
I will spend my time in the lobby.*

MATHER, SPEAKING TO MYRON T. HERRICK,
THE TREASURER OF THE SOCIETY FOR SAVINGS,
IN JUNE OF 1890, ON THE OCCASION OF THE
OPENING OF THE SOCIETY'S NEW HEADQUARTERS
AT 127 PUBLIC SQUARE IN CLEVELAND

From the start the Society for Savings had but one purpose: the encouragement of thrift.

CENTENNIAL CELEBRATION OF THE SOCIETY FOR SAVINGS, JUNE 22, 1949

. . . .

Mutual banks such as Bangor Savings were born of religiously-inspired social conscience.

HERE FOR GENERATIONS, A HISTORY OF THE BANGOR SAVINGS BANK, FOUNDED IN 1852

. . . .

Many savings bank leaders have made extraordinary efforts to reach out to children.

Said Corporation shall receive on deposits sums as small as five cents.

. . . Whenever any deposits shall be made by any minor, the trustees of said Corporation may, at their discretion, pay to such depositor such sum as may be due to him or her, although no guardian shall have been appointed to such minor . . .

"AN ACT TO INCORPORATE THE BOSTON FIVE CENTS SAVINGS BANK," 1854

. . . .

Savings bank leaders have also made extraordinary efforts to welcome and even solicit the smallest of deposits.

The Yorkshire [England] Penny Savings Bank was founded in 1859, under the auspices of Mr. Edward Akroyd . . . About four years ago, Mr. George C. T. Bartley determined to bring about an extension of the penny-bank system to London. This gentleman was already well-known as the honorary secretary of the Provident Knowledge Society, and an apostle of thrift . . . Mr. Bartley now proceeded to deliver speeches, and to write pamphlets and tracts on thrift, experiencing no little difficulty in persuading people that the machinery already provided for saving was not amply sufficient . . . to encourage saving among the actually poor and needy . . . [including] the large class who cannot muster deposits of a shilling and upward . . .

"PENNY BANKS," *ALL THE YEAR ROUND*, MARCH 11, 1876

At the same time, thrift institutions such as savings banks have almost always and in most places been far outnumbered by institutions promoting the opposite of thrift.

Dissipation has her nets drawn across every street. In many of our towns, sobriety has to run a gauntlet of half a dozen spirit-shops in the space of a bow-shot. These are near at hand—open by day, and blazing by night, both on Sabbath and Saturday. Drunkenness finds immediate gratification; while economy has to travel a mile, it may be, for her saving-bank; and that opens its doors to thrift but once or twice a week.

THOMAS GUTHRIE, *SEED-TIME AND HARVEST OF RAGGED SCHOOLS*, 1860

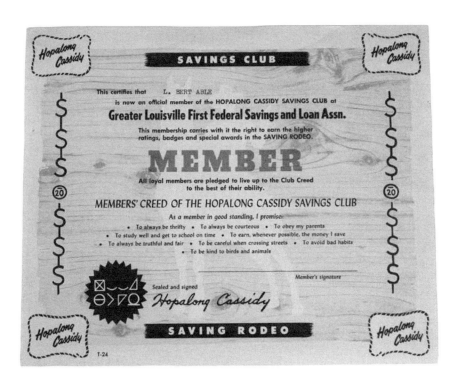

Again, we say that it is not enough to establish savings-banks and expect that people will go to them. We must bring the banks to the people . . . We want to make it as easy for a working man to invest his spare cash in a savings-bank or in a safe insurance or a deferred annuity for his old age, as it is now to invest it in a glass of beer.

LORD DERBY, ADDRESS TO THE PROVIDENT KNOWLEDGE SOCIETY, MAY 9, 1873

. . . .

You, the working promoters of these banks, are the humble and obscure, but no less effective, missionaries of the movement, which is essentially one in favor of civilization. (Renewed applause.) For, rely on it, in all societies, the thriftless class is really the dangerous class. It is not a question of social position. There is not much to choose between the poor Irish tenant, who is ripe for a revolution because he cannot pay his rent, and the ruined lord who is ready to vote that black is white that he may get a place at Court and pay his gambling debt.

LORD DERBY, ADDRESS TO THE LIVERPOOL PENNY BANK ASSOCIATION, JANUARY 16, 1880

. . . .

I think it is possible to have savings banks into which it shall be much easier to put money, and harder to draw it out, except for good reasons, than any which we have at present . . .

My idea is thus, simply to place the money [to be saved] in the hands of honest parties . . . who

keep stores that are frequented by laboring men or women, and especially such stores as are open early in the morning and late at night, or on Sunday. There, a person finding himself or herself with twenty-five or fifty cents in his purse will say: "I will put this change aside . . ." After the first twenty-five or fifty cents have been so placed, the desire to place more will come, as of itself, and finally a habit of saving will take the place of wastefulness . . .
He gets the receipt for it right there. The next day the bank acknowledges having received the money, and he knows that it is safe . . .

I have mentioned the liquor shops as possibly suitable for the purpose of making these deposits. It is of course, easy to cavil at this suggestion. Doubtless most who frequent them go in no mood of saving. But the point is that they are frequented by people who have money to be saved, and those are the ones we wish to appeal to.

H. W. ROSENBAUM, *HANDY SAVINGS BANKS: SUGGESTIONS FOR A NEW PLAN*, 1886

· · · ·

Let's apply this idea to today. Why not think about state lotteries today the same way that Rosenbaum in 1886 was thinking about liquor stores? What if every U.S. establishment selling lottery tickets— the very embodiment of anti-thrift values—was also required to make available, for purchase by individuals, tickets or stamps that contribute to saving? What if state-sponsored lotteries were required to advertise these pro-thrift products?

Here's a suggested ad line for these new products: "Every Ticket Wins!"

Peoples Thrift Savings Bank
FOUNDED 1887, PHILADELPHIA

· · · ·

Did savings banks and the thrift philosophy they embodied change Britain and the U.S. for the better over the course of the nineteenth century? You bet they did.

In 1830, only a small percentage of urban households in the Northeastern United States held assets in financial institutions; by the 1890s, the majority did. Savings banks played a major role in this transformation . . .
JOURNAL OF POLICY HISTORY, 2006

· · · ·

Growth of the U.S. economy in the nineteenth century was stimulated by a substantial increase in the aggregate saving rate . . . We believe that savings banks, by making it easier and safer for individuals to save, encouraged the increase of savings that generated growth at the macrolevel.
THE JOURNAL OF ECONOMIC HISTORY, 2004

· · · ·

In the history of the present century, now so near its close, nothing perhaps will stand out more

Published 1921

conspicuously than the remarkable progress that has been made in the education of the masses in the ways of thrift. Frugality and providence have been enjoined as a duty in every age and country, but the means afforded to the poor for saving and investing with profit are an institution of the nineteenth century.

ARCHIBALD G. BOWIE, *THE ROMANCE OF THE SAVINGS BANKS*, 1898

. . . .

Throughout the banks of the State a more satisfactory condition than ever before is observable. A better class of men are entering into the direction; scandals that once were common, and at one time threatened the whole system, are now rare, and the growing confidence of the people in these

depositories is shown in the vast increase in the sums placed there, which, in the closing year of the century, carried the total deposits in the State up to the long-hoped-for billion-dollar mark.

"HUMOR AND PATHOS OF THE SAVINGS-BANK," *THE CENTURY MAGAZINE*, FEBRUARY 1901

. . . .

The Bank now [1903] began to advertise in magazines and newspapers. Thousands of cards, inviting deposits, were sent to actors and actresses. Every week factories were furnished with hundreds of thousands of pay envelopes—reminding each employee, as he received his money, of the possible rainy day, against which he should provide. Thousands of letters were sent to clergymen around *the world, inviting their assistance in extending the lessons of thrift and economy among those who need the savings bank. Letters and literature were sent to hotels in an effort to keep The Bowery constantly before commercial travelers. Reading notices concerning the work and purposes of the Bank went to editors of country papers.*

A HISTORY OF THE BOWERY SAVINGS BANK

. . . .

There are 657 savings-banks in the United States at this date. The total amount deposited therein is two billion, five hundred and twelve million, four hundred and sixty-eight thousand, four hundred fifty-eight dollars ($2,512,468,458), or more than one-fourth of all deposits in all the banks and trust companies in the entire country.

A HISTORY OF THE CHARLESTOWN FIVE
CENTS SAVINGS BANK, 1904

. . . .

The gospel of thrift should be preached in the highways and byways until the last improvident soul is saved.

GEORGE E. ALLEN, SPEECH TO THE SAVINGS BANK
SECTION OF THE AMERICAN BANKERS ASSOCIATION, 1906

. . . .

In British Savings Banks, the Trustee and Post Office Banks, there are assets of nearly 250,000,000 pounds . . . What a monetary monument of the

founders of thrift! What an enthronement of thrift itself! (Applause.)

. . . There are in our country, apart from the Savings Banks, some thirty-five thousand registered Provident and other Societies in aid of Thrift, with a membership of nineteen and a half millions . . .

MR. J. AVON CLYDE, M.P., SPEAKING TO CONFEREES
ASSEMBLED IN THE MUSIC HALL IN EDINBURGH,
SCOTLAND, TO COMMEMORATE THE CENTENARY OF
SAVINGS BANKS, JUNE 9, 1910

. . . .

Now let us see what the nickels and the dimes of the steady savers have done in the United States. It is the record of the militant march of thrift . . . To-day we have 1,978 savings-banks . . . whose savings pile up to the tremendous total of $4,727,403,950. If this money were distributed among all the people of the country it would mean $48.56 for each of the 95,656,000 men, women, and children in the United States . . . At every turn you find some amazing evidence of the magnitude and power of the savings-banks.

ISAAC F. MARCOSSON, "THE COLOSSAL GROWTH OF
THE SAVINGS-BANK," 1914

. . . .

The expense of its [the school savings bank's] operation is, of course, greater than any interest or income that can come from the funds collected—being about three to one . . . But whatever the expense may be, it is small for a large bank—much smaller in any one year than some commercial banks of no greater deposits spend in a month for advertising, and is amply justified in practice by the benefits bestowed on the great number of children . . . that the people of the American city need education in thrift and economy, and that this system give such an education to the children in the most plastic time of life there can be no doubt, and in my opinion the bank itself as well as the community will profit by it.

NEWTON F. HAWLEY, SPEECH TO THE AMERICAN BANKERS ASSOCIATION, SEPTEMBER 1910

. . . .

School savings systems are now in operation in 46 of the 48 states of the United States, and annual deposits in each of seven states are in excess of one million dollars.

A HISTORY OF SCHOOL SAVINGS BANKING, 1928

. . . .

The rapid growth of small savings during the last thirty years or so was only possible because of the work and devotion of many generations of relatively unknown labourers in the field of thrift, whose reward at the time often seemed meagre enough.

H. OLIVER HORNE, A HISTORY OF SAVINGS BANKS, 1947

. . . .

What romantic stories could be written, if one knew all the facts, about the thrifty men, women

and children who have passed through the portals of the bank, during its one hundred years, on their way to happiness and achievement!

GATEWAY OF PROGRESS, 1857–1957: THE STORY OF NEW JERSEY'S LARGEST SAVINGS BANK, 1957

. . . .

In 1906 the Society's first School Savings Program was started by Arthur Deerin Call, principal of the Henry Barnard School. Mr. Call, a true New Englander, believed firmly in the basic virtue of thrift as well as education. When his pupils strolled into the schoolyard laden with penny candy, his Yankee heart was sorely distressed. He felt they should not be wasting their petty cash on unwholesome sweets, but saving it for worthwhile future needs. Deciding that education in thrift was part of the duty of a good public school, he instructed his teachers to collect deposits from their pupils every Tuesday. This money he personally carried to the Society for Savings . . .

A HISTORY OF THE SOCIETY FOR SAVINGS, HARTFORD, CONNECTICUT

. . . .

Since Thursday was "maid's day off," domestic workers from "up on the hill" congregated in the bank. Having no expenses for room and board, these women, many of them from foreign countries, frequently deposited their entire weekly wages. However, quite as important as the practice of thrift was the pleasure derived

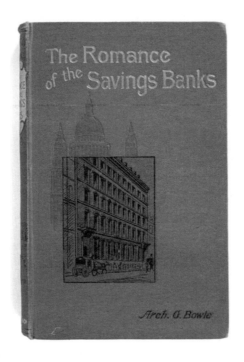

Published 1921

from chatting together in front of the blazing
hearth.

Cordial friendships often developed between
savers and tellers. On holidays depositors would
bring along little gifts of candy, flowers or special
delicacies. A Chinese laundryman, Yip Mow,
who handwashed many of the young tellers' shirts,
used to bring them lychee nuts and tea. Since
handwashed shirts lasted much longer than those
done by commercial laundries, with Yip Mow and
the tellers thrift was a two-way enterprise!

A HISTORY OF THE SOCIETY FOR SAVINGS, HARTFORD,
CONNECTICUT

. . . .

Walter A. Danforth . . . proper and ramrod
straight, ran a tight ship at the bank from

1917 to 1947 . . . Above all, Danforth was a
strong temperance man. He once told an employee
seen coming out of a local saloon on Harlow
Street that "People at Bangor Savings Bank
don't drink. I don't want to see you coming
out of that bar again."

. . . When Walter A. Danforth died in July
in July 1948, the bank promoted the forty-seven-
year-old [Harold L.] Nason to treasurer (then the
equivalent of bank president).

Outside the bank, Nason followed the Bangor
Savings Bank tradition of community involvement.
He served as a Boy Scout leader, president of the
Bangor Rotary Club, treasurer and director of the
Bangor YMCA, trustee of Bangor Public Library,
director of Home for Aged Men and commissioner
of the Bangor Housing Authority.

. . . Most of all, Nason was methodical and

precise. He arrived at the same time every day and wanted the blinds open—all slats in the same direction—precisely at 9 A.M. In the same order and nearly at the same time every day, he came to work, sat down, polished his shoes, reviewed the cash balances and met with a trustee . . . He talked with his wife precisely at noon and left for lunch, returned to the office precisely at 1:30 and read the Wall Street Journal *precisely at 3 P.M. when the bank closed.*

. . . For Nason, the bank was an extension of his person and retirement [in 1975] didn't come willingly or with any enthusiasm. As he prepared to leave, he gave his successor Malcolm Jones one overriding piece of advice and one sincere wish: "Now Mac, don't you let anyone take over this old bank."

After he retired, Nason sometimes walked down State Street, strolled past the bank and looked at the front window display. If it had been in place longer than he felt necessary, he might step inside the building, walk over to McInnis' desk and say, "Alice, I think it's time to change the display."

HERE FOR *GENERATIONS*, A HISTORY OF THE BANGOR SAVINGS BANK

. . . .

Leaders of the U.S. savings bank movement never tired—maybe they did, but they never seemed to tire—of explaining to people that thrift is a big and capacious idea, not a narrow or cramped one.

To the average man the word "thrift" is meaningless. It smacks of saving money and frequent trips to the savings bank. But that is a narrow thrift, and it may not be thrift at all. The thrift I would talk about today is a broader thrift— the thrift that earns largely and spends wisely; the manner of living that results in bank accounts and a peaceful old age as a natural sequence to a well ordered life; the course of conduct that makes for independence and not dependence.

WILLIAM H. KNIFFEN, "THE BROADER THRIFT," ADDRESS TO THE OHIO BANKERS ASSOCIATION, SEPTEMBER 1916

. . . .

Virtue is the Root, Wealth is the Flower

INSCRIPTION IN THE DOME OF THE BUFFALO (NEW YORK) SAVINGS BANK, COMPLETED IN DECEMBER 1926

. . . .

Without the thrift habit the savings bank—yea, the nation—would soon decay, and without the savings bank the thrift habit would lose its chief exponent.

WILLIAM H. KNIFFEN, *THE SAVINGS BANK AND ITS PRACTICAL WORK*, 1928

. . . .

Fundamentally thrift is an expression of good morals.

A. C. ROBINSON, SPEECH TO THE AMERICAN BANKERS ASSOCIATION, 1931

41. Producer and Consumer Cooperatives

IN PRODUCER COOPERATIVES, members join together to increase thrift and reduce waste by cooperatively marketing and selling their goods, in the process eliminating middle men and, by becoming their own bosses, effectively abolishing the distinctions between worker and owner. In consumer cooperatives, members join together to facilitate saving and improve purchasing power by cooperatively buying their consumer goods, again eliminating the middle men and, by becoming owners of their own stores, erasing distinctions between store owner and consumer. Both of these types of cooperative endeavors advance what many progressive reformers have called industrial or economic democracy.

Unlike the cases of countries such as Britain (with its consumer cooperatives) or France or Denmark (with their producer cooperatives), producer and consumer cooperatives have never emerged as mainstream components of the U.S. economy. But these organizations are nevertheless still a part of our national story, visible to anyone curious enough to look, serving partly as standing reminders of roads not taken in the U.S., and even more, as evidence of some significant, if seldom noticed, efforts in our history to promote particular forms of thrift.

Husbands who never knew what it was to be out of debt, and poor wives who, for years never knew what it was to have a sixpence unmortgaged in their pockets, now possess little stores of money sufficient to build them small cottages; they can now afford to go to their own market with money in their pockets. And in that market there is no adulteration, no distrust, no deception.

A DESCRIPTION OF THE FAMOUS ROCHDALE COOPERATIVE STORE, FOUNDED IN ENGLAND IN 1844, IN A PAMPHLET ANNOUNCING THE OPENING OF "THE PHILADELPHIA SAVINGS STORE, ON THE ROCHDALE PLAN," A COOPERATIVE STORE SPONSORED BY THE PHILADELPHIA SAVINGS SOCIETY, 1859

. . . .

First, I learn the folly of being a slave, when I may be free. Secondly, I learn to save my money, and well as to earn it. And, Thirdly, I learn how best to spend it.

"CO-OPERATIVE CATECHISM," FROM THE BRITISH JOURNAL *CO-OPERATOR*, 1860S

. . . .

Co-operators have from the very beginning been proud of the essentially voluntary character of their

movement. They have appealed to consumers to trade at their stores and to become shareholding members with a mixture of appeals to idealism and morality and to self-interest. Mutual trading has been held out as at one and the same time morally superior to profit-making and more advantageous to the consumer from the economic standpoint; and the effect of Co-operation in encouraging thrift has also been strongly emphasized . . .

[The Co-operative movement] grew up, side by side with the Friendly Societies, the popular Savings Banks and the Building Societies, as a agency for the "frugal investment" of working-class savings, and it attracted mainly the thriftier among the workers . . .

G. D. H. COLE, ON THE BRITISH CO-OPERATIVE MOVEMENT IN THE MID-NINETEENTH CENTURY

. . . .

Cole estimates that, by 1950, at least one of every three Britons was connected in one way or another to a cooperative association, in most cases a consumer cooperative.

In 1886, the influential author, journalist, and reformer Albert Shaw—author of *The Outlook for the Average Man* (1907), editor of the *Minneapolis Tribune* and of *The Review of Reviews*, and a thrift partisan who, for example, accepted Edward Filene's invitation in 1919 to join the National Committee on People's Banks, organized to promote credit unions—wrote an in-depth study of the cooperative movement in Minneapolis, Minnesota. What he found is remarkable. He begins

his study with a report on cooperative barrelmaking, or coopering.

Mr. Charles A. Pillsbury . . . promised the cooperative the contract for supplying one of the mills he controlled, and on the strength of that promise the enterprise materialized. In November, 1874, the "Cooperative Barrel Manufacturing Company" was incorporated . . . [and] has been more stable and prosperous than that of any non-cooperative coopering establishment which has ever existed in Minneapolis.

. . . If there is a penny to be made in the manufacture of barrels, the cooperatives make the penny. They use honest materials, and do thorough, honest work; but every man has the spirit of a proprietor and works for the good of the shop. There is no waste of material.

. . . Of the ninety members of the Cooperative Barrel Company, probably from sixty to seventy are married men . . . fully nine-tenths of these family men own their own homes . . . it cannot be too emphatically urged that but for cooperation these men would not have acquired their little homesteads . . . It is interesting also to know . . . that probably two-thirds of the members of [the] company who owned their homes obtained them through the aid of cooperative building and loan associations.

. . . The [cooperative] system is an excellent discipline. It trains all the members to an understanding of ordinary business methods and transactions, conduces to moderation, patience and self-control and fits for the duty of citizenship.

. . . cooperation alone has enabled the coopers to save. Those in the non-cooperative shops have not saved. The regular weekly assessment of $2 or more from wages, to which is added all dividends until stock shares are fully paid for, compels the member to become a capitalist in spite of himself. If he remains two or three years he will retire with savings of several hundred dollars, and with the well-grounded habit of savings.

ALBERT SHAW, "COOPERATION IN A WESTERN CITY," 1886

. . . .

. . . it being fully understood and agreed to that no speculative purposes having reference to the future sale of said land, or any part of it, enters as considerations into the agreement. On the contrary, it is fully understood that the land hereby granted is to be regarded as the home and heritage of generations of honest workmen, and that the present resources of the location, the fertility of the soil, the timber, the beauty of the scenery, and other natural advantages, are to be carefully preserved, and, if possible, increased. To accomplish this, it is hereby declared that no less than one-fourth of the land should be kept covered with timber; that in the use of timber for fuel, buildings or manufactures, sufficient care should be taken to preserve young

and thrifty groves of trees . . . It is also understood that any unnecessary destruction of fish or game is to be discouraged.

RULES OF THE PIONEER COOPERATIVE COMPANY, A COOPERATIVE AGRICULTURAL COLONY, CROW WING COUNTY, MINNESOTA, 1885

. . . .

By 1913, American farmers had organized over 1,180 dairy cooperatives and 960 grain elevator cooperatives . . . [and by the late 1920s had organized] a total of 2,487 dairy cooperatives and over 3,300 grain elevator cooperatives . . .

MARC SCHNEIBERG, WRITING IN *THE SOCIO-ECONOMIC REVIEW*

. . . .

Cooperation depends for its success, not only on its commercial principles of cash payment and deferred benefits, but on the moral qualities of patience, thrift, and loyalty, which make the character known as the "cooperating man."

FRANCIS GREENWOOD PEABODY, *JESUS CHRIST AND THE SOCIAL QUESTION*, 1915

. . . .

These aids to economy [connected to joining a consumer cooperative] and the paying back of savings on cost in a lump sum are found to be great helps and incentives to thrift. Savings is made automatic and thrift easy and dignified. Many co-operators in England have been led to save until they reach the dignity of small capitalists. Some have paid for their homes out of dividends. As Mr. William Maxwell, president of the International Co-operative Alliance, says, they "eat themselves into a home."

EMERSON P. HARRIS, *CO-OPERATION: THE HOPE OF THE CONSUMER*, 1920

. . . .

If the present system of selling were devised expressly to discourage thrift, it could hardly do so more effectually.

HARRIS, *CO-OPERATION: THE HOPE OF THE CONSUMER*

Do not forget! There will be a $25.00 Prize Story Contest each month, stories to be written by members or their wives. Each story must feature thrift, or in some way must be linked up with our Association . . .

TODAY: A MAGAZINE OF THRIFT, PUBLISHED BY THE ASSOCIATION OF ARMY AND NAVY STORES, JUNE 1930

42. Building and Loan Associations

BUILDING AND LOAN associations—later typically called savings and loan associations—are cooperative thrift organizations in which members pool savings and finance homes.

Building and loans are one institutional expression of a larger idea, and at times also of a social movement, centered on the principle of cooperative (or mutual) economic endeavor. As we've seen, in both Europe and the U.S., advocates of cooperation have focused on three key areas—production (e.g., dairy farmers joining together to sell their milk cooperatively), consumption (e.g., a food co-op in which members organize ways to buy fresh food at good prices), and credit (e.g., a cooperative bank or credit union, in which members pool their savings and are eligible to take out loans). Building and loans are examples of this third type of cooperative, focusing on the average consumer's access to credit—in this case, particularly the ability to borrow money to build a home.

Democratically organized, reaching into all areas of the country, and linking the virtue of saving one's money with the classic American dream of owning one's own home, building and loans stand out as our society's paradigmatic thrift institutions—probably the most important and influential thrift organizations in U.S. history. So it's no accident that the greatest thrift movie ever made in America, Frank Capra's *It's a Wonderful Life*, centers on . . . a building and loan association!

It is not an organization for a few to make large profits at the expense of the many; or one wherein the borrower pays a large interest for the benefit of the shareholder who does not borrow. All stand upon equal footing. It does not encourage speculation, but steady savings; and to attain them, there must be industry and frugal habits. It encourages home-building and all the blessings that naturally flow from it.

SEYMOUR DEXTER, *A TREATISE ON CO-OPERATIVE SAVINGS AND LOAN ASSOCIATIONS*, 1889

. . . .

A building association is a mutual, co-operative financial institution . . . Building associations provide the ideal facilities for the practice of thrift. The members save money together.
They lend money to each other.
They divide the profits with each other.
They work together to help each other.
. . . a building association is the practical example,

the concrete expression of the idea of democracy, applied to a financial institution.

HENRY S. ROSENTHAL *CYCLOPEDIA OF BUILDING, LOAN AND SAVINGS ASSOCIATIONS,* 1927

. . . .

Its members pay in their savings, generally in small but regular amounts, to a common fund. From this fund, some of the members receive loans for the purpose of purchasing or constructing homes. Over a period of time all members who so desire can secure such loans.

H. MORTON BODFISH, *HISTORY OF BUILDING AND LOAN IN THE UNITED STATES,* 1931

. . . .

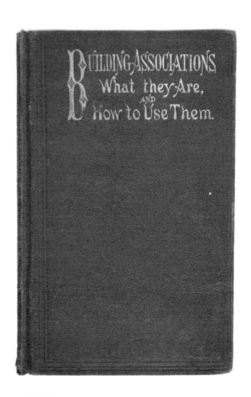

Published 1869

On January 3, 1831, according to the [Frankford, Pennsylvania] Call:

A meeting of sundry inhabitants of the borough of Frankford was held at the house of Thomas Sidebotham for the purpose of forming an association to enable the contributors thereof to build or purchase dwellings houses.

. . . The partnership feature of building associations, one of their most prominent features, is emphasized by the popular name for the Oxford Provident, viz., that of "Club," by which name in Frankford the building associations are popularly known. To this day, in the locality in which they originated and in which almost every man, woman, and child in the community is familiar

with them, they are invariably referred to as the "Building Club."

ROBERT T. CORSON, DESCRIBING THE FOUNDING IN 1831 IN FRANKFORD, PENNSYLVANIA, OF THE OXFORD PROVIDENT BUILDING ASSOCIATION, THE FIRST U.S. BUILDING AND LOAN ASSOCIATION, IN A SPEECH TO THE U.S. LEAGUE OF LOCAL BUILDING AND LOAN ASSOCIATIONS, 1899

. . . .

. . . associations for investing and accumulating the periodical and other contributions of the associators for the creation of a fund, to be finally distributed equally among them, have in other States been found highly conducive to public and individual

Gary Cooper says: "No, partner, this isn't where I work . . . It's where my money works for me. I know my savings are safe here, because wherever you see that insurance emblem displayed you know your savings are protected by an agency of the U. S. Government."

See Gary Cooper in "The Real West" on NBC-TV, March 29th.   Insured Savings and Loan Associations

"Be a thrift-teener...the Insured Savings and Loan way" says Pat Boone. "Thrift-teeners are teenagers who've learned the habit of saving some of their allowance or job money regularly. In my book, it's a pretty good habit to have. "It's the best way to get enough money for the big things you want. And a great place for teenagers to save is at an Insured Savings and Loan. There your money is safe and earns more money for you. "So be a thrift-teener. Start saving at your nearby Insured Savings and Loan Association today. They'll be glad to see you and help you work out your savings plan."

Where you save does make a difference

prosperity, by encouraging and fostering the virtues of temperance, industry, economy, and frugality.

THE FIRST U.S. STATE LAW TO PROVIDE FOR THE GENERAL INCORPORATION OF BUILDING AND LOANS, PASSED BY THE NEW JERSEY STATE LEGISLATURE, 1847

. . . .

But although those institutions [such as savings banks] have done and are doing a vast amount of real good . . . yet there exists in their management and government a tendency to aristocracy, and the keeping down of the working classes . . . In the first place, they are ruled and managed by an entirely different class of men, in whose selection as managers the working people or depositors have no voice; and in the second place, their managers take entire charge of the accumulated funds thus saved . . . This system, therefore, while doing much positive good, does not act in unison with the spirit of the present age to the fullest extent . . . [Whereas the Building Association] has a tendency directly opposite . . .

1st. In that it is perfectly democratic, admitting each individual corporator or member to a full, free and unrestricted voice in the creation and management of Associations . . .

2d. In that it is entirely mutual and equal in distributing its benefits . . .

3d. In that it is much more liberal in it return of profits and gains . . . Having,—owing to its entirely mutual character,—no preferred class to share its profits . . . and no necessity for expensive banking houses and clerk hire; and

4th. In that it is the only plan by which the working man can become his own capitalist, and create a source of wealth from which he can supply all reasonable demands, without the aid or interference of the outside capitalist.

. . . It is the principle of cooperation applied to money.

EDMUND WRIGLEY, *THE WORKING MAN'S WAY TO WEALTH; A PRACTICAL TREATISE ON BUILDING ASSOCIATIONS*, 1869

. . . .

Edmund Wrigley was a thrift nut—a great admirer of Benjamin Franklin and a fervent and influential advocate of building and loans. He was born in Philadelphia in 1831—the same year that, just outside of Philadelphia, America's first building and loan was founded. His father was from Manchester, England, and his mother was a Philadelphia Quaker. Edmund's father died when Edmund was eleven years old, soon after which Edmund began working, first in a printing shop and then in a public library, where he also borrowed and read many books. He spent several years working as a real estate broker. His deep interest in building and loans appears to have begun in about 1850 or 1851. He eventually served as a secretary of several associations, and founded several others. He was widely

viewed as an expert practitioner and as an important pioneer in the movement. For some time, he served as the editor of the *Building Association Journal*, and his second book, published in 1872, and for many years much in demand, was entitled *How to Manage Building Associations: A Director's Guide and Secretary's Assistant*. H. Morton Bodfish, himself an important leader in the field, later described Wrigley this way: "His heart and soul were in the work. He gave freely of his time and talent and himself for the good of the cause . . ."[1]

The form of cooperative enterprise that has attained far greater results in the United States than all others combined, is that of the well-known and almost invariably successful building and loan association.

ALBERT W. SHAW, "CO-OPERATION IN A WESTERN CITY" (MINNEAPOLIS), 1886

. . . .

Hennepin County Catholic Building and Loan Association (135 members)
Mechanics and Workingmens Loan and Building Association (750 members)
Minneapolis Mutual Building and Loan Association (100 members)
Turners' Building Association (180 members, German-speaking)
South Minneapolis Building and Loan Association (175 members, mostly Scandinavian)
North Minneapolis Building and Loan Association (75 members)

Central Building and Loan Association
   (125 members)
East Side Association (85 members)
BUILDING AND LOANS FOUNDED SINCE 1874 IN
MINNEAPOLIS, AS OF 1886

. . . .

*About one thousand homes thus far have been
secured for workingmen in Minneapolis by the
building and loan associations of the city, and their
operations have only fairly begun.*
SHAW, "CO-OPERATION IN A WESTERN CITY," 1886

. . . .

*At the rate the building associations are
now gaining, the time may come when their
accumulated savings at any one time may exceed
those of our savings-banks, and it is doubtful
that any system of savings has been devised which
has such a tendency to produce frugality among
persons of small incomes as the building association
methods.*
PROFESSOR FRANKLIN BENJAMIN SANBORN,
"CO-OPERATIVE BUILDING," A REPORT
PRESENTED TO THE AMERICAN SOCIAL
SCIENCE ASSOCIATION, SEPTEMBER 7, 1888

By 1890, an estimated 5,800 cooperative building and loan institutions were operating in the United States, with a majority of the institutions having been founded only recently, since the late 1870s. Pennsylvania, with about 1,200 building and loans in 1890, had by far the most of any state. The other top building and loan states in 1890 were Ohio (about 800), Illinois (about 600), New York (about 475), and Indiana (about 400).[2]

The Hackensack, New Jersey, lawyer, journalist, and banker William Alexander Linn (b. 1846) was the founding president in 1887 of the Hackensack Mutual Building and Loan Association, an office that he held into the new century. Like his fellow journalist Albert W. Shaw, Linn during these years became a prominent and quite fervent advocate of this form of economic cooperation.

*But I had to work hard and save my money. I
did not dress in expensive clothing and go like a
dude on the streets with a cane. If a man does that
he will never get anything done. I got the idea of
saving and building from some other coachmen I
met at Newport, from Philadelphia, who owned
their own homes in this way.*

*Now, I am rather fond of giving advice, and I
would say to the laboring man who is industrious
and wants a home for himself and his family—
especially if he is a mechanic, or one who works by
the day or month, or piece-work—get into some
corporation like this. When they are paying their*

monthly dues they are really paying for their own houses.

JOHN (LAST NAME WITHHELD), A COACHMAN
FROM ROXBURY, IN BOSTON, MASSACHUSETTS,
SPEAKING TO W. A. LINN ABOUT BUILDING AND LOANS,
ABOUT 1890

. . . .

. . . one of the greatest means for the encouragement of thrift that man has devised.

W. A. LINN, "CO-OPERATIVE HOME-WINNING: SOME
PRACTICAL RESULTS OF BUILDING ASSOCATIONS,"
SCRIBNER'S MAGAZINE, MAY 1890

. . . .

The increase of the building and loan associations in San Francisco has been almost phenomenal.

CALIFORNIA BUREAU OF LABOR STATISTICS, 1890

. . . .

Building Association Congress of the World

A CONFERENCE OF U.S. BUILDING AND LOAN
ASSOCIATIONS HELD IN CHICAGO ON APRIL 14–15, 1892,
LEADING TO THE CREATION OF THE UNITED STATES
LEAGUE OF LOCAL BUILDING AND LOAN ASSOCIATIONS
(FOUNDED 1893) AND THE AMERICAN SAVINGS, BUILDING
AND LOAN INSTITUTE

. . . .

The Irish-American Savings and Loan Association, of Buffalo, is now entering upon its thirtieth year of progress and prosperity with gross resources of $1,903,087, almost all of which is loaned on Buffalo homes bought by members through this thrift-inducing organization.

THE *AMERICAN BUILDING ASSOCIATION NEWS*,
FEBRUARY 1914

. . . .

The editor of the *American Building Association News* in 1914 was the outstanding building and loan leader Henry S. Rosenthal of Cincinnati, Ohio. Rosenthal first became active in the movement in the 1880s. In 1893, he was one of the main founders of the movement's national association, the United States League of Local Building and Loan Associations. In 1888, he published an important book for movement organizers, *Manual for Building and Loan Associations*.

Rosenthal was a committed internationalist. He initially proposed, helped to organize, and prepared a paper for the first International Congress of Building and Loan Associations, held in London on August 11–12, 1914, although he was unable to attend the congress in person, since the *Vaterland*, the ship on which he was to travel, failed to leave the New York harbor on account of the onset of the Great War. He was an active participant, however, in the second International Congress, held in San Francisco on July 30, 1915, in conjunction with the Panama-Pacific International Exposition—a congress which constituted one part of the same broad gathering of thrift organizations and leaders that, as we saw in part three,

The American Home - The Safeguard of American Liberty

THE Peoples Savings AND LOAN ASSOCIATION

Founded 1897

4300 CLARK AVE.   ☎ 961-7500   CLEVELAND, OHIO 44109

had as one of its main organizers S. W. Straus of the American Society for Thrift.

In 1923, Rosenthal published his *Cyclopedia of Building, Loan and Savings Associations*, a terrific book that went through many printings and editions and became a worthy successor to Edmund Wrigley's classic *The Working Man's Way to Wealth*.

When we discuss the abolition of poverty . . . we know it to be a demonstrable fact that if certain educational work is properly done, poverty will rapidly decline. This educational work to alleviate poverty, I take it, is the task before us, who are believers in the worth of the building and loan movement . . . We are all working toward this end because we conceive it to be our duty to our fellow-men to do so, and because we have faith in the co-operative principle. We believe that we are doing a work that is not only an economic necessity and a social blessing, but also a conservation of resources . . .

. . . we can readily see the great possibilities

fun for thrift-builders, young and old

SAVINGS BOOK

Thrifty-50

An exciting challenge for 2 — 4 players

THE SAVINGS & LOAN ASS'N. *Fun* GAME

Issued 1961

of our movement, and we are impressed by the obligation that rests upon us to demonstrate to the public in a more compelling way, not only the necessity for thrift, but also the fact that our institutions are the best media for the exercise of that virtue . . .

HENRY S. ROSENTHAL, "POSSIBILITIES OF THE BUILDING AND LOAN MOVEMENT," AN ADDRESS TO THE SECOND INTERNATIONAL CONGRESS OF BUILDING AND LOAN ASSOCIATIONS, HELD IN SAN FRANCISCO, JULY 30, 1915

. . . .

Your efforts have resulted in educating your people in that greatest philanthropy, that of learning them how to best and nobly help themselves.

CHARLES E. CLARK, PRESIDENT OF THE UNITED STATES LEAGUE OF LOCAL BUILDING AND LOAN ASSOCIATIONS, "OUR PLAIN DUTY TO THE BUILDING AND LOAN ASSOCIATION MOVEMENT OF THE UNITED STATES," ADDRESS TO THE LEAGUE'S ANNUAL CONVENTION, DECEMBER 5, 1914

. . . there is no other financial agency in the country which is attempting to do the stupendous work that those institutions are doing in encouraging systematic thrift on the one hand and in building homes on the other.

CHARLES O. HENNESSY, U.S. LEAGUE OF LOCAL BUILDING AND LOAN ASSOCIATIONS, TESTIMONY BEFORE THE U.S. CONGRESS, OCTOBER 31, 1919

. . . .

Our associations are serving just two classes of customers: receiving the savings of thrifty and far-seeing people, and loaning those funds to members who wish to buy or build a home.

ANN E. RAE, PRESIDENT OF THE NEW YORK STATE LEAGUE OF SAVING AND LOAN ASSOCIATIONS, 1922

*There is one [building and loan association]
for every 9,514 of the people of the United States,
yet comparatively few people know how they
operate. There are more associations than the
total number of national banks, and there are
more than one-third as many as all the banks
combined . . . in 1920, they had a membership
of 7,202,880 persons.*

ELEMENTS OF THE MODERN BUILDING AND LOAN
ASSOCIATION, 1925

. . . .

*Thrift doesn't mean miserliness—it merely means
common sense applied to spending.*

"SAVINGS SHARE STAMPS" BOOKLET OF THE WALTON
CO-OPERATIVE SAVINGS & LOAN ASSOCIATION, WALTON,
NEW YORK, 1931

. . . .

*Thrift, industry, perseverance, and placing a
definite percentage of your pay envelope to your
credit in a building-loan and saving association
puts you on the road to financial independence.
It will also provide for your dependents a fund, if
your earning power should be suddenly stopped or
decreased.*

"PASS BOOK OWERNERSHIP IS THRIFT,"
ADVERTISEMENT, CORRY (PENNSYLVANIA) BUILDING
AND LOAN ASSOCIATION, MAY 1931

*Planned thrift is an admirable characteristic.
World War II has shown us that the American
people can be a thrifty people. The challenge of
peace is to sustain that trait. The encouragement
of thrift is one of the primary purposes of savings
and loan associations such as ours. Buy more bonds!
Keep those you have! Practice thrift!*

HOME LIFE, NEWSLETTER OF THE NILES (MICHIGAN)
FEDERAL SAVINGS AND LOAN ASSOCIATION, OCTOBER 1945

. . . .

*The American people have discovered us. Their
savings have swelled our total assets well beyond
the $20-billion mark—twice the total of five years
ago. In 1952, they will again have chosen us for the
largest share of their thrift patronage. Our growth
rate is so fast that we have serious staff training
problems.*

BEN H. HAZEN, PRESIDENT OF THE UNITED STATES
SAVINGS AND LOAN LEAGUE, ADDRESS TO THE LEAGUE'S
ANNUAL CONVENTION, 1952

. . . .

*Two qualities distinguish our mutual thrift
institutions and have made them indispensable
to the economic well-being of the nation. The first
is that we are specialists in the promotion and
encouragement of thrift. The second is our mutual
form of organization.*

JOHN DELAITTRE, PRESIDENT OF THE NATIONAL
ASSOCIATION OF MUTUAL SAVINGS BANKS, SPEECH TO
THE ANNUAL CONVENTION OF THE U.S. SAVINGS AND
LOAN LEAGUE, 1959

THRIFT ORACLE

TELLS YOU
HOW TO SAVE

SAVE AND HAVE

DIRECTIONS INSIDE

Thrift Oracle, Ashland Building & Loan Company

In 1954, U.S. savings and loan associations for the first time surpassed mutual savings banks in total individual savings, with savings and loans that year holding $27.3 billion of U.S. citizens' savings, compared to $26.3 billion held in mutual savings banks. By 1960, that advantage had widened significantly, with savings and loans reaching $54.7 billion in savings, compared to $35 billion in mutual savings banks.

By 1960, there were more than 6,200 savings and loans in the United States, with annual loans totaling about $15 billion. Savings and loans that year financed about 40 percent of all home purchases in the United States requiring the assistance of borrowed money.[3]

We're a service organization dedicated to more abundant living through the twin goals of thrift and home ownership.

DONALD H. GATES, WINNING THE ANNUAL SPEECH CONTEST OF THE UNITED STATES SAVINGS AND LOAN LEAGUE, 1969

. . . .

By training the young citizen to use the [building and loan] association in accumulating his savings, the officers can establish for themselves a definite basis of future business . . . Not all states allow associations to accept the savings of minors in their own name, but the laws are gradually being changed to permit this practice . . . the added expense to the association is made up in later years through increased business. Immediate returns can well be overlooked in view of the remote ends which are sure to benefit both parties. A special teller's window with a platform above the floor of the lobby is provided by many associations today, so that the child can easily see through it. A sympathetic officer behind such a window soon gains a child's confidence.

ELEMENTS OF THE MODERN BUILDING AND LOAN ASSOCIATION

. . . .

On the following Monday a card reading "Tomorrow is School Thrift Day" was hung in each classroom. The teachers also gave each child two signature cards to take home for their

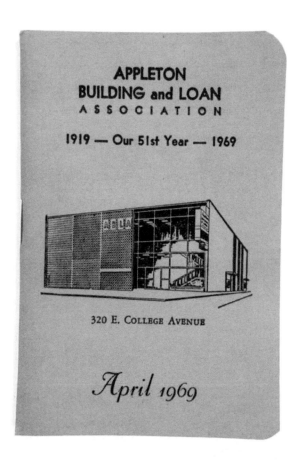

APPLETON BUILDING and LOAN
ASSOCIATION

1919 — Our 51st Year — 1969

320 E. COLLEGE AVENUE

April 1969

parents' signature—one yellow for the association's files, the other white, which also contained an authorization to the school principal to deliver the children's money to the association. Tuesday morning the classroom cards bore the legend "Today is School Thrift Day," and as soon as classes opened, the children were given the opportunity of opening accounts with a minimum of 25 cents. The association is so well satisfied with results that they expect to continue the work whether or not it ever shows a profit.

DESCRIPTION OF A SCHOOL SAVINGS PROGRAM LAUNCHED BY THE SCHOOLS AND THE FRESNO GUARANTEE BUILDING-LOAN ASSOCIATION IN FRESNO, CALIFORNIA, IN MARCH 1924

. . . .

Dan Geyer, staff vice president of the League, discussed the U.S. League's new booklet entitled Thrift: Making Your Wishes Come True. Designed for grade school children, the booklet explains the value of thrift, how saving helps children have things they want and how a savings and loan operates. Mr. Geyer also emphasized that children are our future customers and that we should make special efforts to reach them through promotional activities and by opening our associations to classroom and teacher visits.

SAVINGS AND LOAN ANNALS, 1962

43. Credit Unions

LIKE BUILDING AND LOAN associations, credit unions are cooperative thrift organizations in which members pool their savings and provide one another with access to credit. The modern credit union movement originated in Germany in the mid-nineteenth century, led by pioneers including Herman Schultze-Delitzsch and Friederich Wilhelm Raiffeisen, and it is in Germany that this movement has enjoyed its greatest influence. Raiffeisen's 1866 book, *The Credit Union*, for many years was the unofficial bible of the international credit union movement. In Britain, Henry W. Wolff, who wrote the 1893 book *People's Banks*, became an internationally known advocate of cooperative credit. In Canada, the great turn-of-the-century credit union pioneer was Alphonse Desjardins, from Quebec, who also helped to spread the credit union idea south of the border, in the United States.

In the United Sates, due to the dedicated work of reformers such as Edward Filene, the Boston department-store magnate, and Roy F. Bergengren, the Massachusetts attorney turned national organizer and thrift visionary, the credit union movement took root in the early decades of the twentieth century. The movement's goal was to encourage saving and to provide people of modest means with access to affordable credit, particularly in response to the spread during these years of pawn shops, loan-sharking, and other predatory credit operations, including salary loans, or what we today call payday lending.

. . . a cooperative association formed for the purpose of promoting thrift among its members.

THE DEFINITION OF A CREDIT UNION CONTAINED IN THE MASSACHUSETTS CREDIT UNION ACT, THE NATION'S FIRST GENERAL STATUTE FOR THE INCORPORATION OF CREDIT UNIONS, APRIL 15, 1909

. . . .

. . . loans [by credit unions] shall be made only for the purposes which promise to result in a saving or a profit to the borrower. Each applicant for a loan must state the object for which he desires to borrow, in order that the credit committee, which passes on all loans, may rigidly exclude thriftless and improvident borrowing.

. . . As personal knowledge of the character of the members is essential, the membership in an association must be restricted to citizens of a small community, or of a small subdivision of a large city, or to a small group or organization of individuals.

. . . the principle that loans may be made only for purposes which promise to benefit the borrower, introduces an element of education as to

the distinction between good borrowing and bad borrowing . . . in credit unions, the object of the loan is the first consideration . . .

Operating in a personal manner in small local fields or groups, [credit unions] can teach their members the desirability of saving in a way which the less personal savings bank cannot do.

ARTHUR B. CHAPIN, BANK COMMISSIONER
OF MASSACHUSETTS, 1911

. . . .

What are the functions of a Credit Union?
1. *It encourages thrift by providing a safe, convenient and attractive medium for the investment of the savings of its members through the purchase of shares and the making of savings deposits.*
2. *It promotes industry by enabling its members to borrow for productive and other beneficial purposes.*
3. *It eliminates usury by providing its members, when in urgent need, with a source of credit at reasonable cost, which they could not otherwise obtain.*
4. *It trains its members in business methods and self-government, endows them with a sense of social responsibility, and educates them to a full realization of the value of co-operation.*

A CREDIT UNION PRIMER, 1914

The real "keystone of the system" [of co-operative credit] is the compulsion brought to bear upon members to save, regularly and steadily, and by their savings to raise up a "capital of guarantee," a capital sufficient to command benefits [of access to credit] which are offered, not wholly as an end in themselves, but no less as an inducement to members to practice the great economic virtue of thrift.

. . . [co-operative] banks, then, may not be incorrectly described as . . . savings banks first and credit banks afterward. The want of credit urging people to apply for membership was to be used as a means for turning them into habitual savers, as the first condition for enabling them to satisfy that want.

. . . Master the principle [of co-operative credit institutions], adopt it loyally, and you may allow the rules to take care of themselves. That principle is—that the institution should be absolutely based on self-help, that its government should be democratic, that the quality of its work should be assured by a quickening of the sense of responsibility, by checking, and union, and control.

HENRY W. WOLFF, *PEOPLE'S BANKS*, 1896

. . . .

Credit union pioneers aimed to get rid of, by making no longer necessary, salary-loan operators—what we today call payday lenders—and other "loan sharks."

Credit Union vs. Salary Loans (Notice which ad says "thrifty"!)

Though the salary-loan business is one of great risks, every city in the country is infected with so-called loan sharks. Innocent borrowers must suffer equally with those for whom little social sympathy need be felt.

SAMUEL MCCUNE LINDSAY, "LOANS ON SALARIES AND WAGES," 1908

"But I can't possibly raise the money," cried the unfortunate clerk. "And if you notify my company I'll be fired—and then I can't pay the notes at all."

"Why not fix it this way," suggested [the salary-loan operator], who was aware of both contingencies. "You take out another loan to-day and pay the $14.09, and that will give you two weeks [i.e., until your next pay day] to make some arrangement before the next note is due."

. . . Within a year from the date of his first transaction with the Anaconda Company, Cogg had paid them more than twice the money he had borrowed, and was regularly handing over to them more than half his salary.

FRANK MARSHALL WHITE, "THE STORY OF A DEBT," 1912

. . . .

The People's Banks, or Credit Unions, as they are known in some states . . . aim to promote thrift and to abolish the necessity for loan sharks, and professional money lenders.

NEW YORK TIMES, JUNE 1, 1919

. . . .

They [credit unions] are designed to encourage thrift, and to provide credit facilities for their members. They lessen the strangle-hold of the loan sharks and start people on the way to free themselves from debt.

"LOANING MONEY ON CHARACTER," AN ARTICLE ABOUT CREDIT UNIONS, THE WORLD'S WORK, 1922

. . . .

In Pittsburgh, a few years ago, an investigation showed an appalling amount of loan shark activity among schoolteachers. But the Pittsburgh

schoolteachers now have a credit union. The loan shark is a dim and distant memory.

"THE POOR MAN'S BANK," AN ARTICLE SERIES IN THE PITTSBURGH PRESS, 1935

. . . .

DO YOU KNOW THAT:
Loan Sharks commonly charge 240 percent interest?
Loan Sharks try to prevent you from paying your debt?
Loan Sharks have fifteen ways of fooling you?

LOAN SHARKS AND THEIR VICTIMS, 1940

. . . .

Salary Loans . . . $10 to $80 . . . on your signature only . . . Quick—Confidential . . . For Employed Men & Women . . . Borrow on YOUR Signature Only . . . Employer, Relatives and Friends not Notified . . . Payments Arranged to Suite You Pay Days.

MATCHBOOK AD FOR A PAYDAY LENDING OPERATION CALLED (I'M NOT MAKING THIS UP!) THRIFTY LOAN SERVICE, ABOUT 1950

. . . .

Hey, are you kiddin'?

A BEMUSED CUSTOMER LOOKING FROM THE STREET INTO A STOREFRONT LOAN-SHARKING AND BET-MAKING OPERATION CALLED (I'M NOT MAKING THIS UP!) LIBERTY FINANCE, COMPLETE WITH WINDOW ADS PROMISING, "BE FREE OF WORRY" AND "CREDIT IS YOUR GREATEST ASSET," FROM THE MOVIE 711 OCEAN DRIVE, 1950

When you are in a jam, go to a credit union; don't go to a high-rate lender, as you are just throwing your money away.

ROY F. BERGENGREN, SPEECH IN BOSTON TO
THE AMERICAN ASSOCIATION FOR ECONOMIC
EDUCATION, 1934

. . . .

Roy F. Bergengren was born on June 14, 1879, in Gloucester, Massachusetts. He later moved with his family to Lynn, Massachusetts, where he attended high school. He graduated in 1903 from Dartmouth College and in 1906 from Harvard Law School. He opened a law practice in Lynn, in which, owing to his progressive political convictions, he ended up mostly serving people who were too poor to pay for legal help.

Bergengren knew very little about credit unions when, in 1920, at the age of forty, he was hired by Edward A. Filene, the Boston-based merchant and philanthropist, to be the managing director of the not-very-active Massachusetts Credit Union Association. The decades-long partnership between Filene and Bergengren—Filene as funder and national spokesperson, Bergengren as tireless grassroots leader and strategist—is arguably the most fruitful and consequential partnership in the history of U.S. thrift institutions.

At the outset, Bergengren set four ambitious goals for himself and the movement. First, to organize multiple credit unions in every U.S. state. Second, to organize a credit union league in each state. Third, to win passage of national legislation to support credit unions. And finally, to organize a national credit union association. Amazingly, and to his great credit, he achieved all four goals. I admire this man enormously. Roy F. Bergengren died on November 13, 1955.

A small, shabby office was opened at 5 Park Square, Boston, Massachusetts; it was furnished with some odds and ends of second-hand furniture. It was decided to call the effort the Credit Union National Extension Bureau . . . I well recall the first day. Into an empty office we moved an empty desk, an empty file, and empty chair and an old typewriter. I then sat in the empty chair at the empty desk and wondered how one went about the nationalization of cooperative credit.

ROY F. BERGENGREN, RECALLING HIS FIRST FEW DAYS
AS THE LEADER OF THE CREDIT UNION NATIONAL
EXTENSION BUREAU IN 1921

. . . .

During one of these trips in the spring of 1926 into the Midwest he traveled 4,500 miles in twenty-one days.

A DESCRIPTION OF BERGENGREN'S ACTIVITIES IN
J. CARROLL MOODY AND GILBERT C. FITE, *THE CREDIT
UNION MOVEMENT*

My notes indicate that it was "cold and rainy" and we had "tire trouble" and "got lost." However, we organized four new parish credit unions.

BERGENGREN, RECALLING AN ORGANIZING TRIP HE TOOK TO IOWA IN 1927

. . . .

In February [1928], for example, on one twenty-day trip I covered seventeen cities and towns in seven states and, with much local help everywhere, organized twenty-nine additional credit unions. There were all-day and evening meetings on eighteen of the days . . . In Kansas City we organized four credit unions in one day, something of a record for that time. We got one new league on that trip.

BERGENGREN, RECALLING EARLY 1928

. . . .

Members only had to put in 25 cents to join the credit union when it was first started, but in those days [1929] a quarter wasn't all that easy to come by. It gave our employees who couldn't afford bank accounts an easy way to save 50 or 75 cents a week and to obtain loans.

MRS. JOSEPHINE WEILER, RECALLING IN 1979 THE EARLY DAYS OF THE MONTGOMERY WARD FORT WORTH [TEXAS] CREDIT UNION, WHICH WAS FOUNDED IN 1929

. . . a minor Apostle of Thrift . . .

BERGENGREN, LOOKING BACK, RUEFULLY DESCRIBING HIS ACTIVITIES IN 1929, AT THE HEIGHT OF "THE WILDEST AND MOST IRRESPONSIBLE ERA IN THE HISTORY OF THE STOCK MARKET," AS HE CRISSCROSSED THE COUNTRY WITH HIS COLLEAGUES "LIKE SO MANY UNAPPRECIATED OLD MAIDS, PREACHING THRIFT TO A BEDAZZLED PEOPLE WHO COULD HEAR NOTHING BUT THE SWEET SONGS OF THE LORELEI."

. . . .

I really believe in the usefulness of these credit unions.

PRESIDENT FRANKLIN D. ROOSEVELT, MEMO TO THE U.S. SECRETARY OF THE TREASURY, HENRY MORGENTHAU JR., JUNE 1934

. . . .

. . . the greatest single step forward in the history of the credit union movement.

BERGENGREN, LETTER TO FILENE, CHARACTERIZING THE PASSAGE IN JUNE OF 1934 OF THE FEDERAL CREDIT UNION ACT, WHICH PROVIDED FOR THE INCORPORATION AND REGULATION OF CREDIT UNIONS NATIONALLY, JUNE 21, 1934

. . . .

The Credit Union National Extension Bureau did not come officially to an end until after the board meeting [of its much larger successor organization, the Credit Union National Association, or CUNA] in 1935 . . . It was nearly

HARDTIMES SICKNESS FINANCIAL DISTRESS

CREDIT UNION™

Thrift Credit

The Way to Economic Betterment

"Little Man Under the Umbrella," the main early symbol of the U.S. credit union movement.
Courtesy of the Credit Union National Association, Inc.

time to take my . . . hat permanently from the peg behind the door of Room 23, 5 Park Square, where we had done our best to produce a national credit union in America.

BERGENGREN

. . . .

Sometimes the small facts of history are poetic: 5 Park Square in Boston, where Bergengren's small office was located, was owned by the Franklin Savings Bank.

We shall, in credit unions, drive the usurious money lenders from the temple. We shall in credit unions equalize, by cooperation, those inequalities which make the worker at a modest wage pay more for everything he buys than does the individual whose wealth establishes him as a cash buyer of things. We shall in the credit unions eventually put about the home, for which our member goes forth to earn his daily bread, the protection of life insurance at cost and without exploitation. We shall eventually in the credit union establish such reserves for the worker in times of steady employment that he can withstand the rigors of unemployment without becoming either an object of charity or a ward of the state. We shall, in credit unions, encourage cooperation in its various manifestations as cooperation comes increasingly to supplant an economic system based on unfair profits with a system which operates on the sole basis of the maximum service by man to his fellow man without profit.

BERGENGREN, 1935

. . . .

We are not only pooling our savings, but we are pooling our knowledge about savings and the uses to which savings can be put . . . Our movement is not only democratic in form but democratic in aspiration. It is a movement toward economic democracy.

EDWARD A. FILENE, A SPEECH ABOUT CREDIT UNIONS, EARLY 1937

. . . .

Edward A. Filene, Bergengren's long-time employer and the great financial supporter and visionary of the U.S. credit union movement, was born in Salem, Massachusetts, in 1860. He died in Paris at the age of seventy-seven on September 26, 1937, while attending a meeting of the International Cooperative Alliance. Today, the headquarters of the U.S. credit union movement, located in Madison, Wisconsin, is called "Filene House."

Mr. Filene (and I knew him probably better than anyone else did) never felt that he owned any money. He had a great distaste for material things, lived very modestly, never owned an automobile and was scrupulously careful about small expenditures, all because he felt that he was a trustee for the money that he had earned and that the trustee-ship involved turning his accumulations into the greatest possible disinterested public service.

BERGENGREN, REMEMBERING FILENE

. . . .

When Filene died, Bergengren, ever the organizer, planned and attended thirty-one memorial meetings across the country so that hundreds of credit union leaders and members could pay their last respects and reflect on the meaning of Filene's life.

The credit union in Filene's department store in Boston is one of the largest of any type in the state . . .

CREDIT UNIONS IN MASSACHUSETTS, 1939

. . . .

Credit unions offer people who have few resources a way of getting funds when they need them. I am told that last year, in the United States alone, credit unions had about 4 million members and made *loans totaling close to $1 billion. This is a splendid record. It is a tribute to the values of thrift and self-help and mutual assistance.*

PRESIDENT HARRY S TRUMAN, SPEECH TO THE CREDIT UNION NATIONAL ASSOCIATION, MADISON, WISCONSIN, MAY 14, 1950

. . . .

As the bank is the basis of capitalist economic activity so the credit union is the basis of the co-operative movement . . . It is the business enterprise in which millions of people have experienced for the first time the thrill of co-operative activity and have realized that it is possible to have Christian brotherhood in economic life.

ONTARIO (CANADA) CREDIT UNION LEAGUE, 1942

. . . .

Harold Grant remembers that the credit union office was initially in George Willette's kitchen, with cardboard boxes serving as the filing cabinets. Back then [in 1961], he recalls, a strong sense of voluntarism and purpose was needed for any credit union to survive. Mr. Grant maintains that even today "voluntarism is the key to the success of a credit union."

HISTORY OF THE BARCO FEDERAL CREDIT UNION, WHICH WAS FOUNDED IN 1961 IN MILLENOCKET, MAINE, BY EMPLOYEES OF THE BANGOR AND AROOSTOOK RAILROAD COMPANY

Next to the church, credit unions are the most powerful force for good in America today.

A FREQUENT SAYING OF CONGRESSMAN WRIGHT PATMAN, WHO SERVED TEXAS AS A MEMBER OF THE U.S. CONGRESS FROM 1929 UNTIL HIS DEATH IN 1976

. . . .

. . . from 1940 to the late 1960s, savings in credit unions doubled every five years and in 1970 they represented 3 per cent of all public holdings in thrift institutions.

THE BUSINESS HISTORY REVIEW

. . . .

Nearly 34 million persons, or about one out of every six Americans, belong to a credit union—double the number a decade ago.

WALL STREET JOURNAL, JUNE 22, 1977

. . . .

According to the World Council of Credit Unions, in 2005 more than 86 million Americans, or more than 40 percent of the economically active population, belonged to a credit union.

44. Public Libraries

Here's something interesting I discovered: lovers of thrift tend almost invariably to be lovers of the public library. Once you think about it, it's not hard to see why. Thrift leaders are deeply attracted to the idea of efficiently sharing books and therefore of spreading fruitful knowledge on a mass scale at a relatively low cost. The old-fashioned aristocrat or the gentleman might want to build himself a fine private library. The progressive thrift visionary, on the other hand, wants to use his resources in order to go public and democratic—to build a huge book temple in the middle of the town and invite everyone to join. And keep the fees low! Thrift leaders advocate the cooperative lending of books via public libraries with the same fervor and for exactly the same reasons that they advocate the cooperative lending of money via building and loans and credit unions—both types of institutions are paradigmatic expressions of the thrift idea. Both types of organization are generative, or oriented to thriving. One promotes thrift of money. The other promotes thrift of knowledge. Once you think about it, the two go together naturally.

In the roll call of thrift-loving builders of public libraries, who in the United States is first on the list? Take a guess.

The Junto led to the establishment, by [Benjamin] Franklin, of the Philadelphia Public Library, which became the parent of all public libraries in America.
ELBERT HUBBARD

. . . .

When the fervent thrift advocate Andrew Carnegie wasn't busy making yet more money, or writing essays with titles such as "Thrift as a Duty," to what form of philanthropy was he devoting the greatest share of his time and fortune? Take a guess.

The result of my own study of the question, What is the best gift which can be given to a community? is that a free library occupies the first place, provided the community will accept and maintain it as a public institution . . .
ANDREW CARNEGIE, "THE GOSPEL OF WEALTH," 1889

. . . .

Carnegie chose libraries as his primary philanthropy in large part due to his firm conviction—a belief that has always been central to the thrift ethic—that the best, and in most cases only, way to help people is to help those who can and will help themselves.

The first requisite for a really good use of wealth by the millionaire who has accepted the gospel which proclaims him only a trustee of the surplus that comes to him, is to take care that the purposes for which he spends it shall not have a degrading, pauperizing tendency upon its recipients, but that his trust shall be so administered as to stimulate the best and most aspiring poor of the community to further efforts for their own improvement.

    . . . by placing books within the reach of 37,000 aspiring people which they were anxious to obtain, Mr. [Enoch] Pratt [the founder in 1882 of the Enoch Pratt Free Library of Baltimore] has done more for the genuine progress of the people than has been done by all the contributions of all the millionaires and rich people to help those who cannot or will not help themselves . . . Mr. Pratt is the ideal disciple of the gospel of wealth.

ANDREW CARNEGIE

. . . .

And who is this man from Baltimore, this "ideal disciple of the gospel of wealth," who helped to inspire Carnegie to build libraries across America?

Enoch Pratt, with his public generosity and private thrift.

HENRY P. GODDARD, "SOME DISTINGUISHED MARYLANDERS I HAVE KNOWN," 1909

. . . .

Born in North Middlebrough, Massachusetts [in 1808] . . . he came here [to Baltimore] at the age of twenty-three and established himself in the iron business, which he still continues. Prosperity soon followed—not rapidly, but steadily, because it was based on those qualities of honesty, industry, sagacity and energy which, mingled with thrift, although they cannot be said to insure success, are certainly most likely to achieve it.

GEORGE WILLIAM BROWN, BOARD OF TRUSTEES OF THE PRATT FREE LIBRARY, AT THE LIBRARY DEDICATION CEREMONIES OF JANUARY 4, 1886

. . . .

His large fortune has been accumulated entirely by the labor of his own hands, and is a direct result of a tireless energy and the application of a strict integrity and fixedness of purpose to acquire and a wise economy and sagacity to save.

SKETCH OF ENOCH PRATT'S LIFE, 1886

. . . .

The theme of thrift and the Enoch Pratt Free Library regularly intersect.

As a part of its work in the aid of children the society has established a number of home libraries . . . There are now 14 libraries, each containing about 20 books in a box, which is kept in the home of one of the children. To that particular home a friendly visitor comes once a week . . . The object of these libraries is to develop an interest in the child so that it will of its own volition use the Enoch Pratt and other libraries of Baltimore. Miss Mary Wilcox Brown, the author of The Development of Thrift, *is the secretary of the Children's Aid Society, and the work of the home libraries is due to her efforts.*

REPORT OF THE HENRY WATSON CHILDREN'S AID SOCIETY OF BALTIMORE, *THE LIBRARY JOURNAL*, JANUARY 1900

. . . .

Aid from private sources was received in the establishment of several of the branches [of the Pratt Free Library]. That of Woodbury and Hampden was donated by citizens of that thriving milling suburb, headed by Mr. Robert Poole, who has since 1886 conducted there a free reading-room and circulating library at his own expense. Upon his solicitation, also, a room in this branch library was rented to a savings bank, for the encouragement of thrift among the readers.

A HISTORY OF BALTIMORE, 1912

. . . .

Boxes of books were sent [by the Pratt Free Library] to public and private schools, reformatory institutions, Sunday schools, playgrounds and clubs, post offices [and] police stations, as a desire for them became manifest. The growth of the work became so rapid that it was evident that the endowment of Mr. Pratt could not meet its demands. In 1906, therefore, an appeal was made to Mr. Carnegie for aid. Mr. Carnegie responded favorably, stating in a letter that "Enoch Pratt was my pioneer—I visited him, saw his Library . . . " He [Carnegie] offered to give $500,000 for the erection of twenty branch libraries on city lots . . .

A HISTORY OF BALTIMORE

. . . .

Andrew Carnegie's gifts of libraries had an astonishing impact on the American landscape in the early years of the twentieth century. By 1907, he had provided for more than 1,000 libraries across the United States. Ten years later, the number had grown to 2,865. In Indiana alone, for example, in the slightly more than three years between January of 1901 and March of 1904, Carnegie established and equipped libraries in thirty-nine Indiana cities spread across thirty-six of Indiana's ninety-two counties.[1]

Probably no other single American from the era of the Civil War through the end of World War II—with the possible exception of Frederick Law Olmsted, who designed and successfully advocated for public parks in so many major U.S. cities—has so dramatically altered, in so short a period of time, the physical look and civil society organization of American cities and towns.

IT'S PART OF OUR AMERICAN TRADITION
TO WORK THINGS OUT TOGETHER

The Blockhouse

First homes in many pioneer areas were built within the protection of blockhouse forts. Working together, the families were strong against trouble

How today 10 million of us
ward off money troubles

WORKING things out together in the American tradition has enabled certain groups of people in our country to secure a remarkable degree of protection against money troubles.

These groups are called credit unions. There are more than 20,000 of them in America . . . with almost 10,000,000 members.

A credit union is simply a group of people with some common bond, such as employment in the same company or membership in the same church or club, who operate their own borrowing and savings system under a proven plan. All credit unions are chartered and supervised by federal or state agencies.

This plan was started over 100 years ago when a group hit upon the simple expediency of pool-

ing their savings in a common fund which could be used to help those who needed money for emergencies or any other provident purpose.

That's still the way credit unions operate to-day. The members save their money together a little at a time whenever they can. Saving is encouraged and made easier by the convenient location of the credit union (usually right in the plant or office) and by good returns on the money.

But the greatest service of the credit union is to provide a ready source of understanding credit. A means by which people working together can improve their living standards without getting into financial difficulties. Loans are made at low cost. Actually, in addition to borrowing for emergency purposes, members find it's cheaper

to use a credit union loan and handle major purchases with cash.

The entire credit union idea is democracy in action—people working things out together with dignity of spirit. Management, labor, church and government all heartily endorse credit unions. Anyone employed by a company with 50 or more employees, or belonging to a church, lodge or other group can help get a credit union started. One person informed about credit unions can easily be the instrument of great good to himself and hundreds more where he works or lives.

SEND FOR FREE BOOKLET. Just write and say, "Tell me more about credit unions." Sign your name and address and mail to Credit Union, Dept. 100, Box 57, Madison, Wisconsin.

45

Credit Union ad

The Public Library of Portland, Indiana, was established in January, 1900. A meeting was held at the court house, at which nine directors were appointed . . . Miss Elma Bolton was engaged as librarian, which position she held until the donation was received from Mr. Carnegie, when Miss Nellie Stanley was engaged to take charge until a trained librarian should come in March 1902, to reorganize the Library previous to moving into the new building.

In March 1901, Mr. Carnegie's offer of $15,000 for the erection of a new building was accepted, the building being completed and dedicated September 10, 1902. The new Library building contains a general reading room, children's room, reference room, librarian's room and stack room, with a basement which contains work room, boiler room and two other rooms which, when furnished, will be used for general assemblies. The building is heated by hot water and lighted by electricity.

REPORT FROM THE CARNEGIE FREE LIBRARY OF PORTLAND, INDIANA, *MUNCIPAL AND INSTITUTIONAL LIBRARIES OF INDIANA*, 1904

. . . .

I like a free library because it is free. It is the grand symbol of true genuine democracy . . . It is great for what it does in enabling the poor citizens of Liverpool in passing through her streets to look up and say—"Yes, I am a landlord there." That is the thing that tells . . . They [public libraries] cannot work injury. They must always work for good. They

cannot pauperize; because they are the people's own property . . .

ANDREW CARNEGIE, REMARKS AT THE OPENING OF THE TOXTETH BRANCH OF THE FREE PUBLIC LIBRARY OF LIVERPOOL, ENGLAND, OCTOBER 15, 1902

. . . .

Remember from earlier in the book the businessman, philanthropist, and thrift leader Charles Pratt of Brooklyn, whose Ben Franklin–derived personal motto, "Waste Neither Time Nor Money," was inscribed above the fireplace of the reading room of "The Astral," Pratt's model housing project? Charles Pratt (who appears to be unrelated to Baltimore's Enoch Pratt) also loved libraries, and loved to build them.

From the beginning the Pratt Institute Free Library, organized in 1887 while the Brooklyn Library was still a subscription library and the Brooklyn Public Library which absorbed it had not yet been started, was a free circulating and reference library for the people of Brooklyn . . .

JOSEPHINE ADAMS RATHBONE, "THE PRATT INSTITUTE SCHOOL OF LIBRARY SCIENCE," *THE LIBRARY JOURNAL*, NOVEMBER 15, 1921

. . . .

In 1888 . . . Mr. Charles Pratt . . . [gave] the details of a scheme in which he wished to benefit the working people particularly of his native town [of Watertown, Mass.] . . . he offered to give $5,000 for *the establishment of a fund to furnish periodicals of use particularly to the industrial portion of the community, on the condition that the town would fit up the lower rooms [of the Library] for reading-rooms in a appropriate and substantial manner.*

REPORT ON THE ESTABLISHMENT OF THE ASA PRATT READING ROOM OF THE FREE PUBLIC LIBRARY OF WATERTOWN, MASSACHUSETTS, 1892

. . . .

America has taken the lead in developing the usefulness of Public Libraries . . . in library economy and administration we [in Britain] can learn many lessons from our progressive cousins on the other side of the Atlantic . . . The marvelous growth of the movement in America is extraordinary. Seventy years ago such things as public libraries were almost unknown in America . . . Today they are as common as public schools . . . Public libraries have reached a development in the State of Massachusetts which would probably be impossible to match anywhere else in the world.

PUBLIC LIBRARIES, 1891

The avowed enemies everywhere of Public Libraries are the publicans [owners of drinking establishments], and yet it is acknowledged on all hands that their business creates the necessity of the workhouse and jail, with their huge machinery for management. How long will thrifty and intelligent citizens continue to be governed by this powerful body, who always range themselves against every movement which has for its object the true interests of citizenship?

. . . The presence of Public Library buildings always improve the adjoining property . . . These institutions inculcate by their influence temperate habits and thrift, and as the masses spend less in drink they will have more to spend with the local tradesmen.

PUBLIC LIBRARIES, 1891

45. Thrift Shops

WINSTON CHURCHILL once reportedly said, a dog looks up at you, a cat looks down at you, but only a pig looks you directly in the eye. That's how I feel about thrift shops. Of all the thrift institutions, the thrift shop looks you most directly in the eye, revealing simply and with complete transparency nearly all that thrift is. That's probably why they are called . . . thrift shops!

Thrift shops are probably the thriftiest of all the thrift institutions. Recall from part one the three lodestars of the thrift concept—industry, frugality, and trusteeship. Thrift shops are about one-third of each, without an ounce of fat. Industry: thrift shops historically and still typically encourage work and self-help by providing jobs in the stores for low-income people. Frugality: thrift shops stand front and center for conservation, reuse and repurposing, low and affordable prices, and the toning down of consumerism run amok. Trusteeship: thrift shops are nonprofit charities that seek to give back to the community and serve people in need.

And to top it all off, thrift shops today are . . . **kind of cool.**

As for us, we wear avant-thrift.

LISA ROBERTSON, *SOFT ARCHITECTURE: A MANIFESTO*, 1999

. . . .

Besides the look, there are substantive justifications for thrift store shopping. For starters, where else can you get a wardrobe for under five dollars? Arrive on a blue tag day with a five-spot, and you'll walk home with two pairs of pants, three shirts, a clip-on tie, and between five and ten hit cassette singles . . .

And of course, if overflowing landfills or sweatshop labor stresses you out, thrift stores are a healthy way to release your craving to consume without actually compelling new production. So you get that phatty new outfit without the guilt . . .

. . . the stuff has been loved and then tossed, and somewhere in the pile, there is treasure waiting to be created, with no model to tell you it was "in" this season. Used clothes come with more than just image; they have history. And while critics would say that thrift-shopping has largely become as trendy as the mall, there remains a certain inevitably creative element to assembling an outfit that is indeed unique to you, not mass produced . . . thrift stores have become beacons for people trying to avoid the general plague of consumerism

or seeking something different that you can't
find in the strange cloned netherworld that is
the American mall.

RUSS BARUFFI, *THE COLLEGE HILL INDEPENDENT*, 2003

. . . .

Stores selling consignment, resale and otherwise
"gently used" shoes and clothing have gone
mainstream. The National Association of Resale
and Thrift Stores said it had 25,000 stores—
up from about 20,000 five years ago.

NEW YORK TIMES, JUNE 24, 2006

The clothing swap gained traction in the last
decade as a kicky girls night in; one woman
would invite a dozen friends over to trade
cast-offs, kvetch and drink. But now it has
become a night out, moving to public spaces
like bars and community centers, where anyone
is welcome.

NEW YORK TIMES, JULY 9, 2006

. . . .

"To assist but not pauperize the worthy poor" is
the motto of the clothing bureau which for the

past four years has been conducted by the King's Daughters of Zion and St. Timothy's Protestant Episcopal Church of this city.

NEW YORK TIMES, JANUARY 18, 1897

. . . .

There is a social responsibility for such further utilization of clothing . . . There are in several cities clothing bureaus that solicit gifts of worn clothing and sell them at reasonable prices, the proceeds going to charities, such as the Clothing Bureau and Everybody's Thrift Shop of New York . . .

BENJAMIN R. ANDREWS, ECONOMICS OF THE HOUSEHOLD, 1924

Thrift Shop. *The Red Cross Chapter in Montclair, New Jersey, has for almost five years been operating a shop which sells partially used clothing, household goods, and other articles contributed by members of the community, distributes books and magazines to "shut-ins," students, and prisons, and arranges for the "rehabilitation" of toys to be given away at Christmas . . . the profits on sales over and above all expenses are sufficient to support two scholarships and aid the visiting nurse's service.*

JOURNAL OF HOME ECONOMICS, 1928

. . . .

We Turn Your Trash Into Cash

MOTTO OF THE JUNIOR LEAGUE THRIFT SHOP OF WASHINGTON, DC, 1931

PART FIVE

Movements

IN JULY OF 1950, about forty savings bank leaders from a dozen or so countries spent a week together in Oxford, England. They were the first participants in what eventually became an annual summer school convened by the International Savings Bank Institute, an organization that had been formed in 1925 as the International Thrift Institute. During one portion of that week, the students traveled north to the little village of Ruthwell, in the Scottish border country, to visit the Parish Hall where, in 1810, the Rev. Henry Duncan (whom we met in part three) had established the world's first modern savings bank. The students stood or kneeled in front of the old building and smiled—mostly men, but a few women as well, many wearing overcoats for a crisp Scottish summer day—to have their picture taken.

Sixty-seven years later, in July of 2007, I too traveled to the village of Ruthwell to visit that Parish Hall. I went with my mother. We opened the creaky door, walked in, and saw that we were the only visitors present. A manager emerged from a side room. He asked my mother, "Just traveling through?" She said, "No, my son came all the way from New York City to visit with you." We spent several delightful hours talking to this fellow, Mr. Robert Vallance, who, it turns out, is a scholar and a remarkable authority on Duncan, on Ruthwell, and on the Scottish savings bank movement.

I too had my picture taken in front of that old building. Standing there, posing while my mother adjusted the camera, I thought very intently, and perhaps a little wistfully, of that photograph from 1950 of the summer school students. Are any of those people still living? I'm standing here as one person, I thought, just a tourist. *Those people were part of a movement.*

A few years before 1950, in April of 1945, a terrible world war is ending. There are plans for a United Nations and hopes for a more cooperative, peaceful world in the future. And that spring, Roy F. Bergengren, the credit union organizer, publishes a little book called *I Speak for Joe Doakes*. Even if you are not a thrift nut, the book is worth reading. It's a straightforward, passionate call for economic democracy and cooperation at home and abroad. He wants big changes.

I believe that our next phase of economic life should rather consist of a reformed capitalism, dedicated to the service of man, in fair competition with a rapidly developing and efficient co-operative system . . . In the long run I believe that co-operation will be found to be more consistent with what the forefathers had in mind for American than capitalism.

ROY F. BERGENGREN, *I SPEAK FOR JOE DOAKES*, 1945

Roy Bergengren was a part of a movement. The savings bank leaders who visited Ruthwell were a part of a movement. Social movements by definition are big, sprawling things, but we can often get the feel of them by looking at specific, small moments.

How can we tell whether or not we are looking at a genuine social movement? For starters, the people involved tend to call what they are doing a "movement," rather than, say, a business or a vocation or a political campaign. They also typically want to do considerably more than expand one organization, or change one specific law or institution; they usually want to change minds and policies in general, on a broad scale. For this reason, they are inveterate coalition-builders.

People in social movements almost always have what they believe to be an urgent message. They seek to share that message with everyone, including children. They are constantly looking for converts,

new recruits. They tend to be idealistic. The salary matters and the status matters, but what ultimately drives the best of them is the mission. They believe that they are working for a better world. They feel a sense of comradeship, a sense of shared meaning and sacrifice, with others in the same movement. Many social movements also have, or claim, a universal dimension and message; they often pay much less attention than do others in the society to the languages and skin colors that divide people or to the borders that divide countries.

As we've seen, thrift can be an individual virtue and practice. It can be part of the ethos of a household. It can inspire and build particular institutions. It can determine business strategy. It can help to guide public policy and political debate. The thrift idea does all of these things. But ultimately, and beyond these specific spheres, thrift can also drive social movements. It can be the motivating mission. Thrift can be the vision that brings together idealistic people to work for broad social change.

We call our co-operative credit societies "credit unions." They constitute a single subdivision of the co-operative movement which is becoming important in America and which has reached, with its philosophy, into all parts of the world and to all people.

BERGENGREN, *I SPEAK FOR JOE DOAKES*

Let's briefly look at four notable characteristics, or organizing aims, of thrift movements in Britain and the United States.

46. To Build International Solidarity

I have met credit union people in Switzerland, Holland, Germany, and Belgium. I have talked credit union with men who had the same point of view I had in England and the best informed man I know on all matters pertaining to cooperation is my deeply and highly respected and beloved friend, Dr. G. Fauquet of Paris. When I think of the future, I think of the identity of interest of tram drivers in London and motor men in Kansas City. I think of a universal language, the language of cooperation which will one day do away with passports and customs regulations and invisible lines separating men who have common interests and supercede in quite orderly fashion all of the demagogues and dictators and political bosses of the world, substituting cooperative effort, properly understood and successfully applied.

I shall be dead long before that happens but the catholicity of the cooperative movement is the one hope of the world.

ROY F. BERGENGREN, 1935

. . . .

Thrift Propaganda, especially among the working and middle classes.

AGENDA ITEM, FIRST INTERNATIONAL THRIFT CONGRESS, MILAN, OCTOBER 1924

Asking for the most beautiful and efficacious words written on thrift in the language of each country.

A REQUEST SENT TO DELEGATES ATTENDING THE MILAN CONGRESS

. . . .

That, in this ideal, Thrift finds no place as a theory of self-denial to be practiced solely by the poorer classes, but as a discipline imposing upon all a better social and individual usage of all wealth.

A RESOLUTION ADOPTED BY THE MILAN CONGRESS

. . . .

The claim of "first" almost always becomes complicated. As we've seen, in Edinburgh, Scotland, on June 8–10, 1910, British savings bank leaders had organized what they called an International Thrift Congress to commemorate the centenary of the founding by Henry Duncan of Ruthwell of the first modern savings bank. That Edinburgh conference was attended by delegates from a number of countries, including the United States. In addition, as we've also seen, S. W. Straus and the American Society for Thrift organized what they too called an International Thrift Congress, as a part of the Panama-Pacific International Expo-

Participants in the first International Summer School (10–15 July, 1950, in Oxford) visit the home of Henry Duncan, founder of the Scots Savings Banks

sition in San Francisco on August 11–13, 1915—though apparently few if any delegates from overseas actually attended this gathering.

The 1924 Milan conference, which had grown out of earlier, local efforts to commemorate the centenary of the founding of the famous Lombardy Savings Bank, attracted a total of 354 delegates from 27 countries. It therefore does indeed stand out as the first successful attempt to gather together, for serious collaboration and ongoing mutual exchange, many of the leaders of savings bank movements from around the world, including the United States.

To institutionalize its work, this congress created a permanent organization—the International Thrift Institute, headquartered in Milan—began planning for future congresses, proposed that October 31 be recognized each year in every country as "World Thrift Day," and started a journal, World Thrift.

It was this organization that years later, in 1950, organized the international summer school that met in Oxford and went on the pilgrimage to Ruthwell.

Thrift, precisely because it is par excellence an ethical, economic-social problem, has no boundaries, no nationality . . .

MARQUIS GIUSEPPE DE CAPITANI D'ARZAGO,
PRESIDENT OF THE LOMBARDY SAVINGS BANK,
ADDRESS TO THE FIRST INTERNATIONAL THRIFT
CONGRESS, MILAN, OCTOBER 26, 1924

*A library is slowly being formed in the Institute
... regarding Thrift, and how it is carried out
in the various countries and in its institutions, in
order to form little by little a kind of permanent
encyclopedia of Thrift.*

WORLD THRIFT, 1926

. . . .

*This was the first gentleman in the United
States to answer the call ... He did his utmost,
ably continuing his work for the success of the
undertaking, moved by the vision of the world-wide
function, both economical and moral, of Thrift and
of the Savings banks, upheld by the highest ideals of
international peace.*

AN EXPRESSION OF GRATITUDE FROM THE
INTERNATIONAL THRIFT INSTITUTE TO MILTON W.
HARRISON, SECRETARY OF THE SAVINGS BANK SECTION
OF THE AMERICAN BANKERS ASSOCIATION, FOR HIS
SUPPORT OF THE INTERNATIONAL THRIFT CONGRESS,
ON THE OCCASION OF AN INTERNATIONAL MEETING
OF SAVINGS BANK LEADERS HELD IN PHILADELPHIA ON
OCTOBER 18–22, 1926

. . . .

The Philadelphia conference attracted delegates
from a total of nineteen nations and included
the participation of the International Thrift Institute.[1]

*... the [Second] International Thrift Congress,
which opens to-day at Burlington-gardens, W. [in
London]. There are about 400 delegates, more than
half of whom are from 29 foreign countries ...
The first congress was held at Milan five years ago,
where the movement was founded.*

"WORLD THRIFT," THE TIMES, OCTOBER 8, 1929

. . . .

*It has been a privilege to me to have been able to
identify myself with the inculcation of the habit of
Thrift in Great Britain. I have learnt to know at
first hand something of the magnitude and value
of the work which my own fellow-countrymen
are doing in this connection; but I think I never
realized how world-wide was the Thrift movement,
how vigorous and manifold were its activities, until
I took part in the great and historic gathering of
that International Thrift Congress five years ago in
Milan. (Applause.)*

SIR SPENCER J. PORTAL, ADDRESS TO THE SECOND
INTERNATIONAL THRIFT CONGRESS, LONDON, OCTOBER
8, 1929

. . . .

*What is needed is some way to make saving a
romance and to tempt the young to the high
adventure of thrift. For this purpose of striking
youthful imaginations there is a good deal to say for
holding an Exhibition side by side with the next
Thrift Congress ... the mechanical aids to thrift are
never seen in mass arrayed, and it would gladden
many careful hearts to see how many and how
various are the money-boxes of the world ... It
would also be a valuable part of such an exhibition*

*to have a Chamber of Horrors showing not only
the usual spendthrift's progress, with some real
paneling from the Bankruptcy Court, but also the
most notorious relics of extravagance available—
highly priced bad wines laid out in a setting of evil
waiters, flimsy and ephemeral dresses guarded by
waxen unscrupulous modistes, boxes at bad plays,
and so on through the range of ways in which it is
particularly easy to spend a great deal and get very
little for it.*

"A THRIFT EXHIBITION," *THE TIMES*,
OCTOBER 12, 1929

. . . .

*No fewer than 28 countries joined in observing
"World Thrift Day" last year.*

THE TIMES, OCTOBER 31, 1933

. . . .

The Third International Thrift Congress, drawing
more than 1,000 delegates representing more than
8,000 savings banks in 36 countries, was held in
Paris on May 20–25, 1935.[2]

*Thrift, it is urged by the promoters of World Thrift
Day, is more than the mere practice of saving
money: it implies rather a denunciation of every
form of waste, not only of money, but of time,
energy, talents, and other assets of mankind. It is by
conserving these assets and by directing them into
channels of constructive use that the character and
well-being of the individual and the community*

*can be developed, and a real contribution be made
toward the economic and moral reconstruction of
the world.*

"WORLD THRIFT DAY," *THE TIMES*, OCTOBER 26, 1938

. . . .

France: *. . . Government financial experts are busy
discussing means for financing the war and the
effort to be demanded of French saving . . .*
Germany: *Public statements of the increased
importance of saving in wartime are the order of
the day in Germany . . .*
Great Britain: *During the first three weeks of
the War Savings Campaign which began late in
November . . .*

"INTERNATIONAL THRIFT CHRONICLE," *THRIFT*
(FORMERLY *WORLD THRIFT*), THE JOURNAL OF THE
INTERNATIONAL THRIFT INSTITUTE, 1939

. . . .

International Exchange of Thrift Publicity Posters

*Those of our members who send us 12 copies of
thrift publicity posters will receive in exchange
10 different posters from other countries (2 copies
remaining with us for our Files) with translations
of their wording . . . We hardly need emphasize
the advantage there is in having posters of other
countries available for purposes of comparison and
inspiration . . .*

THRIFT, 1939

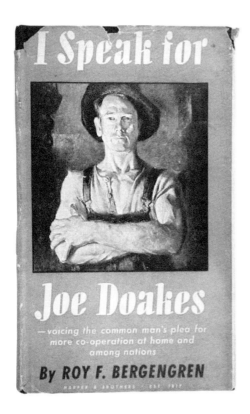

Published 1945

A Japanese savings poster submitted that year shows a row of children marching, carrying the national flag, in military headgear.

Picture this amazing moment. It's 1939. These people have been meeting together, united by a shared desire to promote thrift worldwide, since 1924. Now another world war is beginning. The International Thrift Institute is about to suspend its work. Meanwhile, most of the nations plunging into war with one another are publicly invoking the value of thrift to mobilize their populations for that war. And yet, quite poignantly, as late as 1939, the organization's leaders, as if in some kind of denial, are still seeking to organize an international exchange of thrift publicity posters, "for purposes of comparison and inspiration."

The Fourth International Thrift Conference, to be held in Berlin in 1940, for which the preparations had advanced according to schedule up until the last meeting of the Permanent Committee on 25 May 1939 in Lisbon, could not take place due to the war.

A HISTORY OF THE INTERNATIONAL THRIFT INSTITUTE

. . . .

The last English-language version of the journal *Thrift* coming out of Milan appeared in 1942. In 1943, the Milan headquarters of the International Thrift Institute was destroyed by bombing.[3]

In 1948, the International Thrift Institute resumed its work, establishing its new headquarters in Amsterdam. In 1963, the group changed its name to the International Savings Bank Institute. In 1969, the organization moved to Geneva, and in 1994, to Brussels, where it operates today as the World Savings Bank Institute (WSBI), in conjunction with the Brussels-based European Savings Bank Group.

By the way, the Fourth International Thrift Congress, originally planned for Berlin in 1940, did eventually take place—in Wiesbaden, West Germany, on June 14–16, 1954.

47. To Bring People Together

IN BOTH BRITAIN and the United States, generations of thrift leaders have sought to build broad national coalitions capable of putting thrift high on the public agenda.

A society called the National Thrift Society is now in the course of formation at Oxford, having for its chief object the encouragement of thrift among school-children, the working-classes, servants and artisans.

LORD JOHN MANNERS, 1877

. . . .

The National Thrift Society got started in Oxford in 1878. Apparently the principal founder was T. Bowden Green, who also authored a short biography of Samuel Smiles (*Samuel Smiles, His Life and Work*, 1904). The Society's chairman for some period of time was Dr. Greville Walpole, and its vice president for a number of years was Sir Hugh Owen (1804–81), a Welsh educational reformer and philanthropist who was also a leader for many years of the National Temperance League.[1]

A penny bank, established by the National Thrift Society, was opened last Monday evening at the Board Schools, Portobello-road. There were a large number of depositors, and more than 500 accounts were begun . . .

THE ILLUSTRATED LONDON NEWS, MARCH 12, 1881

. . . .

We hail the appearance of this excellent periodical with pleasure. It is calculated to do much toward the cultivation of habits of thrift and economy . . .

REVIEW OF THE FIRST ISSUE OF *THRIFT*,
THE PUBLICATION OF THE NATIONAL THRIFT
SOCIETY, IN *THE PRACTICAL TEACHER*, MAY 1882

. . . .

Arrangements are now being made by the National Thrift Society for holding a large number of thrift meetings throughout London and the surrounding districts . . . It is estimated that several hundred thousand copies of the society's thrift publications will be distributed at these meetings.

THE TIMES, SEPTEMBER 1, 1883

. . . .

the national thrift movement . . .

AGENDA TOPIC FOR THE FOURTH NATIONAL GATHERING
OF THE AMERICAN ASSOCIATION FOR THE ADVANCEMENT
OF SCIENCE, HELD AT COLUMBIA UNIVERSITY, NEW YORK
CITY, 1916

. . . .

It is astonishing how the idea of thrift has been spreading the last few months.

ARTHUR H. CHAMBERLAIN, CHAIRMAN OF THE
COMMITTEE ON THRIFT EDUCATION OF THE NATIONAL
EDUCATION ASSOCIATION, QUOTED IN THE *NEW YORK
TIMES*, MAY 14, 1916

Arthur Henry Chamberlain of San Francisco was a professor of education and dean at the Throop Polytechnic Institute in Pasadena. Chamberlain's

connections to the U.S. thrift movement of the early twentieth century were numerous. While chairing the NEA's Committee on Thrift Education, he worked closely with S. W. Straus and the American Society for Thrift, serving as that group's educational director. He was also the general editor of the Lippincott "Thrift Text Series," which included both Straus' 1920 book, *History of the Thrift Movement in America*, and Chamberlain's own 1919 book (coauthored with James F. Chamberlain), *Thrift and Conservation: How to Teach It.*

Intelligence—Health—Thrift

MOTTO OF THE CLOTHING FACTS BUREAU OF BOSTON,
MASSACHUSETTS, ESTABLISHED IN NOVEMBER OF 1917
TO PROVIDE PEOPLE WITH RELIABLE INFORMATION ON
MAKING AND PURCHASING CLOTHES

. . . .

. . . [to] make war-taught thrift and the practice of saving through lending to the Government a permanent and happy habit of the American people, the United States Treasury will conduct

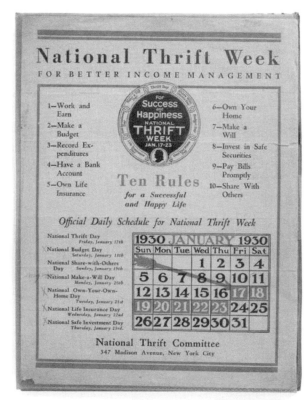

during *1919 an intensive movement to promote wise spending, intelligent saving, and safe investment.*

TO MAKE THRIFT A HAPPY HABIT, U.S. TREASURY
DEPARTMENT, 1918

. . . .

In the United States, a broadly based and quite interesting thrift initiative began in late 1917 under the general leadership of the YMCA and continued for nearly fifty years.

The National Thrift Committee has it origin in 1917, under the sponsorship of the YMCA. Its primary purpose was two-fold—to assist in the promotion of Baby War Bonds in the First World

War and to develop helpful materials in the field of personal money management.

"RESUME OF THE NATIONAL THRIFT COMMITTEE"

. . . .

A luncheon was given yesterday at the Bankers Club by Adolph Lewisohn, Chairman of the National Committee for Thrift, at which plans were discussed for a national thrift week to begin on January 17 next, under the direction of the Y.M.C.A. The date selected for beginning the campaign is the anniversary of the birth of Benjamin Franklin and the plans now under consideration are most comprehensive.

NEW YORK TIMES, DECEMBER 24, 1919

In more than 300 cities National Thrift Week will be launched today to implant the thrift idea . . .

NEW YORK TIMES, JANUARY 17, 1920

. . . .

The thrift campaign in Atlanta is part of a national movement which was inaugurated by the Y.M.C.A. and is now being observed throughout the United States.

THE ATLANTA CONSTITUTION, JANUARY 22, 1920

. . . .

The Home Economics Teacher is the natural leader in the Thrift Movement as it relates to the home.

MARY S. WOOLMAN, CLOTHING, 1920

. . . .

National Thrift Week, designed to impress on the people of this country the importance of thrift, begins tomorrow, on the anniversary of the birth of the great preacher of thrift, Benjamin Franklin.

NEW YORK TIMES, JANUARY 16, 1921

. . . .

The United Stewardship Council of Protestant Churches is an organization representing the stewardship promotion of many of the larger denominations. This Council has secured the endorsements of their various denominations in a united stewardship program which starts January

17th and includes the observation of National Thrift Week through the cooperation of the Churches with local Thrift Week Committees . . .

REPORT OF THE INTERNATIONAL COMMITTEE OF THE YMCA'S OF NORTH AMERICA, 1921

. . . .

. . . this year's [1922's] official slogan, "Spend time and money wisely."

JOHN A. GOODELL, DIRECTOR, NATIONAL THRIFT WEEK, LETTER TO THE NEW YORK TIMES, DECEMBER 31, 1921

. . . .

Efforts are made to establish regular organizations called "Thrift Societies," in conjunction with the building association movement. The main object of these societies is to instill the idea of thrift in time, money and other details of life into the American people . . . The Y.M.C.A. of the United States have inaugurated a so-called "Thrift Week" each year . . . [and in] many states the building associations are utilizing the thrift week as a special one for membership campaigns, and are meeting with good success, especially on [the day of Thrift Week that is called] "Own Your Own Home" day.

CYCLOPEDIA OF BUILDING, LOAN AND SAVINGS ASSOCIATIONS, 1923

. . . .

Miss Hilda Wendt of Michigan City, Indiana, won the first prize for the best essay on Benjamin

NATIONAL THRIFT NEWS

Published by
National Thrift Committee

347 Madison Avenue
New York City

Vol. 9   December, 1927   No. 3

**Special Inside Pro-
gram for "Y"
Work Features
1928 Plans**

**New Skeleton Cam-
paign Gives Oppor-
tunity for Participation
on Restricted Basis**

**The National Thrift
Ten Point
Success Creed**

Work and Earn
Make a Budget
Record Expenditures
Have a Bank Account
Carry Life Insurance
Own Your Home
Make a Will
Invest in Safe Securities
Pay Bills Promptly
Share With Others

"For Success and Happiness"

**Big Rally Formally
Opens Tenth Na-
tional Thrift Week**

**Enthusiastic Meeting
of Executive Com-
mittee Forecasts Best
Year. Adolph Lewis-
ohn again Leads Move-
ment**

Franklin conducted by the National Thrift Committee of the Y.M.C.A., it was announced yesterday. The prizes were offered by J. Robert Stout, President of the Education Thrift Society, Inc.

NEW YORK TIMES, APRIL 18, 1926

. . . .

The publisher J. Robert Stout (born July 23, 1878) of Ridgewood, New Jersey, founded Education Thrift Service in New York City in 1914. For many years—at least through the early 1940s—Stout served as chairman of the executive committee of the YMCA's National Thrift Committee. Stout also cofounded and for years led the International Benjamin Franklin Society, based in New York City, and as a hobby over the years assembled his own collection of books by and about Franklin. Stout was also a generous donor to the Valley Hospital in Ridgewood. He died at the age of eighty-six in March of 1965.[2]

The national character of this movement is often lost to the worker in local fields. Yet the realization that National Thrift Week is not confined to your city is a big factor in our future development. At the same time that you are spreading the gospel of "success and happiness" to your own friends and townsfolk, hundreds of others are doing the very same thing, in every state of the Union.

NATIONAL THRIFT WEEK ANNUAL REPORT, 1926

. . . .

Mrs. T. J. Matheson, state chairman of thrift for the Georgia P.T.A., outlines the following plans for the observance of thrift week in January: "Thrift pictures to us a good provider—one who makes and serves for the happiness of his family and society. Energy, progress and prosperity, acquisition, economy, contentment and generosity are the elements of thrift which we value most. During thrift week in January we are asking each local P.T.A. to observe a 'daddies night' using 'Thrift' as the theme of the evening."

ATLANTA CONSTITUTION, NOVEMBER 21, 1926

. . . .

. . . the Colorado Springs [Girl Scouts] Council, with Mrs. C. S. Morrison as Chairman of their Thrift Committee and leader of their thrift campaign, decided that there was a great deal more to thrift than simply paying your dues of fifty cents year, and that it was their duty to help the Girl Scouts to a true understanding of thrift and a cultivation of thrifty habits.

THE GIRL SCOUT LEADER, DECEMBER 1926

Knowing that you are interested in the coming Thrift Week Campaign, I am taking the liberty of asking you to serve with me upon the Committee for Meetings and Speakers.

LETTER OF CHARLES H. HILLEGEIST OF THE
THRIFT COMMITTEE FOR THE DISTRICT OF COLUMBIA
TO MRS. ANNA K. WILEY OF WASHINGTON, DC,
DECEMBER 23, 1926

. . . .

Careful consideration has been given to the selection of persons well qualified for this particular field of endeavor. We therefore are writing you to urge that you consent to address one or more gatherings during "Thrift Week," delivering a talk of from five to ten minutes duration.

LETTER OF HILLEGEIST TO WILEY, DECEMBER 28, 1926

. . . .

Children, this is National Thrift Week . . . Day by day throughout this week the people all over the country are thinking of the various phases of thrift for the purpose of bringing greater success and happiness into their lives and into the lives of those about them.

. . . And now let us think a moment of what thrift really is. Thrift is not only saving, it also means wise giving and wise spending . . .

. . . a budget has no magic to produce sudden wealth by any short cut route. But in the experience of many families it has put the [family] finances on profit producing foundations so that year after *year, consistent earnings, planned spending, regular savings, careful investing and liberal giving have produced happiness and prosperity, independence in old age, freedom from debt; in short, happiness.*

. . . If a boy or girl has an allowance of a quarter a week, he or she should have a little box or bank in which to put, let us say, 2 cents a week for savings, 2 cents a week for Sunday School, and the rest can go for things he or she needs.

. . . Above all things be thrifty with time. Getting up late, getting late to breakfast, makes it hard for mother, getting to school late makes it hard for the teacher and your loss of time makes everyone else lose time.

Thrift means . . . simplicity of living, a love of nature, and not a love of the artificial pleasures which cost money . . .

America is a land of opportunity. *In closing, is there a better question to ask, than what does each of us intend to do with this opportunity? . . . Are we going to make the best of what we have, or are we going to waste it? Are we going to use our strength and energies and money wisely, or are we going to squander them? Let us begin to-day to follow the advice of Benjamin Franklin and believe that God giveth all things to them who love him and who practice industry in all its phases.*

"THRIFT WEEK, JANUARY 17, 1927," NOTES FOR A TALK TO CHILDREN, FOUND IN THE PAPERS OF ANNA K. WILEY

. . . .

Anna Campbell Kelton was born in 1877, the youngest daughter of a military officer. In 1911,

she married Dr. Harvey W. Wiley, who at that time was chief chemist of the U.S. Department of Agriculture. In addition to the work that she carried out for National Thrift Week, Anna K. Wiley was the president (in 1911, and perhaps also in other years) of the Woman's Suffrage League of the District of Columbia; the president (1912–14, 1922) of the Housekeepers' Alliance; the president (1911–12) of the Washington, DC, chapter of the National Consumers League, and the president (1933–35) of the American Pure Food League.

She had strong views on many subjects related to thrift. To chose one of many possible examples, that of food thrift, she was a firm opponent of the adulteration of bread—"The bleaching of flour has become a national menace," she wrote—and, with her husband, worked long and hard to promote the widespread purchase and consumption of whole wheat bread and breakfast food. In her thrift talk from 1927 cited above, discussing the importance of being "thrifty" with one's health, she told the children in no uncertain terms: "Eat good sensible whole wheat bread . . ." Anna K. Wiley died in 1964.[3]

Dr. Earl Wilfley, pastor of the Vermont Avenue Christian church . . . will impersonate Benjamin Franklin, the apostle of thrift, on whose birthday anniversary this thrift week will open . . . Virtually every luncheon club will devote some time that week to thrift. The subject of thrift will be brought to the attention of every school child—essay, slogan, and poster contests will be employed to put over the thrift message . . . More than 50 organizations in Washington are giving endorsements to the movement . . .

WASHINGTON POST, JANUARY 9, 1927

. . . .

Some hundred odd addresses on the subject [of thrift] were heard at Kiwanis meetings throughout the country . . . An almost equal number of fine thrift meetings were held by the Rotary Clubs of the country. The life and work of Benjamin Franklin were featured at many of these meetings.

NATIONAL THRIFT WEEK ANNUAL REPORT, 1927

. . . .

Fargo, N.D., always a leader in thrift activity, has become a path-finder in still another phase of the work with the establishment . . . of a thrift library which is considered to be one of the most complete of its kind in the country.

NATIONAL THRIFT NEWS (PUBLISHED BY THE NATIONAL THRIFT COMMITTEE OF THE YMCA), SEPTEMBER 1927

. . . .

American Home Economics Association
American Library Association
American Red Cross
American Society for Thrift
Boy Scouts of America
Jewish Welfare Board
Federal Council of Churches
General Federation of Women's Clubs

National Association of Mutual Savings Banks
National Education Association
National Fraternal Congress of America
U.S. League of Local Building and Loan
*   Associations*

SOME OF THE FORTY-SEVEN NATIONAL ASSOCIATIONS SPONSORING NATIONAL THRIFT WEEK, 1928

. . . .

A new Thrift Exhibit has been prepared which is calculated will do valiant service in the interest of the Thrift movement. It contains 12 panels attractively mounted with various materials to be used in the observance of Thrift Week.

NATIONAL THRIFT NEWS, SEPTEMBER 1928

Pacific Coast: . . . *Also the untiring efforts of Andrew Miller and his associate, William Warren, in giving us the greatest publicity we ever had. This not only covered every paper in the State of Oregon, but at Salem the Y.M.C.A. issued an eight-page edition of the* Statesman *devoted entirely to thrift* . . .

Capitol City [Washington, DC]: . . . *Twenty-two thousand four hundred and sixteen white persons and fourteen thousand colored persons heard thrift messages* . . .

"HIGH SPOTS" OF NATIONAL THRIFT WEEK, 1928, AS REPORTED IN *NATIONAL THRIFT NEWS*, APRIL 1928

. . . .

What Constitutes Thrift in the Light of the Present Economic Situation?

RECOMMENDED TOPIC FOR "INSTITUTES" BEING ORGANIZED AROUND THE COUNTRY TO MARK THE OBSERVANCE OF NATIONAL THRIFT WEEK, 1933

. . . .

The Committee's activities were dramatically reduced during the years of the Great Depression, but picked up again in 1939–40, and continued strongly during World War II, focusing on war savings and the elimination of waste to support the war effort.

After the war, the National Thrift Committee was reorganized, primarily under the leadership of the United States Savings and Loan League and its highly respected executive vice president,

Morton Bodfish. In 1947, the Committee moved its main office to Chicago, where the League was headquartered.[4]

It was decided to send to the National Thrift Committee in answer to its request for cooperation on its project of "developing a curriculum for elementary and high schools, using the philosophy of thrift as the subject," . . . *the names of six persons whom the National Thrift Committee might ask to serve on an advisory committee.*

NATIONAL COUNCIL ON FAMILY RELATIONS, 1950

. . . .

In 1949, the National Thrift Committee, under the guidance of the U.S. Savings and Loan League, had seventeen institutional members. By 1959, membership had climbed to about 600, and by 1961, to about 1,100. By 1965, the Committee's last full year of operation, membership stood at about 725—primarily savings and loan associations (584), but also including savings banks (42), commercial banks (39), credit unions (12), and business/insurance (13).[5]

I do want to mention and stress the importance of another organization which exists exclusively to serve the cause of thrift, which is open alike to savings and loans and to savings banks, which is most appropriate common meeting ground for our thrift industries and yet which neither of us supports in anywhere nearly sufficient numbers. I refer to the National Thrift Committee, which has its home

Issued 1918

office in Chicago under the direction of its devoted executive secretary, Miss Helen White.

JOHN DELAITTRE, PRESIDENT OF THE NATIONAL ASSOCIATION OF MUTUAL SAVINGS BANKS, SPEECH TO THE ANNUAL CONVENTION OF THE U.S. SAVINGS AND LOAN LEAGUE, 1959

. . . .

If literature can be made available for club or community observance of National Thrift Week— October 21-27, 1962—we [7,200 Kiwanis clubs] should appreciate knowing the source from which our clubs could obtain it. A kit of promotional materials might be of great help.

REPORT ON BREAKFAST MEETING WITH KIWANIS INTERNATIONAL, SAVINGS AND LOAN ANNALS, 1961

. . . .

It is with regret that we announce the cessation of National Thrift Committee activities on July 1, 1966.

LETTER FROM HERMAN B. WELLS, CHAIRMAN OF THE NATIONAL THRIFT COMMITTEE, JUNE 29, 1966

48. To Organize Sacrifice

THERE HAVE BEEN only two instances of war-time crisis in American history—the escalation of the Vietnam War by President Lyndon Johnson in the 1960s, and the war in Iraq under President George W. Bush—in which, apart from those serving in the military, there have been effectively no appeals to the citizenry to make sacrifices to win the war. I believe that in all other cases, starting of course with our war for independence in the late eighteenth century, our citizens have been asked, in time of national emergency, to make important sacrifices. And in both Britain and the United States, when those appeals are, one of the most important words by far is "thrift."

A Call to Thrift

THE TIMES (LONDON) HEADLINE, DESCRIBING A
MANIFESTO CALLING FOR SACRIFICE AND SAVING
TO WIN THE WAR, DECEMBER 23, 1915

. . . .

45,000 Join Army of Thrift Recuits

NEW YORK TIMES HEADLINE, DESCRIBING
SPREAD OF U.S. WAR-SAVINGS SOCIETIES,
JUNE 25, 1918

WORK HARD . . . SPEND LITTLE . . . SAVE MUCH

BILLBOARD AND NEWSPAPER AD, UNITED KINGDOM,
DURING THE GREAT WAR

. . . .

ARE YOU HELPING THE GERMANS?
You are helping the Germans when you use a motor car for pleasure: when you buy extravagant clothes: when you employ more servants than you need: when you waste coal, electric light or gas: when you eat and drink more than is necessary to your health and efficiency. Set the right example, free labour for more useful purposes, save money and lend it to the Nation and so help your Country.

BILLBOARD AND NEWSPAPER AD, UNITED
KINGDOM, DURING THE GREAT WAR

Some business leaders, for obvious reasons, publicly opposed war-thrift campaigns:

BUSINESS AS USUAL
BEWARE OF THRIFT AND UNWISE
ECONOMY
MONEY BREEDS MONEY
PLACARD DISPLAYED IN SOME U.S.
RETAIL STORE WINDOWS, 1917

. . . .

A dollar down, a dollar a week buys a $50 bond.
Ten dollars down, five dollars a month buys a $100
bond.
Less than ten cents a day buys a baby bond.
AD FOR "PARTIAL PAYMENT PLANS" FOR BUYING LIBERTY
BONDS, 1917

. . . .

The Birth of American Thrift
BOOKLET ENCOURAGING PUBLIC PARTICIPATION
IN THE FIRST LIBERTY LOAN, 1917

. . . .

The biggest thing is this: When you start saving your pennies and nickels and dimes and no longer spend them for chocolate creams and other unnecessary things, Robinson Crusoe does not have to make those unnecessary things. His services are not needed to make unnecessary goods, and he can go to work

for our government, or in other factories making things that will help win the war. And you see where the government will get the money to pay him? It will be the very same money you would have spent for chocolate creams or other things! The reason is that when you buy a Thrift Stamp you are lending your money to the government. When you don't buy chocolate creams (or so forth) and do buy a Thrift Stamp with your 25c, you let Robinson Crusoe stop making chocolate creams and you give the government 25c to hire him (or buy his services) to make goods that will help win the war, So you are helping in three ways! First, you let Robinson Crusoe get away from making goods that are unnecessary; second, you lend money to the government to buy the goods and services it needs, and third, your money goes to pay Robinson Crusoe in his new job of helping our government win the war! That is a great deal for a little money to do, but it does it!

And besides these three things there is a fourth; you are saving your money and putting it where it will earn money for you while you are awake and while you sleep! So I suggest a new rhyme to add to the old one about Robinson Crusoe:

Good old Robinson Crusoe!
Good old Robinson Crusoe!
The Thrift Stamps he bought
Won the war that we fought,
And we all saved and helped him to do so.
ROBINSON CRUSOE AND THRIFT STAMPS,
PAMPHLET FOR CHILDREN, ABOUT 1917

The commission is of course gratified at the success of its work in behalf of food thrift.

CHARLES LATHROP PACK, U.S. NATIONAL
EMERGENCY FOOD GARDEN COMMISSION, 1917

. . . .

The smallest denomination was the 25-cent Thrift stamp. These stamps, as purchased, were placed on Thrift Cards and when sixteen stamps were attached a card had a value of four dollars ($4) if used in the purchase of a War Savings Stamp. The War Savings Stamp . . . was a promise of the government to pay the holder five dollars ($5) on the first of January, 1923.

. . . [Indiana] State Director Oliver launched his campaign on January 7th, 1918 . . . "It is the purpose of the plan," said the announcement, "to encourage the organization of Thrift clubs wherever ten or more people are gathered together . . . and enlist as many manufacturers in this service as possible." . . . February 3, 1918 was set as "Thrift Day" throughout the country . . . The Indiana War Savings Stamp Bulletin quoted one of Ring W. Lardner's "Thrift Jingles" on February 11th as follows:

> *There was a foolish man*
> *   And he bought a foolish block*
> *Of Yaki Hula common,*
> *   And foolish mining stock.*
> *And now he dines on field mice*
> *   And pals with other tramps,*
> *Which never would have happened*
> *   If he'd bought War Savings Stamps*

. . . By the end of March the state was honeycombed with Thrift and War Savings Societies . . . Under the leadership of Felix M. McWhirter, county chairman, a "Thrift Army" had been established in the Marion County schools. More than 15,000 pupils in this county were owners of War Savings and Thrift Stamps at this time, "most of them purchased with money earned from hard labor or from the giving up of the things which children love best."

A great "Thrift Stamp Week" for Indiana was set for May 27th to June 3rd. Elaborate preparations had been made by both state and local War Savings committees to make "Thrift Stamp Week" a period when every individual in Indiana should give something, however little, to the support of his Government.

. . . While the results of the War Savings campaign as to totals in moneys collected for Government use were relatively unimportant, when compared with the billions collected through other forms of financing [such as the Liberty Loans], the spirit of thrift and scientific saving which was engendered by the campaign in many of the people of Indiana and the nation was of great value. It is probable that the habits of generations to come in America were modified by the Thrift campaigns. This is particularly true when it is remembered that the bulk of the Thrift campaigns were directed at the school children and at the employes of large business houses and industries.

Many months after the war had closed the programs of systematic saving that had started among employes, children and other elements of the

Published 1918   Published 1942

population continued uninterrupted. The banks of the state and nation benefited from this new thrift spirit long before the war had been concluded, and in the days following the conflict many plans for adapting the war thrift education to old and new financial businesses rapidly took form.

WALTER GREENOUGH, *THE WAR PURSE OF INDIANA: THE FIVE LIBERTY LOANS AND WAR SAVINGS AND THRIFT CAMPAIGNS IN INDIANA DURING THE WORLD WAR*, 1922

. . . .

I hereby request and urge the people of the State of Indiana to set aside this anniversary day [of the signing of the armistice ending the World War] as a day to begin the practice of thrift and saving . . . I urge that every man, woman and child in Indiana realize, for his own and the common good,

the importance of buying wisely to reduce demand; using wisely to avoid waste; saving regularly to provide for the future; and producing more for his own and his country's welfare. Let us battle against extravagance; let us increase our savings . . .

PROCLAMATION BY INDIANA GOVERNOR JAMES P. GOODRICH, NOVEMBER 11, 1919

. . . .

Perhaps the most important phase of the 1919 activities was the real education in Thrift that was going forward in the schools . . . the State Board of Education adopted a resolution providing for the teaching of Thrift as a special part of the curriculum in schools everywhere in Indiana. This step towards making the Thrift idea permanent became the object of emulation in many states subsequently.

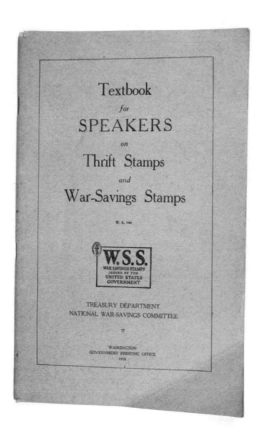

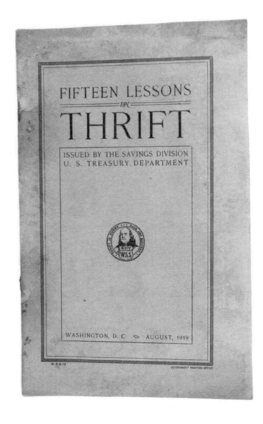

Under the Indiana plan each city and town and county superintendent of schools was a definite part of the Thrift organization. Advertising material was used elaborately in the schools and the response from the school children in the formation of Thrift clubs and the consequent saving of their funds was important.

Printed Thrift lessons were distributed from the state organization. In some schools Thrift stamps actually were on sale, while in others a dual system of buying stamps and making deposits at banks, was in vogue.

GREENOUGH, *THE WAR PURSE OF INDIANA*

Note that in Indiana and across the country, thrift campaigns that had begun as measures to win the war were continued, and in some cases even expanded, after the war had been won. Thrift as a requirement to defeat the enemy turned quite fluidly into thrift as a newly appreciated strategy for building a better society.

In Britain, too, the success of war thrift led to new efforts to promote peace thrift. Very shortly after the shooting stopped, Britain's extensive network of community-based war-savings clubs joined forces with the Post Office Savings Bank and the Trustee Savings Banks to form what the British called their three-pillared "National Savings Movement."[1]

HE IS
PILING UP
HIS
THRIFT STAMPS
ARE YOU?

Buy
Thrift Stamps

It would certainly appear that the system of savings clubs, started during the war, has come to stay, and that it will take its rank with such fundamentally British institutions as the Post Office Savings Bank, the Trustee Savings Banks, the building societies, and the friendly societies. One of the satisfactory features of the position is that there is no conflicting rivalry between theses bodies and the War-Savings Associations. These older institutions have their representative on nearly all the local "Savings Committees," and it is fully realized that all thrift agencies stand to benefit by the intensification of the spirit of thrift.

"THREE YEARS OF WAR SAVINGS: PLANS FOR PEACE THRIFT," *THE TIMES*, MARCH 12, 1919

The National Savings Movement has a wide field open to it, which far transcends the purpose which brought it into being.

"THE NEW THRIFT CAMPAIGN," DESCRIBING THE FIRST MEETING OF THE NEWLY FORMED NATIONAL SAVINGS ASSEMBLY, *THE TIMES*, JANUARY 17, 1920

. . . .

If anyone asked him what were the greatest movements, judged by what we had accomplished in his lifetime, that had taken hold of our national life, he was not sure he would not answer that they were the Boy Scout movement, with its accompanying development of Girl Guides, and *the War Savings Movement, developing into the National Savings Movement. (Cheers.)*

AUSTEN CHAMBERLAIN, M.P., REMARKS TO THE CITY OF LONDON SAVINGS COMMITTEE, JUNE 25, 1924

. . . .

Originally introduced as a war measure, it [the National Savings Movement] has since proved to have a special value in time of peace as an instrument available, in every section of the community, for the encouragement and practice of thrift.

"NATIONAL THRIFT," *THE TIMES*, JULY 4, 1925

. . . .

It was, he concluded, the aim of the National Savings Movement to inculcate thrift, and the true aim of thrift was the formation of character, the cultivation of the homely virtues of frugality, diligence, punctuality, and veracity.

SIR CHARLES ADDIS, PROPOSING A TOAST TO THE NATIONAL SAVINGS MOVEMENT, NOVEMBER 6, 1928

. . . .

Every Savings Certificate and Bond you buy, every deposit you make in the Post Office Savings Bank and Trustee Savings Banks is another nail in the coffin of Nazi tyranny. The savers will beat the enslavers.

LEAFLET DESCRIBING THE "SAVE YOUR WAY TO VICTORY" CAMPAIGN, GREAT BRITAIN, NOVEMBER 1939

In times of war and stress, even more than in days of peace and plenty, meat is a food it pays to buy with thrift and cook with care.

MEAT FOR THRIFTY MEALS, U.S. DEPARTMENT OF AGRICULTURE, 1942

. . . .

Wage war against waste! *It is a home-front necessity to extend the usefulness of bedding fabrics by renovating, making over, mending, and finding new uses for those discarded. Every worn or torn fabric that needs replacement makes a demand on the fabric industry that should be going into the war effort.*

NEW YORK STATE *WAR EMERGENCY BULLETIN*, MARCH 1943

. . . .

YOU CAN HELP BUILD THIS BOMBER! It may sound funny to hear a girl like me say that you can help build a bomber—but it's true just the same . . .

MAKE FEWER CALLS. Materials needed to build new telephone lines are now going to war. So to serve the greatest number of people with the equipment we have, we need to make fewer calls and be brief on all calls.

ADVERTISEMENT APPEARING IN THE *BIRMINGHAM NEWS*, MAY 3, 1943

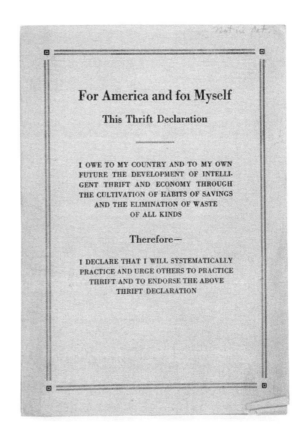

Published 1934

Nationwide housewives were urged to "use it up, wear it out, make it do, or do without." Women were viewed as soldiers and their "kitchen a combination frontline bunker and rear-eschelon miniature war plant." They saved fats and took them to their butcher, where they were exchanged for red points. They were encouraged to save their tin cans by washing the labels off, removing both ends, inserting the extracted tops and bottoms into the cans, and flattening them with their feet. One pound of fat, women were told, contained enough "glycerin to make a pound of black powder—enough for six 75-mm shells or fifty 30-

caliber bullets." If every family would save one can a week, this would save "2,500 tons of tin and 190,000 tons of steel—the equivalent of 5,000 tanks or 38 liberty ships." Both black and white Alabama housewives were told, "Turn in your Kitchen Fat—it's worth two Red-Ration Points." An article headlined "From Frying Pan to Firing Line" offered detailed description of how waste fats were used to manufacture nitroglycerin, dynamite, and gunpowder.

MARY MARTHA THOMAS, *RIVETING AND RATIONING IN DIXIE: ALABAMA WOMEN AND THE SECOND WORLD WAR*

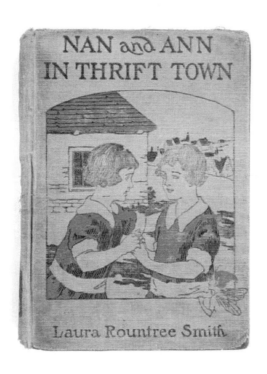

Published 1925

During the war, drives were undertaken to salvage materials that could be used by the Allies. Scrap metal, rubber, nylon and silk were collected. Even kitchen fats could be used in the manufacturing of munitions, and the Casper Girl Scouts collected fats at Halloween rather than asking for traditional handouts. Clothes and old keys were dug out of closets and junk drawers. Athletic equipment and games, discarded canes, old radios, hair clippers, jewelry and phonograph records were salvaged from basements, attics and garages.

A VIEW FROM CENTER STREET, A HISTORY OF CASPER, WYOMING

49. To Train Children

ALMOST ALL BROADLY BASED social movements make special efforts to persuade and recruit the young. In the case of thrift, not only do the main "adult" thrift institutions such as fraternal societies, savings banks, and building and loans typically reach out to children by forming youth departments and offering special services to children, but many thrift leaders commit themselves directly, as the main focus of their work, to passing on the thrift ethic to children, either through community-based thrift education programs, or by seeking to introduce and expand thrift education in the schools.

If this be not enough to vindicate for social economics, or, in a word, "the Art of Thrift and Providence," a claim to be taught to all of our national school-children, I will offer one further argument in this direction. This art must be learned in youth, in early youth, and put in practice from the beginning. A man of thirty may learn to sing, to study mathematics, to make machinery, to write books, to make speeches; but if he wait til then to study thrift he has lost his chance of providence.

WILLIAM L. BLACKLEY, *THRIFT AND INDEPENDENCE: A WORD FOR WORKING MEN*, 1885

A prominent thrift advocate, whom we met briefly in part one, the Rev. Willliam Lewery Blackley was the rector of North Waltham. One of his thrift papers from this period was "Scheme for National Insurance," in which, on grounds of greater thrift, he argued for a national insurance program in Britain—thus in this instance strongly making the case for social (as compared to individual) thrift.

An Act to Provide for Compulsory Instruction in Thrift in the Public Schools.

A BILL PASSED BY THE MASSACHUSETTS LEGISLATURE, 1910

. . . .

Thrift may, therefore, be assumed as a virtue which the schools are to teach.

J. O. ENGLEMAN, *MORAL EDUCATION IN SCHOOL AND HOME*, 1918

Boy Scout Handbook,
1933, Boy Scout Medal

Whereas, Believing that thrift makes for moral strength and contentment, and that waste and extravagance not only cause high prices, but instability and deterioration; be it

Resolved, That the National Congress of Mothers and Parent-Teacher Associations give its unqualified endorsement to the establishment of Thrift instruction as a regular part of the curriculum of the schools of our country . . .

RESOLUTION PASSED BY THE NATIONAL CONGRESS OF
MOTHERS AND PARENT-TEACHER ASSOCIATIONS, 1923

To be sure, we are enjoying great national prosperity at the moment [the late 1920s], but it seems timely to direct our attention to means for its conservation and utilization through universal child training in thrift.

WILLIAM G. SUTCLIFFE AND LINDLEY A. BOND, *SAVINGS BANKS AND SAVINGS DEPARTMENT MANAGEMENT*

. . . .

The need for Public School instruction in the principles of thrift education was never so great or apparent as at the present time.

ARTHUR H. AND JAMES F. CHAMBERLAIN, *THRIFT AND CONSERVATION: HOW TO TEACH IT*, 1919

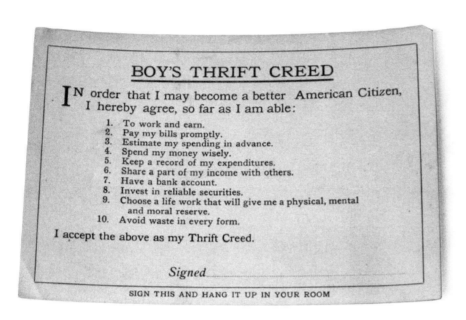

BOY'S THRIFT CREED

IN order that I may become a better American Citizen, I hereby agree, so far as I am able:

1. To work and earn.
2. Pay my bills promptly.
3. Estimate my spending in advance.
4. Spend my money wisely.
5. Keep a record of my expenditures.
6. Share a part of my income with others.
7. Have a bank account.
8. Invest in reliable securities.
9. Choose a life work that will give me a physical, mental and moral reserve.
10. Avoid waste in every form.

I accept the above as my Thrift Creed.

Signed_____

SIGN THIS AND HANG IT UP IN YOUR ROOM

Recall from earlier in this book that Professor Arthur H. Chamberlain of San Francisco was one of his generation's busiest and most prominent thrift advocates. Here, in a remarkable passage, he carefully distinguishes between thrift and conservation, and in the process nicely invokes thrift's classic meanings—of which I trust you by now are fully aware, and which I hope will remind you, in this instance, as it did me, of the proverb we encountered early on in this book: "Planting of trees is England's old thrift."

Use of our principal without waste, whether that principal be a natural resource, money, time, or health, is conservation. So using our principal to cause it to increase is thrift. Conservation applied to our forests will prolong their life for many years. Thrift dictates that we plant both trees and seeds, thus adding . . . to our capital.

CHAMBERLAIN, *THRIFT AND CONSERVATION: HOW TO TEACH IT*

. . . .

September—Punctuality

October—Taste and economy in indoor decoration.

November—Harvest

December—Charity

January—Health

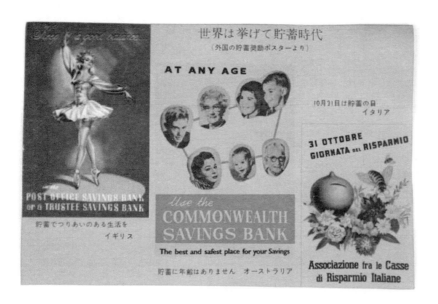

*February—Kindness to animals, feeding
 the birds, etc.*
March—Pride in home, and civic cleanliness
April—Economy of Mother Nature
May—Gardening
June—Dependability

A PROPOSAL FROM TERESA M. LENNEY, A SEVENTH-GRADE
TEACHER IN NEW ROCHELLE, NEW YORK, FOR TEACHING
THRIFT IN SCHOOLS BY EMPHASIZING ONE ASPECT OF
THRIFT FOR EVERY MONTH OF THE SCHOOL YEAR, 1915

. . . .

I love this teacher's ideas—she was honored for her
creative work in this area in 1916 by the American
Society for Thrift. Note that "saving money" did
not make her list of nine main aspects of thrift.

*There is a good old-fashioned word called "thrift."
Every man, woman, boy, and girl ought to know
what it means. It does not stand for stinginess. It is
not the same thing as meanness. But it does mean
taking good care of our money so that we will not
spend it for foolish things. People in Europe know
much more about thrift than the people on this side
of the water. Many Americans earn money quickly,
but spend it still more quickly.*

A CITY READER FOR THE FOURTH YEAR (A CHILDREN'S
SCHOOL BOOK), 1916

. . . .

How do you like my bank?
 I made it myself.
It is as good as any bank you can buy.
 It is pretty, too.
There are ten pennies in it now.
 Here them jingle, jingle!

*. . . When I get twenty-five cents, I shall cut the
   paper and open my bank.
I shall buy a thrift stamp.
You can get a thrift stamp for twenty-five cents.
Jingle, jingle, jingle!
My pennies sing a merry song.*

ANNIE E. MOORE, *PENNIES AND PLANS*, SCHOOL
TEXTBOOK ("A FIRST READER"), 1919

. . . .

Lessons in Thrift *. . . as, "Holding Down the
Candy Habit," "How I Saved for a Rainy Day,"
"Peter Penniless and Willie Wise," "Mending Holes
in My Money Pocket," "Wise Ways to Use Money"
. . . A thrift booklet may be made . . . In the
book may be "Rules for Young Workers," "Thrift
Maxims," and account sheets for records of savings.*

LIVE LANGUAGE LESSONS (A TEACHERS' MANUAL), 1921

*The Women's Division of the National Association
of Mutual Savings Banks has inaugurated a
contest among teachers of the elementary and
continuation schools for the best course of study in
Thrift education which includes instruction in the
right use of time, energy, materials and money. The
contest has the sanction of the National Education
Association. The prizes will be generous enough
to provoke wide interest [and] will be distributed
next June at the Annual Conference of the Mutual
Savings Banks in New York.*

MAGARET J. BACON OF ROCHESTER, NEW YORK,
CHAIRMAN OF THE WOMEN'S DIVISION OF THE NATIONAL
ASSOCIATION OF MUTUAL SAVINGS BANKS, LETTER TO
PRESIDENT CALVIN COOLIDGE, OCTOBER 24, 1923

. . . .

Patriotism*: I believe in the United States of
America. I believe that her progress depends upon
the Industry and Thrift of her people.*
Punctuality*: Therefore, I will devote my time*

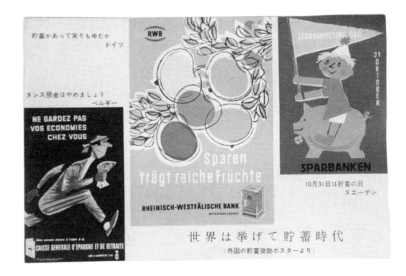

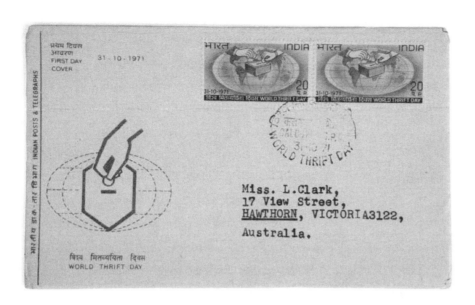

to worthwhile activities and save time by being punctual.

Physical Training: *I will Preserve my Health because without it I have less earning power.*

Conservation: *I will Conserve Materials because materials Cost Money.*

Thrift: *I will Save my Money, because saving leads to security, helpfulness, and happiness.*

I Will Do All These Things for the Welfare of America.

THRIFT CREED ADOPTED BY LOS ANGELES PUBLIC SCHOOLS, ABOUT 1930

. . . .

In the United States, the main founding father of school savings banks—school-based programs that encourage and help children to save money, often in partnership with community-based organizations such as mutual savings banks or build-

ing and loan associations—is J. H. Thiry of Long Island City, New York, a long-time and fervent advocate of teaching children thrift. His main booklet, *The History, Rules and Regulations of the Penny School Savings Bank*, was published in 1886. Another important early publication is Sara Louisa Oberholtzer's *School Savings Banks*, published by the United States Bureau of Education in 1915.

A number of children can easily organize a savings bank. Here is how Hubert, George, William, Carol and Edith organized and managed the Thrift Saving Bank.

FIRST LESSONS IN BUSINESS (FOR 8TH AND 9TH GRADE STUDENTS), 1919

. . . .

The Rochester plan of school savings . . . was due to the vision of the late Howard A. Barrows, who as a member of the Rochester Board of Education was greatly impressed with the importance of training youth in the proper handling of money, thus encouraging at the earliest age the development of the habit of thrift. . .

Having enlisted the interest of the Bank in his plan, Mr. Barrows gave it further impetus by offering, out of his own pocket, a bright new dime to each pupil who started an account in the School Saving Department during the first month of its operation—October, 1915.

A HISTORY OF THE ROCHESTER SAVINGS BANK

. . . .

In every area the schools have been brought into the noble system of thrift, so that the pennies of the children of forty-seven educational establishments are garnered and lent out on hire on behalf of nearly 9,000 youthful depositors.

A CENTURY OF THRIFT, REPORTING ON THE AIRDRIE SAVINGS BANK OF SCOTLAND, 1935

. . . .

Sceptics who question the power of a child's thrift may be surprised at the findings of a recent survey by the American Bankers Association. Through the school savings programs, more than $200,000,000 have been saved since the program's inception in 1885. In New York State . . . there are 285, 988 students participating from public, private, and parochial schools. In 1959–1960, they saved $2,300,000.

"PENNY IS SAID TO START CHILD ON ROAD TO THRIFT," *NEW YORK TIMES*, APRIL 4, 1962

PART SIX

Thrift Wisdom

MORE THAN ANYTHING else, thrift wisdom is proverbial wisdom. As we've seen, thrift ideas link to almost all of life's domains and can be articulated in many different ways, from high-brow poetry, to elementary school math textbooks, to lengthy after-dinner speeches delivered at credit union conferences. Yet despite this delightful diversity, the fact remains that apparently in all societies, the paradigmatic thrift statement is the proverb or maxim—those little droplets of common sense intended to entertain and instruct ordinary people.

Surely a part of Benjamin Franklin's genius, and a key to his enduring popularity, was his grasp of this basic fact. Probably for more than anything Franklin ever said or did—and he said and did quite a lot—he is remembered and loved for his brilliant retrofitting of the thrift wisdom of the ages into the maxims of Poor Richard. In the United States, in particular, and of course in part due to Franklin's influence, generations of thrift leaders have delighted in compiling and dissemi-

nating thrift proverbs, maxims, and short sayings. I began this book by collecting them and have never found research so enjoyable.

The fact that thrift wisdom is ultimately proverbial wisdom ought to tell us several things. First, it suggests that thrift is a democratic virtue. No one is excluded from its prospective reach; no one is denied the right to participate in the ways of thrift. That's why none of these sayings suggest that to be thrifty, you need to be a male or come from a prominent family or be a certain color or have certain accent or religion or be physically powerful or even be particularly smart. Thrift principles can be difficult to live by, but they are almost never difficult to understand. Work hard. Don't waste. Exercise care. Give back. These are ultimately simple ideas, and they are open to everyone.

Second, proverbs and maxims typically urge us to live a certain way. They give us direction. Almost by definition, they counsel. With wit and brevity, they remind us of what is ethically good, often by also reminding us of what works best

Fun-Full Thrift Game

Fun-Full Thrift Game

and what is strategically wise. These sayings therefore make plain that thrift is an inescapably moral idea. Thrift is more about the "ought" than about the "is."

In this book's preface, I mentioned the prominent Harvard professor who insisted at some length at a conference on the history of thrift that thrift is not a virtue. Well, he is certainly free to believe that the thrift ethic is unnecessary or even harmful. (Join the club! Go stand in that long line!) But I'm pretty sure that he meant something different, and much more condescending. He meant that thrift is merely a technique—scrimp and save, put your money in the bank, mend your clothes— that does not rise to the level of a morally complex idea. He meant that thrift is little more than a tool, like a knife or a pair of scissors, and that

whether the tool is used for good or ill depends mainly on who is doing the using, and for what purpose, not on the tool itself.

If this book shows anything—and in particular, if these popular thrift sayings show anything— they show that this professor simply did not know what he was talking about. All by itself, thrift is a big, demonstrably moral idea. If thrift is merely a technique, then so is courage. So is hope. So are all of the classical and modern virtues. We call many of these sayings "proverbs" precisely because, at least in part, they point to a moral standard, and advise us to conform to that standard. Thrift sayings, as familiar to us as household words, seek overall to guide us toward a particular and ethically serious way of living.[1]

50. Proverbs and Maxims

Always taking out of the meal-tub and never putting in, soon comes to the bottom.

. . . .

Ask thy purse what thou should spend.

. . . .

The bless'd source of lib'ral deeds is wise Economy.

. . . .

The best throw upon the dice, is to throw them away.

. . . .

Better to go to bed supperless than get up in debt.

. . . .

Better to say here it is than here it was.

. . . .

Beware of little expenses.

. . . .

The borrower is servant to the lender.

. . . .

Buy what thou hast no need of, and ere long thou shalt sell thy necessaries.

Buying a thing too dear is no bounty.

. . . .

By sowing frugality, we reap liberty, a golden harvest.

. . . .

Charity gives itself rich, covetousness hoards itself poor.

. . . .

Charity is the chief and most charming beauty.

. . . .

Creditors have better memories than debtors.

. . . .

Cut your Coat according to your Cloth.

. . . .

Debt is a heavy Burden to an honest Mind; but thievish Borrowers make light of it.

. . . .

Debt is the worst Poverty.

. . . .

Debtors are liars.

Despise not the day of small things . . .

. . . .

Diligence is the mother of good luck.

. . . .

*Do not buy what you want. Buy what
you need. What you do not need is too
expensive, even if it only costs a penny.*

. . . .

*Do not overspend, God does not
like those who overspend.*

. . . .

*Do what you have to do just now,
and leave it not for tomorrow.*

. . . .

*Early to bed and early to rise, make men more
healthy, more holy, wealthy, and wise.*

. . . .

*Economy is the foundation of human prosperity.
The spendthrift is always in trouble. Prodigality on
the part of any person is an unpardonable sin . . .*

. . . .

Economy is wealth.

. . . .

*Economy is the wealth of the poor
and the wisdom of the rich.*

Eident [Thrifty, diligent] youth makes easy age.

. . . .

Employ thyself in something excellent.

. . . .

An empty bag cannot stand upright.

. . . .

Enough is as good as a feast.

. . . .

Evil gotten, evil spent.

. . . .

Extend your feet to the length of your carpet.

. . . .

Feast today, fast tomorrow.

. . . .

First deserve and then desire.

. . . .

Fly the pleasure that will bit to-morrow.

. . . .

*The foot of the owner is the best
manure for his land.*

. . . .

*A Fop [clotheshorse] of Fashion is the
Mercer's [cloth merchant's] Friend, the
Taylor's Fool, and his own Foe.*

Frae [From] saving comes having.

. . . .

Frugality embraces all the other virtues.

. . . .

Frugality is equal to half a subsistence.

. . . .

Frugality is a great revenue.

. . . .

Frugality is misery in disguise.

. . . .

Frugality may be termed the daughter of Prudence, the sister of Temperance, and the parent of Liberty.

. . . .

The generous man enriches himself by giving; the miser hoards himself poor.

. . . .

Give no great credit to a great promiser.

. . . .

Giving much to the poor, doth increase a man's store.

. . . .

Go to the ant, thou sluggard; consider her ways, and be wise; Which having no guide, overseer, or ruler, Provideth her meat in the summer, and gathereth her food in the harvest.

God keeps him who takes what care he can of himself.

. . . .

God supplies him with more, who lays out his estate well.

. . . .

Good and quickly seldom meet.

. . . .

Good harvests make men prodigal, bad ones provident.

. . . .

Good husbandry is the first step toward riches.

. . . .

A good name is rather to be chosen than great riches, and loving favour rather than silver and gold. The rich and the poor meet together: the LORD *is the maker of them all.*

. . . .

Great businesses turn on a little pin.

. . . .

Hand in use is the father of affluence.

. . . .

The happiness of the body consists in health; that of the mind, in knowledge.

130   THE SATURDAY E

It's Still Smart

To Be Thrifty!

And no wonder, because a Whizzer Bike Motor takes you 125 miles on a gallon of gas . . . six zestful miles for a penny!

America's finest bike motor is precision-engineered for long life, trouble-free performance.

It fits any man's balloon tire bike, and pocketbook.

It's the perfect answer to your commuting problem . . . the greatest travel bargain on wheels . . . and real fun to ride!

Soon, see your local Whizzer Dealer. Take the Whizzer way to low-cost transportation! Ride one, and you'll buy one!

$9755 PLUS TAX

F. O. B. Pontiac, Mich. Complete with gas tank, exhaust stand, and all attachments necessary to motorize your bike.

WHIZZER

AMERICA'S FINEST BIKE MOTOR

CLIP THIS COUPON Now

Whizzer Motor Company, Dept. 509, Pontiac, Mich.

I enclose $99.97, which includes $2.42 Federal Excise Tax (   ) check or (   ) money order. Send me one Whizzer Motor complete, ready for installation. If descriptive literature only is desired, check here (   ).

Name
Street
City   State

If no dealer in your community yet, use this coupon.

The happy are those who are competently furnished with external advantages, act honestly, and live temperately.

Haste makes waste.

. . . .

Haste makes waste, and waste makes want, and want makes strife between the good man and his wife.

. . . .

He becometh poor that dealeth with a slack hand: but the hand of the diligent maketh rich.

. . . .

He is a great fool, who squanders rather than doth good with his estate.

. . . .

He is the only rich man, who understands the use of wealth.

. . . .

He is richest who is contented with least; for content is the wealth of nature.

. . . .

He is well constituted who grieves not for what he has not, and rejoices for what he has.

. . . .

He'll never be a slave, who learns to save.

. . . .

He only is idle, who might be better employed.

He only is rich enough, who hath all that
he desires.

. . . .

He that borrows an' bigs [builds], maks
feasts and thigs [steals], drinks an' is na
dry, these three are na thrifty . . .

. . . .

He that by the plough would thrive,
himself must either hold or drive.

. . . .

He that goes a borrowing, goes a sorrowing.

. . . .

He that sleeps too soundly, let him
borrow the pillow of a debtor.

. . . .

He that spends, more than his goods extend,
merry will not be, and he'll be grieved
with poverty.

. . . .

He that tilleth his land shall have plenty of
bread; but he that followeth after vain persons
shall have poverty enough. A faithful man shall
abound with blessings: but he that maketh
haste to be rich shall not be innocent.

. . . .

He that would thrive, must ask his wife.

He who depends wholly on another's providing for
him, hath but an ill breakfast, and a worse supper.

. . . .

He who pays his debts, begins to make a stock.

. . . .

He who promises, runs into debt.

. . . .

He who trifles away his time, perceives not
death which stands upon his shoulders.

. . . .

He who will thrive, must rise at five.
He who hath thriven, may sleep till seven.

. . . .

He who won't keep a penny, won't
have many.

. . . .

I cannot call riches better than
the baggage of virtue.

. . . .

Idleness is the enemy of the soul.

. . . .

Idleness is the greatest prodigality.

. . . .

If a man empties his purse into his head
no man can take it from him.

Independence thrives of thrift.

. . . .

Industry is Fortune's right hand.

. . . .

*It is a disease of the mind to desire
what is unattainable, and to overlook
the greater wants of others.*

. . . .

*It is equally wrong to be liberal to the
undeserving; and uncharitable to the worthy.*

. . . .

*It is more desirable to distribute the
fruits of one's own industry, than to
reap the benefit of other people's.*

. . . .

Keep some till furthermore come.

. . . .

Keep within compass.

. . . .

Keep the wolf from the door.

. . . .

Labor conquers all things.

. . . .

*Let that which is wanting in income
be supplied by frugality.*

If rich, be not elated; if poor, be not dejected.

. . . .

*If you desire many things, the possession
of many things will seem but little.*

. . . .

*If you want to live and thrive
Let the spider run alive.*

. . . .

Ill gotten gains never thrive.

Let your expenses never exceed your income.

. . . .

Light gains make a full purse.

. . . .

Lightly come, lightly go.

. . . .

Little and often fills the purse.

. . . .

*A little Debt makes a Debtor, but
a great one an Enemy.*

. . . .

Luxury is attained through thrift.

. . . .

Make hay while the sun shines.

. . . .

A man ought to obey reason, and not appetite.

. . . .

*Many one blames their Wife,
for their own unthrift.*

. . . .

*The master makes the house to be
respected, not the house the master.*

. . . .

*The most certain gain comes from
carefully using what you have.*

Necessity sharpens Industry.

. . . .

Neither a borrower nor a lender be.

. . . .

Never spend money before you have it.

. . . .

No alchemy like saving.

. . . .

No man is free who does not command himself.

. . . .

Nothing is so hard to bear well, as prosperity.

. . . .

*Nothing is so precious as leisure, not
because one should be idle, but because
one should do what he wills.*

. . . .

Oft change, small thrift.

. . . .

*The only means that man has to assimilate himself
to God, is to do good, and to speak truth.*

. . . .

Out of debt, out of danger.

. . . .

A penny spared is twice got.

A place for everything, and everything
in its place.

. . . .

A pound of care will not pay an ounce of debt.

. . . .

Poverty screams, wealth whispers.

. . . .

Practice thrift, or else you'll drift.

. . . .

Prefer labour before idleness, unless you
esteem rust more than brightness.

. . . .

Prefer loss to unjust gain.

. . . .

Prudent men woo thrifty women.

. . . .

Resolve not to be poor: whatever
you have, spend less.

. . . .

Riches are like muck, stink in a heap; but
spread abroad, make the earth fruitful.

. . . .

Riches do not consist in the possession
of wealth, but in the use of it.

Riches well got, and well used, are
a great Blessing.

. . . .

The right-thinking person is anything but
negligent in acquiring money, never a
wrong-doer in seeking it, and cautious of
extravagance and waste in disbursing it.

. . . .

A rolling stone gathers no moss.

. . . .

Save money and money will save you.

. . . .

Save your white penny for your black day.

. . . .

Saving is getting.

. . . .

Scatter with one hand, gather with two.

. . . .

The secret of thrift is foresight.

. . . .

Seest thou a man diligent in his business?
He shall stand before kings; he shall
not stand before mean men.

. . . .

The slothful man saith, There is a lion
without, I shall be slain in the streets.

A small leak will sink a great ship.

. . . .

Spare well that you may spend well.

. . . .

Spending is quick, earning is slow.

. . . .

Sweet to take, but bitter to pay.

. . . .

Take care of the pence: the pounds
will take care of themselves.

. . . .

Take heed to your charge, keep within
measure, and you will be rich.

. . . .

There are no gains, without pains.

. . . .

A thing lasts longer mended than new.

. . . .

Think of ease, but work on.

. . . .

Those who exercise continency and frugality,
have a higher relish of pleasure, and are less
affected with pain, than those who are
the most diligent and assiduous in the
pursuit of delight and indulgences.

Three littles make a man rich on a sudden;
little wit, little shame, and little honesty.

. . . .

Thrift comes too late when th'
Purse is grown too low.

. . . .

Thrift is better than an annuity.

. . . .

Thrift is half thy store.

. . . .

Thrift is the Philosopher's Stone.

. . . .

Thrift must begin with little savings.

. . . .

Thrifty people spend more.

. . . .

A thrifty wife is better than a great income.

. . . .

Thrive honestly, or remain poor.

. . . .

Thrush paid for is better than turkeys owed for.

. . . .

Time wasted is existence, used is life.

Fun-Full Thrift Game

Tine [Lose] thimble, tine thrift.

. . . .

Tithe, and be rich.

. . . .

To be engaged, is good and useful; to be idle, is pernicious and evil. They who do good are employed; but they who spend their time in vain recreations, are idle.

. . . .

To a good spender, God is treasurer.

. . . .

Undertake deliberately; but having begun, persevere.

. . . .

Use it up, Wear it out, Make it do, Do without.

. . . .

Waste not, want not.

. . . .

The way to immortality is to live well.

. . . .

The ways of thrift are the ways of pleasantness.

. . . .

We ought to aim at such pleasures as follow labour, not at those which precede it.

Wealth gotten by vanity shall be diminished;
but he that gathereth by labour shall increase.

. . . .

Whan thrift and you fell first at a fray,
You played the man, for ye made thrift run away.

. . . .

 Whan thrift is in the towne, yee be
in the feeld.
. . . Whan thrift was in the field,
ye ware in the towne.

. . . .

 What you can do alone, expect not
from another.

. . . .

When ill actions acquire wealth,
the infamy is the greater.

. . . .

Where one blade of grass grew
before, thrift makes two grow.

. . . .

Who shall keep well sheep and been [bees],
Sleep or wake, their thrift comes in.

Who wastes what he has, is mad.

. . . .

Whoever puts himself into another's
power, becomes a slave.

. . . .

Wilful waste makes woeful want.

. . . .

Wise and good is better than rich and great.

. . . .

A woman can throw out with a spoon
in the kitchen more than a man
can bring in with a shovel.

. . . .

Work provides easy chairs for old age.

. . . .

Your thrift's as gude [good] as the
profit o' a yeeld [your] hen.

CONCLUSION

The Possibilities of American Thrift

BEGINNING IN EARNEST in the eighteenth century, people from around the world—mostly from Europe and Africa, but soon enough from nearly everywhere—came or were taken to the North American continent, whereupon they took the land from its native people and established across that land a European-influenced, English-oriented, but ultimately distinctive civilization. From this mix, something new emerged. "What then is the American, this new man?" asked the immigrant J. Hector St. John Crevecoeur in his 1782 book, *Letters from an American Farmer.*[1] It's a great question. With respect to thrift, let's try to answer it.

THE INHERITANCE

The main American idea is freedom. We move west, we go where we please, we do what we will. We do not have to bend the knee. We do not have to obey our fathers. We are slow to recognize

limits. Listen to Walt Whitman, the great poet of American democracy:

From this hour I ordain myself loos'd of limits
  and imaginary lines,
Going where I list, my own master total and
  absolute.[2]

Must I bend the knee? Is there something larger than individualism? For many of us, of course, still significantly shaped by biblical culture and the old ideas, the main answer to these questions is "Yes." We bow before God. We disavow the notion that we own ourselves. We recognize, and try not to eat, the forbidden fruit. But for growing numbers of us, and in some respects now for the country as whole, the main answer is "No." Whitman again:

Whimpering and truckling fold with powders for
  invalids, conformity goes to the fourth-remov'd,
I wear my hat as I please indoors or out.

Why should I pray? why should I venerate and be
   ceremonious?
Having pried through the strata, analyzed to a
   hair, counsel'd with doctors and calculated close,
I find no sweeter fat than sticks to my own bones.[3]

Surveying the origins and content of core American values today, Everett C. Ladd describes "a uniquely insistent and far-reaching individualism—a view of the individual person which gives unprecedented weight to his or her choices, interests, and claims." Ladd concludes: "The American idea of freedom is of the 'leave me alone' variety."[4] Even the ideal of equality, the other master value of American culture, is most frequently understood to mean equal opportunity, or equality of freedom.

In this sweet land of liberty, one part of our inheritance—one outgrowth of our biblical culture, one of the old ideas—is thrift. As we've seen, the concept of thrift in English-speaking societies is more than anything else a restatement, in secular terms, of the Judeo-Christian concept of stewardship.

Recall the three related lodestars of this thrift ideal. *Industry*: Work hard. *Frugality*: Don't waste. *Trusteeship*: Give back. What have we Americans done to date with this ideal, this little jewel from our inheritance? What might we decide to do with it in the future?

Do you recall, from part one, the views in 1920 of Edward Bok, who as a child had emigrated to the U.S. from Holland? Bok was shocked and dismayed by American extravagance and wastefulness, and rightly called it a lack of thrift. But at the same time, he was moved and inspired by what he called "the American spirit of initiative"[5]—which of course is also an aspect of thrift.

Industry is the part of thrift at which American typically excel. Americans are almost always up and doing. We take lots of initiative and risks. We work very hard and, compared to the other rich countries, take few vacations and put in very long hours. Much of this work turns out to be quite creative. All of this initiative and industry, of course, has paid off for us materially. We are a fabulously rich country—a gaudy, over-the-top society in which, as Tom Wolfe puts it, the guy who cleans swimming pools in East Hampton is wearing a Rolex watch and is on his third wife. Americans are industrious!

On trusteeship—what we have is not ours alone, but is held by us in trust, for the benefit of others—Americans overall can point to much that is good. By many measures, we seem to be a generous people. Our system of private philanthropy is probably the most robust in the world. A recent British study, for example, finds that U.S. charitable donations in 2005 amounted to about 1.7 percent of the nation's gross national product (GNP)—a significantly higher proportion than in any of the other surveyed nations.[6]

One important reason for our comparative generosity, of course, is our affluence. Giving a lot is easier for people who have a lot. Another key reason is that our tax laws encourage private giving. A third reason is that among the rich modern societies, we are the most religious, and religiosity tends in general to correlate with charitable giving. A fourth and also significant reason is that the United States is a low-tax society. In areas such as social insurance and welfare services, much of what we in the U.S. do privately and often locally, through our philanthropies, other rich countries do publicly and nationally, through their tax-supported governmental agencies. This fact can complicate our attempt to measure things fairly. To take just one obvious example, it suggests that France, with its high taxes and low charitable giving, may be doing just as well if not better on this particular dimension of thrift than the United States, with its low taxes and high charitable giving.

Regarding the dimension of the thrift ethic that emphasizes frugality—carefulness, conservation and reuse, avoidance of waste, and the disavowal of personal extravagance—the United States by almost any measure is . . . a disaster. In almost every category, we lead the world in waste. What Americans waste every day shocked young Edward Bok a century ago, and it shocks most visitors to our country today. In the John le Carré novel, *Tinker, Tailor, Soldier, Spy*, the English school teacher in front of his class grabs a crayon and with frustration draws a globe, with Britain in the middle: "To the west, America, he said, full of greedy fools fouling up their inheritance."[7] It's a point of view.

Wonderfully blessed with natural resources, it would be hard to argue that, to date, we have been anything other than poor stewards of those resources. My favorite animal has always been the American buffalo. From *Buffalo Bill's Own Story*:

They could afford to remunerate me well, because the meat would not cost them anything . . . During my engagement as hunter for the company—a period of less than eighteen months—I killed 4,280 buffaloes . . .[8]

From Tom McHugh's *The Time of the Buffalo*:

Indian wastefulness increased as the white man began to offer tempting goods in exchange for buffalo products. In 1832, for instance, when George Catlin first arrived at Fort Pierre, South Dakota, he was informed that a few days earlier "party of five or six hundred Sioux Indians . . . came into the Fort with fourteen hundred fresh buffalo tongues . . . for which they required but a few gallons of whiskey, which was soon demolished, indulging them in a little, and harmless, carouse." When the traders became more numerous and offered more attractive barter, some Indians started to kill buffalo for their hides alone, thus degrading themselves to the level of the white hunters.[9]

From David A. Dary's *The Buffalo Book*:

What has often been reported to be the world's record for buffalo killing on the southern plains was set by Thomas C. Nixon during the early 1870s . . . Shortly Nixon's judges arrived and counted the dead buffalo. In forty minutes Nixon had killed 120 buffalo . . . [B]y 1884, hide hunting as a business on the northern plains had all but ended. What is believed to be

*the last carload of buffalo robes and hides from
the northern plains was shipped from Dickinson in far western Dakota in 1884.*[10]

From Larry McMurtry's beautifully researched
novel, *Streets of Laredo*:

*Years before, when the buffalo were being
killed, a large remnant of the great southern
herd had wandered south, off the plain and
into the sandhills. There they were pursued by
the Kiowa and Commanche, and by the most
unremitting of the buffalo hunters, in a last
great frenzy of killing. The skins were piled in
great heaps, awaiting wagons to transport them
east. But the hide market collapsed, and the
wagons never came. The towering heaps of hides
slowly rotted.*[11]

I single out the buffalo for a moment not in
order to delve into the particulars of that sad and
difficult issue, but partly because of the buffalo's
iconic importance in our national history, and
mostly because our record of stewardship in this
case, for good and for ill, resembles closely enough
our record of stewardship regarding numerous
other aspects of our inherited natural resources.
What explains such a record? Surely much of the
answer is that, for most of our history, we have
been a rapidly growing society with a steadily
westward-moving frontier. Listen to Frederick
Jackson Turner, the great historian of the American frontier, speaking at a university commencement ceremony in 1910:

*To the pioneer the forest was no friendly resource
for posterity, no object of careful economy . . .
fired with the ideal of subduing the wilderness,
the destroying pioneer fought his way across the
continent, masterful and wasteful, preparing
the way by seeking the immediate thing, rejoicing in rude strength and wilful achievement.*[12]

When it comes to the frugality and conservation dimensions of the thrift ethic—even after
we've noted the important qualifications and the
historical reasons why—we as a society clearly
have much to confess, and much to amend—at
least insofar as our criterion is that little jewel, the
thrift principle.

Oh, and did I mention our national performance on frugality when it comes to our money?
Let's face it, when compared to other countries,
we are a nation of spendthrifts. Especially in recent
years, we have not only spent our money as fast as
we have earned it, we have actually begun to spend
it *faster* than we earn it! At both the governmental level, with our very large and perhaps struc-
tural budget deficits, and at the level of individual
citizens and families, with our huge and growing levels of consumer debt and with our (as of
2006) negative savings rate, over-indebtedness has
become an American way of life. Whether, and
how long, this trend can continue unabated without producing a major financial crisis is a topic
that economists today are hotly debating. But this
much is clear: When it comes to money, we Americans are almost anything but frugal!

DIVISIONS AND CHALLENGES

So far we've been measuring Americans' thrift overall, as a nation, but now let's zoom in a bit closer, and observe several regional, sociopolitical, and institutional distinctions and challenges. I am a Southerner, from Mississippi, so let's begin with region. The diffusion of the thrift ethic in the United States has been very regionally uneven, with the South lagging far behind (or far ahead, depending on your point of view). While in Britain, for example, the savings bank movement fairly quickly reached every area of the nation, in the U.S. the savings banks never picked up much steam in the South, or even in the Sunbelt as a whole. Roughly speaking, the same is true for other cooperative thrift institutions, such as building and loans and credit unions. Regionally, ground zero for the U.S. thrift tradition is the Northeast, particularly Massachusetts. The Deep South is on the other end of the scale.

As with so much in the South, the main underlying issue is probably race. We can start with slavery, a labor system that is inimical to thrift. For me, one of the most chilling quotations in this book is Henry Adams's comment in 1857 about the poor quality of roads in the slave state of Virginia: "Bad roads meant bad morals." Or consider the observation from about the same time by the novelist Nathaniel Hawthorne, commenting disdainfully on

the natural shabbiness, and decayed, unthrifty look of a Virginian village . . . there would be a

less striking contrast between Southern and New England villages, if the former were as much in the habit of using white paint as we are.[13]

Or this remarkable formulation, also from 1857, from George Fitzhugh, who passionately despised thrift as a cultural value and passionately supported Southern slavery:

The only difference [between the South and the North] is, we love our slaves, and we are ready to defend, assist and protect them; you hate and fear your white servants, and never fail, as a moral duty, to screw down their wages to the lowest, and to starve their families, if possible, as evidence of your thrift, economy and management—the only English and Yankee virtues.[14]

What do we make of these propositions? Amazingly, people on opposite sides of the slavery question in the nineteenth century actively shared the view that thrift—with its good roads, whitewashed fences, and wage-labor system—was mainly an "English and Yankee virtue," whereas the South, with its preindustrial codes of chivalry and gentlemanliness and its ruling elite served by slaves, was largely guided by values quite distinct from, and even opposed to, the value of thrift.

In the twentieth century, issues linked to race and racism continued to deform and miniaturize Southern thrift. Consider the issue of building new thrift institutions. For most of the century, anyone wanting to establish or advance a thrift institution in the South faced a cruel choice—

serve either whites only or blacks only, as a part of a Jim Crow system in which, under the best of circumstances, it was by definition necessary to create two networks of savings banks (or public libraries, or credit unions, or building and loans) in every locale in which, were race not an issue, only one would be necessary; or alternatively, seek to serve both races through the same networks and institutions, and be assured of strong and possibly violent resistance from whites.

The main result, not surprisingly, has been the marked and general retardation of Southern public thrift institutions, a handicap from which the South even today, especially the Deep South, has not recovered. If there is to be a new thrift movement in America in the years ahead—and that is a goal to which I am committed—it will have to be truly national in scope, and much of the hardest and most necessary work will need to take place in the South.

A second divide within American thrift concerns marriage and family life. Put simply, the thrift ethic tends to correlate, and overlap significantly, with an ethic of marriage and family life. Most of my work to date has been in the areas of marriage and families. For more than two decades, I have followed the scholarly and public debates on these issues quite closely, and as a result I believe that I know the current lines of demarcation fairly well. When I began my research on thrift, I certainly did not imagine or look for any connections between thrift and my other main field of study. They seemed like two entirely separate issues. And in many ways, of course, they are.

But in other ways, they are not. I now see linkages on several levels. First, there is a clear kinship between the values comprising the thrift ideal and the values usually associated with well-functioning marriages and families. Both the thrift ethic and the marriage ethic, for example, depend on foresight, patience, consistent effort, taking other people's needs into account, and building good things over time, as opposed to depending on luck or being pushed and pulled by short-term considerations or the desire for instant personal gratification. For this reason, in individuals, the two ethics often tend to go together. Alternatively, someone who goes through his money too fast and too carelessly is probably also prone to go through other things, such as wives and lovers, too fast and too carelessly.

And should we really be surprised by this convergence? A family, after all, can be described as a locally based, usually small-scale cooperative organization whose members help one another economically as well as in other ways. A building and loan association can be described in pretty much the same way! I am not suggesting that the two are the same—obviously they are not. But I am suggesting that as institutions they have some interestingly similar forms, and that those similar forms tend to generate similar and overlapping values, habits, and personality traits.

Finally, and to me most revealingly, public arguments dismissing or attacking thrift tend to be virtually identical in structure to public arguments dismissing or attacking marriage and the family as institutions. For me, this was quite a discovery!

There was never a golden age of family life . . .

STEPHANIE COONTZ, *THE WAY WE REALLY ARE*, 1997

. . . .

There was never a golden age of thrift.

JACKSON LEARS, "THE AMERICAN WAY OF
DEBT," *NEW YORK TIMES MAGAZINE*, 2006

. . . .

I know the Rutgers University historian Jackson Lears because he wrote a paper, and was also a lead advisor, for the scholarly conference on the history of thrift that I helped to organize in the fall of 2005. I also know the historian Stephanie Coontz.

For years, in books with titles such as *The Way We Never Were*, Coontz has essentially argued that family fragmentation has always been with us, that there was never a golden age of the family, and that people who worry about the weakening of the family are worried about the wrong thing and are therefore part of the problem. And not just Coontz. This nearly exact formulation is an easily recognizable and widely deployed rhetorical template among intellectuals who champion family diversity and criticize customary family forms, such as marriage.

Imagine my shock of recognition, then, when I learned from my erstwhile conference associate Jackson Lears, in his dismissal of thrift in the *New York Times*, that debt has always been with us, that there was never a golden age of thrift, and that people who worry about the weakening of thrift

are worried about the wrong thing and are therefore part of the problem. Professor Lears, meet Dr. Coontz!

By the way, on the merits, what should we make of this repeated insistence on never a golden age? If you have perused this cyclopedia, you have seen literally hundreds of pro-thrift arguments from scores of thrift leaders across British and U.S. history. Do you recall even one of these advocates basing his or her main argument on the idea that there was once a golden age of thrift? I don't. Here are a few additional and quite typical comments on this point from some leading thrift advocates.

Good husbandry is no English vertue, it may have been brought over, & in some places where it has been planted it has thriven well enough, but 'tis a foreign species, it neither loves, nor is beloved by an Englishman . . .

DANIEL DEFOE, *GIVING ALMS NO CHARITY*, 1704

. . . .

One point wherein the American people are exceedingly deficient is that of method. We are energetic; we are audacious; we are confident in our own capacities and in our national destiny; but we are not a systematic, a frugal, economical people . . . the differences between our people and the Europeans are immense.

HORACE GREELEY, *AN ADDRESS ON SUCCESS IN BUSINESS*, NOVEMBER 11, 1867

. . . possibly it is because we make our money faster than most other countries that we spend it faster also. The Americans equal us, perhaps exceed us, in both respects, and it may be that a certain absence of caution, a certain reluctance to contemplate the possibility of things going wrong, a vague confidence that the future must be even more prosperous than the present, are traits of character inherent in, and inseparable from, the nature of a progressive and energetic people.

. . . Our English people have always been, as they are now, patient of labor, anxious to raise themselves; not envious of those who succeed (and that is a great matter); willing to make great exertions in pursuit of wealth, but less able, in general, to keep it when acquired than acquire it; and rather too much inclined to consider the squandering of capital as a sign of a general disposition, and the propensity to save as evidence of selfishness and meanness.

LORD DERBY, ADDRESS TO THE PROVIDENT
KNOWLEDGE SOCIETY, MAY 9, 1873

. . . .

Having worked over and exhausted our soil from one ocean to the other, we are going back and learning the business of farming all over again, under permanent conditions . . . There must now come a mature period of positive rural prosperity, following the lax and shiftless days since the first freshness of the soil was exhausted by pioneers who made the clearings.

ALBERT SHAW, *THE OUTLOOK FOR
THE AVERAGE MAN*, 1907

The country passed through a period of prosperity and suddenly acquired wealth, but nobody thought to teach this new generation of women the value of money or how to spend it to best advantage . . . This is unjust. Give the American woman lessons in thrift along the modern lines of income and expenditure, and she will work out her splendid salvation.

"WHAT DO YOU DO WITH FATHER'S MONEY?"
LECTURE TO MEMBERS OF THE NATIONAL
HOUSEWIVES' LEAGUE, ABOUT 1915

. . . .

Do these people seem historically deluded? Do they need a reminder from Professor Lears not to kid themselves about a lost golden age? Of course not. In fact, far from succumbing to illusions about a golden age of thrift, the typical thrift jeremiad throughout U.S. history (and including today) has stated almost exactly the opposite! Over and over, we are warned that we Americans have never been a particularly thrifty people, but that due to current challenges, we need to change our ways. (Put me in that category of belief as well!) So this "never a golden age" trope from contemporary scholars is almost completely nonhistorical, and therefore intellectually irrelevant, except insofar as it has become in recent years a form of partisan name-calling—a way of suggesting that everyone who might favor (fill in the blank) is a naive person ready to indulge in historical make-believe.

There are other similarities between the two arguments. Both Lears and Coontz, for example, seek to reduce all arguments in favor of (fill in the blank) to the level of hypocritical finger-pointing, or what Lears in his essay terms "moralism," which is very bad.

More generally, as examples of scholarship, both of these argument are breathtakingly insubstantial—top-heavy with political theorizing and self-assured pronouncements, but very skimpy with the facts. From Lears, for example, *in an essay on debt in the U.S.*, there is not one word, and nary a number, on actual trends regarding savings and indebtedness in the United States. Nor is there a single mention of any of the actual institutions, from savings banks to credit unions, that thrift leaders over time have created to address problems of savings and over-indebtedness. Instead, we get sentences such as: "In fact, debt is as American as cherry pie." Thanks for the insight!

So there are more convergences between the thrift ethic and the family ethic than I had originally assumed. Of course, I am sure that many lovers of the conventional family are thriftless, just as I am sure that many unmarried and solo-living people are committed to thrift and could be important leaders of a future thrift movement. And though I have my doubts, I concede that there may also be some prominent public intellectuals out there who can't stand thrift, but love customary family forms.

At the same time, these multiple convergences—normative, institutional, and regarding the shape of the respective public arguments—seem to me to be too striking to ignore. They clearly suggest that, looking to the future, American thrift values are likely to rise or fall in rough tandem with American family values, and that our thrift institutions are likely to face the same types of criticism and share the same general fate as our family institutions. This fact changes some calculations. I used to assume, when considering the possibility of a thrift renewal movement in the United States, that my old friends from movements to strengthen the family would not have a dog in this new fight one way or the other. Now I believe, and hope, differently.

A third and (for us, for now) final challenge within American thrift concerns one of those topics about which Professor Lears, with his exclusive identification of thrift as "moralism," had zero to say: the role of institutions and institutional change in shaping outcomes for individuals.

An important trend in our generation is sharply rising levels of individual and societal debt and a steady decline in savings. Debt payments now consume about 15 percent of the average American family's income. About 20 percent of low-income families spend at least 40 percent of their income in debt payments. Nearly half of all credit card holders have missed payments in the past year, and an estimated one in seven U.S. families is dealing with a debt collector. In 2005 and 2006, for the first time since the Great Depression, and in the context of historically low unemployment, Americans overall spent more than they earned, meaning that our national savings rate has now dropped to below zero. Nearly two-thirds of Americans report that they do not save enough.[15] "Crisis" is an overused word, but it may be fair to say that much of America, using borrowed money to cover the costs of today's needs and wants, and without adequate savings, is now experiencing a crisis of over-indebtedness.

Why? Is it because too many Americans are making foolish choices? Is it because they lack thrift? In part, yes. But probably an even bigger part of the answer is that powerful institutions—let's call them anti-thrift institutions—are increasingly soliciting and sponsoring those foolish choices. Consider payday lenders, those modern successors to the old salary loan companies, whose flagrantly predatory practices in the early decades of the twentieth century highlighted the need for, and in that sense helped give rise to, the modern credit union movement. These old practices have now returned with a vengeance. Today there are more payday lending operations in California than there are McDonald's franchises.

Or consider the explosion in recent years of rent-to-own stores, especially in poorer neighborhoods. Or auto title lenders. Or check-cashing shops—an industry that more than doubled in size from 1998 to 2002.[16] Or chain pawn shops. Or consider our newly aggressive credit card companies, now sending cards with buy-me-now gimmicks through the mail to nearly everyone in sight, including college students with no income.

Or consider the public sector's very own, enormously influential anti-thrift institutions, the state lotteries and other forms of state-sponsored gambling. Until 1964, there was not one government-sponsored lottery in the United States. Today there are forty-three, all of them working

24/7, using the most sophisticated advertising that money can buy in order to extract billions of dollars of gambling revenue from the paychecks of the poor, working class, and middle-income players who are its core customer base.

Economic historians have recognized that savings banks stood in direct competition with the lottery . . . Savings banks were designed to compete with purveyors of vice, with tavern keepers, with lottery and policy dealers, with gambling-house proprietors . . .

ANNE FABIAN, *CARD SHARPS, DREAM BOOKS AND BUCKET SHOPS: GAMBLING IN 19TH CENTURY AMERICA*

. . . .

Lotteries and thrift simply do not go together. I live in New York, and the main ad slogan of the New York State Lottery is, "You Never Know!" If those who hate our country wanted to come up with the single best slogan to insinuate into every American's head in order to eviscerate the habits and character traits associated with thrift—not to mention a few other little things, like self-government and democracy—that slogan almost certainly would be, "You Never Know!"

Individuals make choices. In a pro-thrift culture, individual choices are typically guided by, as well as rewarded and at times even required by, authoritative pro-thrift institutions. But in today's increasingly pro-debt culture, people who would pursue thrift must typically rely almost *entirely* on their own individual knowledge and willpower, including the willpower to ignore the constant and seductive "money for free" messages coming at them courtesy of today's regnant anti-thrift institutions. That's why, in a debt-oriented culture such as ours, it's not just that more people are making bad choices, it's also that society's main institutions are *promoting* those bad choices, while they simultaneously ignore, downplay, and often even block realistic avenues for individual thrift.

As we've seen, earlier generations of thrift visionaries build important thrift institutions that helped millions of people. They organized fraternal societies. They founded savings banks. Taught young people thrift in schools. Started food co-ops and community gardens. Organized producer cooperatives. Built libraries. Raised homes through building and loan associations. Democratized access to credit through credit unions.

Duncan of Ruthwell. Sikes of Huddersfield. Franklin. Beecher. Child. Pratt. Washington. Straus. Walker. Bergengren. In my view, these people are true heroes. What they did was so important. Do we have people like them today? Do they possess the vision and capacity to build new thrift institutions to meet the new circumstances and needs of this generation?

In this entire area, our greatest challenge in the coming years is to create powerful new thrift institutions that can provide realistic alternatives to today's anti-thrift institutions. Put more simply, our challenge is to replace today's debt culture with a thrift culture.

WHICH AMERICA?

I want to conclude this book by asking you to reflect briefly on this 1957 observation on successful American business leaders ("Titans") from Max Lerner:

There is one division which cuts across most of the Titans of the earlier prewar era of America—the split between the puritan and the magnifico. J. Piermont Morgan, the greatest of all the Titans, was a magnifico in the sense that he operated on a scale of magnificence. So also were [James J.] Hill, [John W.] Gates, [Jay] Gould, several of the early Du Ponts, and [Charles Tyson] Yerkes himself. There was a lustiness and grandeur of scope in their private as in their business lives. They bet and gambled, lived conspicuously, gave parties, sailed yachts, were seen in the European capitals; there were legends of the stables of women they kept; they built palatial homes and crammed them with art treasures rifled from the museums and collections of Europe. There was native optimism in them; in business as in private life they were "bullish" . . .

There was another strain, however, represented by Daniel Drew, the Rockefellers, Henry Ford: not the strain of magnificence but of the taut Puritan qualities. These men came out of small towns and remained at home in small-town America. They were abstemious, church-going, taught Sunday-school classes. They spent little on themselves, and what they did they spent quietly. Like Rockefeller, they handed out shiny dimes; like Ford, they ploughed everything back into the business. They had the eccentricities in which men can indulge when they sit on top of a pyramid of power. They were apt to be gloomy men and presented a stern vision of the world, at once unsmiling and unrelenting. Yet they were probably closer than the magnificos to the theological roots of capitalism: the demonstration of virtue through success, the doctrine of calling, the gospel of work and thrift.

MAX LERNER, *AMERICA AS A CIVILIZATION*, 1957

. . . .

When I think of this same basic division today, I think of Donald Trump and Warren Buffet. Donald Trump, one of Max Lerner's magnificos if ever there was one, is a billionaire real-estate mogul and owner of gambling casinos, who has also in recent years become a best-selling author, TV and radio star, and tabloid media celebrity—the latest and possibly most shameless in a long line of out-sized American gamers who get famous by being rich and stay rich by being famous.

If we ever need a poster boy for "Thrift—*Not!*" we surely have one in Donald Trump. For him, everything is about high living and fast bucks, or what Trump calls "the art of the deal." He is a caricature of egotism. Much of his money is from his gambling interests. He leaves behind him a trail of indebtedness and messy bankruptcies. He is a man whose core philosophy seems to be that bigger is always better and that more is always good. A man who cannot have his name on too many buildings or billboards, or in letters too large. A deep craving for glitz, flash, and conspicuous consumption—

Donald Trump was bling before bling was a word. Quantities of bragging that, in most places, would gag a horse.

Heaven help us, we all, or at least most of us, have a bit of Donald Trump in us. After all, is it *always* wrong to want it, have it, and flaunt it? As Lerner recognized, being a magnifico in America can be quite exciting and, often enough, lots of fun! I imagine that more than a few Americans play the lottery today hoping that they'll get lucky and become a somewhat smaller-scale version of Donald Trump, a hometown magnifico. In any case, there is a reason why so many, and growing numbers, of our signs across the country have the word "Trump" emblazoned on them. If Trump were a U.S. city, he would doubtless be Las Vegas or Atlantic City, but there is also a sense in which *all* of our cities, and our society as a whole, have been moving steadily in recent decades in a Trump-like direction.

Warren Buffet is also a famous billionaire. But any similarity to Trump ends there. Buffet lives modestly in Omaha, Nebraska. He eats lunch at the Dairy Queen. He has never borrowed money in business, and has never been in debt. Throughout his career, nearly everyone associated with him has made money, usually lots of it. Lerner describes his American puritans as typically "gloomy men" who are "at once unsmiling and unrelenting." But Buffet seems to be cheerful enough, and by all accounts has a great sense of humor.

He could not be less interested in "the art of the deal." As an investor, he emphasizes the fundamentals and looks for companies that are likely to thrive over time. He filed his first tax return at age thirteen, for his paper route, and took a $25 deduction for his bicycle. Because he does not believe that the children of rich men, including his own children, should inherit all or even most of their fathers' estates, he recently announced plans to give most of his money away. He argues that "huge fortunes that flow in large part from society should in large part be returned to society."[17] He keeps receipts and is a stickler over small sums of money. For years—until he gave it to a charity auction—the license plate on his car read "THRIFTY."

Most of us have a bit of Warren Buffet in us, or at least would like to. There is much to admire here. And as Lerner's observations suggest, Buffet's America—the America of "the demonstration of virtue through success, the doctrine of calling, the gospel of work and thrift"—runs quite deep in our history and still looms large today as an aspect of our collective identity and a shaper of our possibilities.

The question for us today is, which America? Looking ahead, in which direction do we want to go? Do we want as a society to become a bit more like Trump? Or a bit more like Buffet? To me, the answer is clear enough. Moreover, the stakes are quite high. If I had to pick the best word to describe the Trump direction, it would be "waste." For the Buffet direction, by far the best word, and possibly the only truly adequate word, is "thrift."

Acknowledgments

My deepest debts regarding this project are to Sir John Templeton, and his son, Dr. Jack Templeton, of the John Templeton Foundation. They have provided money, for which I am grateful, but they have also done much more. Both of these men are thrift visionaries—they have the true spirit of the thrift idea, and have given generously not only of their resources, but of themselves, to pass that spirit along to others. When I had a chance to meet Sir John several years ago, he said simply, "We need a history of thrift!" Since then, I have thought about that short sentence many times. Sir John, I hope that this book contains some of the raw material, a few of the working notes, that can shine a light on that history.

For encouragement and much assistance, I am also very grateful to Raina Sacks Blankenhorn, Sorcha Brophy-Warren, Kozue Ishi, Phillip Longman, Bonnie Robbins, Alex Roberts, Deb Strubel, Barbara Dafoe Whitehead, Kendra Worsley, Arthur Schwartz and Kimon Sargeant of the John Templeton Foundation, and Laura G. Barrett and Natalie Lyons Silver of Templeton Foundation Press.

Appendix A: Do You Know What Thrift Is? (A Quiz)

Five Words or Less Per Answer:

1. Thrift is:

2. The opposite of thrift is:

3. The best thing about thrift is:

4. The worst thing about thrift is:

5. Best all-time thrift book:

6. Best all-time anti-thrift book:

7. Best all-time thrift movie:

8. Best all-time anti-thrift movie:

9. All-time most admirable U.S. thrift millionaire:

10. All-time most notorious U.S. anti-thrift millionaire:

11. All-time most beneficial U.S. thrift institution:

12. All-time most destructive U.S. anti-thrift institution:

13. All-time greatest thrift visionary:

14. All-time greatest anti-thrift visionary:

15. If thrift was an animal, it would be:

16. If thriftlessness was an animal, it would be:

17. If thrift was a U.S. city, it would be:

18. If thriftlessness was a U.S. city, it would be:

19. If thrift was a color, it would be:

20. If thriftlessness was a color, it would be:

21. If thrift was a movie star, it would be:

22. If thriftlessness was a movie star, it would be:

23. The world's most thrifty nation:

24. The world's least thrifty nation:

25. Most valuable current pro-thrift idea:

You can share your answers, and learn mine, by taking this quiz online at www.newthrift.org.

Appendix B: Puritans and Quakers

BEFORE ENDING this inquiry, let's briefly go back to Benjamin Franklin. After all, when it comes to thrift, Franklin is surely, to borrow a phrase from the magnificent boxer Muhammad Ali, "The Greatest of All Time." Studying him is always a good investment. At the same time, with winning modesty, Franklin often stated that he took all his ideas on "industry and frugality" from others. This statement begs the question: which others?

Two main answers are the Puritans and the Quakers. Remember, Franklin grew up in Puritan Boston and lived most of his life in Quaker Philadelphia. And each of those great religious movements—the Puritanism that arose in England in the sixteenth century with the goal of "purifying" the Church of England of any traces of Catholicism, and the Quakers who broke away from the Puritans in the mid-seventeenth century to form their own religious practice and community—had much to say about the meaning and purposes of thrift in human affairs. Franklin clearly owed the most to the Puritans, and in particular to the Rev. Cotton Mather. In essence, Franklin absorbed the Puritan thrift ethic, dropped much of its theological content and context, and brilliantly translated it, with some help from his Quaker neighbors, as "the way to wealth" for his fellow Americans and for the world. It worked splendidly.

Here is a more formal way to pose the same question: what are the religious and cultural roots of Franklin's thrift?

Seriously and frequently meditate on the account that men are to give of using their wealth. We are not lords of our riches, but stewards; and a steward must give an account of his stewardship.
THE PURITAN DIVINE WILLIAM GOUGE, SERMON ON "OF WELL-USING ABUNDANCE," 1655

. . . .

To get our goods honestly, to keep them safely, and to spend them thriftily.
THE PURITAN DIVINE JOHN COTTON, *SPIRITUAL MILK FOR BOSTON BABES*, A CHILDREN'S PRIMER THAT WAS THE FIRST AND ONE OF THE MOST INFLUENTIAL BOOKS OF ITS KIND WRITTEN BY AN AMERICAN, 1656

. . . .

But that which did not a little amuse the merchandisers was, that these pilgrims set very light by all their wares. They cared not so much as to look upon them; and if they called upon them to buy, they would put their fingers in their ears, and cry, "Turn away mine eyes from beholding vanity," and look upward, signifying that their trade and traffic was in heaven.

One chanced mockingly, beholding the carriage of the men, to say unto them, "What will ye buy?" But they, looking gravely upon him, said, "We buy the truth."

THE NONCONFORMIST WRITER AND PREACHER JOHN BUNYAN, *THE PILGRIM'S PROGRESS*, PROBABLY THE MOST FAMOUS PUBLISHED CHRISTIAN ALLEGORY AND ONE OF THE MOST INFLUENTIAL BOOKS IN THE ENGLISH LANGUAGE, 1678

. . . .

Every grace is nourished by the Word, and without it there is no thrift in the soul.

JOHN BUNYAN, *FEAR OF GOD*, 1679

. . . .

The question is, How they use that which they labour so hard for, and save so sparingly. If they use it for God, and charitable uses, there is no man taketh a righter course. He is the best servant for God, that will be laborious and sparing, that he may be enabled to do good.

THE PURITAN DIVINE RICHARD BAXTER, *DIRECTIONS AGAINST COVETOUSNESS*

. . . .

If God shows you a way in which you may lawfully get more than in another way (without wrong to your soul or to any other), if you refuse this, and choose the less gainful way, you cross one of the ends of your Calling, and you refuse to be God's steward . . . every penny which is laid out . . . must be done as if by God's own appointment.

THE PURITAN DIVINE RICHARD STEELE, *THE TRADESMAN'S CALLING*, 1684

. . . .

As to these modern Seducers [Quakers], they are not men of Arms but a herd of silly insignificant People, aiming rather to heap up Riches in Obscurity, than to acquire a Fame by an heroick Undertaking. They are generally Merchants and Mechanicks, and are observed to be very punctual in their Dealings, Men of few Words in a Bargain, modest and compos'd in their Deportment, temperate in their Lives and using great Frugality in all Things . . . they are singularly Industrious . . .

GIOVANNI PAOLO MARANA, DESCRIBING QUAKERS IN HIS VERY POPULAR BOOK, *LETTERS WRIT BY A TURKISH SPY*, 1684

. . . .

Frugality is good, if Liberality be join'd with it. The first is leaving off superfluous expenses; the last bestowing them to the Benefit of others that need.

WILLIAM PENN, WHO IN 1682 FOUNDED THE COLONY OF PENNSYLVANIA AS A SAFE PLACE FOR QUAKERS TO LIVE AND PRACTICE THEIR FAITH, *SOME FRUITS OF SOLITUDE*, 1693

Diligence is another virtue useful and laudable among men: it is a discreet and understanding application of one's self to business; and avoids the extremes of idleness and drudgery . . . Shun diversions; think only of the present business, till that be done . . . it is the way to wealth . . .

Frugality is a virtue too, and not of little use in life, the better way to be rich, for it has less toil and temptation. It is proverbial, a penny saved is a penny got; it has a significant moral; for this way of getting is more in your own power and less subject to hazard, as well as snares, free of envy, void of suits, and is beforehand with calamities . . . But have a care of the extreme: want not with abundance, for that is avarice, even to sordidness; it is fit you consider children, age and casualties, but never pretend those things to palliate and gratify covetousness. As I would have you liberal but not prodigal; and diligent but not drudging; so I would have you frugal but not sordid. If you can, lay up one half of your income for those uses, in which let charity have at least the second consideration . . .

WILLIAM PENN, *WILLIAM PENN'S ADVICE TO HIS CHILDREN*, 1699

. . . .

. . . thou must remember that the more frugall thou art the more will by thy Stock . . . Come back plain. This will be a reputation to thee and recommend thee to the best and most Sensible people.

THE PROMINENT PHILADELPHIA QUAKER MERCHANT ISAAC NORRIS, WRITING TO HIS SON JOSEPH, 1719

There is another combination of virtues strangely mixed in every lively, holy Christian: and that is, diligence in worldly businesses, and yet deadness to the world. Such a mystery as none can read but they that know it.

THE PURITAN DIVINE COTTON MATHER, *A CHRISTIAN AT HIS CALLING*, 1701

. . . .

I tell you with Diligence a man may do marvellous things . . . Let your Business Engross the most of your Time . . . Be stirring about your Business as Early as is Convenient. Keep close to your Business.

. . . Suite your Expenses unto your Revenues: Take this Advice, O Christians; 'Tis a Sin, I say 'Tis ordinarily a Sin, and it will at length be a Shame, for a man to Spend more than he Gets, or make his Layings out more than his Comings in.

MATHER, *A CHRISTIAN AT HIS CALLING*

. . . .

This may be said of all our estates: what God gives us, is not given us for ourselves, but, "for the Lord."

MATHER, *ESSAYS TO DO GOOD*, 1710

. . . .

Assert the liberty of thinking on the noblest question that can be asked, What good may I do in the world?

MATHER, *ESSAYS TO DO GOOD*

The noblest question in the world is What Good may I do in it?

BENJAMIN FRANKLIN, *POOR RICHARD'S ALMANAC*, 1737

. . . .

From a Child I was fond of reading . . . There was also a Book of Defoe's called an Essay on Projects *and another of Dr. Mather's called* Essays to do Good, *which perhaps gave me a Turn of Thinking that had an influence on some of the principal future Events of my Life.*

FRANKLIN, *AUTOBIOGRAPHY*, 1784

. . . .

The diary of Samuel Sewall [born in 1652 and died in 1730] not only narrates the homely activities of Boston in the evening of the theocracy, antiquis moribus, prisca fide, but it unconsciously reveals the transformation of the English Puritan into the New England Yankee. The sober Boston citizens who on the Sabbath droned Windsor and York tunes, and took notes of long sermons, on week-days plied their gospel of thrift with notable success . . .

Like those kindred spirits, Defoe and Franklin, the dominant inspiration of [Sewall's] life was prudential . . . To acquire wealth and honors, to occupy a dignified position among his fellows, was the dominant ambition of his life. With excellent thrift he fixed his affections upon the only child of a wealthy merchant, the richest heiress in the colony . . . He understood how desirable it is to put money in one's purse; so he made a great alliance and proved himself a shrewd husbandman as well as a kind husband. From commerce and land speculation and money lending and the perquisites of many offices, he accumulated steadily . . . He did not forget his prudence even in his generosities, but set down carefully in his diary what his benefactions cost, that there might be no mistake when he came to make his reckoning with the Lord.

VERNON PARRINGTON, *MAIN CURRENTS OF AMERICAN THOUGHT*, 1927

Notes

PART 1

1

1. Clara B. Burdette, ed., *Robert J. Burdette: His Message* (Pasadena, CA: Clara Vista Press, 1922), 305–6, 310.

2

1. Carl Van Doren, *Benjamin Franklin* (New York: Viking Press, 1938), viii.
2. See Edmund Malone, ed., *The Plays and Poems of William Shakespeare* (London: C. Baldwin, 1821), 17:89–90.

3

1. Robert Louis Stevenson, *A Christmas Sermon* (New York: Charles Scribner's Sons, 1900), 8.
2. W. Somerset Maugham, *Of Human Bondage* (New York: Modern Library, 1915), 15.
3. "How the Good Wife Taught Her Daughter," in *The Babee's Book: Medieval Manners for the Young: Done Into Modern English from Dr. Furnivals' Texts by Edith Rickert* (London: Chatto and Windus, 1908), 40.

6

1. A cogger is one who lives by cheating; a swindler.
2. A ding-thrift is a spendthrift: one who dings, or drives away, thrift.

PART 2

9

1. For Shakespeare's plays in their estimated historical order, see W. J. Craig, ed., *Shakespeare: Complete Works* (London: Oxford University Press, 1905), 1165–66. William Shakespeare was born about 1564, completed his first plays in the late 1580s, and died on April 23, 1616.

PART 3

20

1. John Greenleaf Whittier, "Introduction," in *Letters of Lydia Marie Child* (Boston: Houghton, Mifflin and Company, 1883), vii.
2. Lydia Marie Child, *The American Frugal Housewife: Dedicated to Those Who Are Not Ashamed of Economy*, 27th ed. (New York: Samuel S. & William Wood, 1841; published as *The Frugal Housewife* in 1829), 6.

23

1. See *Under Golden Dome: The History of Buffalo Savings Bank* (Buffalo: Buffalo Savings Bank, 1982), 177.

27

1. "Sir Edward Brabrook: Thrift and Social Insurance," *The Times*, March 21, 1930. See also "Discussion on Sir Edward Brabrook's Paper," *Journal of the Royal Statistical Society* 71, no. 4 (December 1908): 612–18; Edward Brabrook, "The Economic and Social Value of Thrift," in M. E. Sadler, ed., *Moral Instruction in the Schools* (London: Longmans, Green, and Co., 1908), 1:343–45; *Catalogue of the Library of the Royal Statistical Society* (London: Royal Statistical Society, 1908), 3, 34; and "In Memorium: Sir Edward Brabrook," *Folklore* 40, no. 2 (1929): 189–90.

29

1. B. O. Flowers, *Progressive Men, Women, and Movements of the Past Twenty-Five Years* (Boston: New Arena, 1914), 294.

31

1. George C. T. Bartley, *Domestic Economy: Thrift in Every-Day Life. Taught in Dialogues Suitable for Children of All Ages* (London: C. Kegan & Paul, 1878), 194–95.

33

1. See "Editorial," *Education* 36, no. 3 (November 1915): 192–93, 197; and "Editorial," *Education* 36, no. 4 (December 1915): 263. See also "Thrift" in Ellsworth D. Foster, ed., *The World Book* (Chicago: World Book, 1918), 7:5802. Numerous state and local organizations as well, such as state associations of savings banks, also organized essay contests for school children on thrift.

PART 4

39

1. David T. Beito, "To Advance the 'Practice of Thrift and Economcy': Fraternal Societies and Social Capital, 189-1920," *Journal of Interdisciplinary History* 29, no. 4 (Spring 1999): 585. See also Beito, *From Mutual Aid to the Welfare State: Fraternal Societies and Social Services, 1890–1967* (Chapel Hill: University of North Carolina Press, 2000).
2. Cited in Beito, "To Advance," 586. See also B. H. Meyer, "Fraternal Insurance in the United States," in Robert La Follette, ed., *The Making of America* (Chicago: Making of America Company, 1906), 10:232–48.
3. See Beito, "To Advance," 602–6; *The Reformer*, January 27, 1900;

William Taylor Thom, "The True Reformers," U.S. Department of Labor *Bulletin*, no. 4 (Washington, DC: Government Printing Office, 1902); *From Slavery to Bankers*, a twenty-one-page pamphlet published in 1907 by the "Grand Fountain" (the headquarters, the main lodge) of the United Order of True Reformers; W. P. Burrell and D. E. Johnson Sr., *Twenty-Five Years History of the Grand Fountain of the United Order of True Reformers* (Richmond: United Order of True Reformers, 1909); and John N. Ingham and Lynne B. Feldman, *African-American Business Leaders: A Biographical Dictionary* (Westport, CT: Greenwood Press, 1974), 112–20. See also David M. Fahey, *The Black Lodge in White America: "True Reformer" Browne and His Economic Strategy* (Lanham, MD: University Press of America, 1994). The Du Bois quote is cited in Ingham and Feldman, *African-American Business Leaders*, 119; however, William Taylor Thom in the above-cited Labor Department *Bulletin* from 1900 uses this same language to describe and praise the True Reformers. The circumstances surrounding the founding of the True Reformers Savings Bank are recounted in some detail in Burrell and Johnson, *Twenty-Five Years History*; and also in Booker T. Washington, *The Story of the Negro: The Rise of the Race from Slavery* (New York: Doubleday, Page and Company, 1909), 2:215–16.

40

1. Kate Brownlee Sherwood, "Characteristics of Richard Mott," *Magazine of Western History* 10, no. 1 (May 1889): 39.
2. David D. Field, *The Genealogy of the Brainerd Family* (New York: John F. Trow, 1857), 122; J. Disturnell, *The Great Lakes* (New York: Charles Scribner, 1863), 189; John Jay Knox, *History of Banking in the United States* (New York: Bradford Rhodes & Company, 1900), 668–69; Daniel J. Ryan, *History of Ohio* (New York: Century History Company, 1912), 4:501.

42

1. H. Morton Bodfish, *History of Building and Loan in the United States* (Chicago: United States Building and Loan League, 1931), 237.
2. *Thirteenth Annual Report of the Bureau of Statistics of Labor and Industries of New Jersey, 1890*, 85–86. Lawrence V. Conway, *Savings and Loan Principles* (Chicago: American Savings and Loan Institute Press, 1960), 33.
3. Conway, *Savings and Loan Principles*, 45–46, 85, 367.

44

1. R. R. Bowker, "Introduction," in Theodore Wesley Koch, *A Book of Carnegie Libraries* (White Plains, NY: H. W. Wilson Company, 1917), vii–viii. W. E. Henry, ed., *Municipal and Institutional Libraries of Indiana* (St. Louis: Louisiana Purchase Exposition Commission of Indiana, 1904), 1.

Part 5

46

1. Trevor Craddock and Maurice Cavanough, *125 Years: The Story of the State Savings Bank of Victoria, 1842–1966* (Melbourne: Savings Bank of Victoria, January 1, 1967), 41.

2. *50 Years: International Savings Bank Institute* (Geneva: International Savings Bank Institute, 1974), 22. See also *Third International Thrift Conference* (Milan: International Thrift Institute, 1937).
3. "Minutes of the Seventeenth Meeting of the Permanent Committee, 24th September 1948," in *International Thrift Institute: Report on the Activities and Financial Statement for the Period October 1st, 1948, to December 31st, 1949*, p. 3, document courtesy of the World Savings Bank Institute, Brussels; and *50 Years: International Savings Bank Institute*, 17, 24.

47

1. See Benjamin Vincent, *Haydn's Dictionary of Dates* (New York: G. P. Putnam's Sons, 1906), 911; "Sir Hugh Owen," in Sidney Lee, ed., *Dictionary of National Biography* (New York: Macmillan and Co., 1895), 42:417–18; and "Thrift," *The Times*, January 28, 1880.
2. William Starr Myers, ed., *Prominent Families of New Jersey* (Baltimore: Geneological Publishing Co., 2000; first published 1945), 1:64. See also, "Thrift Committee Will Push Program," *New York Times*, January 12, 1942; and Stout's obituary in the *New York Times*, March 14, 1965.
3. The 1926 letters to Wiley and notes for her 1927 thrift talk are from the "Housekeepers' Alliance 1922–23" folder in the Anna Kelton Wiley Papers, located in the Library of Congress, available online as a part of the Library of Congress' collection, "Prosperity and Thrift: The Coolidge Era and the Consumer Economy, 1921–1929." See also "Dr. Harvey W. Wiley Weds," *New York Times*, February 28, 1911.
4. "Resume of the National Thrift Committee," memorandum, n.d. (probably 1965 or 1966), p. 1, courtesy of The Lilly Library, Indiana University, Bloomington, Indiana.
5. "Resume of the National Thrift Committee."

48

1. For an overview of results of the movement as of 1926, see "Ten Years of Thrift: Record of 'The Savings Movement,'" *The Times*, October 21, 1926.

Part 6

1. All scripture is from the King James Version. Unless otherwise noted, sayings attributed to ancient persons are taken from *Proverbs; or, The Manual of Wisdom*, 2nd ed. (London: Tabart & Co., 1804), 115, and following.

Conclusion

1. J. Hector St. John Crevecoeur, *Letters from an American Farmer* (New York: Fox, Duffield & Company, 1904; first published 1782), 54.
2. Walt Whitman, "Song of the Open Road," in *Leaves of Grass* (Garden City, NY: Doubleday & Company, 1954), 125. The poem was written in 1856.
3. Whitman, "Song of Myself," *Leaves of Grass*, 41. The poem was written in 1855.
4. Everett C. Ladd, *The American Ideology: An Exploration and*

a Survey of the Origins, Meaning, and Role of American Values (Washington, DC: American Enterprise Institute, March 1992), 2, 9.

5. Edward Bok, *The Americanization of Edward Bok* (New York: Charles Scribner's Sons, 1923; first published 1920), 15.

6. *International Comparisons of Charitable Giving* (West Malling, UK: Charities Aid Foundation, 2005).

7. John le Carré, *Tinker, Tailor, Soldier, Spy* (New York: Alfred A. Knopf, 1974), 12.

8. William F. Cody, *Buffalo Bill's Own Story of His Life and Deeds* (New York: John R. Stanton, 1917), 114–15.

9. Tom McHugh, *The Time of the Buffalo* (New York: Alfred A. Knopf, 1972), 283.

10. David A. Dary: *The Buffalo Book: The Full Saga of the American Animal* (Athens, OH: Swallow Press, 1989), 107, 119.

11. Larry McMurtry, *Streets of Laredo* (New York: Simon & Schuster, 1993), 86.

12. Frederick Jackson Turner, Commencement Address at the University of Indiana, 1910, as reprinted in Turner, *The Frontier in American History* (New York: Henry Holt and Company, 1920), 270. Turner's most famous paper, "The Significance of the Frontier in American History," originally presented to the American Historical Association in 1893, is also reprinted in this volume.

13. Nathaniel Hawthorne, "Chiefly About War Matters," *Atlantic Monthly*, July 1862, reprinted in *The Writings of Nathaniel Hawthorne*, vol. 17, *Miscellanies* (Boston: Houghton, Mifflin and Company, 1900), 396. Hawthorne also writes (p. 385) of "a normal lack of neatness in the rural life of Virginia, which puts a squalid face even upon a prosperous state of things."

14. George Fitzhugh, *Cannibals All! or, Slaves Without Masters* (Cambridge: Havard University Press, 1960; first published in 1857), 220.

15. David Blankenhorn, Sorcha Brophy-Warren, Alex Roberts, and Barbara Dafoe Whitehead, *For a New Thrift: An Appeal to Prospective Colleagues* (New York: Institute for American Values, January 2008), 4. My discussion in the next several paragraphs of the current U.S. debt culture and the rise of anti-thrift institutions draws heavily, and in several instances verbatim, on this coauthored publication. More specifically, I want to acknowledge with gratitude that the terms "debt culture" and "anti-thrift institutions," which I think are enormously valuable analytic concepts, came mainly from my coauthor Barbara Dafoe Whitehead.

16. Gerald Goldman and James R. Wells, Jr., *Check Cashers Are Good Bank Customers* (Hackensack, NJ: Financial Service Centers of America, 2002), 1.

17. Carol J. Loomis, "Warren Buffet Gives It Away," *Fortune*, July 10, 2006.

Quote Citations

INTRODUCTION

The fact or condition of . . . "Thrift," *Oxford English Dictionary*, 2nd ed. (Oxford: Clarendon Press, 1989), vol. 17. Hereafter "OED"; citations below are either from volume 17 ("thrift") or volume 19 ("unthrift").

. . . there are few words . . . Richardson Campbell, *Provident and Industrial Institutions: Being Records and Historical Sketches of Various Thrift Associations* . . . (Manchester, UK: Board of Directors, Rechabite Buildings, n.d.), 1.

There are several species . . . "Thrift," *Encyclopedia Britannica*, 11th ed. (New York: Encyclopedia Britannica Company, 1911), 26:890.

Thrift, that sovereign . . . Maria Ossowska, *Bourgeois Morality* (London: Routledge & Kegan Paul, 1986; first published in Polish in 1956), 104.

The very word "thrift" . . . John Lubbock, *The Use of Life* (New York: Macmillan, 1894), 41.

The word has . . . Ellsworth D. Foster, ed., *The World Book* (Chicago: World Book, 1918), 7:5801.

PART ONE

1

And if it be asshe . . . The Rev. Walter W. Skeat, ed., *The Book of Husbandry*, by Master Fitzherbert (London: Trubner & Co., 1882; reprinted from the 1534 edition), 82.

Farmington seems to us . . . Irving Todd, publisher of the *Hastings Conserver*, commenting in that publication in 1863. Cited in David Schreier, "How the 'Village of Farms' Became a City: A Brief History of Farmington Incorporation in 1872," from the Web site of the Farmington Area Historical Society: http://www.geocities.com/fahsmn/farmington.htm

. . . I would select . . . James Fenimore Cooper, *The Pioneers: Or, the Sources of the Susquehanna* (New York: Stringer and Townsend, 1852), 8.

. . . in the rear of . . . Nathaniel Hawthorne, "The Custom-House – Introductory."

The Scarlet Letter: A Romance (New York: Doubleday & McClure Co., 1898; first published 1850), 7.

No grace has . . . Sermon 30, as cited in Richard Chenevix Trench, *A Select Glossary of English Words Used Formerly in Senses Different From Their Present* (New York: Redfield, 1859), 209. Edward Reynolds, who served as bishop of Norwich, was born in 1599 and died in 1676.

O love and summer . . . Walt Whitman, "The Sleepers," 1855, in *Leaves of Grass*, vol. 1 (Garden City, NY: Doubleday, Page and Company, 1902), 208.

An Olde Thrift . . . Richard Churton, *An Olde Thrift Newly Revived. Wherein is declared the manner of Planting, Preserving, and Hus-banding Young Trees. . .*, 1612, as cited in Donald McDonald, *Agricultural Writers:From Sir Walter of Henley to Arthur Young, 1200–1800* (London: Horace Cox, 1908), 202.

On sandy wastes . . . James Knox, *The Triumph of Thrift: The Story of the Savings Bank of Airdrie* (Airdrie, Scotland: Baird & Hamilton, 1927), 17. Howe became the first bishop of Wakefield in 1888.

Phi. What I pray you? . . . King James VI of Scotland, *Daemonologie*, 1597, book 1, chapter 2.

Planting of trees . . . *Proverbs; or, The Manual of Wisdom* (London: Tabart and Co., 1804), 74. Editor's name not given.

. . . the rules of thought are . . . G. K. Chesterton, "The Thrift of Thought," *America* 15, no. 2 (April 22, 1916).

Shall we apologize . . . Albert Shaw, *The Outlook for the Average Man* (New York: Macmillan Company, 1907), 61–62, 127.

There is a use . . . Mary E. Richmond, *Friendly Visiting Among the Poor: A Handbook for Charity Workers* (New York: Macmillan Company, 1903), 110.

This cow had a cough . . . Report from Dr. E. E. Salmon, *Index to the Executive Documents of the House of Representatives for the Second Session of the Forty-Eighth Congress, 1884–1885* (Washington, DC: Government Printing Office, 1885), 451.

. . . a thrifty growth . . . Herman Melville, "The Valley of Martair" in *Omoo: A Narrative of Adventures in the South Seas*. (Boston: Dana Estes and Co., 1892; first published 1847) 232.

. . . whose old roots furnish . . . Henry David Thoreau, *Walden* (Boston: Houghton, Mifflin, and Company, 1897), 2:399–400.

2

But by my thrift . . . Chaucer, *Canterbury Tales*, "The Reeve's Tale" (4049–50). All Chaucer excerpts are as they appear in Larry D. Benson, ed., *The Riverside Chaucer*, 3rd ed. (Boston: Houghton Mifflin Company, 1987).

The entrie unto immortal . . . Miles Coverdale, *Erasmus' Paraphrases*, 1549, no. 5. Cited in OED, "thrift."

Fellow, learn to . . . John Ford, *Love's Sacrifice*, in *Works of John Ford*, (London: James Toovey, 1869), 2:102.

For he does men . . . "A Miracle of St. James," in Frederick James Furnival, ed., *Early English Poems and Lives of Saints* (London: A. Asher & Co., 1862), 59. Date of 1305 from OED, "thrift."

Hir chaffare [merchandise] . . . Chaucer, *Canterbury Tales*, "The Man of Law's Tale" (138).

Hire armes smale . . . Chaucer, *Troilus and Criseyde* (iii, 1247–50).

I have a mind . . . William Shakespeare, *The Merchant of Venice* (i, 1), about 1596. All Shakespeare quotes are from *Shakespeare: Complete Works* (London: Oxford University Press, 1976).

I kan right now . . . Geoffrey Chaucer, *Canterbury Tales*, "The Man of Law's Tale," Introduction (46), 1380s.

I sitte at hoom . . . Chaucer, *Canterbury Tales*, "The Wife of Bath's Tale" (238).

Now good thrifte [luck, fortune] come . . . Thomas Hoccleve, *The Regiment of Princes*, 1411, in *Hoccleve's Works* (London: Kegan Paul, Trench, Trubner & Co., 1925), 15.

Now good thrift [good luck, good fortune] have he . . . Chaucer, *Troilus and Criseyde* (ii, 847), 1380s.

Of al this noble town . . . Chaucer, *Troilus and Criseyde* (ii, 737), 1380s.

She took hire . . . Chaucer, *Troilus and Criseyde* (iii, 211), 1380s.

Slip-thrift . . . A game invented in England during the reign of King Henry VIII.

There are such dicing-houses . . . Hugh Latimer, sermon preached before King Edward VI, April 12, 1549, in *Sermons by Hugh Latimer* (London: J. M. Dent & Co., 1906), 170. Hugh Latimer, the bishop of Worcester, was born about 1470 and died on October 16, 1555. "What a picture of thrift does good old Hugh Latimer give in one of his sermons!" —from "An Old Boy," *Notes for Boys (and their Fathers) on Morals, Mind and Manners* (London: Elliot Stock, 1885), 54.

Also: "He that drinks, or spends his thrift at dice." —from *The Famous History of the Life and Death of Captain Thomas Stukeley* (1605), in Richard Simpson, ed., *The School of Shakespeare* (London: Chatto and Windus, 1878), 1:195.

The Way to Thrift . . . The title of a poem, in which a mother advises her daughter on the ways of wise living, late fourteenth century. See *The Babee's Book: Medieval Manners for the Young: Done Into Modern English from Dr. Furnivals' Texts by Edith Rickert* (London: Chatto and Windus, 1908), 186.

Ye prowd galantts hertless . . . *Songs and Carols*, about 1470, author unknown. Apparently published by Percy Society, no. 56. This poem is also excerpted in Alfred Guy Kingan L'Estrange, "Anglo-Saxon Humour," *History of English Humour* (London: Hurst and Blackett, 1878).

3

Annual income, twenty pounds . . . Charles Dickens, *David Copperfield*, 1850.

Be thriftie . . . George Herbert, "The Church-porch," in *The Temple: Sacred Poems and Private Ejaculations* (London: T. Fisher Unwin, 1893; first published 1633), 6–7.

Behold th' ensamples . . . Edmund Spencer, *The Faerie Queene*, 1596, book 2, canto 12, stanza 9. All Spencer citations unless otherwise noted are from *The Works of Edmund Spencer* (London: Edward Moxon, 1845).

But to thrive . . . Rev. William Lewery Blackley, *Thrift and Independence: A Word for Working Men* (London: Society for Promoting Christian Knowledge, 1885), 15.

By all the world contributed . . . Walt Whitman, "The Prairie States," 1880, in *Leaves of Grass*, vol. 1 (Garden City, NY: Doubleday, Page and Company, 1902), 177.

Cut my coat . . . *Godly Queen Hester*, about 1529. See John Heywood, *Proverbs and Epigrams* (London: Spencer Society, 1867; first published 1562; 2nd ed. published 1566), 16. The phrase is also used in John Lyly, *Euphrates and His England* (1580). See also *Proverbs; or, The Manual of Wisdom* (London: Tabart and Co., 1804), 110.

The Earl had a reputation . . . Views of the fourth Earl of Bedford (1593–1641), "General Introduction," in F. H. W. Sheppard, ed., *Survey of London* (London: Central Books, 1970), 36:1–18. The remarks from the Earl are taken from his commonplace book.

For husbandrie weepeth . . . Thomas Tusser, *Five Hundred Pointes of Good Husbandrie* (London: Trubner & Co., 1878; based on the edition of 1580 collated with those of 1573 and 1577), 160.

God pays debts . . . Robert Browning, "Dramatic Idyls, Second Series," in *The Complete Works of Robert Browning* (New York: Kelmscott Society, 1898), 11.193.

His thrift waxes . . . "How the Good Wife Taught Her Daughter," from a version from about 1430, in *The Babee's Book: Medieval Manners for the Young: Done Into Modern English from Dr. Furnivals' Texts by Edith Rickert* (London: Chatto and Windus, 1908), 40.

If much were mine . . . Christina G. Rossetti, "Christ Our All In All," in *Verses* (London: Society for Promoting Christian Knowledge, 1896), 30.

In this respect . . . Hinton Rowan Helper, *Compendium of The Impending Crisis of the South* (New York: A. B. Burdick, 1860; *Impending Crisis of the South* first published 1857), 43.

Industry is the parent . . . Henry Ward Beecher, *Lectures to Young Men on Various Important Subjects*, 2nd ed. (Salem: John P. Jewett & Co., 1846), 25, 30–31.

It is required that . . . The Puritan divine William Ames, *Conscience with the Power and Cases Thereof*, published 1643, cited in Donald E. Frey, "Individualist Economic Values and Self-Interest: The Problem in the Puritan Ethic," *Journal of Business Ethics* 17 (1998): 1575, 1580.

Let wealth come . . . Robert Herrick, "The Well-wishes at Weddings," in Alfred Pollard, ed., *Works of Robert Herrick* (London: Lawrence & Bullen, 1891), 2:21–23.

The new America of . . . John Dos Passos, writing about Henry Ford in *The Big Money* (New York: Harcourt, Brace and Company, 1936), 56.

The scope of thrift . . . Thomas A. Edison, cited in Franklyn Hobbs, *The Secret of Wealth* (New York: Cosimo Classics, 2005; first published 1923), 19.

She was so thrifty . . . Henry Wadsworth Longfellow, "The Courtship of Miles Standish," in *The Complete Poetical Works of Henry Wadsworth Longfellow* (Boston: Houghton Mifflin Company, 1914), 181.

. . . those principles which . . . *The Two Carpenters; Fruits of Sloth and Thrift Illustrated* (Philadelphia: American Sunday-School Union, 1847), 5–6, 8.

Thrift is the best . . . Eliza Cook, describing "diamond dust" (short wise sayings), in *Eliza Cook's Journal*, no. 13, July 28, 1849, collected in *Eliza Cook's Journal* (London: John Owen Clarke, October 1849), 1:192. Eliza Cook was born in Southwark, England, on December 24, 1818, and died in Wembledon on September 23, 1889. An author and reformer, she wrote, edited, and published *Eliza Cook's Journal*, a weekly, from 1849 to 1854; Samuel Smiles was a frequent contributor. The saying "Thrift is the best means of thriving" seems to have been first used in print in about 1838 by "Two Brothers," Julius Charles Hare and Augustus William Hare. See *Guesses at Truth, By Two Brothers* (London: Taylor and Walton, 1847), 329.

Thrift is the fuel . . . Sir Philip Sidney, *Countess of Pembroke's Arcadia*, about 1580 " . . . provision is the foundation of hospitality, and thrift the fuel of magnificence." Cited in James Wood, *Dictionary of Quotations* (London: Frederick Warne and Co., 1899), 359. Sir Philip Sidney was born in 1554 and died in 1586.

To lose sensibility . . . Wallace Stevens, "Esthetique du Mal," 1945.

4

Among the recollections . . . Henry Snell, *Men, Movements and Myself* (London: J. M. Dent and Sons, 1936), 6.

And I must needs . . . Samuel Pepys, letter to his father, May 16, 1663, in *The Letters of Samuel Pepys and His Family Circle* (Oxford: Clarendon Press, 1955), 3.

The book will be . . . Review of *Pennies and Plans*, in Benjamin R. Andrews, *The Elementary School Journal* 20, no. 7 (March 1920): 558.

The buyer must cling . . . Mary Schenk Woolman, *Clothing: Choice Care Cost* (Philadelphia: J. B. Lippincott Company, 1922; first published 1920), 108.

Children Should Save . . . Ad, Pennsylvania Trust Company, early 1900s, reprinted in William H. Kniffen Jr., *The Savings Bank and Its Practical Work* (1912), 482.

Decent burial was . . . George Eliot, *Adam Bede* (New York: Harper, 1860), 89.

It has been usual . . . John Maynard Keynes, *A Treatise on Money,* vol. 2, 1930, as cited in R. F. Harrod, *The Life of John Maynard Keynes* (New York: Harcourt, Brace and Company, 1951), 406–7. Harrod (p. 406) states that, for Keynes, thrift could be either a virtue or a vice, depending on the circumstances, but also "broadly through history Keynes did not think that thrift had been the major virtue."

Lee, who's also . . . "Andrew Lee '07 Named Truman Scholar," news release, Claremont McKenna College, April 10, 2006.

Lesson 23: THRIFT . . . George C. T. Bartley, *Domestic Economy: Thrift in Every-Day Life. Taught in Dialogues Suitable for Children of All Ages* (London: C. Kegan & Paul Co., 1878), 44, 51–52, 64–65.

Bartley was also the manager of the "National Penny Bank" in Britain and the well-known author of a series of short publications for children called "Provident Knowledge Papers." Each publication cost one penny. Titles included:

> *Insuring one's life: How to set about it by small payments, weekly or otherwise*;
>
> *Penny Banks in every town, village, and manufactory: How to start them*;
>
> *Penny Banks in every elementary school: Why they should exist, and how to start them*;
>
> *A Penny a-week; or, Who earns enough to put by anything? or, Is a shilling, sixpence, threepence, twopence, or one penny a-week worth putting by?*; and *What's the good of saving?*

(These publication titles are presented in an appendix in *Domestic Economy*.)

In 1881, W. L. Blackley wrote of Bartley's "Provident Knowledge Papers" that "no more useful present than a bound set could be made to any young person starting in life, or to the library of any elementary school." See W. L. Blackley, "The Post Office, and Aids to Thrift," *The Contemporary Review* 39 (January–June 1881): 780.

Bartley also wrote *The Poor Law and Its Effects on Thrift: With Suggestions for an Improved Out-Door Relief; or, Thrift as the Out-Door Relief Test.*

Little Bo-Peep has . . . *Thrift—After Mother Goose* (Chicago: Continental and Commercial Trust and Savings Bank, 1920).

The last page of the booklet says: "If you believe in teaching THRIFT to your children, we suggest that you start a savings account for them at this bank."

Money saved . . . T. D. MacGregor, *The Book of Thrift: Why and How to Save and What to Do With Your Savings* (New York: Funk and Wagnalls Company, 1915), 284.

Mrs. Ward mended . . . Louisa May Alcott, "The King of Clubs and the Queen of Hearts," *Hallberger's Illustrated Magazine* 2 (1876): 684.

My fair, no beauty . . . Alice Meynell, "The Lover Urges the Better Thrift," in *Collected Poems of Alice Meynell* (New York: Duey Press, 2007; first published 1913). Meynell was born in 1847 in London and died in 1922.

Of course, it is . . . James M. Spinning, Superintendent of Schools of Rochester, New York, writing in *The Thrift Advocate* 7, no. 8 (June 1934): 1. *The Thrift Advocate* was "published periodically by the Rochester Savings Bank to encourage thrift in the school and home."

Paradise is that old . . . Emily Dickinson, "Paradise is that old mansion," about 1868, in *Poems by Emily Dickinson* (Raleigh, NC: Hayes Barton Press, 2007), 1119.

That there shall be . . . Chapter 21, Laws of Kentucky, 1920, reprinted in W. Espey Albig, *A History of School Savings Banking: In the United States and Its European Beginnings* (Savings Bank Division, American Bankers Association, 1928), 30–31.

There are today . . . John Maynard Keynes, "Saving and Spending," radio address, January 14, 1931. The text of the talk appears in J. Maynard Keynes, "The Problem of Unemployment – II," *The Listener*, January 14, 1931, 46–47.

They who are Sparing . . . Rev. Thomas Secker, *Sermons* (1770) III, v, 104, as cited in OED.

Thrift is the art . . . J. S. Kirtley, "Thrift," in Kirtley and Henry Hopkins, *Half-Hour Talks on Character Building* (New York: A. Haming, 1910), 192.

Thrift means . . . "A Day in Honour of Thrift," letter of October 30, 1933, signed by Kingsley Wood, Postmaster-General; Mottistone, National Savings Committee; and Spencer Portal, Trustee Savings Banks Association.

We must save . . . Sir Charles Sedley, speech to Parliament, March 1690, in "Second Parliament of King William: First Session," *The History and Proceedings of the House of Commons* (1742), 2:373–84. Also in George L. Craik and Charles Macfarlane, *The Pictorial History of England*, vol. 4 (New York: Harper & Brothers, 1848), 20.

Whatever might be . . . Nathaniel Hawthorne, *The Blithedale Romance* (Boston: Ticknor, Reed, and Fields, 1852), 76.

The whole secret . . . Mary Wilcox Brown, *The Development of Thrift* (New York: Macmillan Company, 1899), 5.

5

As for the argument . . . Agnes Lambert, "Thrift Among the Children," *The Nineteenth Century* 19, no. 110 (April 1886): 551.

As I have said . . . Ernest Belfort Bax, "Unscientific Socialism," *To-day*, January–June 1884; as appearing in Bax, *The Religion of Socialism* (Freeport, NY: Books for Libraries Press, 1972; first published 1902), 94–95.

Ay! I have come . . . Oscar Wilde, "The Duchess of Padua," 1883, in *The Complete Works of Oscar Wilde: The Duchess of Padua, An Ideal Husband* (New York: Nottingham Society, 1907), 30.

But the theatre . . . Booth Tarkington, *The Magnificent Ambersons* (Garden City, NY: Doubleday, Page & Co., 1918), 18–19.

Figure out the cost . . . Jeremiah W. Jenks, *Life Questions of School Boys* (New York: Young Men's Christian Associations, 1916), 45, 94–95, 104.

For as a thrifty wench . . . John Donne, "Satyre 2," in *The Satires, Epigrams, and Verse Letters* (Oxford: Oxford University Press, 1967), 9.

    Donne died in London on March 31, 1631; many of his poems were published posthumously. His five "satyres" were likely composed during the years 1593 through 1597.

For instance, it appears . . . President Franklin D. Roosevelt, excerpts from a Press Conference, July 31, 1935. From the website of the American Presidency Project: http://www.presidency.ucsb.edu/ws/index.php?pid=14903&st=58+thriftiest+people&st1=family+trust+method#

He [Sir William Temple] loved fame . . . Thomas B. Macaulay, "Sir John Temple," *Edinburgh Review*, October 1838, appearing in Macaulay, *Critical and Historical Essays* (London: Longmans, Green, and Co., 1866), 3. William Temple was born in 1628 and died in 1699.

Her thrift was . . . Gail Hamilton, "An American Queen," *North American Review* (October 1886), as reprinted in Lydia Hoyt Farmer, *What America Owes to Women* (Buffalo, NY: Charles Wells Moulton, 1893), 260. Zilpah P. Grant was born in 1794 and died in 1874.

Hoarding millions . . . Andrew Carnegie, "Thrift as a Duty," in *The Youth's Companion*, September 1900, also appearing in Carnegie, *The Empire of Business* (New York: Doubleday, 1902), 98.

I mistook her . . . Margaret Cavendish, *Playes*, 1662, part 2, act 5.

It may be said . . . "Philip of Pokanoket," in Washington Irving, *The Sketch Book of Geoffrey Crayon, Gent.* (New York: Maynard, Miller & Co., 1906; first published 1819), 412.

. . . it should be . . . Thomas Nixon Carver, "The Relationship of Thrift to Nation Building," in *Principles of National Economy* (Boston: Ginn and Company, 1921), 203.

Long enough has . . . William J. Bryan, *The First Battle: A Story of the Campaign of 1896* (Chicago: W. B. Conkey Company, 1896), 257.

Mrs. Manson Mingott . . . Edith Wharton, *The Age of Innocence*, 1920, book I, chapter 2.

No man of . . . Arthur D. Ficke, "Youth and Age," in *Mountain Against Mountain* (New York: Doubleday, Doran and Company, 1929), 41. Arthur Davison Ficke was born in 1883 and died in 1945.

The peculiarity of . . . Max Weber, *The Protestant Ethic and the Spirit of Capitalism* (New York: Charles Scribner's Sons, 1958; first published in German in 1904–5), 51.

So devotion is . . . Bishop Joseph Hall, *Meditations and Vows, Divine and Moral* (New York: E. P. Dutton and Co., 1901), 45. Joseph Hall was born in 1574 and died in 1656. Much earlier, the Latin writer of maxims Publius Syrus had a similar idea:

    A coward calls himself cautious, a miser thrifty.
    (*Timidus se vocat cautum, parcum sordidus.*)
    Publilius Syrus, *Maxims*, first century BCE

"So you came to . . . William Faulkner, "Thrift," *Saturday Evening Post*, September 6, 1930.

Some economists may . . . Lord Derby, "National Thrift," *The Times*, March 13, 1880.

Thrift by derivation . . . G. K. Chesterton, *As I Was Saying* (New York: Dodd, Mead, & Company, 1936), 228.

Thrift is the watchword . . . Jacob A. Riis, *How the Other Half Lives* (New York: Charles Scribner's Sons, 1890), 106.

THRIFTY, an old miser . . . A character in Otway's *The Cheats of Scapin*, in *The Modern British Drama*, vol. 5, *Operas and Farces* (London: William Savage, 1811), 8–20.

Two passions . . . William Wordsworth, "The Excursion," in *The Excursion: A Poem* (London: Edward Moxon, 1847; first published 1814), 230–31.

Whatever thrift is . . . "Lord Rosebery on Thrift," *The Times*, December 29, 1908. Archibald Philip Primrose, fifth Earl of Rosebery (1847–1929), was a leader of the Liberal Party in the United Kingdom and served as prime minister in 1894–95.

Why should money . . . Ben Brierly, *Tales and Sketches of Lancashire Life: Marlocks of Merriton. Red Windows Hall* (Manchester, UK: Abel Heywood & Son, 1884), 181.

. . . a wise and . . . Linda Thayer Guilford, in *The Uses of a Life: Memorials of Mrs. Z. P. Grant Banister* (New York: American Tract Society, 1885), 219.

The word thrift . . . California Building-Loan League, *Report of the Annual Convention* (San Francisco: California Building-Loan League, 1922), 67–68, as cited in Heather A. Haveman, Hayagreeva Rao, and Srikanth Paruchuri, "The Winds of Change: The Progressive Movement and the Bureaucratization of Thrift," *American Sociological Review* 72 (February 2007): 127.

    That year the League also adopted a code of ethics pledging to fight against (p. 47) the "waste of time, money, effort, material or natural resources." This formulation is quite similar to a thrift poster from 1929: "Real thrift is the saving and intelligent use of health, time, and property of all kinds, including money."

6

And looks the . . . Henry Wadsworth Longfellow, "The Village Blacksmith," in *Complete Poetical Works of Henry Wadsworth Longfellow*, 14–15.

Be assured that . . . Cited in Henry Stephens Randall, *The Life of Thomas Jefferson* (Philadelphia: J. B. Lippincott, 1871), 476.

Believe me when . . . William E. Gladstone, Rectorial Address, University of Edinburgh, April 1860, cited in John Morley, *Life of William Ewart Gladstone* (London: Macmillan Company, 1903), 634. William Gladstone was born in Liverpool on December 29, 1809, and died in the village of Hawarden (near Chester) on May 19, 1898. He served four times as Britain's prime minister, taking office for the first time in 1868 and leaving it for the last time in 1894.

But in another instance . . . William Blackstone, *Commentaries on the Laws of England*, Book One (Philadelphia: Rees Welsh & Company, 1902; first published 1765), 273. Also, "The Roman law made no distinction between unthrifts and idiots." —Sir H. Cairns, *The Times* (London), January 2, 1862.

But when a man . . . Rev. Joseph Butler, sermon delivered March 31, 1748, in William E. Gladstone, ed., *Butler's Works* (Oxford: Clarendon Press, 1896), 2:391. In the index to this volume (p. 462), Gladstone summarizes Butler's argument with the proposition that "thrift may be charity."

. . . By diligence and . . . Ralph Waldo Emerson, "Prudence," in *Essays First and Second Series, English Traits, Representative Men, Addresses* (New York: Hearst's International Library Co., 1914), 152–53.

. . . carefulness, that . . . "Sir Roger de Coverley," in *The Spectator*, about 1711. "Sir Roger de Coverley" is a fictitious character, a country gentleman, created by Joseph Addison and Richard Steele, writing in *The Spectator*, a daily publication from London in 1711 and 1712 for which they were the principal writers. The phrase allegedly from Sir Roger (and probably penned by Steele)

is used in 1925 by Emma, Lady Wilson, of Kippen House, Dunning, in Scotland, as reported in James Knox, *The Triumph of Thrift: The Story of the Savings Bank of Airdrie* (Airdrie, Scotland: Baird & Hamilton, Ltd., Publishers, 1927), 299.

Also: ". . . the skill of the purse is the cardinal virtue of this life . . . frugality is the support of generosity . . ."—Richard describing "Sir Roger de Coverly," *The Spectator*, no. 107, July 3, 1711, reprinted in Will D. Howe, ed., *Selections from Addison and Steele* (New York: Charles Scribner's Sons, 1921), 176.

Also, "For the true root of generosity is carefulness . . ." — Dinah Maria Mulock Craik, "On Living in Perspective," *Fraser's Magazine* (October 1866): 504. Craik is the author of *John Halifax, Gentleman* (1859).

A credit union . . . Roy F. Bergengren, *Credit Union North America* (New York: Southern Publishers, 1940), 8, 18–20.

Ecology, for example . . . Mark Wegierski, "Beyond left-right," *Enter Stage Right* (Web publication), posted March 8, 2004.

From a purely . . . Horace Plunkett, *Ireland in the New Century* (London: John Murray, 1904), 273. Sir Horace Plunkett (October 24, 1854–March 26, 1932) was an agricultural reformer and a supporter of agricultural cooperation who in 1894 founded the Irish Agricultural Organization Society.

The future orientation . . . Elliot Liebow, *Tally's Corner: A Study of Negro Streetcorner Men* (Boston: Little, Brown and Company, 1967), 65.

Genuine thrift is . . . John M. Templeton Jr., MD, *Thrift and Generosity* (Philadelphia: Templeton Foundation Press, 2004), 12, 75.

Gladstone's love . . . "Gladstone's Thrift and Generosity," *The Times*, June 27, 1936.

Happy Jack shook . . . Thornton W. Burgess, *Happy Jack's Thrift Club* (Boston: Savings Division of the First Federal Reserve District, 1918).

He looked like . . . Herman Melville, *Moby Dick, or, The White Whale* (Boston: L. C. Page & Company, 1892; first published 1851), 52.

How would you . . . Harry C. McKown, *Adventures in Thrift* (Topeka, KS: School Activities Publishing Co., 1946), 301.

It has been . . . Mark Junge, *A View From Center Street: Tom Carrigen's Casper* (Casper, WY: McMurry Foundation, 2003), 251.

I've never borrowed . . . From the third of three lectures to Notre Dame faculty, MBA students, and undergraduates, Spring 1991. Cited in Timothy L. O'Brien, "Fortune's Fools: Why the Rich Go Broke," *New York Times*, September 17, 2006.

Luxury, Extravagance . . . John A. Goodell, "Thrift Movement Tackles Problem of Reckless Spending," *Bankers Magazine* 66 (January 1928): 125–26, as cited in Alfred L. Roe, "Bankers and Thrift in the Age of Affluence," *American Quarterly* 17, no. 4 (Winter 1965): 623.

. . . the man of thrift . . . "Hezekiah Thrift," in *The Spectator*, October 14, 1712. Richard Steele is the author of this issue. *The Spectator* (London: Geo. B. Whittaker, 1827), 7:509.

A man who . . . Cited in H. Oliver Horne, *A History of Savings Banks* (London: Oxford University Press, 1947), 137. David King, who died in 1883, was for many years pastor of Greyfriars United Presbyterian Church, the first dissenting church in Glasgow.

Many men marvell . . . *Harrington's Epigrams*, 1633, cited in Robert Nares, ed., *A Glossary; or, Collection of Words, Phrases, Names, and Allusions to Customs, Proverbs, Etc.* (London: John Russell Smith, 1867), 1:177. Note that the composer of this poem links thrift and thrive.

Maybe we should . . . Vaclav Havel, "Our Moral Footprint," *New York Times*, September 27, 2007. The playwright and political leader Vaclav Havel was the first post-communist president of the Czech Republic.

Necessary frugality . . . Richard Baxter, *Directions about Prodigality and sinful Waste,* in *The Practical Works of The Rev. Richard Baxter* (London: James Duncan, 1830), 6:364–65.

Now, we have . . . John Ruskin, lecture on "The Political Economy of Art," delivered July 10, 1857, cited in Ruskin, *The Political Economy of Art: or, A Joy Forever* (New York: John Wiley & Sons, 1886), 14–15.

Old Uncle Thrift . . . Laura Roundtree Smith, *The Treasure Twins: The Merry Book of Thrift* (Chicago: Albert Whitman & Company, 1923), 89.

On the whole . . . Thomas Carlyle, "The Hero as a Man of Letters," Lecture 5, delivered May 10, 1840. Cited in Thomas Carlyle, *On Heroes, Hero-Worship, and the Heroic in History* (Boston: Houghton Mifflin and Company, 1907), 257.

One of the most . . . William Foote Whyte, *Street Corner Society: The Social Structure of an Italian Slum* (Chicago: University of Chicago Press, 1955; first published 1943), 106.

The penny savings . . . in Robert A. Woods and Albert J. Kennedy, eds., *Handbook of Settlements* (New York: Charities Publication Committee, 1911), 273.

The Persistent Peddler . . . Laura Rountree Smith, *Nan and Ann in Thrift Town* (Chicago: M. A. Donohue & Company, 1925), 77.

Pick up that pin . . . Freeman Hunt, *Worth and Wealth: A Collection of Maxims, Morals and Miscellanies for Merchants and Men of Business* (New York: Stringer & Townsend, 1856), 247–48. According to Louis B. Wright, Hunt's book was the model for a later, quite similar book: T. L. Haines, *Worth and Wealth. Or the Art of Getting, Saving, and Using Money* (Chicago: Haines Brothers, 1883). See Louis B. Wright, "Franklin's Legacy to the Gilded Age," *Virginia Quarterly Review* 22, no. 2 (Spring 1946): 273–74.

Raw Haste . . . Alfred, Lord Tennyson, "Love Thou Thy Land, With Love Far-Bought," 1833, in *The Works of Alfred Lord Tennyson* (London: Macmillan and Co., 1886), 66.

Real thrift is . . . Cited in Turo-Kimmo Lehtonen and Mika Pantzar, "The Ethos of Thrift: The Promotion of Bank Saving in Finland During the 1950s," *Journal of Material Culture* 7, no. 2 (2002): 224. The authors (p. 228) add:

It is important to realize that "thrift" meant—and still means—much more than negative restriction. Rather, it was a name given to a heterogeneous set of practices, of working diligently, of taking care of oneself and others—in addition to being careful with the way one uses money. When promoting saving, the banks felt the need to describe in detail the question of what forms this activity could take.

. . . the science of . . . Laurance S. Rockefeller, "The Case for a Simpler Life-Style," *Reader's Digest*, February 1976, 61–62.

9. A SCOUT IS THRIFTY . . . The Ninth Scout Law, *Boy Scouts of America Handbook* (New York: Boy Scouts of America, 1916), 36.

So that the . . . "Human Responsibility," in Eugene R. Smith, ed., *The Gospel in All Lands* (New York: Mission Society of the Methodist Episcopal Church, November 1900), 514.

38. Some mouth'd like . . . Edmund Spencer, *The Faerie Queene*, 1596, book 2, canto 11, stanza 12.

Spend upward . . . Theordore T. Munger, *On the Threshold* (Boston: Houghton, Mifflin and Company, 1881), 97–98. See also the book review in *The Century Magazine* 23, no. 1 (November 1881): 154.

The spirit of thrift . . . Cited in S. W. Straus, *History of the Thrift Movement in America* (Philadelphia: J. B. Lippincott Company, 1920), 101.

Stay out of . . . George R. Barnes of Prudential Financial, three financial rules for young fathers presented at a "Meeting the Fatherhood Challenge" conference at the Apollo Theater, New York City, February 3, 2007.

Staying married . . . Economics professor Jay Zargorsky, on the main ways to get rich, May 2007, cited in Selena Maranjian, "You Don't Have to be Einstein to Get Rich," *Slate*, posted May 18, 2007.

Summed up: Thrift . . . M. W. Harrison, "Do You Know What Thrift Is?" in Bennett B. Jackson, Norma H. Deming, and Katherine I. Bemis, eds., *Thrift and Success* (New York: Century Club, 1919), 7–8.

Talk economy . . . Cited in Merle Miller, *Lyndon: An Oral Biography* (New York: Putnam, 1980).

. . . that thrift . . . Gen. W. H. Noble, "The Chinese Ailanthrus," *The Gardener's Monthly and Horticulturalist* 19, no. 221 (May 1877): 132.

There is a close . . . "An Old Boy" (Edward Bellasis), *Notes for Boys (and their Fathers) on Morals, Mind and Manners* (London: Elliot Stock, 1885), 53.

There was no man . . . "Lord Rosebery on Thrift," *The Times*, December 29, 1908. Speaking in this instance to the annual meeting of the Edinburgh Savings Bank, Lord Rosebery also said:

> If I wanted to train a child to be thrifty . . . I should teach him to abhor waste. I do not mean waste of money. That cures itself because very soon there is no money to waste, but I mean waste of material, waste of something which is useful, which may not represent any money value to the waster.

Rosebery defined thrift elegantly: "Thrift means care, forsight, tenderness for those dependent on you." And: ". . . I regard that as the greatest blessing resulting out of thrift—independence of character."

They must recognize . . . Herbert A. Smith, U.S. Forest Service, 1924, cited in *Thrift Education*, 24.

Thinges thriftie . . . Thomas Tussser, *Five Hundred Pointes of Good Husbandrie* (London: Trubner & Co., 1878), 234.

Things are in . . . Emerson, "Ode, Inscribed to William H. Channing," 1846, in Emerson, *Poems* (Boston: Houghton Mifflin Company, 1918), 78. See also Samuel Straus, "'Things Are in the Saddle,'" *The Atlantic Monthly*, November 1924, 577–88.

This, then, is . . . Andrew Carnegie, "The Gospel of Wealth," in *The Gospel of Wealth and Other Timely Essays* (New York: Century Club, 1901), 15. Carnegie's famous essay on "The Gospel of Wealth" was first published in two parts, "Wealth" and "The Best Fields of Philanthropy," in *The North American Review* in June and December of 1889, respectively.

From Stephen Girard's obituary in the *Saturday Evening Post* more than a half-century earlier, in 1831:

> . . . this munificent donor considered himself merely as an agent, or steward, who was to account for the manner in which he disposed of his vast wealth; and . . . his anxious wish was to make such a disposition of it as would produce the greatest possible good . . . he has discharged his duty, and fulfilled his destiny like a philanthropist and benefactor, and left behind him those who for generations will revere his name and cherish his memory . . . Mr. Girard looked upon the wealth and prosperity of individuals

as blessings that are given in trust, to be used and disposed for the common good.

Cited in Sigmund Diamond, *The Reputation of American Businessmen* (Cambridge: Harvard University Press, 1955), 10.

In December of 1868, while staying at the St. Nicholas Hotel in New York City, Andrew Carnegie wrote the following to himself in the form of a memorandum:

> Thirty-three and an income of $50,000 per annum! By this time two years I can so arrange all my business as to secure at least $50,000 per annum. Beyond this never earn—make no effort to increase fortune, but spend the surplus each year for benevolent purposes . . . Man must have an idol—the amassing of wealth is one of the worst species of idolatry—no idol more debasing than the worship of money. Whatever I engage in I must push inordinately; therefore should I be careful to choose the life which will be the most elevating in its character.

Cited in Andrew Carnegie, *Autobiography* (Boston: Houghton Mifflin Company, 1920), 157–58.

Thrift . . . is . . . "World Thrift Day," *The Times*, October 26, 1938.

Thrift is a universal . . . M. S. N. Menon, "The Mad World of Capital," *The Tribune* (Chandigarh, India), March 26, 1999.

Thrift is making . . . Dora Morrell Hughes, *Thrift in the Household* (Boston: Lothrop, Lee & Shepard Co., 1918), 11–12.

Thrift is a word . . . Henry S. Rosenthal, *Cyclopedia of Building, Loan and Saving Associations*, 5th ed. (Cincinnati: American Building Association News Publishing Co., 1927), 15.

Thrift means . . . James Platt, "Thrift," in *Life* (New York: G. P. Putnam's Sons, 1889), 177.

The true thrift . . . Ralph Waldo Emerson, *The Conduct of Life* (Boston: Houghton Mifflin Co., 1904), 126.

Thy heart's . . . John Lyly, *Sapho and Phao* (i, 1), 1584, in *The Complete Works of John Lyly*, Vol. 2 (Oxford: Clarendon Press, 1902), 373.

To catch Dame . . . Robert Burns, "Epistle To a Young Friend," May 1786, in James Barke (ed.), *Poems and Songs of Robert Burns* (London: Collins, 1955), 130.

To earn what . . . J. O. Engleman, *Moral Education in School and Home* (Chicago: Benj. H. Sanborn & Co., 1918), 219.

To inspire higher . . . Cited in Woods and Kennedy, *Handbook of Settlements*, 47.

To the New England . . . Henry Adams, *The Education of Henry Adams: An Autobiography* (Boston: Houghton Mifflin Company, 1918; first published 1906), 47.

To promote right . . . Mission statement of the Cheerful Home Settlement, 421 Jersey Street, Quincy, Illinois, founded February 1903, cited in Woods and, *Handbook of Settlements*, 81.

Upheld by truth . . . Robert A. Macfie, "Plain Words to Young Men," in *Brotherhood, Fellowship, and Acting Together* (London: Elliot Stock, 1883), 19.

The virtues are . . . Emerson, *Conduct of Life*, 113.

Warren Buffett's 2001 . . . "$73,200 for Buffett's Town Car," *New York Times*, September 23, 2006.

Waste is worse . . . Thomas A. Edison, 1847, cited in Franklyn Hobbs, *The Secret of Wealth* (Chicago: Franklyn Hobbs and Company, 1923), 19.

We are going . . . President Lyndon Johnson, speech delivered in Washington, D.C., December 4, 1964.

From the website of the American Presidency Project: http://www.presidency.ucsb.edu/ws/index.php?pid=26743

We believe in . . . Thrift creed adopted by Roosevelt High School in Seattle, cited in Carobel Murphey, *Thrift Through Education* (New York, 1929), frontispiece, as cited in Alfred L. Roe, "Bankers and Thrift in the Age of Affluence," *American Quarterly* 17, no. 4 (Winter 1965): 626.

We decided that . . . Helen Atwater, American Home Economics Association, 1924, cited in *Thrift Education*, 11.

We have worked . . . Miss E. A. Shelton, Camp Fire Girls, 1924, cited in *Thrift Education*, 20.

What is Thrift? . . . U.S. Treasury Department, "Material for a Thrift Talk," in *Textbook for Speakers on Thrift Stamps and War-Savings Stamps* (Washington, DC: Government Printing Office, 1918), 26. This excerpt borrows from Bolton Hall's 1916 book, *Thrift*. See p. 148.

Whatcha gonna do . . . Norman Blake, "Chattanooga Sugar Babe," 1998.

When I came . . . Edward Bok, *The Americanization of Edward Bok* (New York: Charles Scribner's Sons, 1923; first published 1920), 434–35.

Where did Donald . . . From the third of three lectures by Warren Buffett to Notre Dame faculty, MBA students, and undergraduates, Spring 1991.

Why walkes . . . Robert Herrick, "Upon Flimsey," in George Saintsbury, ed., *The Poetical Works of Robert Herrick* (London: George Bell & Sons, 1893), 1:208. Robert Herrick was born in 1591 and died in 1674.

. . . wise spending . . . "7 Watchwords of Thrift," *New York Times*, January 14, 1934.

Wisedome is great . . . John Lyly, *Euphes: The Anatomy of Wit; Euphes and His England* (Westminster: A. Constable and Co., 1900; *Euphes and His England* first published 1580), 229–30, 237, 430, 474, 476.

Work, earn . . . "Financial creed" recommended by the National Thrift Committee of the YMCA, in "Lewisohn Defines Thrift," *New York Times*, December 23, 1928.

Your request for . . . Cited in M. Lincoln Shuster, *The World's Great Letters* (New York: Simon and Schuster, 1940), 311–13.

PART TWO

7

For we brought . . . 1 Timothy 6:7–10 (KJV)

He who has . . . Cited in R. H. Tawney, *Religion and the Rise of Capitalism* (Middlesex, UK: Penguin Books, 1938; first published, as lectures, in 1922), 38.

Thrift is care . . . Immanuel Kant, lecture at Konigsberg, April 25, 1775. The great German philosopher Immanuel Kant was born on April 22, 1724, in Konigsberg, where he spent his entire life, and died on February 12, 1804.

. . . truth and commerce . . . Stanislaw Orzechowski, *The Polity of the Kingdom of Poland*, 1564, as cited in Maria Ossowska, *Bourgeois Morality* (London: Routledge & Kegan Paul, 1986; first published in Polish in 1956), 33.

Whoever buys . . . Corpus Juris Canonici (Corpus of Canon Law), compiled about 1150. Sometimes attributed to St. Chrysostom, who died in 407 CE, this passage was incorporated into canon law via the *Decretum* of Gratian. See G. G. Coulton, *The Medieval Scene* (Cambridge: Cambridge University Press, 1961; first published 1930), 141; and Britton J. Harwood, "Chaucer and the

Silence of History: Situating the Canon's Yeoman's Tale," *PMLA* 102, no. 3 (May 1987): 339.

8

Avaunt, you drudge . . . Philip Massinger, *A New Way to Pay Old Debts* (iii, 2), in F. Cunningham, ed., *The Plays of Philip Massinger* (London: Alfred Thomas Crocker, 1868), 403.

Consider the ravens . . . Luke 12:24, 27–31 (KJV)

O my friends . . . Ralph Waldo Emerson, Divinity School Address, Cambridge, Massachusetts, July 15, 1838, in *The Collected Works of Ralph Waldo Emerson* (C.C. Bigelow, 1884), 121.

9

Above all things . . . Letter excerpt published in Washington Irving's, *The Life of Oliver Goldsmith* (New York: John. B. Alden, 1886), 80–81. See also Katharine C. Balderston, ed., *The Collected Letters of Oliver Goldsmith* (Cambridge, UK: Cambridge University Press, 1928), 60–61; and Richard C. Taylor, "Goldsmith's Frst Vicar," *The Review of English Studies* 41, no. 162 (May 1990): 194.

But the age . . . Edmund Burke, *Reflections on the Revolution in France*, 2nd ed. (London: J. Dodsley, 1790), 113.

Domestic slavery . . . George Fitzbugh, *Sociology of the South*, as quoted by John Patrick Diggins, *The Lost Soul of American Politics* (Chicago: University of Chicago Press, 1986), 141.

I have already . . . Jonathan Swift, *A Modest Proposal* (1729), in Robert A. Greenberg and William B. Piper, *The Writings of Jonathan Swift* (New York: W. W. Norton & Company, 1973), 505.

. . . I was not . . . William Dean Howells, *My Literary Passions* (New York: Harper & Brothers, 1895), 42.

"A lost cent" . . . David Bosworth, *From My Father, Singing* (Wainscott, NY: Pushcart Press, 1986), 13. Later (p. 102), the novel's narrator reports these thrift-oriented aphorisms "lock like Puritan stocks around my wrist."

My great-uncle Ben . . . Harry Graham, "The Seven Deadly Virtues: No. 1—THRIFT," *The Graphic Midsummer Number*, July 15, 1911.

This was increased . . . Arthur Train, *Puritan's Progress* (New York: Charles Scribner's Sons, 1931), 334.

With your neat . . . Vachel Lindsay, "The Virginians Are Coming Again," *The American Mercury*, July, 1928; reprinted in Lawrence E. Spivak and Charles Angoff. eds., *The American Mercury Reader* (Philadelphia: Blakiston Company, 1944), 230–31.

Woful profusion . . . Henry Vaughn, "To His Friend," in E. K. Chambers, ed., *The Poems of Henry Vaughn, Silurist* (London: Lawrence & Bullen, 1896), 2:70.

10

Finally, the very . . . "Savings Banks," *Encyclopedia Britannica* (Chicago: Encyclopedia Britannica, 1954), 20:18.

The further through . . . Ogden Nash, "A Penny Saved Is Impossible," 1942. Copyright © 1940 by Ogden Nash. Reprinted by permission of Curtis Brown, Ltd.

Hang consideration . . . Philip Massinger, *The Renegado* (i, 3), in Cunningham, ed., *The Plays of Philip Massinger*, 137.

. . . he laughs . . . Review of *The Songs of Scotland, Ancient and Modern*, in *The Literary Gazette*, no. 468, January 7, 1826, 3.

He said, "I will" . . . Lucy Larcom, "Thriftless," in *Wild Rose of Cape Ann and Other Poems* (Boston: Houghton, Mifflin and Company, 1881), 195–96.

. . . he [Mr. Hunt] told . . . *The Diary of Samuel Pepys* (London: J. M. Dent & Sons, 1906), 2:190.

In his passion . . . Zona Gale, "Period Realism," *Yale Review*, September 1933, as reprinted in William H. Cordell, ed., *Molders of American Thought, 1933–1934* (Garden City, NY: Doubleday, Doran & Company, 1934), 293.

I am a lusty . . . F. W. Fairholt (ed.), " 'The Civic Garland,*"* in *Early English Poetry, Ballads, and Popular Literature of the Middle Ages*, vol. 19 (London: T. Richards, 1846), 48–49.

. . . I am writing . . . *The Complete Poetical Works of Keats*, Cambridge ed. (Boston: Houghton Mifflin Company, 1899), 310–11. See also, below, in section on "Benjamin Franklin," excerpt from John Keats, October 1818.

I found out . . . William Faulkner, *The Wild Palms* (New York: Penguin Books, 1948), 78.

I never was . . . Nathaniel Hawthorne, *English Note-Books*, 1853–58, as cited in Julian Hawthorne, *Nathaniel Hawthorne and His Wife: A Biography* (J. R. Osgood, 1885), 127.

It is stupid . . . Malcolm Cowley, *Exile's Return* (New York: F. W. Norton & Co., 1934), 60.

Let neist day . . . Scottish poem from the eighteenth century, written or collected by Allan Ramsay (1686–1758), as cited in Wallace Notestein, *The Scot in History* (New Haven, CT: Yale University Press, 1947), 181.

Let the world . . . See John Heywood, "Be Merry, Friends," in John Payne Collier, ed., *A Book of Roxburghe Ballads* (London: Longman, Brown, Green, and Longmans, 1847), 138. Heywood, also a famous collector of proverbs, was born in about 1497 and died in about 1580.

. . . money won . . . "Eddie Felson," in the movie *The Color of Money*, 1986

No, I ain't . . . Bob Dylan, "Maggie's Farm," 1965. Copyright © by Warner Bros. Inc. Copyright renewed 1993 by Special Rider Music. All rights reserved. International copyright secured. Reprinted by permission.

Now I shall laugh . . . Sir William D'avenant, *The Wits* (ii, 3), 1636, in *The Dramatic Works of Sir William D'avenant* (Edinburgh: William Paterson, 1872), 2:162.

(Passionately seen) . . . Walt Whitman, "Song of the Banner at Daybreak," 1865 in *Leaves of Grass*, vol. 1 (Garden City, NY: Doubleday, Page and Company, 1902), 53.

Taught to wanton . . . J. A. Symonds, "An Exhortation to Liberality by the Example of the Rose," in Eleanor Vere Boyle ("E.V.B."), ed., *Ros Rosarum: Dew of the Ever-Living Rose* (London: Elliot Stock, 1885), 251. J. A. Symonds was born in 1840.

These thriftless . . . George Gascoigne, *The complaynt of Philomene*, 1575, in Gasciogne, *English Reprints* (Birmingham: 1 Montague Road, 1868), 87.

'Tis even a . . . Thomas Middleton, *Women Beware Women*, about 1622 (i, 3), in *The Complete Works of Thomas Middleton*, vol. 6 (Boston: Houghton Mifflin Company, 1885), 254. See also Christopher Ricks, "Word-Play in *Women Beware Women*," *The Review of English Studies*, New Series, 12, no. 47 (August 1961): 245.

The utilitarian habits . . . Josiah Gilbert Holland ("Timothy Titcomb"), *Lessons in Life: Series of Familiar Essays* (New York: Charles Scribner, 1864; first published 1861), 323–24.

We owe something . . . Jennie Jerome Churchill, about 1915, cited in Ralph G. Martin, *Jennie: The Life of Lady Randolph Churchill* (Englewood Cliffs, NJ: Prentice-Hall, 1971), 375. Jennie Jerome Churchill, an American beauty and socialite whose first marriage was to Lord Randolph Churchill and who was the mother of Winston Churchill, was born in Brooklyn, New York, on January 9, 1854, and died in London on June 9, 1921.

WILL SUMMER . . . Thomas Nashe, *Summers Last Will and Testament,* in *The Unfortunate Traveller and Other Works* (New York: Penguin Classics, 1972) 154–57.

11

But things are . . . Clifford F. Thies, "The Paradox of Thrift: RIP," *Cato Journal* 16, no. 1 (Spring/Summer 1996): 119. In this book, the excerpts from Marx (1844) and Carver (1920) also address issues connected to what John Maynard Keynes and others later called the paradox of thrift.

By attempting . . . Campbell R. McConnell, *Elementary Economics* (New York: McGraw-Hill, 1960), 261–62.

Dr. [Alvan L.] Barach . . . "Thrift Habit Held Retarding Recovery," *New York Times*, January 29, 1934.

Excessive Saving . . . Uriel H. Crocker, 1884, *The Cause of Hard Times* (Boston: Little, Brown, and Company, 1896), 97. See also Crocker, "Saving versus Spending," *Atlantic Monthly*, December 1878.

I was brought up . . . Joan Striefling, "Thoughts on Thrift," *New York Times*, May 29, 1980.

The identification of . . . A. F. Mummery and J. A. Hobson, *The Physiology of Industry: Being an Exposure of Certain Fallacies in Existing Theorie of Economics* (London: John Murray, 1889), 99, as cited in John M. Robertson, *The Fallacy of Saving: A Study in Economics* (London: Swan Sonnenschein & Co., 1892), 112.

It is a paradox . . . Paul A. Samuelson, *Economics*, 4th ed. (New York: McGraw-Hill, 1958), 237.

Keynes's successors . . . Robert H. Frank, "Why Do Americans Save So Little and What Might Be Done to Increase Savings?" forthcoming.

. . . the most serious . . . Lawrence H. Summers, "The United States and the Global Adjustment Process," speech at the Third Annual Stavros S. Niarchos Lecture, Institute for International Economics, Washington, DC, March 23, 2004.

. . . prodigality . . . Bernard Mandeville, *The Fable of the Bees; or Private Vices, Public Virtues* (New York: Capricorn Books, 1962; first published 1714), 31–32, 74–76, 121.

Prodigality is a vice . . . Nicholas Barbon, *A Discourse of Trade*, 1690 as cited in Leonard Games, *The Economics and Ideology of Free Trade* (Northampton, MA: Edward Elgar Publishing, 2003), 20.

So that the . . . John M. Robertson, *The Fallacy of Saving: A Study in Economics* (London: Swan Sonnenschein & Co., 1892), 83.

There is a widespread . . . T. N. Carver, "The Relation of Thrift to Nation Building," in "The New American Thrift," *The Annals of the American Academy of Political and Social Science* 87 (Philadelphia: American Academy of Political and Social Science, 1920), 5.

12

Another panacea for . . . F. M. Sprague, *Socialism: From Genesis to Revelation* (Boston: Lee and Shepard Publishers, 1983), 230, 235.

But this lady . . . Jane Addams, "The Subtle Problems of Charity," *The Atlantic Monthly* 83, no. 496 (February 1899): 167, 170. Addams also criticizes thrift in Addams, "Exaggerated Nationalism and International Comity," *Survey Graphic*, April 1934, as reprinted in William H. Cordell, ed., *Molders of American Thought, 1933–*

1934 (Garden City, NY: Doubleday, Doran & Company, 1934), 46–47.

The doctrine of . . . The U.S. socialist leader and presidential candidate Norman Thomas, as cited in Arthur Richmond (ed.), *Modern Quotations for Ready Reference* (New York: Dover Publications, 1947), 228. Norman Thomas was born on November 20, 1884, in Marion, Ohio, and died on December 19, 1968.

Each class would . . . Oscar Wilde, *The Picture of Dorian Gray*, in *The Writings of Oscar Wilde* (New York: Wm. H. Wise & Company, 1931), 3:30–31.

I know the miners . . . M. D. Eder, "On Thrift," *The New Age* 6, no. 8 (December 23, 1909): 177.

Intemperance, unthrift . . . John A. Hobson, "Moral Aspects of Poverty," in *Problems of Poverty: An Inquiry Into the Industrial Condition of the Poor* (Whitefish, MT: Kessinger Publishing, 2004; first published 1891), 111–13.

Most esteemed . . . Cited in *Nadezhda K. Krupskaya, Memories of Lenin* (New York: International Publishers, 1930), 2:111.

One school . . . Karl Marx, *Economic and Philosophical Manuscripts*, in *Early Writings* (London : Penguin Books, 1992), 361–62.

The palliatives over . . . William Morris, "Art and Socialism," lecture delivered January 23, 1884, http://www.marxists.org/archive/morris/works/1884/as/as.htm

Political economy . . . Marx, *Economic and Philosophical Manuscripts*, in *Early Writings*, 360–61.

. . . a poor person . . . George Bernard Shaw, *The Intelligent Woman's Guide to Socialism and Capitalism* (New York: Brentano's Publishers, 1928), 128–29, 493. Here is Shaw discussing what he views as the class biases in thrift as a cultural value in his 1884 novel *The Unsocial Socialist*:

> In a year or two his liberal payments enabled the mason to save sufficient to start as an employer, in which capacity he soon began to grow rich, as he knew by experience exactly how much his workmen could be forced to do, and how little they could be forced to take. Shortly after this change in his circumstances he became an advocate of thrift, temperance, and steady industry, and quitted the International Association, of which he had been an enthusiastic supporter when dependent on his own skill and taste as a working mason.

And here he is again in 1907, referring to a character in Shakespeare's *As You Like It*: "That servile apostle of working-class Thrift and Teetotalism . . ."

See Bernard Shaw, "Toujours Shakespeare," in *Dramatic Opinions and Essays with an Apology* (New York: Brentano's Publishers, 1907), 2:121. George Bernard Shaw, *An Unsocial Socialist*, (New York: Brentano's Publishers, 1917), 195.

Sometimes the poor . . . Oscar Wilde, *The Soul of Man Under Socialism*, in *The Writings of Oscar Wilde*, 5:7.

. . . thrift is an . . . William H. Dawson, *German Socialism and Ferdinand Lassalle* (New York: S. Sonnenschein & Co., 1899), 75. Karl Johann Rodbertus, along with Karl Marx, Frederick Engels, and Ferdinand Lassalle, was a founder of modern German socialism. He was born on August 12, 1805, and died in 1875.

Thrift is very well . . . Algernon Sidney Crapsey, *The Rise of the Working-Class* (New York: Century Co., 1914), 244, 249.

Thrift was invented . . . Cited in William Edward Hartpole Lecky, *Democracy and Liberty* (Indianapolis, IN: Liberty Fund, 1981; first published 1896), 2:326.

13

. . . greed, for . . . "Gordon Gekko," in the movie *Wall Street*, 1987.

. . . Hasbro is . . . Jill Lepore, "The Meaning of Life," *The New Yorker*, May 21, 2007.

How can the . . . William H. Whyte Jr., *The Organization Man* (Garden City, NY: Doubleday Anchor Books, n.d.; first published 1956), 19–20.

Commenting on Whyte's analysis of mid-twentieth-century America, the sociologist C. Wright Mills said of Whyte: "He understands that the work-and-thrift ethic of success has grievously declined—except in the rhetoric of top executives; that the entrepreneurial scramble to success has been largely replaced by the organizational crawl." Mills's comment is cited in Michael T. Kaufman, "William H. Whyte, 81, Author of 'The Organization Man,'" *New York Times*, January 13, 1999.

I reckon few . . . James Collier, ed., *Letters of John Cockburn of Ormistoun to His Gardener, 1727–1744* (Edinburgh: Scottish Historical Society, 1904), 50.

I suppose you . . . Collier, *Letters*, 79–80. Letter of October 17, 1742.

In fact, the . . . Joseph C. Sindelar, *Father Thrift And His Animal Friends* (Chicago: Bekeley-Cardy, 1918), 13–14.

In recent weeks . . . "Wall St. Bonuses: So Much Money, Too Few Ferraris," *New York Times*, December 25, 2006.

It was not . . . Theodore Dreiser, *The Financier* (New York: Penguin, 1995; first published 1912), 21.

Yet above al . . . Andrew Borde, *The Fyrst Boke of the Introduction of Knowledge* (London: N. Trubner & Co., 1870; first published 1542), 117.

Part Three

14

As I have mentioned . . . Daniel Defoe, *Roxana, or, The Fortunate Mistress*, 1724, in *The Novels and Miscellaneous Works of Daniel Defoe: Roxana and Mrs. Christian Davies* (London: George Bell and Son, 1881), 146–47.

[Benjamin Franklin's] great . . . Vernon Louis Parrington, *Main Currents of American Thought* (New York: Harcourt, Brace and Company, 1927), 1:166. See, below, section on Benjamin Franklin.

But he saved . . . "Robinson Crusoe," *The Golden Book of Favorite Songs: A Treasury of the Best Songs of Our People* (Chicago: Hall and McCreary Company, 1915), 106.

But I was gotten . . . Daniel Defoe, *Robinson Crusoe* (New York: Charles Scribner's Sons, 1920, first published 1719), 73, 102–3, 201–2.

. . . Daniel Defoe . . . Richardson Campbell, *Rechabite History: A Record of the Origin, Rise, and Progress of the Independent Order of Rechabites* (Manchester, UK: Independent Order of Rechabites, 1911).

Defoe was . . . James Sutherland, *Defoe* (London: Methuen & Co., 1950; first edition published 1937), 150.

European thrift . . . S. W. Straus, "Promotion and Practice of Thrift in Foreign Countries," in "The New American Thrift," *The Annals of the American Academy of Political and Social Science* 87, 190.

Expensive living . . . Daniel Defoe, *The Complete English Tradesman*, 1726 in John S. Keltie, ed., *The Works of Daniel Defoe* (Edinburgh: William P. Nimmo, 1870), 557.

It is but a . . . Daniel Defoe, *An Essay Upon Projects* (UK: Dodo Press, undated; first published as *Essay on Projects*, 1697), 59–60, 63–65.

Lesson 22: THRIFT . . . George C. T. Bartley, *Domestic Economy: Thrift in Every-Day Life. Taught in Dialogues Suitable for Children of All Ages* (London: C. Kegan & Paul Co., 1878), 63–64.

Modern Robinson . . . Chapter title in Harry C. McKown, *Adventures in Thrift* (Topeka, KS: School Activities Publishing Co., 1946), 215.

One of the narrow . . . Cited in William Dana Orcutt, *The Miracle of Mutual Savings* (New York: Bowery Savings Bank, 1934), 22.

15

1. Be frugal . . . John Wesley, rules for the "stewards" (or adminstrators) of the Methodist movement, cited in "A Plain Account on the People Called Methodists," in James H. Potts, ed., *Living Thoughts of John Wesley* (New York: Eaton & Mains, 1891), 23.

For I look upon . . . John Wesley, in Potts, ed., *Living Thoughts of John Wesley*, 28.

Gain all you . . . John Wesley, *The Use of Money*, in Bishop Herbert Welch, ed., *Selections from the Writings of Rev. John Wesley, M.A.* (Nashville, TN: Abingdon, 1942), 411, 414, 417–18.

. . . I do not see . . . John Wesley, August 4, 1786, in Welch, *Selections from the Writings*, 208.

I must double . . . John Adams, diary, May 24, 1773, in L. H. Butterfield, ed., *Diary and Autobiography of John Adams* (Cambridge: Harvard University Press, 1961), 82.

Never let your . . . John Wesley, letter to a Methodist, February 7, 1776, in Welch, *Selections from the Writings*, 381.

Will you tell me . . . John Adams, letter to Thomas Jefferson, December 1819, cited in Patricia O'Toole, *Money and Morals in America: A History* (New York: Clarkson Potter/Publishers, 1998), 63.

A year or . . . John Wesley, in Potts, *Living Thoughts of John Wesley*, 27. See also Rev. Joseph B. Wakeley, *Anecdotes of the Wesleys* (New York: Carlton & Lanahan, 1870), 252.

16

Above all, he . . . Joseph Dennie, *The Port Folio*, cited in Esmond Wright, "Introduction," in *Benjamin Franklin: A Profile* (New York: Hill and Wang, 1970), ix.

Also who soo . . . *The Treatyse of Fysshinge wyth an Angle* (London: William Pickering, 1827; reprinted from *The Book of St. Albans of 1496*), 5–6. Interestingly, regarding the issue of thrift, we also are advised by this author (p. 89):

> Also ye shall not use this forsayd crafty dysporte for no covetysenes [covetousness] to the encreasynge & sparynge [sparing, saving] of your money oonly, but pryncypally for your solace & to cause the helthe of your body, and specyally of your soule.

See also Thomas Satchell, ed., *An Older Form of the Treatyse of Fysshinge wyth an Angle* (London: W. Satchell & Co., 1883). Washington Irving mentions this "treatyse" affectionately in his charming essay, "The Angler," in Irving, *The Sketch Book* (New York: Macmillan Company, 1924; first published 1819), 343.

. . . always taking . . . Benjamin Franklin, *The Way to Wealth*, in J. A. Leo Lemay, ed., *Benjamin Franklin: Writings* (New York: Library of America, 1987). Unless otherwise noted, all excerpts from Franklin's writings cited here are from this text.

And I hope it . . . Letter to George Whatley, May 23, 1785, 1106.

The Art of . . . Benjamin Franklin, *Poor Richard's Almanac*, 1749.

As the Stamp . . . Franklin, letter to his wife, April 6, 1766, 818.

At this time . . . Benjamin Franklin, "The Art of Making Money Plenty in Every Man's Pocket" in *The Posthumous and Other Writings of Benjamin Franklin* (H. Colburn, 1819), 108–9.

Avarice and . . . Franklin, *Poor Richard's Almanac*, 1734.

Bankers who . . . "National Thrift Week," *California Bankers Association Bulletin* (December 1926), 570, as cited in Alfred L. Roe, "Bankers and Thrift in the Age of Affluence," *American Quarterly* 17, no. 4 (Winter 1965): 621.

Be always . . . Franklin, *Poor Richard's Almanac*, 1741.

Be industrious . . . Franklin, letter to John Alleyne, August 9, 1768, 837.

Ben Franklin is . . . Elbert Hubbard, *Let Thrift Be Your Ruling Habit* (East Aurora, NY: Roycrofters, 1917), 12.

Beware of . . . Franklin, *Poor Richard's Almanac*, 1745.

Buy what thou . . . Franklin, *The Way to Wealth*.

By a credible . . . Louis B. Wright, "Franklin's Legacy to the Gilded Age," *Virginia Quarterly Review* 22, no. 2 (Spring 1946): 279.

Content and Riches . . . Franklin, *Poor Richard's Almanac*, 1743.

The Credit Union . . . Cited in Roy F. Bergengren, *Crusade: The Fight for Economic Democracy* (New York: Exposition Press, 1952), 109.

Deny Self . . . Franklin, *Poor Richard's Almanac*, 1735.

Did I gain . . . George Chapman, Ben Johnson, and John Marston, *Eastward Hoe* (i, 1), 1605, in Robert Dodsley, ed., *A Select Collection of Old Plays* (London: J. Nichols, 1780), 4:205.

Diligence is the . . . Franklin, *Poor Richard's Almanac*, 1736

The diligent Spinner . . . Franklin, *The Way to Wealth*, 1758.

Dost thou love . . . Franklin, *Poor Richard's Almanac*, 1746.

Early to bed . . . Franklin, *Poor Richard's Almanac*, 1735.

Employ thy time . . . Franklin, *Poor Richard's Almanac*, 1740.

Every little . . . Franklin, *Poor Richard's Almanac*, 1737.

A fat Kitchen . . . Franklin, *The Way to Wealth*.

Fifteen years ago . . . "Benjamin Franklin—Early Advocate of Thrift," in *Home Life* (Niles, MI: Niles Federal Savings and Loan Association, January 1946), 4.

Fond pride of . . . Franklin, *The Way to Wealth*.

For Age and . . . Franklin, *Poor Richard's Almanac*, 1755.

For my own part . . . Franklin, letter to his daughter-in-law, Mrs. Sarah Bache, January 26, 1784, 1088.

Fly pleasures . . . Franklin, *Poor Richard's Almanac*, 1738.

Franklin represented . . . Charles Angoff, *A Literary History of the American People* (York: Tudor Publishing Company, 1935), 2:296.

5. FRUGALITY. . . . Franklin, *Autobiography*, 1784, 1385.

The frugality of . . . Herman Melville, *Israel Potter: His 50 Years of Exile* (Boston: Northwestern University Press, 1855), 81–82.

God helps . . . Franklin, *Poor Richard's Almanac*, 1758.

Great frugality . . . Franklin, letter to Joseph Priestly, July 7, 1775, 905–6.

Have you somewhat . . . Franklin, *Poor Richard's Almanac*, 1742.

. . . he that . . . Franklin, *The Way to Wealth*.

He that idly . . . Franklin, *Poor Richard's Almanac*, 1737.

He that riseth . . . Franklin, *Poor Richard's Almanac*, 1742.

He was the . . . Wayne Whipple, *The Story of Young Benjamin Franklin* (Philadelphia: Henry Altemus Company, 1916), 254.

. . . here was Franklin . . . Thomas Mellon, *Thomas Mellon and His Times* (Pittsburgh: University of Pittsburgh Press, 1994; first published 1885), 33.

His maxims were . . . Mark Twain, "The Late Benjamin Franklin," 1870, reprinted in Charles Neider, ed., *The Comic Mark Twain*

Reader (Garden City, NY: Doubleday & Company, 1977), 388–90.

His mighty . . . William Carlos Williams, *In the American Grain*, 1925, as cited in Peter Baida, *Poor Richard's Legacy* (New York: William Morrow and Company, 1990), 42.

Hope of gain . . . Franklin, *Poor Richard's Almanac*, 1734.

I began now . . . Franklin, *Autobiography*, 1784, 1368–69.

I can remember . . . D. H. Lawrence, "Benjamin Franklin," in *Studies in Classic American Literature* (New York: Viking Press, 1964; originally published 1923), 14. Lawrence (p. 21) sees the United States "on her muck-heaps of gold, strangled in her own barbed wire of shalt-not ideals and shalt-not moralisms"; he also (p. 13) calls Franklin "the economic father of the United States."

I send you . . . Franklin, letter to Benjamin Webb, April 22, 1784, in Albert Henry Smyth, ed., *The Writings of Benjamin Franklin* (New York: Macmillan Company, 1906), 9:197.

I was charmed . . . Franklin, letter to his daughter-in-law, Mrs. Sarah Bache, June 3, 1779, 1009–10.

. . . I live here . . . Benjamin Franklin, letter to his wife, June 22, 1767, in John Bigelow, ed., *Life of Benjamin Franklin* (J. B. Lippincott & Co., 1875), 529.

Industry need . . . Franklin, *Poor Richard's Almanac*, 1739.

. . . it is prodigious . . . Franklin, letter to Thomas Brand Hollis, October 5, 1783, in *The Writings of Benjamin Franklin* (New York: Macmillan & Co., Ltd., 1906), 104.

Keep thy . . . Franklin, *The Way to Wealth*.

The keynote of . . . Mary R. Parkman, *Conquests of Invention* (New York: Century Co., 1923), 159.

Live with . . . Robert Herrick, "Expences Exhaust," in Pollard, *Works of Robert Herrick*, 1:13.

Lost Time is . . . Franklin, *Poor Richard's Almanac*, 1758

Many have been . . . Franklin, *The Way to Wealth*.

New England has . . . Theodore T. Munger, *On the Threshold* (Boston: Houghton, Mifflin and Company, 1881), 78–79.

The noblest question . . . Franklin, *Poor Richard's Almanac*, 1737.

Now I have . . . Franklin, *Poor Richard's Almanac*, 1736.

One of the . . . Max Weber, *The Protestant Ethic and the Spirit of Capitalism* (New York: Charles Scribner's Sons, 1958; first published in German in 1904–5), 180.

The Parliament remains . . . Franklin, letter to Samuel Cooper, April 27, 1769, in *Writings of Benjamin Franklin*, 203.

A penny sav'd . . . Franklin, *Poor Richard's Almanac*, 1737.

. . . a philosophical . . . John Keats, letter to George and Georgiana Keats, October 25, 1818. Letter available at John-Keats.com.

Poor Richard appeals . . . Editorial, *New York Times*, January 21, 1938, cited in Dixon Wecter, *The Hero in America* (Ann Arbor: University of Michigan Press, 1963; first published 1941), 54.

Pride breakfasted . . . Franklin, *The Way to Wealth*.

Pride is . . . Franklin, *The Way to Wealth*.

Remember that TIME . . . Franklin, *Advice to a Young Tradesman*, 1748, 320–21.

The said sum . . . Franklin's will, June 23, 1789, in *Benjamin Franklin* (Philadelphia: McCarthy & Davis, 1834), 1:194–95.

The second Vice . . . Franklin, *Poor Richard's Almanac*, 1748.

Sloth, like Rust . . . Franklin, *Poor Richard's Almanac*, 1745.

. . . the subject of . . . Eustace Budgell, *The Spectator*, January 24, 1712, in G. Gregory Smith, ed., *The Spectator* (London: J. M. Dent & Co., 1898), 4:120–21, 123–24.

For another issue of this publication from which Franklin probably did, or at least certainly could have, borrowed consid-erable thrift wisdom, see *The Spectator*, no. 509, from October 14, 1712, subtitled "Discharging the part of a good economist" and signed by one "Hezekiah Thrift" (and actually written by Richard Steele).

Though Franklin . . . Carl Van Doren, "Meet Dr. Franklin," in *Meet Dr. Franklin* (Philadelphia: The Franklin Institute, 1943), 9.

The thrifty maxim . . . Franklin, *Poor Richard's Almanac*, 1734.

'Tis easier . . . Franklin, *The Way to Wealth*.

To show how . . . *Outlines Suggested for Teaching Thrift in the Elementary Schools* (Washington, DC: U.S. Treasury Department, 1919), 11.

Wealth is not . . . Franklin, *Poor Richard's Almanac*, 1734.

. . . we should . . . Franklin, letter to Madame Brillon, November 10, 1779, 931–32.

What maintains . . . Franklin, *The Way to Wealth*.

Who is rich . . . Franklin, *Poor Richard's Almanac*, 1744.

Who then are . . . "Information to Those Who Would Remove to America," 1782, in Smyth, *Writings of Benjamin Franklin*, 3:607–8, 613.

Women and Wine . . . Franklin, *The Way to Wealth*.

17

Although Dr. Duncan . . . Franklin J. Sherman, *Modern Story of Mutual Savings Banks* (New York: J. J. Little and Ives Company, 1934), 30.

And next . . . Alexander Cargill (ed.), *Memorial of the Celebration of the Centenary of Savings Banks* (Edinburgh: T. and A. Constable, 1910), 100.

At first sight . . . Rudyard Kipling, "Independence," Rectorial Address, St. Andrews University, October 1923, as cited in Rev. John L. Dinwiddie, *The Ruthwell Cross and the Ruthwell Savings Bank*, 2nd ed. (Dumfries, Scotland: Robert Dinwiddie, 1933), 131.

Entering the shop . . . George John C. Duncan, *Memoir of the Rev. Henry Henry Duncan, D. D. of Ruthwell* (Edinburgh: William Oliphant & Sons, 1848), 101.

From this time . . . Duncan, *Memoir*, 103–4. The memoir, written by Duncan's son, describes (p. 104) "the overburdened and weary individual, on whom had thus at once devolved the care of a thousand infant institutions."

It has been . . . Duncan, a pamphlet defending Parish Banks, about 1815.

It may be . . . Henry Duncan, testimony to Parliament, about 1816. See the appendix in Duncan, "A Letter to John H. Forbes, Esq. Advocate; Containing an Answer to Some Remarks and Statements in His "Observations on Banks for Savings" and His "Letter to the Editor of the Quarterly Review" (Edinburgh: Oliphant, Waugh, and Innes, 1817), 55.

It was in . . . Duncan, *Memoir*, 95–96. The memoir also bluntly adds (p. 108): "This was no scheme of charity. He [Duncan] abhorred the dependent spirit which any general plan contingent on the benevolence of the rich must have engendered . . ."

Justice leads us . . . *The Quarterly Review* 16, no. 32 (October 1816): 102.

. . . the most ridiculous . . . William Cobbett, on "the Savings Bank Scheme," January 4, 1817, in Cobbett, "A New Year's Gift to Old George Rose," *Register*, January 4, 1817, as cited in Horne, *History of Savings Banks*, 76. George Rose was a member of Parliament proposing a bill to recognize and protect the newly forming savings banks in Britain. The bill, aided in part by Duncan's strong advocacy, became law in the spring of 1819. Cited in Sophy Hall,

Dr. Duncan of Ruthwell (Edinburgh: Oliphant, Anderson & Ferrier, 1910), 67, 69–70.

. . . the name of . . . Cited in "A Century of Thrift," *The Times*, May 10, 1910.

No sooner were . . . Duncan, *Memoir*, 96–97.

The proposal to . . . Knox, *Triumph of Thrift*, 49.

That every depositor . . . Amendment to the "Rules and Regulations," adopted by the Ruthwell Parish Bank about 1816. See Henry Duncan, *Letter to John H. Forbes*, 30.

That strange . . . Duncan, letter to Mary Lundie, 1833, in Duncan, *Memoir*, 352.

Two funds shall . . . Duncan's "Rules and Regulations" for parish banks, 1815, in Henry Duncan, *Corrected Copy of the Rules and Regulations of the Parent Institution in Ruthwell and Directions for conducting the Details of Business* (Edinburgh, 1815), as reprinted in Noel Dinwiddie, *The Life and Times of the Reverend Dr. Duncan of Ruthwell: A Bicentenary Tribute* (Dumfries, Scotland: n. p., 1974), 14–23. See also Duncan, *Memoir*, 103.

What does your . . . Cited in Duncan, *Memoir*, 115; Dinwiddie, *Life and Times*, 12.

Why he . . . Henry Duncan, *The Young South Country Weaver; or, A Journey to Glasgow: A Tale for the Radicals; and, Maitland Smith, the Murderer, A True Narrative* (Edinburgh: Waugh & Innes, 1821), 26–27.

18

I appreciate very . . . Cited in Knox, *Triumph of Thrift*, 298.

My father succeeded . . . Knox, *Triumph of Thrift*, 68–69.

The next day . . . Knox, *Triumph of Thrift*, 71–73.

The next name . . . James Knox, recalling his grandfather, in Knox, *Triumph of Thrift*, 45.

. . . one of the . . . George Blake, *A Century of Thrift: The Romance of the Airdrie Savings Bank* (Airdrie: Baird & Hamilton, 1935), 9.

They imagine . . . James Knox, speech on the occasion celebrating his fifty years of service to the Airdrie Savings Bank, December 15, 1926, cited in *Airdrie and Coatbridge Advertiser*, December 18, 1926, reprinted in Knox, *Triumph of Thrift*, 346–47.

19

Christianity teaches . . . Catharine E. Beecher and Harriet Beecher Stowe, *The American Woman's Home: or, Principles of Domestic Science; Being a Guide to the Formation and Maintenance of Economical, Healthful, Beautiful, and Christian Homes* (New York: J. B. Ford and Company, 1872; first published 1869), 247.

I was pleased . . . Benjamin Franklin, "An Economical Project," in Smyth, *Writings of Benjamin Franklin*, 9:184.

Many were opposed . . . Beecher, *American Woman's Home*, 308.

Moreover, would not . . . Beecher, *American Woman's Home*, 449–50.

This practice . . . Alas, Beecher was not alone in her strongly favorable opinion of early rising. Benjamin Franklin, of course, famously endorsed it with his "Early to bed, early to rise . . ." maxim in *Poor Richard's Almanac* of 1735. But Franklin was hardly the first. As we saw in section three concerning Franklin, in *The Treatyse of Fysshynge wyth an Angle*, published in *The Book of St. Albans* of 1496, we are reminded that an "olde englysshe proverbe" states that "who soo woll ryse erly shall be holy, helthy, & zely [fortunate]." And in Fitzherbert's *The Book of Husbandry* of 1534 we are similarly told: "At grammer-scole I lerned a verse, that is this . . . Erly rysyng maketh a man hole in body, holer in soule, and rycher in goods." (See *The Treatyse of Fysshinge wyth an Angle*, 6; and the Rev. Walter

W. Skeat, *The Book of Husbrandry, By Master Fitzherbert*, 101.)

America's first millionaire, John Jacob Astor (1763–1848), also had strong views on this subject. As he put it: "The man who makes it the habit of his life to go to be at nine o'clock, usually gets rich and is always reliable . . . such a man will in all probability be up early in the morning . . . Rogues do their work at night." Quoted in *Elbert Hubbard's Scrap Book* (New York: Wm. H. Wise & Co., 1923), 211.

Those who, like me, remain ultimately unpersuaded, or at least unmoved, on this issue may wish late one night to peruse an entire volume devoted only to this subject: *Early Rising, A Natural, Social, and Religious Duty* (Northampton, UK: Abel & Sons, 1855). Or perhaps a briefer text, a colloquy on "The Early Rising"—described as "a very learned Chastisement of Sloth"—by the great Dutch scholar, theologian, and humanist Erasmus (born about 1466), in *Colloquies of Erasmus* (London: Reeves & Turner, 1878), 2:211–20.

Or for an even thriftier (that is, economical, sparing, efficient) iteration, this short piece of verse from Armstrong, published in an 1823 U.S. school textbook for children:

How foolish they who lengthen night,
And slumber in the morning light!

See Lindley Murray, ed., *The English Reader* (Baltimore: Cushing & Jewett, 1823), 138.

. . . young girls . . . Catharine E. Beecher, *A Treatise on Domestic Economy, For the Use of Young Ladies at Home, and at School* (New York: Harper & Brothers, 1854; first published 1842), 5–6.

She was right that Christianity in her generation strongly stressed this point. Here is a "Reader," a schoolbook for young children, published in the United States in 1823:

If idly lost, no art or care
The blessing can restore;
And Heav'n requires a strict account
For every misspent hour.

See Murray, *English Reader*, 126.

20

And yet this . . . Phillips's remarks appear as an appendix in John Greenleaf Whittier, *Letters of Lydia Marie Child* (Boston: Houghton Mifflin and Company, 1883), 266.

Her [Child's] . . . Whittier, *Letters of Lydia Marie Child*, xiv.

. . . No false pride . . . Lydia Marie Child, *The American Frugal Housewife: Dedicated to Those Who Are Not Ashamed of Economy*, 27th ed. (New York: Samuel S. & William Wood, 1841; published as *The Frugal Housewife* in 1829), 4–6.

Pig's head is . . . Child, *American Frugal Housewife*, 46, 90–91.

So Mrs. Child . . . Thomas Wentworth Higginson, "Lydia Marie Child," in *Contemporaries* (Boston: Houghton Mifflin and Company, 1900), 117.

The true economy . . . Child, *American Frugal Housewife*, 3.

True economy is . . . Child, *American Frugal Housewife*, 7.

21

But a very small . . . Reprinted from the *Quarterly Review* as Samuel Smiles, *Workmen's Earnings, Strikes, and Savings* (London: John Murray, 1861), 38, 73.

Economizing for . . . Samuel Smiles, *Self-Help: With Illustrations of Character and Conduct*, Revised Edition (Boston: Ticknor and Fields, 1866), 285.

He [Orison Swett Marden] . . . Margaret Connolly, *The Life Story* of *Orison Swett Marden* (New York: Thomas Y. Crowell Company, 1925), vii, as cited in Richard M. Huber, *The American Idea of Success* (New York: McGraw-Hill Book Company, 1971), 149.

. . . I bethought . . . Samuel Smiles, *The Autobiography of Samuel Smiles* (New York: E. P. Dutton and Company, 1905), 304.

I know that . . . Smiles, letter to the *Leeds Mercury*, November 1850, in Smiles, *Autobiography*, 156.

Idleness consumes . . . Samuel Smiles, *Life and Labor; or, Characteristics of Men of Industry, Culture and Genius* (n.p.: Pioneer Press, 1889), 185.

The man who . . . Thomas Mackay, preface, in Smiles, *Autobiography*, xii.

Many popular books . . . Smiles, *Self-Help: Character, Conduct and Perseverance*, rev. ed. (New York: A. L. Burt, n.d.; apparently published between 1905 and 1911; original edition first published 1859), 289.

Misery is the . . . Smiles, *Workmen's Earnings, Strikes, and Savings* 14.

My object in . . . Smiles, *Autobiography*, 222.

National progress is . . . Smiles, *Self-Help: Character . . .*, 2–3. See also Smiles, *Men of Invention and Industry* (New York: Harper & Brothers, 1885).

The power of . . . Smiles, *Self-Help: Character. . .*, 294.

Prodigality is . . . Samuel Smiles, *Thrift; Or, How To Get On In The World* (New York: John B. Alden, 1884; first published 1875), 14.

The respectable man . . . Smiles, *Self-Help: Character. . .*, 296–97.

Samuel Smiles was . . . G. D. H. Cole, *Labour in the Commonwealth: A Book for the Younger Generation* (London: Headley Bros. Publishers, 1918), 131–32. See also L. L. P. (book reviewer), *Journal of the Royal Statistical Society* 82, no. 2 (March 1919): 239.

Simple industry . . . Samuel Smiles, *Self-Help: Character. . .*, 289.

Smile's Self-Help . . . Orison Swett Marden, *Pushing to the Front* (Petersburg, NY: Success Company, 1911; originally published 1894), 809.

Some of man's . . . Smiles, *Thrift*, 26. See also Smiles, *Self-Help*, 275.

Such progress . . . Horne, *History of Savings Banks*, 229.

There was nothing . . . Smiles, *Self-Help*, xi.

Thrift began . . . Smiles, *Thrift*, 13.

Thrift does not . . . Smiles, *Thrift*, 231.

Thrift is in . . . Smiles, *Thrift*, 38.

To provide for . . . Smiles, *Self-Help*, 293–94.

Within a short . . . Horne, *History of Savings Banks*, 228.

22

. . . at the present . . . Sikes, letter to Gladstone advocating post-office savings banks, 1859, cited in Donald Macleod, ed., *Good Words for 1887* (London: Isbister and Company, 1887), 336.

Equally with . . . "A Century of National Thrift," *The Times*, May 17, 1910

. . . he gave . . . Archibald G. Bowie, *The Romance of the Savings Banks* (London: S. W. Partridge & Co., 1898), 39–40.

His first idea . . . Horne, *History of Saving Banks*, 171–72.

The idea was . . . Horne, *History of Saving Banks*, 172.

If a committee . . . Charles Sikes, advocating penny banks in a letter published in the *Leeds Mercury*, February 23, 1850, cited in Smiles, *Workmen's Earnings, Strikes, and Savings*, 77.

It is self-help . . . Cited in *Thirteenth Annual Report of the Bureau of Statistics of Labor and Industries of New Jersey, 1890* (Trenton, NJ:

Trenton Electric Printing Company, 1891), 3. See also "A Message from Gladstone," *New York Times*, April 1, 1890.

Mr. Sikes' . . . Smiles, *Workmen's Earnings, Strikes, and Savings*, 45.

. . . popular thrift . . . Cited in "Mr. Gladstone on Thrift," *The Times*, June 19, 1890.

The Post Office . . . Horne, *History of Saving Banks*, 181.

The post-office savings . . . Gladstone, remarks to the House of Commons, 1888, cited in "Postal Savings Banks," *Encyclopedia Americana* (New York: Encyclopedia Americana Corporation, 1918), 3:192.

The summer of . . . Horne, *History of Saving Banks*, 174, 176–77.

23

At the annual . . . *The Eighteen Fifties: Being a Brief Account of School Street, The Province House and The Boston Five Cents Savings Bank* (Boston: Boston Five Cents Savings Bank, 1926), 97.

In the month . . . Alonzo H. Evans, "Historical Address," May 2, 1904, in *The Boston Five Cents Savings Bank: Fiftieth Anniversary of Incorporation* (Boston: George E. Ellis Co., 1904), 11.

Of all financial . . . *Eighteen Fifties*, 105.

Whenever any . . . Charter, Boston Five Cents Savings Bank, 1854, in *Boston Five Cents Savings Bank*, 12.

Wilmot R. Evans . . . *Eighteen Fifties*, 101, 103.

24

At first I . . . Charles Sumner Young, ed., *Clara Barton: A Centenary Tribute* (Boston: Gorham Press, 1922), 202.

Economy, prudence . . . Young, *Clara Barton*, 194.

The main interest . . . Clara Barton, *The Red Cross* (Albany, NY: J. B. Lyon Company, 1898), 198.

"Miss Barton . . . Alice Hubbard, tribute to Clara Barton, July 1912, in Alice Hubbard, "The Clara Barton Memorial," *The Fra* 9, no. 4 (July 1912): 112–13. Alice Hubbard was the wife of Elbert Hubbard.

. . . she was . . . Description in 1917 of Clara Barton in Percy H. Epler, *The Life of Clara Barton* (New York: Macmillan Company, 1917), 373.

There must be . . . Young, *Clara Barton*, 202.

We went over . . . Letter to the Erie *Dispatch*, March 18, 1884, as reprinted in Barton, *Red Cross*, 130–31.

25

The difference . . . Ad, *The Thrift*, 1921, in *Prattonia: The All-Pratt Year Book, 1921* (New York: The Pratt Institute, 1921), 274.

Here was a . . . S. W. Straus, 1920, in *History of the Thrift Movement in America* (Philadelphia: J. B. Lippincott Company, 1920), 209.

Mr. Pratt was . . . *Prattonia*, 18–19.

Pratt Institute . . . Florence N. Levy, ed., *American Art Annual: 1898* (New York: Macmillan Company, 1899), 307.
See John J. McLaurin, *Sketches in Crude-Oil* (Harrisburg, PA: John J. McLaurin, 1898), 420–21, and James E. Homans, ed., *Cyclopedia of American Biography* (New York: Press Association Compilers, 1918), 8:192.

The Thrift . . . Homans, *Cyclopedia of American Biography*, 192.

Thrift Hall . . . The location of the Office of the Registrar, today, at the Pratt Institute.

. . . to promote . . . Statement of purpose of "The Thrift," in "Mr. A. C. Bradford on Thrift and Investing," *The World's Work* 36 (June 18, 1918): 133.

Waste Neither . . . Charles Pratt's motto, inscribed above the fireplace in the reading room of "The Astral," the model housing project for working-class residents of Brooklyn, financed by Pratt, and completed in 1886. What was originally the reading room is today the boiler room of "The Astral" apartments, located at 184 Franklin Street (Franklin!) in Brooklyn. The inscription is still there; I saw it in the summer of 2007. The motto "Waste Neither Time Nor Money" is taken from Benjamin Franklin's *Advice to a Young Tradesman* (1748).

26

Arithmetic problems . . . Describing the curriculum in Wanamaker's school for young employees, in Russell H. Conwell, *The Romantic Rise of a Great American* (New York: Harper & Brothers Publishers, 1924), 89.

The habit of . . . Conwell, *Romantic Rise of a Great American,* 196.

He was always . . . Orison Swett Marden, *Little Visits with Great Americans* (New York: Success Company, 1905), 94.

He was very . . . Henry W. Ruoff, describing Wanamaker in his book, *Leaders of Men, or, Types and Principles of Success* (Springfield, MA: King-Richardson Company, 1903), 595.

I am more . . . Wanamaker, in his capacity as U.S. postmaster general, 1891, in *An Additional Argument by the Postmaster-General in Favor of the Establishment of Postal Savings Depositories, With Appendices,* U.S. Senate, 52nd Congress, 1st Session (Washington, DC: Government Printing Office, April 1892), 64. The document (p. 1) urges the establishment of postal savings banks "to act as the guardian of moneys for people residing in sections of the country where there are no savings banks . . ." and, as evidence in favor of the plan, points (p. 44) to "the universal sentiment of the public press of the country seeking continually at the hands of the Government the establishment of these institutions as an incentive to thrift and a remedy for the ills of extravagance."

I have always . . . John Wanamaker, *Maxims of Life and Business* (Mechanicsburg, PA: Executive Books, 2004), 13.

I regard the . . . Wanamaker, writing to the World's Sunday School Convention, 1920, in Conwell, *Romantic Rise of a Great American,* 11. See also, for children, Olive W. Burt, *John Wanamaker: Boy Merchant* (Indianapolis, IN: Bobbs-Merrill Company, Inc., 1952).

It is told of . . . Orison Swett Marden, writing about Wanamaker, 1905, in *Little Visits with Great Americans,* 100.

John Wanamaker . . . William H. Tolman, *Social Engineering: A Record of Things Done by American Industrialists Employing Upwards of One and One-Half Million of People* (New York: McGraw Publishing Company, 1909), 184. See Chapter 6: "Thrift."

Many young people . . . Joseph H. Appel, *The Business Biography of John Wanamaker* (New York: Macmillan Company, 1930), 323.

. . . the [Penny Savings] . . . Conwell, *Romantic Rise of a Great American,* 136.

Robinson Crusoe . . . John Wanamaker, in Appel, *Business Biography of John Wanamaker,* 15.

To do a full . . . Conwell, *Romantic Rise of a Great American,* 85.

While still in . . . Appel, *Business Biography of John Wanamaker,* 324.

27

I must, however . . . See Henry W. Wolff, *People's Banks: A Record of Social and Economic Success* (London: P. S. King & Son, 1896), xii.

Thrift: . . . that . . . Edward Brabrook, "Thrift," Presidential Address to the Economic Association of the British Association, 1904, as cited in *The Times,* March 21, 1930.

28

Among the sworn . . . Marden, *Pushing to the Front,* 761–63.

The art of saving . . . Orison Swett Marden, *Thrift* (New York: Thomas Y. Crowell Company, 1918), 37.

Cheerfulness and . . . Orison Swett Marden, *Economy: The Self Denying Depositor and Prudent Paymaster at the Bank of Thrift* (New York: Thomas Y. Crowell & Company, 1901), 48.

The great thing . . . Marden, *Thrift,* 38, 70, 77.

The habit of . . . Marden, *Economy,* 7.

Ignorance is . . . Marden, *Economy,* 44.

Liberality often . . . Marden, *Economy,* 51–52.

The term thrift . . . Marden, *Thrift,* 1.

Thrift is neither . . . Orison Swett Marden, "Be Good to Yourself," reprinted in Bennett B. Jackson, Norma H. Deming, and Katherine I. Bemis, eds., *Thrift and Success* (New York: Century Club, 1919), 123.

The word thrift . . . Marden, *Pushing to the Front,* 2:753.

29

If you have a . . . Bolton Hall, *Three Acres and Liberty* (New York: Macmillan Company, 1922; first published 1907), 30.

Let us save . . . Bolton Hall, *Thrift* (New York: B. W. Huebsch, 1916), 246. The book was also published in 1923 as *The New Thrift.*

. . . most of us . . . Hall, *Three Acres and Liberty,* 249.

Pleasure is . . . Hall, *Thrift,* 246.

The prudent man . . . Hall, *Thrift,* 12–13. See above, "Material for a thrift Talk" (p. 47) in which the author clearly borrows from Hall's book.

Thrift, economy . . . Hall, *Thrift,* 246.

Thrift, the power . . . Hall, *Thrift,* 11.

30

The cheap article . . . Elbert Hubbard, *Little Journeys* (New York: Wm. H. Wise & Co., 1916), 1:xxvii.

An employee . . . Thomas Sewall Adams and Helen L. Sumner, *Labor Problems: A Text Book* (New York: Macmillan Company, 1905), 361.

The habit of . . . Elbert Hubbard, *Thrift* (New York: Hartford Lunch Co., 1916), 7, 13–15.

He valued . . . Felix Shay, *Elbert Hubbard of East Aurora* (New York: Wm. H. Wise & Co., 1926), 279.

In point of . . . Hubbard, "Benjamin Franklin," in *Little Journeys,* 3:50.

A man who . . . Elbert Hubbard, *The Philosophy of Elbert Hubbard* (New York: Wm. H. Wise & Co., 1934), 178.

The Reward for . . . Felix Shay, *Elbert Hubbard of East Aurora,* 329.

So a Roycrofter . . . "Autobiographical," in Hubbard, *Little Journeys,* 1:xviii–xix.

The Value of . . . Hubbard, "Twelve Things for Roycofters to Remember," in Hubbard, *Philosophy of Elbert Hubbard,* 44.

31

As soon as . . . Booker T. Washington, *Up From Slavery: An Autobiography* (Garden City, NY: Doubleday & Company, 1900), 51–53.

But, of course . . . Washington, *Up From Slavery,* 33–34.

But what are . . . Washington, address to the National Educational Association, July 10, 1896, in University of Illinois Press, *Booker T. Washington Papers* (1889–1895), 4:190.

The Booker T. Washington Papers (multiple volumes) are published online by the University of Illinois Press: http://www.historycooperative.org/btw/Vol.1/html/index.html

For a long time . . . Washington, *Up From Slavery,* 176.

If through me . . . Washington, address to Harvard University Alumni, June 24, 1896, in *Washington Papers,* 4:183.

In meeting men . . . Washington, *Up From Slavery,* 229.

In short . . . August Meier, "Booker T. Washington and the Negro Press: With Special Reference to the *Colored American Magazine,*" *The Journal of Negro History* 38, no. 1 (January 1953): 78.

. . . *the most* . . . Andrew Carnegie, describing Booker T. Washington, 1910, in Peter Krass, *Carnegie* (Hoboken, NJ: John Wiley & Sons, 2002), 466.

Mr. Washington . . . Andrew Carnegie, *Autobiography* (Boston: Houghton Mifflin Company, 1920), 276–77.

My friends . . . Washington, address to the Alabama State Teachers' Association, June 8, 1892, in *Washington Papers,* 3:234.

The night-school . . . Washington, *Up From Slavery,* 196–97.

No man ever . . . Roy F. Bergengren, *I Speak for Joe Doakes* (New York: Harper & Brothers Publishers, 1945), 26.

On New Year's . . . Washington, letter to Emily Howard of Tuskegee, Alabama, January 12, 1894, in *Washington Papers,* 3:383.

The slave system . . . Washington, *Up From Slavery,* 17-18.

So far as . . . Cited in W. E. B. DuBois, *The Autobiography of W. E. Burghardt DuBois: A Soliloquy on Viewing My Life from the Last Decade of Its First Century* (Boston: International Publishers, 1968), 245

The students . . . Washington, *Up From Slavery,* 126.

The thing that . . . Washington, *Up From Slavery,* 278.

. . . *we are* . . . Washington, speech at the unveiling of the Robert Gould Shaw Monument, May 31, 1897, in *Washington Papers,* 4:288.

We must make . . . Washington, address in Birmingham, January 1, 1900, in *Washington Papers,* 5:393.

We should not . . . Washington, address in Boston, July 30, 1903, in *Washington Papers,* 7:236.

The young women . . . Albert Shaw, "Negro Progress on the Tuskegee Plan," *American Review of Reviews* (April 1894): 439.

32

The aim of . . . Martha Berry, "Uplifting Backwoods Boys in Georgia," in *The World's Work,* July 1904, as reprinted in Doyle Mathis and Ouida Dickey, eds., *Martha Berry: Sketches of Her Schools and College* (Atlanta: Wings Publishers, 2001), 198.

Be a lifter . . . Cited in Mathis and Dickey, *Martha Berry,* 204, 221.

The Bible . . . Cited in Elizabeth P. Myers, *Angel of Appalachia: Martha Berry* (New York: Julian Messner, 1968), 175.

Culture may rest . . . Albert Shaw, "Martha Berry and Her Patriotic Work," *The American Review of Reviews* (June 1925): 596.

Everything that . . . Shaw, "Martha Berry and Her Patriotic Work," 596.

He [my father] . . . Mathis and Dickey, *Martha Berry,* 32.

. . . *it is of* . . . Mathis and Dickey, *Martha Berry,* 195.

. . . *teaching the* . . . Shaw, "Martha Berry and Her Patriotic Work," 596.

They need . . . Mathis and Dickey, *Martha Berry,* 191.

33

The American people . . . "Society Founded to Teach the American People Thrift," *New York Times,* November 2, 1913. Apparently

the Society was organized in 1913; Straus reports that the first "formal" meeting took place in Chicago at the City Club on January 13, 1914.

. . . *the American Society* . . . "Buying What We Want," *The Atlanta Constitution,* January 25, 1914.

As a result . . . Straus, *History of the Thrift Movement in America,* 105.

At one meeting . . . Frank Morton Todd, *The Story of the Exposition* (New York: G. P. Putnam's Sons, 1921), 5:81. See also "Editorial," *Education* 36, no. 3 (November 1915), 192–93, 197; and "Editorial," *Education* 36, no. 4 (December 1915): 263. The essay contest, funded by Straus and administered by the National Education Association, took place; the essay submission deadline was March 1, 1916; more than 150,000 U.S. school children participated in the contest.

If we are to . . . Straus, "Promotion and Practice of Thrift in Foreign Countries," issue devoted to "The New American Thrift," *The Annals* (Philadelphia: American Academy of Political and Social Science, January 1920), 87:196.

Individual thrift . . . "Society Founded to Teach the American People Thrift," *New York Times,* November 2, 1913.

Laying aside . . . This excerpt from Straus's 1915 address to the Thrift Congress appears as "Meaning of Thrift" in a guidebook for public school teachers published in 1922. See *Public School Methods* (Chicago: School Methods Publishing Co., 1922), 64.

More than . . . "4,000,000 Save," *New York Times,* June 30, 1926.

My first thrift . . . Straus, *History of the Thrift Movement,* 64–65.

No human virtue . . . Strauss, *History of the Thrift Movement,* 193.

Saving money . . . Straus, "The Greater Thrift," an address delivered to the annual convention of the National Education Association, July 1, 1916, in "Nation's Educators Open Great Meeting," *New York Times,* July 2, 1916; and Straus, *History of the Thrift Movement,* 143, 145–46.

To this end . . . Report of the National Conference on Thrift Education, in "Introduction," *Thrift Education* (Washington, DC: National Education Association, September 1924), 4.

We are going . . . "Europeans Can Teach Americans Thrift," *New York Times,* June 14, 1914.

34

I felt like . . . Cited in L. H. Hammond, *In the Vanguard of a Race* (New York: Council of Women for Home Missions and Missionary Education Movement of the United States and Canada, 1922), 110.

Let us have . . . Cited in "Record of 1901," in Maggie L. Walker, *Historical Report of the R. W. G. Council, I. O. Saint Luke* (Richmond: Everett Waddey Co., 1917), 23.

Over fifteen thousand . . . Hammond, *In the Vanguard,* 113.

. . . *save some* . . . Cited in David T. Beito, "To Advance the 'Practice of Thrift and Economy': Fraternal Societies and Social Capital, 1890–1920," *Journal of Interdisciplinary History* 29, no. 4 (Spring 1999): 60. I have also benefited from this essay's overall discussion of Walker's career of the goals of the Independent Order of Saint Luke.

Succor and . . . Walker, *Historical Report,* 26.

We teach . . . Cited in Hammond, *In the Vanguard,* 114.

35

. . . *he started* . . . Beth Day, *The Little Professor of Piney Woods: The Story of Professor Laurence Jones* (New York: Julian Messner, 1955), 28.

His childhood hero . . . Day, *Little Professor of Piney Woods*, 18.

It is hoped . . . Laurence Jones, *The Spirit of Piney Woods* (New York: F. H. Revell, 1931), 7.

It was clear . . . Laurence C. Jones, *Piney Woods and Its Story* (New York: Fleming H. Revell Company, 1922), 56–57.

[My father gave] . . . Jones, *Piney Woods and Its Story*, 20–21.

Piney Woods . . . Charitable gifts from Iowa chapters of the Daughters of the American Revolution, 1918, cited in *Twenty-Second Report of the National Society of the Daughters of the American Revolution: March 1, 1918 to March 1, 1919* (Washington, DC: Government Printing Office, 1921), 87.

So many times . . . Charles E. Barker, letter to Laurence Jones, May 10, 1916. Letter reprinted in D. J. Harris and Charles E. Baker, *Little Journeys to Piney Woods School*, no. 3, pamphet, n.d. Dr. Charles Barker was formerly a dietician and trainer, or "Physical Advisor," to President William Howard Taft. His 1947 book is *With President Taft in the White House*. For many years, Barker was a popular lecturer, especially to youth audiences and to parents, for Rotary International. Two of his booklets connected to these talks are *A Father's Responsibility to His Son* and *A Mother's Relation to Her Daughter*. Dr. Barker died in 1948. This letter from 1916 appears to have been sent under the aegis of the Chicago office of the Redpath Lyceum Bureau, or what was called "Redpath Chautauqua," due to its connections to the Chautauqua movement.

Taking what . . . Cited in Leslie Harper Purcell, *Miracle in Mississippi: Laurence C. Jones of Piney Woods* (New York: Carlton Press, 1956), 229.

". . . they [my parents] . . . Cited in Alferdteen Harrison, *Piney Woods School: An Oral History* (Jackson: University Press of Mississippi, 1982), 28–29.

The things . . . Quoted in Purcell, *Miracle in Mississippi*, 117.

To be good . . . Cited in Purcell, *Miracle in Mississippi*, 55.

. . . to make . . . Jones, *Piney Woods and Its Story*, 151.

We closed . . . Jones, *Piney Woods and Its Story*, 75, 84.

When we . . . *The Times Republican*, Marshalltown, Iowa, 1930s, cited in Purcell, *Miracle in Mississippi*, 90.

36

But I didn't . . . Frank Capra, *The Name Above the Title* (New York: Vintage Books, 1985; first published 1971), 383.

. . . a figment . . . Reviews of *It's a Wonderful Life*, cited in Capra, *Name Above the Title*, 382–83.

POTTER . . . The movie *It's a Wonderful Life*, 1946, as published online at: http://www.imsdb.com/scripts/It's-a-Wonderful-Life.html

Through the . . . Capra, *Name Above the Title*, 6–7.

Part Four

For better or . . . Mary Douglas, *How Institutions Think* (Syracuse, NY: Syracuse University Press, 1986), 128.

37

Although I have . . . Smiles, *Autobiography*, 19–20.

The American . . . Horne, *History of Savings Banks*, 289.

Has no child . . . Robert Lynd, "The Money-Box," in *English Essays of To-day* (London: Oxford University Press, 1936), 117–18, 120–22. The essay is excerpted from Lynd's 1925 book, *The Money-Box*.

. . . he and his . . . Cited in Knox, *Triumph of Thrift*, 109–10.

I send you . . . From a speech delivered on June 9, 1910 in Edinburgh by Mr. J. Avon Clyde, M.P., as reported in Alexander Cargill (ed.), *Memorial of the Celebration of the Centenary of Savings Banks* (Edinburgh: T. and A. Constable, 1910), 103.

[In] the Barber . . . *The History of Richmond in the County of York* (1814), 300; the author of this book is anonymous, but appears, based on subsequent publications, to have been Christopher Clarkson. Cited in Mrs. Gutch, *County Folk-Lore* (London: David Nutt, 1901), 2:280. The author is here describing customs in Yorkshire.

In the issue of the famous London journal *The Spectator* of October 14, 1712, the author signing his name "Hezekiah Thrift" complains that "the beadles and officers have the impudence at Christmas to ask for their box, though they deserve the strapado." See *The Spectator*, no. 509, October 14, 1712, in N. Ogle, ed., *The Spectator*, 7:223.

In 1895, the antiquarian authority John Brand writes: "This [practice of putting money in a money-box to assist the needy and reward the industrious, particularly at Christmas-time] is still retained in barbers' shops. A thrift-box, as it is vulgarly called, is put up against the wall, and every customer puts in something." See John Brand, *Observations on the Popular Antiquities of Great Britain* (London: George Bell and Sons, 1895), 1:496.

In the British . . . "December," *All The Year Round*, New Series, 41, no. 993, December 10, 1887, 512.

From the eighteenth-century British potter Josiah Wedgewood: "The medieval potter also manufactured at an early date . . . thrift-boxes, which were small: and wide bottles with imitation stoppers, and a slit on the side for the introduction of money." *The Gentleman's Magazine and Historical Review* in 1860 refers to "the well-known medieval and modern thrift-boxes of earthenware"; and the 1871 catalogue of London's Museum of Practical Geology, listing specimens of medieval pottery found in Britain, refers to an "earthenware money-box, or thrift-box . . ."

See *The Life of Josiah Wedgewood, from His Private Correspondence and Family Papers* (London: Hurst and Blackett, 1865), 1:76. (Josiah Wedgewood was born on July 12, 1730, and died on January 3, 1795.) "Works of the Romano-Gaulish Ceramists," *The Gentleman's Magazine and Historical Review*, New Series, 9 (December 1860): 607. Henry de la Beche, Trenham Reeks, and F. W. Rudler, *Catalogue of Specimens in the Museum of Practical Geology*, 2nd ed. (London: George E. Eyre and William Spottiswoode, 1871), 91.

. . . the introduction . . . Blake, *Century of Thrift*, 36.

The money-box . . . "The Money-Box in History and in Ethnography," *World Thrift*, no. 12 (Milan: International Thrift Institute, 1928), 24. If you are interested in the early history of the thrift or money box, beginning with the Greeks, this learned little treatise is quite a read!

1. That thrift . . . Cited in *Proceedings of the New York State Stenographers' Association*, Twentieth Annual Meeting, August 22–23, 1895 (Elmira, NY: Advertiser Association, 1895), 21.

There was at . . . James Nasmyth, "My School-days," in Samuel Smiles, ed., *James Nasmyth: Autobiography* (London: John Murray, 1897; first published 1883), 83–84.

They that know . . . Albert H. Plumb, *When Mayflowers Blossom: A Romance of Plymouth's First Years* (New York: Fleming H. Revell Company, 1914), 196.

Thrif or Thrift-box . . . John Trotter Brockett, *A Glossary of North Country Words* (Newcastle upon Tyne: T. and J. Hodgson, 1825),

217. See also Thomas Wright, ed., *Dictionary of Obsolete and Provincial English* (London: Henry G. Bohn, 1857), 2:958.

The Thrift Box . . . The Thrift Box; or, The Manufacturer's Guide to Health, Wealth and Comfort, &c., by "A Looker On" (Leeds: Edward Baines, n.d.). The pamphlet concludes with extracts from a letter of April 1804 from the Rev. William Gilpin to his parishioners. An original copy of the document is in the New York Historical Society.

. . . the thrift-box . . . Cited in James Raine, *Saint Cuthbert* (Durham: F. Humble, 1828), 117. Raine also refers (p. 129) to "the halt, the maimed, and the blind . . . casting in their mites into the thrift box of St. Cuthbert."

Thrift-boxes of . . . The Rev. B. Smith, "The Missing Thrift-Box (Kindness to Parents)," *The Wesleyan Sunday-School Magazine,* New Series, 7 (March 1872), in *The Wesleyan Sunday-School Magazine and Journal of Education for the Year 1872,* New Series, 7 (London: Wesleyan Conference Office, 1872), 49–51.

When you were . . . Benjamin Smith, *Sunshine in the Kitchen; or, Chapters for Maid-Servants* (London: Wesleyan Conference Office, 1872), 92–93.

38

The first activities . . . Straus, *History of the Thrift Movement in America,* 71.

The first school . . . Harold Waldstein Foght, *The American Rural School* (New York: Macmillan Company, 1910), 186–87.

Our motto was . . . Mrs. Francis King, *Pages from a Garden Note-Book* (New York: Charles Scribner's Sons, 1921), 261.

The school garden . . . Frederick L. Holtz, *Nature-Study: A Manual for Teachers and Students* (New York: Charles Scribner's Sons, 1908), 258–59.

. . . she always . . . Alice M. Rathbone, "Our Hardy Flowers," in Wilhelm Miller, ed., *How to Make a Flower Garden* (New York: Doubleday, Page & Company, 1903), 48.

There is nothing . . . Louise Klein Miller, *Children's Gardens for School and Home, A Manual of Cooperative Gardening* (New York: D. Appleton and Company, 1904), 5.

Thrift is not . . . John C. Stone, "Problems of Thrift and Economy," in *Junior High School Mathematics*, book 1 (Chicago: Benj. H. Sanborn & Co., 1922), 99–100.

When one wanders . . . R. Clipston Sturgis, "English Gardens," in A. D. F. Hamlin, R. Clipston Sturgis, John Galen Howard, and K. Honda, *European and Japanese Gardens* (Philadelphia: Henry T. Coates & Co., 1902), 93.

Your food bill . . . "Victory Gardening Pays Big Dividends," *Home Life* (Niles, MI: Niles Federal Savings and Loan Association, April 1945), 6.

39

Among various . . . "West Ham: Worthies, Entertainments, Sports and Pastimes," in W. R. Powell, ed., *A History of the County of Essex* (London: Oxford University Press, 1973), 6:64–67.

The Archbishop of . . . "The Archbishop of York on Thrift," *The Times*, London, January 29, 1883.

The fraternal . . . George W. Walts, commissioner of the California Bureau of Labor Statistics, 1890, in *Fourth Biennial Report of the Bureau of Labor Statistics of the State of California* (Sacramento: State Printing Offfice, 1890), 111.

Friendly Societies . . . Richardson Campbell of the Independent Order of Rechabites (a friendly society), discussing friendly societies in

Britain, in Campbell, *Provident and Industrial Institutions: Being Records and Historical Sketches of Various Thrift Associations . . .* (Manchester, UK: Rechabite Buildings, n.d.; probably published about 1926), 233–34. The Order of Rechabites were a "teetotal" (protemperance, or antialcohol) friendly society. The society's ritual as of 1835 thus includes these words:

Swiftly our moments pass away,
And soon they all will disappear;
May we endeavor while 'tis day
To stop the drunkard's mad career.

See Richardson Campbell, *Rechabite History: A Record of the Origin, Rise, and Progress of the Independent Order of Rechabites* (Manchester, UK: Independent Order of Rechabites, 1911). Discussing Joseph Livesy, one of the Order's founders, Campbell also writes:

To this course he [Livesy] was disposed by that passage in the autobiography of Benjamin Franklin (between whose character and Mr. Livesy's there were striking points of resemblance), in which he relates his experience as a journeyman printer in London, 1725, when he abstained from ale, and tried to convince his fellow-workmen that their favorite beverage was not a strengthening one; but they went on spending their money, drinking their ale, as Franklin says, "Keeping themselves always under."

One by one . . . Ritual of the Ladies of the Maccabees of the World, 1910, as cited in David T. Beito, "To Advance," 589.

Our Order . . . Ladies Review, the journal of the Ladies of the Maccabees, January 1916, as cited in Beito, "To Advance," 591. Founded in 1892, the Ladies of the Maccabees, with more than 200,000 members as of 1920, became the largest fraternal organization in the U.S. run exclusively by women.

The parish was . . . "Climping," in T. P. Hudson, A. P. Baggs, and H. M. Warne, eds. *History of the County of Sussex* (1997), 5:126–47.

There is . . . Albert C. Stevens, "Fraternal Insurance," *American Monthly Review of Reviews* 21, no. 1 (January 1900): 59.

To discipline . . . Cited in Beito, "To Advance," 604.

40

Again, we say . . . "Lord Derby on Thrift," *The Times*, May 10, 1873.

Annual income . . . Charles Dickens, *David Copperfield* (Oxford: Oxford University Press, 1981; first published 1850), 169.

At some distance . . . Charles Dickens, *Complete Works of Charles Dickens: Oliver Twist, Pictures from Italy, American Notes*, Landport ed. (Rahway, NJ: Merson Company, n.d.; *American Notes* first published 1842), 65–66.

The Bank now . . . William Dana Orcutt, *The Miracle of Mutual Savings* (New York: Bowery Savings Bank, 1934), 80–81.

By the end . . . Alan L. Olmstead, *New York City Mutual Savings Banks, 1819–1861* (Chapel Hill: University of North Carolina Press, 1976), 5–6.

Dissipation has . . . Thomas Guthrie, *Seed-time and Harvest of Ragged Schools; or, A Third Plea, with New Editions of the First and Second Plea* (Edinburgh: Adam and Charles Black, 1860), 99.

The expense of . . . Newton F. Hawley, speech to the American Bankers Association, September 1910, cited in William H. Kniffen, *The Savings Bank and Its Practical Work*, 4th ed. (New York: Bankers Publishing Company, 1928), 506–7.

From the start . . . Centennial celebration of the Society for Savings, June 22, 1949, *In Our Second Century: Society for Savings in the City of Cleveland, The First Hundred Years* (Cleveland: Society for Savings, 1949), 5.

Fundamentally thrift . . . A. C. Robinson, "The Moral Values of Thrift," *American Bankers Association Journal* 24 (October 1931): 209, as cited in Alfred L. Roe, "Bankers and Thrift in the Age of Affluence," *American Quarterly* 17, no. 4 (Winter 1965): 620.

The gospel of . . . George E. Allen, speech to the Savings Bank Section of the American Bankers Association, 1906.

Growth of the . . . George Alter, Claudia Goldin, and Elyce Rotella, "The Savings of Ordinary Americans: The Philadelphia Saving Fund Society in the Mid-Nineteenth Century," *The Journal of Economic History* 54, no. 4 (December 1994): 736.

He was a . . . Joseph Conrad, "Thrift—And the Child," in *Chance* (London: Methuen Co., 1913), 66–67.

I think it . . . H. W. Rosenbaum, *Handy Savings Banks: Suggestions for a New Plan* (New York: 1886).

. . . the idea of . . . Levi P. Smith, "Background and Potential of Thrift Institutions," in *Savings and Loan Annals, 1952* (Chicago: United States Savings and Loan League, 1953), 24.

In British Savings . . . Alexander Cargill (ed.), *Memorial of the Celebration of the Centenary of Savings Banks* (Edinburgh: T. and A. Constable, 1910), 102, 109.

In business . . . Kate Brownlee Sherwood, "Characteristics of Richard Mott," *Magazine of Western History* 10, no. 1 (May 1889): 35.

In 1830 . . . R. Daniel Wadhwani, "Protecting Small Savers: The Political Economy of Economic Security," *The Journal of Policy History* 18, no. 1 (2006): 141.

In four years . . . Oliver Optic, *The Savings Bank; or How to Buy a House*, early nineteenth century, partially reprinted in Freeman Hunt, *Worth and Wealth: A Collection of Maxims, Morals and Miscellanies for Merchants and Men of Business* (New York: Stringer & Townsend, 1856), 276.

In the history . . . Bowie, *Romance of the Savings Bank*, 5.

In 1906 the . . . *Passbook—To a Proud Past and a Promising Future* (Hartford, CT: Society for Savings, 1969), 80.

It is strictly . . . Cited in *In Our Second Century*, 4. See also *Two-Score-Years-and-Ten: Being the Story of the Rise and Progress of the Society for Savings in the City of Cleveland, of the City of Cleveland* (Cleveland: Society for Savings, 1899).

It [the savings bank] . . . Charles E. Knowles, *History of the Bank for Savings in the City of New York* (New York: Bank for Savings in the City of New York, 1936), 42.

Lessons of Thrift . . . A book published in 1820, illustrated by Robert Cruikshank. A copy is in the Kline/Roethke Collection, Stanford University.

Mutual banks . . . Dean Lawrence Lunt, *Here for Generations: The Story of a Maine Bank and Its City* (Frenchboro, ME: Islandport Press, 2002), xv.

My life work . . . *In Our Second Century*, 19.

Now let us . . . Isaac F. Marcosson, "The Colossal Growth of the Savings-Bank," *Munsey's Magazine* (February 1914): 102.

A pamphlet . . . George Alter, Claudia Goldin, and Elyce Rotella, "The Savings of Ordinary Americans: The Philadelphia Saving Fund Society in the Mid-Nineteenth Century," *The Journal of Economic History* 54, no. 4 (December 1994): 739.

Peoples Thrift . . . Founded 1887, Philadelphia.

The Portsmouth . . . Cited in "Sketch Furnished by Mr. Hackett," in Emerson W. Keyes, *A History of Savings Banks in the United States* (New York: Bradford Rhodes, 1876), 1:201.

The primary law . . . Maxims of Richard Mott, in Sherwood, "Characteristics of Richard Mott," 40.

The promotion . . . "Savings Banks," in *Encyclopaedia Britannica*, 24:244.

The rapid growth . . . Horne, *A History of Savings Banks*, 1.

Total Number of . . . An appendix in Charles E. Knowles, *History of the Bank for Savings in the City of New York* (New York: Bank for Savings in the City of New York, 1936), 172.

Said Corporation . . . "An Act to incorporate The Boston Five Cents Savings Bank," in *Boston Five Cents Savings Bank*, 12, 25.

Savings Banks . . . Announcement in the Boston *Christian Disciple*, December 1816, cited in Sherman, *Modern Story of Mutual Savings Banks*, 46.

School savings . . . W. Espey Albig, *A History of School Savings Banking: In the United States and its European Beginnings* (Savings Bank Division, American Bankers Association, 1928), 36.

Since Thursday . . . A history of the Society for Savings, Hartford, Connecticut, in *Passbook*, 77.

There are 657 . . . A history of the Charlestown Five Cents Savings Bank, 1904, in Augustus W. Stover, *A Retrospect on the Fiftieth Anniversary of the Incorporation of the Charlestown Five Cents Savings Bank* (Boston: Charlestown Five Cents Savings Bank, 1904), 39.

This is the . . . Editorial, *New York Times*, on the founding of The Bowery Savings Bank, 1834, cited in Oscar Schisgall, *Out of One Small Chest: A Social and Financial History of the Bowery Savings Bank* (New York: AMACOM, 1975), 11.

Throughout the banks . . . Richard Boughton, "Humor and Pathos of the Savings-Bank," *The Century Magazine* 61, no. 4 (February 1901): 494–95.

To the average . . . William H. Kniffen, "The Broader Thrift," address to the Ohio Bankers Association, September 1916, reprinted in Kniffen, *Savings Bank and Its Practical Work*, 35.

. . . to induce . . . John Pintard, letter of April 3, 1816, proposing the creation of the first savings bank in New York City, cited in Olmstead, *New York City Mutual Savings Banks*, 6.

Virtue is . . . Inscription in the dome of the Buffalo (New York) Savings Bank, completed in December 1926, cited in *Under Golden Dome: The History of Buffalo Savings Bank* (Buffalo: Buffalo Savings Bank, 1982), 81.

Walter A. Danforth . . . Lunt, *Here For Generations*, 179–80, 209–11, 214.

We see that . . . William E. Cox, "The Ethics of the Savings Bank," address to the Savings Bank Section, American Bankers Association, at its Annual Convention, held in New Orleans, LA, November 23, 1911.

What romantic . . . *Gateway of Progress, 1857–1957: The Story of New Jersey's Largest Savings Bank through Its First Century of Service* (Newark: Howard Savings Institution, 1957), 46.

Without the thrift . . . Kniffen, *Savings Bank and Its Practical Work*, 75.

. . . wrote leaden . . . Charles Dickens, *Hard Times* (New York: Signet Classic, 1961; first published 1854), 57.

The Yorkshire . . . "Penny Banks," *All The Year Round*, New Series, 15, no. 380 (March 11, 1876): 559–61.

You, the working . . . "Lord Derby on Thrift," *The Times*, January 17, 1880.

41

By 1913 . . . Marc Schneiberg, "Who's on Path? Path Dependence, Organizational Diversity and the Problem of Institutional Change in the U.S. Economy, 1900–1950," *Socio-Economic Review* 5 (2007): 60.

Cooperation depends . . . Francis Greenwood Peabody, *Jesus Christ and the Social Question* (New York: Macmillan Company, 1915), 283.

Co-operators have . . . G. D. H. Cole, *The British Cooperative Movement in a Socialist Society* (London: George Allen & Unwin Ltd., 1951), 53–54, 155–56. Cole also writes (p. 155) that British Co-operative Societies "got their first legal recognition as thrift agencies" and points out (p. 50) that "the savings bank element in Co-operative trading remains important . . ."
See also "Co-operative Trading as a Means of Thrift," in Rev. William Lewery Blackley, *Thrift and Independence: A Word for Working Men* (London: Society for Promoting Christian Knowledge, 1885), 53–54.

Do not forget . . . *Today: A Magazine of Thrift* (New York: Association of Army and Navy Stores, June 1930), inside cover.

First, I . . . "Co-operative Catechism," from the British journal *Co-operator*, 1860s, reprinted in Frederick Harrison, "Industrial Co-operation," *Fortnightly Review*, no. 16 (January 1, 1866), in George Henry Lewes, ed., *The Fortnightly Review*, vol. 3, November 15, 1865, to February 1, 1866 (London: Chapman and Hall, 1866), 501. The journal *Co-operator* was edited by Henry Pitman, an important British Victorian-era co-operative advocate, who probably wrote the "Catechism" himself and first presented it as a part of a lecture.

Husbands who . . . A pamphlet announcing the opening of "The Philadelphia Savings Store, on the Rochdale Plan," a cooperative store sponsored by the Philadelphia Savings Society, 1859. See *The Philadelphia Savings Store, on the Rochdale Plan* (Philadelphia: Philadelphia Savings Society, 1859). I read the pamphlet courtesy of the New York Historical Society.

If the present . . . Emerson P. Harris, *Co-operation: The Hope of the Consumer* (New York: Macmillan Company, 1920), 121.

. . . it being . . . Cited in Albert Shaw, "Cooperation in a Western City," *Publications of the American Economic Association* 1, no. 4 (September 1886): 53.

Mr. Charles A. Pillsbury . . . Shaw, "Cooperation in a Western City," 15, 41, 25–26, 43, 166–67.

These aids . . . Harris, *Co-operation*, 67.

42

About one thousand . . . Shaw, "Cooperation in a Western City," 93.

The American people . . . Ben H. Hazen, president of the United States Savings and Loan League, address to the League's annual convention, 1952, in *Savings and Loan Annals 1952*, 4.

. . . associations . . . The first U.S. state law to provide for the general incorporation of building and loans, passed by the New Jersey state legislature, 1847, in *Eighth Annual Report of the Bureau of Statistics of Labor and Industries of New Jersey, 1885* (Trenton: John L. Murphy, 1885), 281. See also *Thirteenth Annual Report of the Bureau of Statistics of Labor and Industries of New Jersey, 1890* (Trenton: Trenton Electric Printing Company, 1891), 3.

At the rate . . . Professor Franklin Benjamin Sanborn, "Co-operative Building," a report presented to the American Social Science Association, September 7, 1888, as cited in Symour Dexter, *A Treatise on Co-operative Savings and Loan Associations* (New York: D. Appleton and Company, 1889), iii, 44. The Massachusetts attorney and author Franklin Benjamin Sanborn (b. December 15, 1831) was a founder and for many years the secretary of the American Social Science Association.

Building Association Congress . . . A conference of U.S. building and loan associations held in Chicago on April 14–15, 1892, leading to the creation of the United States League of Local Building and Loan Associations (founded 1893) and the American Savings, Building and Loan Institute, cited in Horace F. Clark and Frank A. Chase, *Elements of the Modern Building and Loan Associations* (New York: Macmillan Company, 1925), 485–86. The Institute sponsored the Clark and Chase textbook, and also worked with YMCA schools around the country. See also "Building Associations' Congress to Be Held in London, England," *The American Building Association News* 34, no. 4 (April 1914): 149–52.

A building association is . . . Henry S. Rosenthal, *Cyclopedia of Building, Loan and Savings Associations*, 5th ed. (Cincinnati: American Building Association News Publishing Co., 1927), 9, 15–16.

But although those . . . Edmund Wrigley, *The Working Man's Way to Wealth; A Practical Treatise on Building Associations: What They Are and How to Use Them* (Philadelphia: James K. Simon, 1869), 2–3, 5–6, 78.

But I had to . . . Cited in W. A. Linn, "Co-operative Home-Winning: Some Practical Results of Building Associations," *Scribner's Magazine* 7, no. 61 (May 1890): 573.

By training . . . Clark and Chase, *Elements of the Modern Building and Loan*, 323–24.

Dan Geyer . . . *Savings and Loan Annals, 1962*, 267–68.

The form of . . . Shaw, "Cooperation in a Western City," 80.

Hennepin County . . . Building and loans founded since 1874 in Minneapolis, as of 1886, in Shaw, "Cooperation in a Western City," 84–93.

The increase of . . . *Fourth Biennial Report of the Bureau of Labor Statisitcs of the State of California* (Sacramento: State Printing Office, 1890), 220. The report also (p. 220) forthrightly cheerleads: "Building and loan associations foster a spirit of thrift and economy by offering a splendid investment for small savings."

It is not . . . Dexter, *Treatise on Co-operative Savings and Loan Associations*, 40.

Its members . . . H. Morton Bodfish, *History of Building and Loan in the United States* (Chicago: United States Building and Loan League, 1931), 1.

The Irish-American . . . "Monthly Dues," *The American Building Association News* 34, no. 2 (February 1914), in *American Building Association News 1914* (Cincinnati: American Building Association News Company, 1915), 81. *The American Building Association News* began publishing in 1880, from Cincinnati and Chicago.

On January 3, 1831 . . . Cited in Clark and Chase, *Elements of the Modern Building and Loan*, 458–59. Frankford in 1854 became a part of the city of Philadelphia, whereas in 1831 it had been a part of Oxford Township. Most of the original members of the Oxford "Club" were wage earners in the textile trade. Also, in 1845, in Philadelphia, another early building and loan association was formed; this one was called the "Franklin Building Association" (Clark and Chase, *Elements of the Modern Building and Loan*, 458).

. . . one of the . . . Linn, "Co-operative Home-Winning," 586. Linn also researched and wrote an article on the history of building and loans that was published in the June 1889 issue of *Scribner's Magazine*. Together these two works appeared as a chapter called "Building and Loan Associations" in Russell Sturgis, John W. Root, Bruce Price, Donald G. Mitchell, Samuel Parsons Jr., and W. A. Linn, *Home in City and Country* (New York: Charles Scribner's Sons, 1893).

Linn appears to have been an interesting guy. Two of his books are *Horace Greeley* (1903) and *Rob and His Gun* (1902), a story for young people about hunting.

On the following . . . Description of a school savings program launched by the schools and the Fresno Guarantee Building-Loan Association in Fresno, California, in March 1924, cited in Clark and Chase, *Elements of the Modern Building and Loan*, 329–31.

Our associations are . . . Report of Miss Ann E. Rae at the 35th Annual Convention of the New York State League of Savings and Loan Associations (1922), as cited in Clark and Chase, *Elements of the Modern Building and Loan*, 4.

Planned thrift is . . . "Peacetime Bonds," *Home Life* (Niles, MI: Niles Federal Savings and Loan Association, October 1945), 13.

. . . there is no . . . Charles O. Hennessy, president of the Franklin Society for Home Building and Saving and chairman of the Federal Legislative Committee of the U.S. League of Local Building and Loan Association, testimony before the Committee on Banking and Currency of the U.S. House of Representatives, October 31, 1919, regarding the Federal Building Loan Act (Washington, DC: Government Printing Office, 1919), 4.

There is one . . . Clark and Chase, *Elements of the Modern Building and Loan*, 1–2.

Thrift doesn't . . . "Savings Share Stamps" booklet of the Walton Co-operative Savings & Loan Association, Walton, New York, 1931.

Thrift, industry . . . "Pass Book Owernership is Thrift," advertisement, Corry (Pennsylvania) Building and Loan Association, May 1931, in booklet titled *Building a Greater Corry* (Corry, PA: Corry Building and Loan Association, May 1931), 1.

Two qualities . . . *Savings and Loan Annals, 1959*, p. 38.

We're a service . . . *Savings and Loan Annals, 1969*, 43.

When we discuss . . . Henry S. Rosenthal, "Possibilities of the Building and Loan Movement," in *The Second Convention of the International Congress of Building and Loan Associations* (Cincinnati: American Building Association News Publishing Co., 1915), 30–31.

Your efforts . . . Charles E. Clark, president of the United States League of Local Building and Loan Associations, "Our Plain Duty to the Building and Loan Association Movement of the United States," address to the League's annual convention, December 5, 1914, reprinted in *The American Building Association News* 34, no. 12 (December 1914), in *American Building Association News 1914*, 542.

43

As the bank . . . Ontario Credit Union League, *Outline for Credit Union Study Groups in the Province of Ontario* (Toronto: Ministry of Agriculture, 1942), 3.

"But I can't" . . . Frank Marshall White, "The Story of a Debt," *The World's Work* 13, no. 3 (January 1912), in *The World's Work* 23, November 1911 to April 1912 (Garden City, NY: Doubleday, Page & Company, 1912), 348.

. . . a cooperative . . . Cited in J. Carroll Moody and Gilbert C. Fite, *The Credit Union Movement: Origins and Development, 1850–1970* (Lincoln: University of Nebraska Press, 1971), 36.

The credit union in . . . Joseph S. Snider, *Credit Unions in Massachusetts* (Cambridge: Harvard University Press, 1939), 68.

The Credit Union National . . . Roy F. Bergengren, *Crusade: The Fight for Economic Democracy* (New York: Exposition Press, 1952), 245.

Credit unions offer . . . President Harry S. Truman, speech to the Credit Union National Association, Madison, Wisconsin, May 14, 1950.

Published online by the American Presidency Project: http://64.233.169.104/search?q=cache:aG0m4-DhLa8J:www.presidency.ucsb.edu/ws/index.php%3Fpid%3D13493+Harry+S.+Truman,+Credit+Union+National+Association,+Madison&hl=en&ct=clnk&cd=1&gl=us

DO YOU KNOW . . . William Trufant Foster, *Loan Sharks and Their Victims*, Public Affairs Pamphlet, no. 39, 1940.

7. *During one of* . . . A description of Bergengren's activities in Moody and Fite, *Credit Union Movement*, 111.

. . . from 1940 . . . Review article by Herman E. Kroos, *The Business History Review* 46, no. 2 (Summer 1972): 257.

. . . the greatest . . . Cited in Moody and Fite, *Credit Union Movement*, 166.

Harold Grant . . . Cited in John W. Zerillo and Ted Desveaux, *A History of the Maine Credit Union Movement* (Portland: Maine Credit Union League, 2004), 33, 102.

I really believe . . . Cited in Bill Sloan, *Credit Where Credit Is Due: A History of the Credit Union Movement in Texas, 1913–1984* (Dallas: Taylor Publishing Company, 1984), 2. Several years earlier, on May 25, 1929, in a speech to the Georgia Credit Union League meeting in Warm Springs, then New York Governor Franklin D. Roosevelt, referring to the "injunction against usury," spoke of "the biblical character of the credit union." As cited in Bergengren, *Crusade*, 141.

In February [1928] . . . Bergengren, *Crusade*, 121.

. . . loans [by credit unions] . . . Arthur B. Chapin, *Credit Unions: Statement and Suggestions in Regard to Organizing and Managing a Credit Union in Massachusetts* (Boston: Wright and Potter Printing Co., 1911).

Members only . . . *Credit Where Credit Is Due*, 37.

. . . a minor Apostle . . . Cited in Bergengren, *Crusade*, 137, 166.

Mr. Filene . . . Roy F. Bergengren, *Credit Union North America* (New York: Southern Publishers, 1940), 94.

My notes . . . Bergengren, *Crusade*, 113.

Nearly 34 million . . . *Wall Street Journal*, June 22, 1977, cited in Sloan, *Credit Where Credit Is Due*, 273.

Next to the . . . Cited in Sloan, *Credit Where Credit Is Due*, 337–38.

The People's Banks . . . "Conference Decides to Ask Congress to Make Credit Unions National Institutions," *New York Times*, June 1, 1919.

The real "keystone" . . . Wolff, *People's Banks*, 80–81, 398.

A small, shabby . . . Roy F. Bergengren, *CUNA Emerges* (Madison, WI: Credit Union National Association, 1935), 23.

They [credit unions] . . . Editors, "Loaning Money on Character," *The World's Work*, 43, no. 4 (February 1922): 355.

Though the salary-loan . . . Samuel McCune Lindsay, "Loans on Salaries and Wages," *The American Review of Reviews* (December 1908), in *The American Review of Reviews* 38 (July–December 1908): 725.

We are not . . . Bergengren, *Crusade*, 290.

We shall . . . Bergengren, *CUNA Emerges*, 198.

What are the . . . Arthur H. Ham and Leonard G. Robinson, *A Credit Union Primer* (New York: Division of Remedial Loans, Russell Sage Foundation, 1914), 13. This and other excerpts of the pamphlet are reprinted in Harold G. Moulton, *The Financial Organization of Society* (Chicago: University of Chicago Press, 1921), 709–14.

When you are . . . Cited in Morris R. Neifeld, *Cooperative Consumer Credit* (New York: Arno Press, 1979; first published 1936), 96.

44

Aid from . . . Clayton Colman Hall, ed., *Baltimore: Its History and Its People* (New York: Lewis Historical Publishing Company, 1912), 1:650.

America has . . . Thomas Greenwood, *Public Libraries: A History of the Movement and a Manual for the Organization and Management of Rate-Supported Libraries* (London: Cassell & Company, 1891), 524, 527.

As a part . . . Report of the Henry Watson Children's Aid Society of Baltimore, *The Library Journal* 25, no. 1 (January 1900): 32.

The avowed . . . Greenwood, *Public Libraries*, 22, 85.

Born in North . . . George William Brown, "Oration," in *The Enoch Pratt Free Library of Baltimore City* (Baltimore: Isaac Friedenwald, 1886), 76.

Boxes of books . . . Hall, *Baltimore*, 650.

Enoch Pratt . . . Henry P. Goddard, "Some Distinguished Marylanders I Have Known," *Maryland Historical Magazine* 4, no. 1 (March 1909): 40.

The first requisite . . . Carnegie, *Gospel of Wealth and Other Timely Essays*, 21–22, 29–30.

From the beginning . . . Josephine Adams Rathbone, "The Pratt Institute School of Library Science," *The Library Journal*, November 15, 1921, in *The Library Journal* (January–December 1921): 46:935.

His large fortune . . . "A Sketch of the Founder," in *The Enoch Pratt Free Library of Baltimore City*, 121. Charles Pratt died on September 17, 1896.

I like a . . . Cited in Peter Cowell, *Liverpool Public Libraries* (Liverpool: Free Public Library, 1903), 177, 181.

In 1888 . . . Twenty-Fifth Annual Report of the Board of Trustees of the Free Public Library of the Town of Watertown, Massachusetts (Watertown: Fred. G. Barker, 1893), 24.

The Junto . . . Elbert Hubbard, "Benjamin Franklin," in *Little Journeys* (New York: Wm. W. Wise & Co., 1916), 3:47. Franklin discusses starting the first "Public Subscription Library" in Philadelphia, and the fact that it was soon "imitated by other Towns and in other Provinces," in his *Autobiography*. See Franklin, *Works*, 1379–80.

The Public Library . . . Report from the Carnegie Free Library of Portland, Indiana, in W. E. Henry (ed.), *Municipal and Institutional Libraries of Indiana* (St. Louis: The Louisiana Purchase Exposition Commission of Indiana, 1904), 121.

The result of . . . Carnegie, *Gospel of Wealth and Other Timely Essays*, 27.

45

As for us . . . Lisa Robertson, "Soft Architecture: A Manifesto," 1999, in Robertson, *Occasional Work and Seven Walks from the Office for Soft Architecture: Essays* (Toronto: Coach House Books, 2006).

Besides the look . . . Russ Baruffi, *The College Hill Independent*, 20, published weekly, online, by students from Brown University and the Rhode Island School of Design. Search terms: russ baruffi college hill independent.

The clothing swap . . . Melena Ryzik, "Walk a Mile in My Shoes (and My Shirt)," *New York Times*, July 6, 2006.

Stores selling . . . Hillary Chura, "Savings Outweigh Any Stigma at Upscale Consignment Shops," *New York Times*, June 24, 2006.

There is a . . . Benjamin R. Andrews, *Economics of the Household* (New York: Macmillan Company, 1924), 419.

Thrift Shop. . . *Journal of Home Economics*, 1928.

"To assist". . . "For the Worthy Poor," *New York Times*, January 18, 1897. See also "Clothing for the Poor," *New York Times*, October 23, 1894.

We Turn Your . . . Motto of the Junior League Thrift Shop of Washington, DC, 1931, cited in Susan Strasser, *Waste and Want: A Social History of Trash* (New York: Henry Holt and Company, 2002), 279.

PART FIVE

I believe that . . . Roy F. Bergengren, *I Speak for Joe Doakes: For Co-operation at Home and Among Nations* (New York: Harper & Brothers Publishers, 1945), 4.

We call . . . Bergengren, *I Speak for Joe Doakes*, 92.

46

Asking for the . . . First International Thrift Congress: Milan, 26–31 October 1924 (Milan: Organizing Committee of the Congress, 1925), 11.

The Fourth . . . A history 50 Years: International Savings Bank Institute (Geneva: International Savings Bank Institute, 1974), 22, 24.

France: . . . "International Thrift Chronicle," *Thrift*, 14, no. 12 (1939): 314–16.

I have met . . . Bergengren, *CUNA Emerges*, 196–97.

International Exchange of . . . *Thrift* 14, no. 1 (1939).

It has been . . . Second International Thrift Congress (1930), 140.

A library . . . *World Thrift* 1, no. 2 (1926): 13.

No fewer than . . . "The Nest Egg," Letter to the Editor, *The Times*, October 31, 1933. See also "World Thrift Day," *The Times*, October 31, 1933.

. . . the [Second] . . . "World Thrift," *The Times*, October 8, 1929.

That, in this . . . First International Thrift Congress, 262.

This was the . . . World Thrift 2, no. 1 (1927): 5. See also Milton W. Harrison, "Do You Know What Thrift Is?" in Jackson, Deming, and Bemis, *Thrift and Success*, 3–8.

Thrift, it is . . . "World Thrift Day," *The Times*, October 26, 1938.

Thrift, precisely . . . First International Thrift Congress, 144.

Thrift Propaganda . . . J. Knox, *Triumph of Thrift*, 282.

What is needed . . . "A Thrift Exhibition," *The Times*, October 12, 1929, See also, regarding the London conference, "The Growth of Thrift," *The Times*, October 9, 1929; and "The Prince on Thrift," *The Times*, October 12, 1929.

47

American Home Economics . . . National Thrift News 10, no. 1 (April 1928): 4.

Arrangements are . . . The Times, September 1, 1883. The latest public reference I found for the National Thrift Society is in 1908: "At its 30th anniversary meeting on Saturday the National Thrift Society decided to offer 30 pounds (in sums of 15, 10, and 5) to the three men or women who produced the three best records of industrial thrift (in respect to savings) covering a period of not less than 30 years. Members of friendly and building societies and depositors in Post Office or trustee savings banks in any part of the British Isles will be eligible for the prizes." See "Rewards for Thrift," *The Times*, April 13, 1908.

Careful consideration . . . Letter of Hillegeist to Wiley, December 28, 1926, found in the papers of Anna K. Wiley, located in the Library of Congress, available online as a part of the Library of Congress' collection, "Prosperity and Thrift: The Coolidge Era and the Consumer Economy, 1921–1929."

Children, this . . . "Thrift Week, January 17, 1927," notes for a talk to children, found in the papers of Anna K. Wiley.

. . . the Colorado . . . *The Girl Scout Leader* 3, no. 12 (December 1926): 1.

Dr. Earl Wilfley . . . "Dr. Wilfley to Lead in Thrift Campaign Covering Country," *Washington Post*, January 9, 1927.

Efforts are made . . . Rosenthal, *Cyclopedia of Building, Loan and Savings Associations*, 56–57.

Fargo, N.D. . . . *National Thrift News* 9, no. 2 (September 1927): 2.

The Home Economics . . . Woolman, *Clothing*, 233.

I do want . . . *Savings and Loan Annals, 1959*, 36–37.

If literature . . . *Savings and Loan Annals, 1961*, 179.

In more than . . . "Start Week's Thrift Drive," *New York Times*, January 17, 1920.

Intelligence— . . . Woolman, *Clothing*, 218, 220.

It is astonishing . . . "50,000 Teachers To Gather Here," *New York Times*, May 14, 1916.

It is with . . . Letter from Herman B. Wells, chairman of the National Thrift Committee, June 29, 1966.

It was decided . . . Christine Newark, "Economic Basis of the Family," *Marriage and Family Living* 12, no. 4 (November 1950): 144. This journal was published by the National Council on Family Relations.

A 1965 or 1966 memorandum from the National Thrift Committee reports as one of its program highlights since about 1950: "Educational kits for both primary and secondary schools, accepted by state boards of education, with referrals to local schools. Thousands of such kits have been circulated." See "Resume of the National Thrift Committee," memorandum, n.d. (probably 1965 or 1966), p. 1, courtesy of The Lilly Library, Indiana University, Bloomington, Indiana.

Knowing that . . . Letter of Charles H. Hillegeist of the Thrift Committee for the District of Columbia to Mrs. Anna K. Wiley of Washington, DC, December 23, 1926.

A luncheon was . . . "Plan for Thrift Week," *New York Times*, December 24, 1919. See also "Draw Up Decalogue as Frugality Guide," *New York Times*, October 19, 1919.

Miss Hilda Wendt . . . "Michigan City Girl Wins Essay Contest," *New York Times*, April 18, 1926. The winning essays from a statewide thrift essay contest among students in 1916 in Ohio are in *The Ohio Education Monthly* 65, no. 7 (July 1916): 299–304.

Mrs. T. J. Matheson . . . "State Thrift Chairman Issues Plans for Thrift Week Observance," *The Atlanta Constitution*, November 21, 1926.

The national character . . . *Annual Report, 1926: National Thrift Week* (New York: National Thrift Committee of the YMCA, n.d.), 4.

The National Thrift . . . "Resume of the National Thrift Committee," 1.

The National Thrift Committee was organized by the YMCA in November of 1917; its founding (and long-time) chairman was Adolph Lewisohn. See "Message from the Chairman," *National Thrift News* 10, no. 1 (April 1928): 2.

. . . the national thrift movement . . . Cited in "The Progress of Science: The Convocation Week Meeting and Columbia University," *The Scientific Monthly* 4, no. 1 (January 1917): 95.

National Thrift Week . . . "Thrift Week," *New York Times*, January 16, 1921. See also, "Thrift Week Opens, Honoring Franklin," *New York Times*, January 17, 1921.

A new Thrift . . . "Thrift Exhibit Will Be Used at Conventions," *National Thrift News* 10, no. 2 (September 1928): 4.

Pacific Coast . . . "High Spots in 1928 Observance of National Thrift Week," *National Thrift News* 10, no. 1 (April 1928): 3.

A penny bank . . . From an essay about the Trinidadian Henry Sylvester Williams, a leader of the Pan African Movement of the late nineteenth and early twentieth centuries, in *The Illustrated London News*, March 12, 1881: "During this time Williams earned some money through lecturing for the Church of England Temperance Society. This took him to all parts of the British Isles speaking under the auspices of parish churches. He also lectured on thrift for the National Thrift Society whose chairman, Dr Greville Walpole, wrote that William's 'heroic struggle to make ends meet won his admiration because the little he was able to earn by his lectures simply defrayed the cost of living.'"

See Deborah John, "Henry Sylvester Williams," Web site of *Race and History* (raceandhistory.com), posted May 26, 2000.

A society . . . Lord John Manners, 1877, cited in J. Hennicker Heaton, "The Postal Savings-Banks of Great Britain," *The Arena* 33, no. 182 (January 1905), in B. O. Flower, ed., *The Arena* (Trenton, NJ: Albert Brandt, 1905), 33:36.

Some hundred . . . *Tenth Anniversary Report of the National Thrift Movement* (New York: National Thrift Committee of the YMCA, 1927), 14.

. . . this year's . . . "National Thrift Week," *New York Times*, January 15, 1922. (The letter is dated December 31, 1921; it was published on January 15, 1922.) Regarding Thrift Week 1922, see also "National Thrift Week," *New York Times*, January 15, 1922.

Goodell's letter says the YMCA assumed sponsorship of the thrift initiative in 1918, but many other sources, including numerous sources from the YMCA itself, state that 1917 was in fact the year that the YMCA became the leader of this initiative.

Goodall also writes:

Mr. [Charles H.] Norton admittedly was the originator of the National Thrift Day idea. Later, at the request of many business organizations, the Young Men's Christian Association . . . accepted responsibility for this patriotic, educational movement . . . For months [Mr. J. Henry Smythe, of New York City's Thrift Committee of 100] has generously contributed time and ideas to thrift headquarters [at the YMCA] . . .

Charles H. Norton was born in 1851 and lived in Philadelphia (according to Goodell's letter to the *Times*) and, beginning in 1922, Hartford, Connecticut. Norton was the inventor of heavy-duty precision grinding machines that became integral to automobile and other modern industrial technologies. He died in 1942.

The thrift campaign . . . "Business Men Urge Thrift By Workers," *The Atlanta Constitution*, January 22, 1920.

. . . [to] make . . . *To Make Thrift a Happy Habit*, U.S. Treasury Department, 1918, cited in Peter Tufano and Daniel Schneider, "Reinventing Savings Bonds," Working Paper (Draft), March 30, 2005.

The United Stewardship . . . "The International Committee of Young Men's Christian Associations of North America," in Samuel

McCrea Cavert, ed., *The Churches Allied for Common Tasks: 1916–1920* (New York: Federal Council of the Churches of Christ in America, 1921), 291.

We hail the . . . Review of the first issue of *Thrift*, the publication of the National Thrift Society, in *The Practical Teacher* 2, no. 3 (May 1882): 156. T. Bowden Green was among the contributors to this first issue. See also "Thrift," *Illustrated London News*, January 1882, reprinted in George Augustus Sala, *Living London* (London: Remington & Co., 1882), 22–23.

What Constitutes . . . "National Thrift Week Dated For 16th Annual Observation," *New York Times*, December 25, 1932.

48

ARE YOU HELPING . . . Cited in Isaac F. Marcosson, *The War After the War* (New York: John Lane Company, 1917), 151. See also "New Thrift Posters," *The Times*, July 15, 1916.

The biggest thing . . . Ellis Parker Butler, *Robinson Crusoe and Thrift Stamps* (Newark: National War Savings Committee for New Jersey, n.d.).

The Birth of . . . John Muir, *The Birth of American Thrift* (New York: John Muir, 1917)—booklet encouraging public participation in the First Liberty Loan. Through the Liberty Loan, citizens purchased government-issued bonds to finance the war effort.

BUSINESS AS . . . Cited in Thomas Nixon Carver, *War Thrift* (New York: Oxford University Press, 1919), 58.

The commission is . . . Charles Lathrop Pack, "Urban and Suburban Food Production," *Annals of the American Academy of Political and Social Science* 74 (November 1917): 204.

A dollar down . . . Ad for "Partial Payment Plans" for buying Liberty Bonds, 1917, cited in Muir, *Birth of American Thrift*, 12.

During the war . . . Mark Junge, *A View From Center Street: Tom Carrigen's Casper* (Casper, WY: McMurry Foundation, 2003), 218. Junge also writes (p. 218) that Casper citizens during World War II were both "encouraged to buy government bonds" and "asked to save ten percent of their income."

Every Savings . . . Leaflet describing the "Save Your Way to Victory" campaign, Great Britain, November 1939, cited in "More Savings Groups: Thrift Encouraged by New Bonds," *The Times*, November 25, 1939.

I hereby request . . . Cited in Walter Greenough, *The War Purse of Indiana: The Five Liberty Loans and War Savings and Thrift Campaigns in Indiana During the World War* (Indianapolis: Indiana Historical Commission, 1922), 232.

If anyone asked . . . Cited in "National Thrift," *The Times*, June 26, 1924.

In times of . . . Lucy M. Alexander and Fanny Walker Yeatman, *Meat for Thrifty Meals*, Farmers' Bulletin, no. 1908 (Washington, DC: Bureau of Home Economics, U.S. Department of Agriculture, 1942), 1.

It was, he . . . Cited in "National Thrift: Growth of Savings Movement," *The Times*, November 7, 1928.

It would certainly . . . "Three Years of War Savings: Plans for Peace Thrift," *The Times*, March 12, 1919.

The National Savings . . . "The New Thrift Campaign," *The Times*, January 17, 1920. See also "Thrift Still Needed," *The Times*, January 17, 1920.

Nationwide housewives . . . Mary Martha Thomas, *Riveting and Rationing in Dixie: Alabama Women and the Second World War* (Tuscaloosa: University of Alabama Press, 1987), 99–100.

Originally introduced . . . "National Thrift," *The Times*, July 4, 1925.

Perhaps the most . . . Greenough, *War Purse of Indiana*, 228.

The smallest denomination . . . Greenough, *War Purse of Indiana*, 203–6, 208–9, 211–12, 201.

Wage war . . . *War Emergency Bulletin* 598, in cooperation with the New York State War Council (March 1943): 1.

WORK HARD . . . Cited in Marcosson, *War After the War*, 139.

YOU CAN HELP . . . Advertisement appearing in the *Birmingham News*, May 3, 1943, reproduced in Thomas, *Riveting and Rationing in Dixie*, 83. Another ad (reproduced on p. 52) appearing in the *Birmingham News* in 1944 asks, "Did someone say this is a *man's* war?" and answers the question by showing a busy woman in an office at a typewriter above the caption, "Saving the Nation by Saving Time."

49

An Act to . . . Cited in Sara Louisa Oberholtzer, "School Savings Banks," United States Bureau of Education *Bulletin* no. 46 (Washington, DC: Government Printing Office, 1915), 15.

How do you . . . Annie E. Moore, Thrift Series, *Pennies and Plans: A First Reader* (New York: Macmillan Company, 1919), 1-2.

If this be . . . Blackley, *Thrift and Independence*, 139.

In every area . . Blake, *Century of Thrift*, 36.

Lessons in Thrift . . . Howard R. Driggs, *Live Language Lessons: Teachers' Manual* (Chicago: University Publishing Company, 1921), 119-120.

The need for . . . Arthur H. Chamberlain and James F. Chamberlain, *Thrift and Conservation: How to Teach It* (Philadelphia: J. B. Lippincott Company, 1919), 17. See also Arthur H. Chamberlain, "Thrift Education in the Public Schools," in *Thrift*, Proceedings of the Committee on Thrift Education (Pittsburgh, PA: National Council of Education, July 29, 1918).

A number of . . . J. A. Bexell, *First Lessons in Business* (Philadelphia: J. B. Lippincott & Company, 1919), 147.

Patriotism: . . . *Thrift in Education* (Los Angeles: Los Angeles Banks School Saving Association, 1931), 6, as cited in Alfred L. Roe, "Bankers and Thrift in the Age of Affluence," *American Quarterly* 17, no. 4 (Winter 1965): 626.

The Rochester plan . . . Jack W. Speare, *In Rochester: 100 Years Ago and Now* (Rochester: Rochester Savings Bank, 1931), 39.

Sceptics who . . . "Penny Is Said to Start Child on Road to Thrift," *New York Times*, April 4, 1962.

September—Punctuality . . . Teresa M. Lenney, "An Outline of a Method By Which the Principles of Thrift May Be Taught in Our Public Schools," appearing as an appendix in Chamberlain, *Thrift and Conservation*, 219.

There is a . . . Abby Porter Leland, *A City Reader for the Fourth Year* (New York: Charles E. Merrill Company, 1916), 176.

Thrift may . . . J. O. Engleman, *Moral Education in School and Home* (Chicago: Benj. H. Sanborn & Co., 1918), 221.

To be sure . . . William G. Sutcliffe and Lindley A. Bond, *Savings Banks and Savings Department Management* (New York: Harper & Brothers Publishers, 1930), 351.

Use of our . . . Chamberlain, *Thrift and Conservation*, 83.

Whereas, Believing . . . Resolution passed by the National Congress of Mothers and Parent-Teacher Associations, 1923, reprinted in Albig, *History of School Savings Banking*, 32.

The Women's . . . The letter is from the "Housekeepers' Alliance 1922–23" folder in the Anna Kelton Wiley Papers.

Always taking out . . . Editor (n.n.), *Proverbs; or, The Manual of Wisdom*, 2nd ed. (London: Tabart & Co., 1804), 3.

Ask thy purse . . . Scottish, cited in Stephen L. Spandoudis, "Quotations #5: Proverbial Wisdom," TheOtherPages.org, Quotations Home Page. Available at http://www.theotherpages.org/quote-05a.html, accessed Feb. 5, 2008.

The bless'd source . . . Lindley Murray, *Introduction to the English Reader* (Baltimore: Cushing & Jewett, 1823), 124.

The best throw . . . *Proverbs; or, The Manual*, 86.

Better to go to bed . . . A. W. Moore, *The Folk-Lore of the Isle of Man* (London: D. Nutt, 1891), 187.

Better to say here . . . Thomas Fuller, ed., *Gnomologia: Adagies and Proverbs* (London: B. Barker, A. Bettesworth, & C. Hitch, 1732), 34.

Beware of little . . . *Proverbs; or, The Manual*, 13.

The borrower is . . . Proverbs 22:7b (KJV).

Buy what thou hast . . . *Proverbs; or, The Manual*, 13.

Buying a thing too . . . *Proverbs; or, The Manual*, 16.

By sowing . . . Agesilaus of Spartacited in John C. Shepard, ed., "Frugality," *Giga Quotes*. Available at http://www.giga-usa.com/quotes/topics/frugality_t001.html, accessed Feb. 5, 2008.

Charity gives . . . Cited in Henry W. Ruoff, *Leaders of Men, or, Types and Principles of Success* (Springfield, MA: King-Richardson Co., 1903), 501.

Charity is the chief . . . *Proverbs; or, The Manual*, 17.

Creditors have better . . . *Proverbs; or, The Manual*, 17.

Cut your Coat . . . Fuller, *Gnomologia*, 46. This saying may date from the sixth to fourteenth centuries.

Debt is a heavy . . . Fuller, *Gnomologia*, 47.

Debt is the worst . . . Fuller, *Gnomologia*, 47.

Debtors are liars . . . Fuller, *Gnomologia*, 47.18.

Despise not the day . . . Cited as an "old adage" in *Boston Five Cents Savings Bank*, 26.

Diligence is . . . *Proverbs; or, The Manual*, 18. In *Don Quixote*, Cervantes uses this saying in chapter 63.

Do not buy what . . . Cato the Censor, as quoted by Seneca, *Epistoloe Ad Lucilium*, number 94, cited in Shepard, "Cato (Marcus Porcius Cato "the Elder")," *Giga Quotes*. Available at http://www.giga-usa.com/quotes/authors/marcus_porcius_cato_2_a002.html, accessed Feb. 5, 2008.

Do not overspend . . . Holy Qu'ran, 6: 141.

Do what you have to . . . Vicesimus Knox, *Elegant Extracts* (London: C. & J. Riverton, 1824), 739.

Early to bed . . . *Proverbs; or, The Manual*, 20. Benjamin Franklin's shorter version became popular.

Economy is the foundation . . . *Bahá'í Scriptures*, p. 453, cited in J.E. Esslemont, *Bahá'u'lláh and the New Era: An Introduction to the Bahá'í Faith* (Wilmette, IL: Bahá'í Publishing Trust, 1950), 102. 'Abdu'l-Bahá is the son of and successor to Baha'u'llah, the founder and prophet of the Baha'i religion. 'Abdu'l-Bahá was born in 1844 and died in 1921.

Economy is wealth. Cited as a well-known old adage in many places, including in Lewis Harvie Blair, *Unwise Laws* (New York: Putnam's Sons, 1886), 62.

Economy is the wealth . . . Henry Davidoff, *A World Treasury of Proverbs from Twenty-Five Languages* (New York: Random House, 1946), 114. Stated as "Economy, the poor man's mint" in Martin F. Tupper, *Proverbial Philosophy* (New York: Wiley & Putnam, 1846), 140.

Eident [Thrifty, diligent] youth makes . . . Alexander Hislop, *The Proverbs of Scotland* (Edinburgh: Alexander Hislop & Co., 1868), 86.

Employ thyself . . . Cleobulus quoted in *Proverbs; or, The Manual*, 118.

An empty bag . . . Samuel Smiles writes: "The proverb says that 'an empty bag cannot stand upright'; neither can a man who is in debt." See Smiles, *Self-Help*, 282.

Benjamin Franklin published three different versions of this proverb: "An empty bag cannot stand upright" (1740); "An empty sack can hardly stand upright; but if it does, 'tis a stout one" (1750); and "'Tis hard for an empty bag to stand upright" (1758). See Carl Van Doren, "Concluding Paper," *Meet Dr. Franklin* (Philadelphia: Franklin Institute, 1943), 233.

Enough is as good . . . *Proverbs; or, The Manual*, 20.

Evil gotten . . . *Proverbs; or, The Manual*, 21.

Extend your feet . . . Arabic cited in Sulayman Hayyim, *Persian-English Proverbs* (Tehran: Beroukhim, 1956), 72.

Feast today . . . Wolfgang Mieder, Stewart A. Kingsbury, and Kelsie B. Harder eds., *Dictionary of American Proverbs* (New York: Oxford University Press, 1992), 204.

First deserve . . . *Proverbs; or, The Manual*, 24.

Fly the pleasure . . . *Proverbs; or, The Manual*, 23.

The foot of the owner . . . *Proverbs; or, The Manual*, 97.

A Fop [clotheshorse] of Fashion . . . Fuller, *Gnomologia*, 5.

Frae [From] . . . Cited in Sandy Stevenson, "Scottish Proverbs (F)," *Tour Scotland*. Available at http://fife.50megs.com/scottish-proverbsf.html, accessed Feb. 6, 2008.

Frugality embraces all . . . Marcus Tullius Cicero, John Edward King, trans, *Tusculan Disputations* (New York: G. P. Putnam's Sons, 1927), 245.

Frugality is equal . . . Solomon Ibn Gabirol, *Mibhar ha-Peninim Choice of Pearls,* about 1050.

Frugality is a great . . . Cicero, *Paradoxa*, VI, iii, about 45 BCE: "*Magnum vectigal est parsimonia*" quoted in John Devoe Belton, *A Literary Manual of Foreign Quotations* (New York: G. P. Putnam's Sons, 1891), 106. Cicero's dates are 106–43 BCE. Also, "Thrift is good revenue," in Henry G. Bohn, ed., *A Hand-Book of Proverbs* (London: George Bell and Sons, 1888), 530. Also, from *The Times* (London), October 10, 1930: "Thrift which is not only a great virtue but also 'a great revenue,' as Tacitus [*sic*] told us long ago when he wrote *magnum vectigal est parsimonia*." For a famous incident in the history of British oratory, involving Edmund Burke's use of this maxim, see Chauncey A. Goodrich, ed., *Select British Eloquence* (New York: Harper & Brothers, 1853), 207.

Frugality is misery . . . Publilius Syrus, *Sententiae*, number 223 cited in Henry Davidoff, *A World Treasury of Proverbs from Twenty-Five Languages* (New York: Random House, 1946), 114.

Frugality may be termed . . . Samuel Johnson, *The Rambler*, number 57, October 2, 1750, cited in Samuel Johnson, *The Works of Samuel Johnson LL.D.: With an Essay on His Life by Arthur Murphy* (New York: Alexander V. Blake, 1896), 97.

The generous man . . . Dutch, Danish. Dwight Edwards Marvin, *Curiosities in Proverbs* (New York: G. P. Putnam's Sons, 1916), 139.

Give no great credit . . . *Proverbs; or, The Manual*, 27.

Giving much . . . *Proverbs; or, The Manual*, 26.

Go to the ant . . . Proverbs 6:6–8.

God keeps him . . . *Proverbs; or, The Manual*, 29.

God supplies him . . . *Proverbs; or, The Manual*, 28.

Good and quickly . . . *Proverbs; or, The Manual*, 26.

Good harvests . . . Proverbs; or, The Manual, 28.

Good husbandry . . . Proverbs; or, The Manual, 27.

A good name . . . Proverbs 22:1–2.

Great businesses . . . Proverbs; or, The Manual, 26.

Hand in use is . . . Cited in Wallace Notestein, *The Scot in History* (New Haven: Yale University Press, 1947), 280.

The happiness of . . . Thales, quoted in *Proverbs; or, The Manual*, 138.

The happy are . . . Solon, quoted in *Proverbs; or, The Manual*, 138.

Haste makes waste. . . John Heywood, *Proverbs* (London: George Bell and Sons, 1874; first published 1546), 6.

Haste makes waste, and waste makes . . . Proverbs; or, The Manual, 40.

He becometh . . . Proverbs 10:4.

He is a great . . . Proverbs; or, The Manual, 35.

He is the only . . . Proverbs; or, The Manual, 34.

He is richest . . . Socrates, quoted in *Proverbs; or, The Manual*, 120.

He is well . . . Democritus, quoted in *Proverbs; or, The Manual*, 120.

He'll never be a slave . . . Cited in Knox, *Triumph of Thrift*, 23, 336. This saying may date from 65–8 BCE: "He will always be slave, who does not know how to live with a little." See Horace, *Epistles* Book 1, letter 10.

He only is idle . . . Socrates quoted in *Proverbs; or, The Manual*, 121.

He only is rich . . . Proverbs; or, The Manual, 38.

He that borrows . . . Bohn, *Hand-Book*, 239.

He that by the plough . . . Proverbs; or, The Manual, 33. Benjamin Franklin also incorporated this proverb into *Poor Richard's Almanac* and *The Way to Wealth*.

He that goes a borrowing . . . Proverbs; or, The Manual, 39.

He that sleeps . . . Lord Derby, in "Lord Derby on Thrift," *The Times*, January 17, 1880; and cited earlier by Samuel Johnson in *The Adventurer*, no. 41, March 27, 1753. See *The Works of Samuel Johnson* (London: F. C. and J. Riverton, 1823), 11:388–89. Also cited in Robert Christy, *Proverbs, Maxims and Phrases* (New York: Putnam's Sons, 1887), 279.

He that spends . . . Adapted from "He that dothe more expende, thanne his goodes wyll extende, meruayle it shall not be, thoughe he be greved with povertee." See Skeat, *Book of Husbandry,* 99.

He that tilleth . . . Proverbs 28:19–20.

He that would thrive . . . Benjamin Franklin, discussing his wife in his *Autobiography*, cites this adage as "an English Proverb" (see Bigelow, *Autobiography of Benjamin Franklin*, 210). In 1562, John Heywood says, "And he that would thrive, must ask leave of his wife," in *Proverbs and Epigrams*, 28. Also, from *The Book of Husbandry* of 1534: "For there is an olde common sayenge, that seldom doth the housebande thryve, withoute the leve of his wyfe." See Skeat, *Book of Husbandry*, 93.

He who depends . . . Proverbs; or, The Manual, 34.

He who pays . . . Proverbs; or, The Manual, 37.

He who promises . . . Proverbs; or, The Manual, 33.

He who trifles . . . Proverbs; or, The Manual, 34.

He who will thrive . . . Proverbs; or, The Manual, 30.

He who won't keep . . . See Mary Turner and Ferne Shelton, eds., *Pioneer Proverbs: Wit and Wisdom from Early America* (High Point, NC: Hutcraft, 1971), 8.

I cannot call riches . . . Francis Bacon, "Essay 34, Of Riches," *Essays, Civil and Moral* (1597) in *The Essays of Francis Bacon*, Clark Sutherland Northrup ed. (Boston: Houghton Mifflin, 1908), 110.

Idleness is the enemy . . . Rule 48, *The Rule of St. Benedict* cited in Ralph Louis Woods, *A World Treasury of Religious Quotations* (New York: Hawthorn Books, 1966), 460.

Idleness is the greatest. . . F. Edward Hulme, *Proverb Lore* (London: Elliot Stock, 1906), 210. Hulme cites Chaucer: "Idlenesse is the gate of all harmes."

If a man empties . . . Robert Christy, ed., *Proverbs, Maxims and Phrases of All Ages* (New York: G. P. Putnam's Sons, 1893), 2:180. See also Hulme, *Proverb Lore*, 213. Scores of authors have attributed this saying to Benjamin Franklin, but I can find no place in his actual writings where he says it. But while we're at it, let's reflect briefly on sayings about emptying one's purse into one's head (and into other places).

A German proverb says, "Better an empty purse than an empty head." In *The Ring and the Book* (1868–69), Robert Browning tells of young scholars:

Who gaze at storied portal, statued spire,
And go home with full head but empty purse.

More cynically, in a story called "The Travelling Tutor," published in 1849, we are told: "Find me a young fellow with a full purse and an empty head, and I will give him a full head and an empty purse. I will teach him how to live like a gentleman; and it will not be my fault if he does not die like a beggar."

A poem by George Meredith from 1893 is called "The Empty Purse, A Sermon to Our Later Prodigal Son." It concerns a young spendthrift who, as a result of suffering and humiliation stemming from his "empty purse," finds the wiser path, i.e., the path to thrift. A 1919 lecture by Charles Reynolds Brown, "The Value of an Empty Purse," conveys basically the same story and the same moral. Recall also the more pessimistic assessment reflected in the proverb appearing just above: "Thrift comes too late when th' Purse is grown too low."

So here are the various empty-purse propositions contending for our allegiance: an empty purse can be a good teacher. That good teacher might be too late. An education fills your head but empties your purse. If you must choose between an empty head and an empty purse, choose the latter. Emptying your purse into your head pays off. For my money, the last one—the one that so many have understandably (if apparently wrongly) attributed to Franklin—is the best and the truest.

See Christy, *Proverbs, Maxims and Phrases*, 2:179. Robert Browning, *The Ring and the Book* (New York: Thomas Y. Crowell & Co., 1897), 370. Leicester F. A. Buckingham, "The Travelling Tutor," *The American Review*, no. 16 (April 1849), in *The American Review*, New Series, 3, vol. 9 (New York: Nassau Street, 1849), 350. Mary Sturge Henderson, *George Meredith: Novelist, Poet, Reformer* (London: Methuen & Co., 1907), 48–59. Charles Reynolds Brown, *Yale Talks* (New Haven: Yale University Press, 1919), 24–38.

If rich, be not . . . Socrates quoted in *Proverbs; or, The Manual*, 125.

If you desire . . . Democritus quoted in *Proverbs; or, The Manual*, 122.

If you want . . . This saying has been attributed to American Quakers, but it is cited as a "popular saying" of Kent, England, in Charles Dickens, *All the Year Round: A Weekly Journal*, vol. 22 (London: Chapman & Hall, 1879), 252.

Ill gotten gains . . . Also "Gain ill-gotten is loss." Hulme, *Proverb Lore*, 226.

Independence thrives . . . Edward Counsel, *Maxims: Political, Philosophical, and Moral*, 2nd ed. (Melbourne: A. H. Massina, 1892), 68.

Industry is . . . Hulme, *Proverb Lore*, 209.

It is a disease . . . Bias quoted in *Proverbs; or, The Manual*, 122.

It is equally . . . Diogenes quoted in *Proverbs; or, The Manual*, 124.

It is more desirable . . . Bion quoted in *Proverbs; or, The Manual*, 124.

Keep some till . . . Cited in Christy, *Proverbs, Maxims and Phrases, 1887,* 575.

Keep within . . . Also, "Holde and kepe measure." Also, "Eate within thy tedure [tether]." Also, "After thy faculty or thy honour, make thyne expences, leste thou spende in shorte space that thynge, that thou shouldest lyve by longe." All from Skeat, *Book of Husbandry,* 99.

Keep the wolf from . . . Cited in Ebenezer Cobham Brewer, *Dictionary of Phrase and Fable* (Philadelphia: H. Altemus, 1898), 1309.

Labor conquers . . . Cited in Henry W. Ruoff, *Leaders of Men, or, Types and Principles of Success* (Springfield, MA: King-Richardson Co., 1903), 245.

Let that which is . . . Alfred Henderson, *Latin Proverbs* (London: Sampson Low, Son & Marston, 1869), 380. "*Quod cessat ex reditu, frugalitate suppleatur.*"

Let your expenses never . . . Leon Battista Alberti, *The Family in Renaissance Florence, Book 3, I Libri Della Famiglia,* trans. Renee Neu Watkins (Long Grove, IL: Waveland Press, n.d.), 115.

Light gains . . . "Le petit gain remplit la bourse." Cited in Bohn, *A Hand-Book,* 110.

Lightly come . . . Cited in William Jacobson, ed., *The Works of Robert Sanderson* (Oxford: University Press, 1854), 3:207. Sanderson quotes this maxim as he defines the old word "ding-thrift" as "spendthrift."

Little and often . . . Also "Slender profits and often are better than large ones and seldom." ("Kleiner Profit und oft, is besser wie grosser und selten.") Cited in James Wood, *Dictionary of Quotations* (London: Frederick Warne and Co., 1899), 219. In the eighth century BCE, Hesiod said it this way: "If thou shouldst lay up even a little upon a little, and shouldst do this often, soon would even this become great." See *Works and Days,* line 360. Cited in John Bartlett, *Familiar Quotations,* 10th ed. (New York: Blue Ribbon Books, 1919), 880.

A little Debt . . . Fuller, *Gnomologia,* 9.

Luxury is . . . Anna Steese Richardson, *Adventures in Thrift* (Indianapolis: Bobbs-Merrill, 1916), 1.

Make hay while the . . . Is stated as "Whan the sunne shinneth make hay" in Heywood, *Proverbs and Epigrams,* 6.

A man ought . . . Alcamenes quoted in *Proverbs; or, The Manual,* 115.

Many one blames their . . . Kelly, *Scottish Proverbs,* 250, as cited in *Oxford English Dictionary.*

The master makes . . . *Proverbs; or, The Manual,* 101.

The most certain gain . . . Ellsworth D. Foster, ed., *The World Book* (Chicago: World Book, 1918), 7:5801 (wording slightly revised by David Blankenhorn).

Necessity sharpens . . . Fuller, *Gnomologia,* 150.

Neither a borrower . . . William Shakespeare, *Hamlet* (i, 3).

Never spend money before . . . Thomas Jefferson's first of ten new commandments, cited in George H. Knox, ed., *Thoughts That Inspire* (Des Moine, IA: Personal Help Pub. Co., 1909), 42.

No alchemy . . . *Proverbs; or, The Manual,* 67.

No man is . . . Pythagoras quoted in *Proverbs; or, The Manual,* 129.

Nothing is so hard . . . *Proverbs; or, The Manual,* 67.

Nothing is so precious . . . Socrates quoted in *Proverbs; or, The Manual,* 129.

Oft change . . . Thomas Tusser, *Five Hundred Pointes of Good Husbandrie* (London: Trubner and Co., 1878; based on the edition of 1580; collated with those of 1573 and 1577), 170.

The only means . . . Pythagoras quoted in *Proverbs; or, The Manual,* 138.

Out of debt . . . Fuller, *Gnomologia,* 163.

A penny spared . . . *Proverbs; or, The Manual,* 1.

A place for everything . . . Charles Dickens says this "rule of life" was taught him and he calls it a "fine old-fashioned maxim." See Charles Dickens, *All the Year Round: A Weekly Journal,* vol. 33, March 29, 1884 (London: Charles Dickens and Evans, 1884), 446.

A pound of care . . . Ibid., 3.

Poverty screams . . . Swiss.

Practice thrift . . . Cited in Wood, *Dictionary of Quotations,* 355.

Prefer labour . . . Plato quoted in *Proverbs; or, The Manual,* 131.

Prefer loss . . . Chilo quoted in *Proverbs; or, The Manual,* 131.

Prudent men . . . "Kluge Manner suchen wirthliche Frauen." Cited in Wood, *Dictionary of Quotations,* 219.

Resolve not to be poor . . . Samuel Johnson, letter to James Boswell, December 7, 1782. Cited in James Boswell, *The Life of Samuel Johnson* (London: Everyman's Library, 1992; first published, 1791), 1048.

Riches are like muck . . . *Proverbs; or, The Manual,* 77.

Riches do not . . . Socrates quoted in *Proverbs; or, The Manual,* 133.

Riches well got . . . Fuller, *Gnomologia,* 173.

The right-thinking . . . Yahya ibn Adi, *The Reformation of Morals* (Provo, UT: Brigham Young University Press, 2002), 101 (section 5.9). In his systematic enumeration of the main virtues and vices, and his insistence on steadily striving for moral perfection, Yahya resembles in striking ways a man who lived in another place some eight centuries later, Benjamin Franklin.

A rolling stone . . . Tusser, *Five Hundred Pointes of Good Husbandrie,* 170. As Tusser puts it (in point 77): "The stone that is rolling can gather no mosse, for maister and servant, oft changing is losse." Many years later, Benjamin Franklin did much to popularize this proverb.

Save money . . . Jamaican. Cited in G. Llewellyn Watson, *Jamaican Sayings* (Tallahassee: Florida A & M University Press, 1991), 269.

Save your white . . . Arabic. *Arabic Proverbs.* Available at http://astro.temple.edu/~trad/final-project/arabic-proverbs.html, accessed Feb. 6, 2008.

Saving is . . . Fuller, *Gnomologia,* 174.

Scatter with one . . . Welsh. Cited in Bohn, *A Hand-Book,* 267.

The secret . . . Alfred M. Hitchock, *Junior English Book* (New York: Henry Holt, 1927), 351.

Seest thou . . . Proverbs 22:29.

The slothful man . . . Proverbs 22:13.

A small leak . . . *Proverbs; or, The Manual,* 3.

Spare well . . . Hulme, *Proverb Lore,* 229.

Spending is . . . Russian. Cited in "Proverbs," *GigaQuotes.* Available at http://www.giga-usa.com/quotes/topics/proverbs_t288.html, accessed Feb. 6, 2008.

Sweet to take . . . Manx: *Millish dy ghoaill, agh sharoo dy eeck.* Cited in Moore, *The Folk-Lore of the Isle of Man,* 187.

Take care . . . Cited in Wood, *Dictionary,* 409.

Take heed . . . Adapted from "Take hede to thy charge, kepe measure, and thou shalt be ryche." See Skeat, *Book of Husbandry,* 16.

There are no gains . . . *Proverbs; or, The Manual,* 85.

A thing lasts longer . . . Cited in J. Ellis Barker, *The Rise and Decline of the Netherlands* (London: Smith, Elder, & Co., 1906), 18.

Think of ease . . . *Proverbs; or, The Manual,* 83.

Those who exercise . . . Socrates quoted in *Proverbs; or, The Manual,* 141.

Three littles make . . *Proverbs; or, The Manual,* 86.

Thrift comes too late . . . Cited as an "old Proverb" in "A Translation of the First Epistle of Seneca to Lucilius," *Poetic Miscellanies of Mr. John Rawlet* (London: Edmund Parker, 1687), 108. See Seneca, about 64, *Epistolae Ad Lucilium*, epis. 1, section 5: "*Sera parsimonia in fundo est*."

Also, Hesiod: "At the beginning of the cask and at the end take thy fill, but be saving in the middle; for at the bottom, saving comes too late." Cited in Bartlett, *Familiar Quotations*, 880.

The Portuguese variation on this maxim is *Bolsa vazia o homo sesuda mas tarde*. (An empty purse makes a man wise, but too late.) Cited in James Puckle, *The Club; or, A Grey Cap for a Green Head. Containing Maxims, Advice & Cautions, Being a Dialogue between a Father & Son* (London: Chiswick Press, 1900; first published 1723), 137.

Thrift is better than . . . Christy, *Proverbs, Maxims and Phrases* (1887), 351.

Thrift is half . . . Marzieh Gail, trans., *Sayings of 'Ali*, National Spiritual Assembly of the Baha'is of the United States, World Order 3, no. 10 (Jan. 1938): 390.

Thrift is the Philosopher's . . . Fuller, *Gnomologia*, 219.

Thrift must begin . . . Cited in Wood, *Dictionary*, 485.

Thrifty people spend . . . In 1920 in "The Relation of Thrift to Nation Building," the economist T. N. Carver wrote:

When we realize that thrift consists in spending money wisely, instead of unwisely, we shall very easily see that the thrifty man spends exactly as much money as the thriftless man, provided he has as much money to spend. Moreover, in the long run, the thrifty man will spend more, because he will have more to spend than the thriftless man; and the thrifty community will be a community in which more money is spent than in the thriftless community.

See T. N. Carver, "The Relation of Thrift to Nation Building," "The New American Thrift," *The Annals of the American Academy of Political and Social Science* 87 (1920): 5.

A thrifty wife is . . . C. H. Spurgeon, *The Salt-Cellars* (London: Passmore and Alabaster, 1889), 1:38.

Thrive honestly . . . Hulme, *Proverb Lore*, 226.

Thrush paid for . . . Christy, *Proverbs, Maxims and Phrases,* 224.

Time wasted is . . . Hulme, *Proverb Lore*, 208.

Tine [Lose] thimble . . . Bohn, *Hand-Book*, 258.

Tithe, and be . . . Cited in Cotton Mather, *Essays to Do Good; Addressed to All Christians, Whether in Public or Private Capacities* (New York: American Tract Society, n.d.; first published 1710), 90.

To be engaged . . . Socrates, quoted in *Proverbs; or, The Manual*, 136.

To a good spender . . . Fuller, *Gnomologia*, 254.

Undertake deliberately . . . Bias quoted in *Proverbs; or, The Manual*, 142.

Use it up. . . Repeated often by Zelma Ferdinandt of Anoka, Minnesota, to her niece, Diane Weaver. Miss Ferdinandt was born in about 1914 in Wisconsin. When she opened cans in her kitchen, she saved the tin shavings to use as ornaments on her Christmas tree.

During World War II, several versions of this slogan appear to have been widely disseminated by the U.S. Office of Price Administration, as part of the war conservation effort. See Strasser, *Waste and Want*, 231–32.

Waste not . . . Stated as "Waste makes Want" in Fuller, *Gnomologia*, 236.

The way to . . . Antisthenes quoted in *Proverbs; or, The Manual*.

The ways of thrift . . . Cited in David T. Beito, "To Advance," 591.

We ought to . . . Antisthenes quoted in *Proverbs; or, The Manual*, 144.

Wealth gotten . . . Proverbs 13:11.

Whan thrift and you . . . Heywood, *Proverbs*, 75.

Whan thrift is in . . . Heywood, *Proverbs*, 156.

What you can do . . . *Proverbs; or, The Manual*, 109.

When ill actions . . . Democritus quoted in *Proverbs; or, The Manual*, 145.

Where one blade of grass . . . This phrase has a fine history, much of it clearly related to the idea of thrift. For example, from the year 1562: "The lesse Semperuiuum, that we call thrift or great stone crop, groweth in walles, rockes, mudwalles . . . it hath manye stalkes coming from one root." See *Herbal* II, 133, as cited in OED.

Also, from Jonathan Swift's *Gulliver's Travels* (1726): "And he gave it for his opinion, that whoever could make two ears of corn, or two blades of grass, to grow upon a spot of ground where only one grew before, would deserve better of mankind, and do more essential service to his country, than the whole race of politicians put together."

From Albert Shaw, *The Outlook for the Average Man* (New York: Macmillan, 1907), 61–62, 127.: "Shall we apologize for making two blades of grass grow where one grew before? Shall we look askance at the man who is diligent in business, and whose thrift and energy give him control of productive capital, the use of which ameliorates the condition of an entire neighborhood?"

From William Kniffen, *Savings Bank and Its Practical Work*, 51: "If he who makes two blades of grass grow where only on grew before is entitled to rank as a philanthropist, what shall it be said of the institution [the savings bank] that builds homes and schools and railroads and court houses and asylums where *none* were built before?"

From Andrew Carnegie, *Autobiography*, 144–45.: " . . . he who makes two blades of grass grow where one grew before is a public benefactor . . . "

From Laurence Jones, founder of the Piney Woods School, in *Piney Woods and Its Story*, 151: " . . . to make two blades of grass grow where only one grew before . . . "

Who shall keep well . . . This saying may have originated from Charles Butler's *Feminine Monarchie, or, The Histori of Bees*, 3rd ed., 1634. I got this citation from *Dictionary of Proverbs* (Herfordshire, UK: Wordsworth Editions Limited, 2006), 577. The proverb, in modern English, is also cited in Margaret Warner Worley, *The Honey-Makers* (Chicago: A. C. McClurg, 1899), 344.

Who wastes what he . . . Cited in John B. Leeds, *The Household Budget* (Philadelphia: Innes & Sons, 1917), 183.

Whoever puts . . . Pompey quoted in *Proverbs; or, The Manual*, 145.

Wilful waste makes . . . William George Smith, *Oxford Dictionary of English Proverbs* (Oxford: Clarendon Press, 1935), 562. Also: "For want is nexte to waste, and shame doeth synne ensue" —Richard Edwards, *Paradise of Dainty Devices*, 1576.

Wise and good . . . Fuller, *Gnomologia*, 254.

A woman can throw out . . . Dora Morrell Hughes, *Thrift in the Household* (Boston: Lothrop, Lee & Shepard, 1918), 11–12.

Work provides . . . Hulme, *Proverb Lore*, 208.

Your thrift's as guide . . . Bohn, *Hand-Book*, 265.

Conclusion

The country passed . . . "What Do You Do With Father's Money?" lecture to members of the National Housewives' League, about 1915, cited in Anna Steese Richardson, *Adventures in Thrift* (Indianapolis: Bobbs-Merrill Company, 1916; first published 1915), 14–15.

Economic historians . . . Ann Fabian, *Card Sharps, Dream Books and Bucket Shops: Gambling in 19th Century America* (Ithaca, NY: Cornell University Press, 1990) 51.

Good husbandry . . . Daniel Defoe, *Giving Alms no Charity*, 1704, in *The Works of Daniel Defoe* (Edinburgh, William Nimmo, 1872), 546–47.

Having worked . . . Albert Shaw, *The Outlook for the Common Man* (New York: Macmillan Company, 1907), 125–26.

One point wherein . . . Horace Greeley, *An Address on Success in Business* (New York: S. S. Packard, 1867), 26–27.

. . . possibly it is . . . Cited in "Lord Derby on Thrift," *The Times*, May 10, 1873.

There is one division . . . Max Lerner, *America as a Civilization* (New York: Simon and Schuster, 1957), 278.

There was never a golden age of family . . . Stephanie Coontz, *The Way We Really Are: Coming to Terms with America's Changing Families* (New York: Basic Books, 1997), 2.

There was never a golden age of thrift . . . Jackson Lears, "The American Way of Debt," *New York Times Magazine*, June 11, 2006.

Appendix B

As to these . . . Cited in Frederick B. Tolles, "Quaker Business Mentors: The Philadelphia Merchants," Wright, *Benjamin Franklin: A Profile*, 8.

Assert the liberty . . . Mather, *Essays To Do Good*, 14.

But that which . . . John Bunyan, *Pilgrim's Progress* (New York: Grosset & Dunlap, n.d.), 106. Bunyan was born in Beforshire, England, on November 28, 1628, and died in London on August 31, 1688. He spent a number of years in prison for his dissenting religious views, but at the time of his death was one of the nation's most influential writers and preachers. Interestingly for our purposes, he strongly disagreed with the Quakers and for years participated in fierce polemics against them.

The diary of . . . Vernon Louis Parrington, *Main Currents of American Thought* (New York: Harcourt, Brace and Company, 1927), 1:88, 90.

Diligence is . . . William Penn, *William Penn's Advice to His Children*, 1699, chapter 3, numbers 10–11. Available at http://www.qhpress.org/quakerpages/qwhp/advice3.html, accessed Feb. 6, 2008.

Every grace is . . . John Bunyan, *The Fear of God* (London: Religious Tract Society, 1839; first printed 1679), 153. See also the Rev. W. Morley Punshon, "John Bunyan," in *Biographical and Historical Lectures* (London: Nisbet, 1881), 472.

From a Child . . . Franklin, *Autobiography*, in Franklin, *Writings*, 1317.

Frugality is good . . . William Penn, *Some Fruits of Solitude*, number 50 (Lombard Street, George-Yard: Thomas Northcott, 1693). William Penn was born in 1644 and died in 1718.

The French essayist and moralist Joseph Joubert (1754–1824) writes: "Be saving, but not at the cost of all liberality. Have the soul of a king and the hand of a wise economist."

The question is . . . Richard Baxter, *Directions Against Covetousness, The Practical Works of the Rev. Richard Baxter* (London: James Duncan, 1830), 23:78. Baxter was born on November 12, 1615, and died on December 8, 1691.

I tell you . . . Cotton Mather, *A Christian at His Calling* (B. Green and J. Allen for S. Sewall Jr., 1701).

If God shows . . . Richard Steele, *The Tradesman's Calling* (J. D. for Samuel Sprint, 1684). Richard Steele was born in 1629 and died in 1692.

The noblest question . . . Franklin, *Poor Richard's Almanac*, 1737.

Seriously and . . . William Gouge, *A Learned Commentary on the Whole Epistle to the Hebrews*. William Gouge was born in Middlesex County, England, in 1575 and died in 1653. His son, the Rev. Thomas Gouge, also a Puritan minister, is the author of *Riches Increased by Giving: or, The Right Use of Mamon: Being the Surest and Safest Way of Thriving* (Harrisonburg, VA: Sprinkle Publications, 1992; originally published 1650).

. . . thou must . . . The prominent Philadelphia Quaker merchant Isaac Norris, writing to his son Joseph, 1719, cited in Tolles, in Wright, *Benjamin Franklin*, 16.

There is another . . . The Puritan divine Cotton Mather, *A Christian at His Calling*, 1701.

This may be . . . Mather, *Essays To Do Good*, 87.

To get our . . . John Cotton, the grandfather of Cotton Mather, was born on December 14, 1585, and died on December 23, 1652. This children's primer was originally published in 1646 in England under the title *Milk for Babes*.

Index